Inventing Arguments

BRIEF EDITION

Inventing Arguments

BRIEF THIRD EDITION

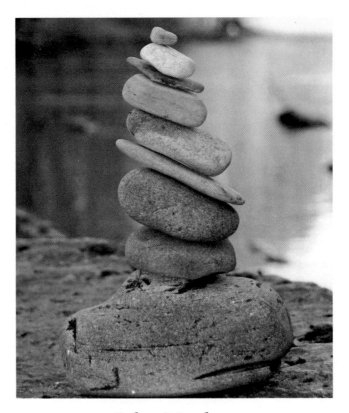

John Mauk
Northwestern Michigan College

John Metz
Kent State University at Geauga

WADSWORTH
CENGAGE Learning

Australia • Brazil • Japan • Korea • Mexico • Singapore • Spain • United Kingdom • United States

Inventing Arguments:
Brief Third Edition
John Mauk, John Metz

Senior Publisher: Lyn Uhl

Publisher: Monica Eckman

Acquisitions Editor: Margaret Leslie

Senior Development Editor: Leslie Taggart

Development Editor: Stephanie Pelkowski Carpenter

Assistant Editor: Amy Haines

Editorial Assistant: Danielle Warchol

Media Editor: Janine Tangney

Executive Marketing Manager: Stacey Purviance

Marketing Manager: Melissa Holt

Marketing Coordinator: Brittany Blais

Marketing Communications Manager: Courtney Morris

Content Project Manager: Corinna Dibble

Senior Art Director: Jill Ort

Manufacturing Planner: Betsy Donaghey

Rights Acquisition Specialist: Mandy Groszko

Production Service: Lachina Publishing Services

Text Designer: Greg Johnson

Cover Designer: Hanh Luu

Cover/title page image: © 2011 PHILWEBBPHOTOGRAPHY/Getty Images

Compositor: Lachina Publishing Services

For product information and technology assistance, contact us at
Cengage Learning Customer & Sales Support, 1-800-354-9706

For permission to use material from this text or product, submit all requests online at **www.cengage.com/permissions.**
Further permissions questions can be e-mailed to
permissionrequest@cengage.com.

Library of Congress Control Number: 2011932605

ISBN-13: 978-0-8400-2776-4
ISBN-10: 0-8400-2776-1

Wadsworth
20 Channel Center Street
Boston, MA 02210
USA

Cengage Learning is a leading provider of customized learning solutions with office locations around the globe, including Singapore, the United Kingdom, Australia, Mexico, Brazil and Japan. Locate your local office at **international.cengage.com/region**

Cengage Learning products are represented in Canada by Nelson Education, Ltd.

For your course and learning solutions, visit **www.cengage.com.**
Purchase any of our products at your local college store or at our preferred online store **www.cengagebrain.com.**
Instructors: Please visit **login.cengage.com** and log in to access instructor-specific resources.

Printed in the United States of America
1 2 3 4 5 6 7 15 14 13 12 11

Brief Contents

Contents

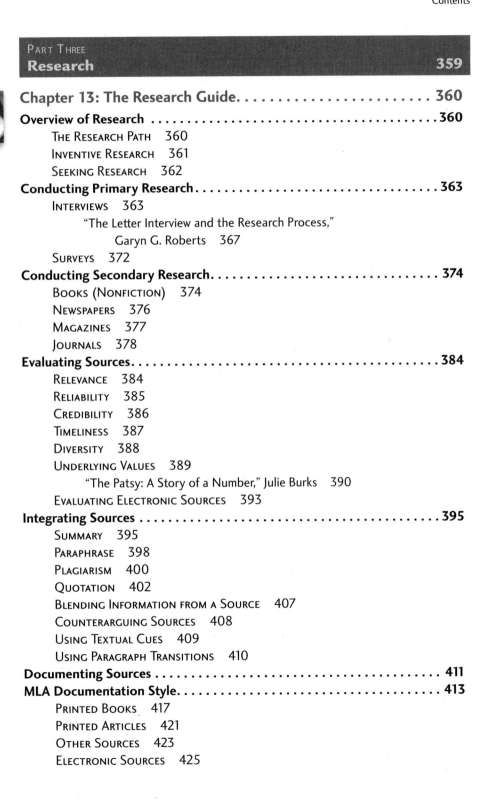

Note to Instructors

Teaching argument to first- and second-year college students requires a good amount of distillation: various theories must be condensed into a reasonable number of terms and concepts. Instructors face the dilemma of how much time to spend hashing over argument intricacies versus hashing out student ideas. (Ultimately, these courses are about student writing, after all.) We've tried to address this tension head on, creating what we think of as a *syllabus-able* argument text—one that has a kind of practical logic but that also does justice to the complexities of the argument tradition.

Most college writing teachers accept the premise that argument is always tied to particular rhetorical situations. Continuing with the Sophistic tradition, most of us believe that the study of argumentative public discourse must emerge from public situations. Therefore, *Inventing Arguments* draws attention to the real material and intellectual affairs of student writers. It teaches students to build arguments from the rhetorical matter swirling around them, including but not limited to the essays, articles, reports, and images they encounter in the classroom.

As instructors ourselves, we've found that students need help getting beyond common argument topics and lifeless support strategies. To succeed in academic argument, and the critical thinking it requires, students must go beyond announcing common opinions and relying on basic factual support. They need help inventing unique positions, developing appeals, and coming to revelatory insights. To these ends, *Inventing Arguments* has three major pedagogical goals:

1. To help students recognize the rhetorical moves they encounter daily and understand how those moves animate their lives.

2. To foreground the *invention* of arguments (the discovery and development of increasingly complex claims and counterarguments).

3. To help students enter arguments in a sophisticated fashion—by attending to the voices and tensions already lurking within and around a topic. When students tune in to the claims, values, and beliefs of others, their own arguments gain intensity and complexity.

To succeed in academic argument, and the critical thinking it requires, students must go beyond announcing common opinions and relying on basic factual support. They need help inventing unique positions, developing appeals, and coming to revelatory insights.

The Structure of Inventing Arguments

Part One: Entering Argument

Chapter 1 introduces basic terms *(argument, rhetoric, invention)* and offers assignments to help students genuinely engage the concepts. The activities throughout, we hope, put students in a powerful intellectual place where they can examine some basic assumptions about rhetoric, their relationship to argument, and the opinions swirling around their lives. Thereafter, the chapters of Part One walk through the main elements of argument—from the most to the least explicit: Claims, Support, Opposition, and Hidden Layers. We hope that these initial chapters distill the most important concepts: three types of claims, three major forms of support, three ways to engage opposition.

The assignments at the end of each brief chapter grow in complexity. First students identify major elements of arguments (in Chapters 1 and 2), then summarize arguments (in Chapters 3 and 4), and then work toward analyzing arguments (in Chapters 5 and 6). In other words, the assignments walk students slowly up to formal rhetorical analysis—which is the focus of Chapter 6.

Part Two: Inventing Argument

We hope that students get one primary point from this book: *Arguments make ideas.* In other words, we hope students learn not only to assert and defend claims but also to develop increasingly complex ideas. Chapters 7–12 help students transform initial opinions into thoughtful academic arguments. The Invention sections, in particular, *model* and *dramatize* the intellectual acts behind academic writing. (Generally, we've always thought it unfair to value intellectual complexity, or even demand it from students, without teaching it—without modeling and dramatizing it.) We hope the particular prompts, questions, and activities help animate your classrooms and vitalize student projects.

Beyond the writing prompts, *Inventing Arguments* offers a range of sample essays and arguments. Students often yearn for models, while instructors want students to explore beyond models. It's a constant pedagogical tension. We tried to address this tension by including sample essays in each chapter, but also displaying the intensive thinking behind those models. We've also found that students can easily become lost in a sea of readings—that too many readings can steal time and energy away from writing projects. Therefore, we've limited the essays in Chapters 7–12 to four samples, including one annotated piece of student or commissioned writing.

Part Three: The Research Guide

We designed the Research Guide with the student in mind—not only with the common questions and problems that students experience but also with the resources and opportunities available to them. We hope that this section teaches students to think of research as a process of reading, entering, and inventing arguments. It includes the common strategies for primary research, print and electronic research, and offers less common, but crucial, advice for evaluating sources that rely on the use of statistics.

New Features in *Inventing Arguments*

NEW CHAPTER: ANALYZING ARGUMENT

We are glad to see writing programs across the country increasing their focus on rhetorical analysis—on helping students understand how arguments work. This new chapter (Chapter 6) walks carefully through the process of analyzing a written argument. It also gives specific strategies for analyzing visual texts and film. The chapter has three accessible sample analyses and draws from them to illustrate key moves. And because we teach rhetorical analysis in our own classes, we have learned the particular pitfalls and struggles that students experience with the process—for instance, the sometimes blurry line between analysis and summary or between analysis and evaluation. The chapter clearly highlights these common pitfalls to help students avoid them.

CHAPTERS 1fi5, ARGUMENT, CLAIMS, SUPPORT, OPPOSITION, AND HIDDEN LAYERS

Beginning with questions such as *What is argument?* and *What is academic argument?*, each brief chapter in the first portion of the book leads students further into the layers of argument. To help students focus on the main concepts, we have eliminated jargon and condensed explanations where possible. Our aim is to give students a manageable introduction to the most important elements of argument: claims, support, opposition, and hidden layers (such as assumptions and spin, an argument in disguise).

STATISTICAL FALLACIES

Many instructors know that students can fall victim to the automatic reverence for numbers. Students often see a statistic and imagine that it's inherently sound, inherently true, and entirely usable. Therefore, we have added new material to the Evaluating Sources section of the Research Guide. The new material explains that statistics are as prone to fallacy as any other form of support. The chapter makes the case that statistics are simply someone's argument put in numerical form. We have also included a short essay, "The Patsy: The Story of a Number," by an accountant who explains some common misconceptions and common allures of numerical persuasion.

LITERARY WORKS AS SUPPORT

We find that fiction, poetry, and drama are often used in formal, and even popular, argumentative essays, the type of essays featured in *Inventing Arguments*. For this edition, we address this strategy in the support sections of the Invention chapters (7–12). Therein, we show students how to use literature as passing or extended allusions. We also placed a more thorough discussion about literature (as a form of argumentative support) in Chapter 3.

Unique Pedagogical Tools

WHAT DO OTHERS CLAIM? WHAT DO I CLAIM?

This activity in each Part Two chapter helps students understand the rhetorical situation and reinforces an essential and often overlooked skill: distinguishing one's own thinking from other voices. These questions also get at the rhetorical theory at the center of the book, namely that better ideas emerge from the juxtaposition of (and tension between) perspectives.

MORE SAMPLE CLAIMS

Each chapter features an "Inventing a Claim" section, which helps students with the heavy intellectual work of narrowing their ideas to a revelatory thesis—one that reveals a new dimension to a topic. And each chapter offers a list of revelatory thesis statements about a variety of topics—so students can see the possibilities for their own projects.

INVENTION QUESTIONS/INVENTION WORKSHOPS

Each chapter in Part Two relies on key questions. These questions are well marked within each section so that you can assign them in class or as homework. The questions are also featured in Invention Workshops— classroom activities designed to help students maximize the rhetorical situation of the classroom. (We've found, and heard, that these workshops animate classroom sessions while keeping the focus on student projects.)

A Final Note

As college composition instructors, we are always in danger of becoming custodians of grammar and arrangement—of format, style, and conformity. We are always (and already) in danger of losing the vitality of the Sophistic tradition, which emphasized invention and rhetorical situation. In writing this pedagogy, we tried to remind ourselves that the formal study of argument emerged from roughly the same place and the same time in history as the practice of democracy. We hope this book does justice to the critical work of the composition classroom—work that keeps both rhetoric and democracy alive.

Acknowledgments

For years, we have thought that invention is the key to good writing. But in developing this book, we have come to believe that invention can change the world. In the process of indulging and promoting this belief, we have been fortunate for the support and contributions of savvy cohorts. We offer our humble gratitude to everyone involved in the initial creation of this book—those who have moved on to various other projects and lives; to Stephanie Pelkowski Carpenter for staying on our team, for managing our ideas and our vexations, for digging up answers and brewing up new questions, for helping us to re-craft, re-tool, and re-invent; to Steve Mockensturm for vitalizing the visual spectrum; to Greg Johnson for carefully designing and re-designing these pages; to Matthew Orgovan for managing the project and addressing details; to Lisa Koehler for attentive copyediting; to Jill Dougan for securing a long list of text permissions and communicating throughout the process; and to Sara Golden for researching photo permissions with speed and transparency. At Cengage Wadsworth, we are grateful to our acquisitions editor, Margaret Leslie, for sustaining the forward momentum of this project and, generally, keeping the publishing wind at our backs; to Leslie Taggart for overseeing development; to Corinna Dibble for managing production; to Mandy Groszko for overseeing permissions; to Amy Haines and Danielle Warchol who provided timely assistance throughout; to Stacey Purviance, Melissa Holt, and the excellent marketing crew; to the English specialists throughout the country, and to the intensive sales folks throughout the country who give spirit, feet, and faces to our pedagogy. Thanks also to our students and colleagues who have graciously joined us in our efforts to transcend what is and to invent what could be. Finally, thanks to our families and friends for enduring another edition. We are driven by your collective support.

Any textbook project requires hearty professionals who offer their time and energy to help steer the pedagogy in valuable directions. Once again, we relied heavily on the insights of our reviewers and were often humbled at their prowess. We are indebted to the following teachers, theorists, rhetoricians, and scholars:

John Boyd, Ball State University
Glenda Buenger, William Penn University
Katawna Caldwell, Eastfield College
Anne Cassia, Merritt College
Naomi Clark, University of Missouri
Maureen Connolly, Elmhurst College
Robert Cooper, Eastfield College–Dallas County Community College

Joseph Couch, Montgomery College
Drucella Crutchfield, Southeastern University
Susan Davis, Arizona State University
Brooke Eubanks, Central Arizona College
Clarence Hundley, Thomas Nelson Community College
Elizabeth Huston, Eastfield College
Melanie Jenkins, Snow College
Elizabeth Joseph, Eastfield College
Cecilia Kennedy, Clark State Community College
Ronald Miller, Francis Marion University
Shawn Miller, Francis Marion University
Dan Morgan, Scott Community College
Michael Morris, Eastfield College
Susan Nyikos, Utah State University
Ildiko Olasz, Northwest Missouri State University
Elizabeth Oldfield, Southeastern Community College
Thomas Owen, Eastfield College
Yolanda Page, University of Arkansas at Pine Bluff
Amy Ratto Parks, University of Montana
Amy Patrick, Western Illinois University
Martha Payne, Ball State University
Luke Rolfes, Northwest Missouri State University
Rod Romesburg, Rollins College
Nancy Rowe, Loyola University
Greg Siering, Ball State University
Shawn Smolen-Morton, Francis Marion University
Larissa Washington, Eastfield College
Sandra Young, Sacred Heart University

Note to Students

Many thousands of students across the country are presently taking a course on argumentation and academic writing. Since it's a requirement for nearly all two-year and four-year college degrees in America, a fair question would be *What's so important about argument?* Among all the possible answers, instructors seem to give a few consistently:

- Because argumentation is a vital tool for thriving in academic life.
- Because supporting assertions in public and professional situations will define much of students' post-college life.
- Because sound argumentation is essential for maintaining a democracy.
- Because students need training in argument to defend against government and corporate propaganda.
- Because getting things done requires bringing others into your way of thinking.
- Because adept arguers are adept thinkers (and vice versa).

In short, most of us who teach these courses know that once you enter public life, you enter argumentative life. Chances are you will be called on almost daily to make assertions about your work, your rights, your faith, your freedom to be without faith, your family, your country, your own hopes. You will have to argue for yourself and others, and for the world that you want to inhabit. And even if you don't make such arguments, others will. Voices all around you will try to define how you should live and think and even hope.

With these ideas in mind, we have tried to create an argumentative experience—a series of chapters that will immerse you in the complexities and nuances of argument. We hoped to create an experience for and *about* students—about the real situations that surround you and define your lives.

Part One: Entering Argument

These chapters introduce the basic and not-so-basic layers of argument. As you will see, there are many terms and tools—and your instructor may highlight some more than others. As the chapters in this section proceed, they increase in complexity—beginning with the most essential and visible layers of argument and evolving into the most evasive or hidden aspects. We have tried to keep the main and most common terms as headings. In other words, if you understand (and know how to apply) the terms in bold throughout these chapters, you will be well on your way to understanding the function and power of academic argument.

Part Two: Inventing Argument

From our perspective, this is the heart of the book. It's where you, the writer, get mired in your own situation and develop arguments from the ground up. We consider these chapters the big assignment projects in the book—where you will apply the tools learned in Part One. Of course, the projects you take on will depend upon your course, your instructor, and your college's particular objectives, but we designed these chapters to facilitate real arguments in your life. Following the ancient Greeks (who invented this whole study), you will learn the most from arguing in real situations. And don't forget, the classroom is a real situation. We hope you'll see these chapters as opportunities to dig up, reveal, and argue about something that matters in your community.

Part Three: The Research Guide

If your college course is like most throughout the country, you will be responsible for learning the nuances of formal research and documentation. It may sound intimidating—or wildly boring. But it doesn't have to be. We see research as another part of invention. The strategies offered in this section can be applied to any of the writing projects in Chapters 7–12. This section helps you work with interviews, surveys, print sources (such as books, journals, magazines, and newspapers), and electronic sources (such as websites, databases, and online books). It explains important skills such as paraphrase, summary, and quotation and covers the documentation formats for the Modern Language Association (MLA) and the American Psychological Association (APA).

Peace,
John Mauk and John Metz

Argumentation: (1) The act of asserting, supporting, and defending a claim; (2) The art of discovering and defending what should be thought, what should be done; (3) The art of changing others' minds while not losing your own.

Inventive writers
learn to see the
lurking arguments.

Part One

ENTERING ARGUMENT

Inventing Arguments

What Is Argument?

Argument is the act of asserting, supporting, and defending a claim. It is an intellectual and a social process. People are surrounded by argument. It can be said that public life is argumentative—that people are vying to be heard, trying to assert their vision of the world to anyone who will hear it. But argument can work in more subtle ways in the form of advertisements, songs, billboards, posters, slogans, and stories. While our daily language may not be full of explicit debate, it is full of underlying values and unstated assumptions. When people make a point about a favorite song or an interesting class, they are hinting at an entire argument, which entails a set of values and assumptions about social worth.

American history can be seen, and is often taught, as a series of arguments. The Founding Fathers were exemplary arguers, and Thomas Jefferson's Declaration of Independence may be one of the most politically significant arguments the world has seen. Arguments have driven American history: the evolution of its colonies and states, the development of a federal government, the drawing of borders, the accumulation of territory, the removal of Native Americans, the institution of slavery, the abolitionist movement, the South's secession from the Union, the Civil War, Reconstruction, the emergence of public education, the extension of voting rights, the Industrial Revolution, the development of unions, the rise of monopoly capitalism, the Works Progress Administration during the Great Depression, the nation's role in World War I and II, the Japanese-American internment camps, the Civil Rights movement, the Vietnam War, *Roe vs. Wade*, Watergate, the L.A. riots, the Iran-Contra scandal, the war on drugs, biotechnology, the nation's intervention in Iraq, state marriage amendments, ballot counting—the list goes on and on. All of these events and situations have been layered with fevered arguments and advocates competing to take the country in one direction instead of another. Today, we need only to turn on the television to hear argument stacked atop argument. From CNN to Comedy Central, news anchors and standup comedians alike are leading participants in collective arguments.

What Is Academic Argument?

Although history seems fraught with bold arguments among classes, religions, rulers, and countries, the vast majority of arguments are subtler: small exchanges of ideas with participants urging others to accept their positions. Most often, argument does *not* include beating an opponent, taking up arms, or preaching to an audience, but involves making a debatable position appear reasonable or acceptable. And this is the primary motive behind academic argument: *to make others see the wisdom of a position or perspective.*

Academic disciplines are arenas of argument. Many college students are surprised to discover the degree to which their fields of study have grown from internal debates. In composition studies, for instance, some scholars, called expressionists, have argued that ideas come from inside a writer's consciousness; other scholars, known as social constructionists, have argued that ideas emerge from the influence of social conditions that surround a writer; still other scholars have tried to combine these views. Or consider psychology: Sigmund Freud did not simply announce his theories on psychoanalysis to receptive audiences. He presented his theories as arguments. In fact, every major figure in a field of study, from chemistry to engineering, has been an arguer as much as anything else.

Many scholars say that academic disciplines provide their own language of argument. In other words, engineers learn how to make arguments within the framework of engineering, chemists learn how to argue using the language of chemistry, and so forth. They learn the formulas, language, and equations required to enter the ongoing arguments of their discipline. It might even be said that academic disciplines teach students how to view the world. Biologists, for instance, may come to believe that the world is knowable and that the origins of life can be discovered. Philosophers may come to believe that nothing can be known outside of a particular time and place. Psychologists may come to believe that people have control over their decisions. These beliefs and assumptions may rest quietly beneath the daily thoughts and work of biologists, philosophers, and psychologists, but they have significant impact on what gets said and done. And eventually, all those who practice within a discipline are affected by the assumptions (and the arguments) that have accumulated during their studies.

Outside the academic tradition is a popular saying: "People are entitled to their own opinions." But we should investigate this statement because it poses a problem for those interested in the study of argument. It suggests that people's opinions are set in stone. But people do not simply keep their opinions. Instead, they trade them for others. Thus, to say that *people are entitled to their own opinions* greatly oversimplifies the human consciousness, which is actually a complex process of building, transforming, and trading opinions. It ignores how people really work in the world of ideas, and it ignores the power of language to shape our perspectives on the world around us.

Although the saying "People are entitled to their own opinions" seems open-minded, the statement most often means, "What other people think doesn't matter to me." This statement is often used to dismiss others' opinions; it is used to stop exploration and cut people off from others' arguments. But in a democratic society, in which everyday citizens help constitute policy, vote for political agendas, and conclude verdicts, other people's opinions do matter. What people think about labor, war, abortion, human rights, water pollution, corporate power, and so forth impacts the civilization that we all inhabit. More than anything else (more than money, weapons, or even good looks), other people's opinions influence how we live. Because most of us do not live on our own islands, cut off from the influence of culture, law, and policy, others' opinions directly filter into our everyday behaviors and thoughts. And that is why argument is so important.

Activities

1. With several others, debate the following: *Why do opinions change?* Share your initial thinking, and then explore other possibilities. Consider particular opinions you once held but that changed.

2. In a small group, make a list of careers that people prepare for in college, such as doctor, accountant, marketing specialist, nutritionist, and so on. Then discuss how a college education teaches students in each field to view the world in a particular way.

3. What arguments make up the national debate about the war in Afghanistan?

4. What arguments are put forth in the preamble of the Declaration of Independence?

What Is Rhetoric?

Rhetoric is a process of recognizing and using the most effective strategies for influencing thought. The Greek philosopher Aristotle defined rhetoric as the ability to see the available means of persuasion for each particular case. In other words, rhetoric is more than a tool for changing people's minds; it is also the study of how people are persuaded into their beliefs. People who study rhetoric and writing are interested in how opinions form and change. They study the relationship between language and belief, and they examine the cultural conditions around people and their everyday use of language.

In its classical Greek origins (circa fifth-century BCE), rhetoric was a primary field of study. In many ways, it was the glue between various academic pursuits because it focused on how ideas (regardless of content) are used, shared, communicated, implemented, and manipulated. The study of rhetoric was the study of social and intellectual activity. Today, in popular use, rhetoric has a significantly smaller domain and is sometimes narrowly associated with empty or dishonest language.

The cartoon on page 9 may point to a truth about politics, but *rhetoric is not about dishonesty*. Rhetoric is most often used honestly to communicate ideas and to bring others into one's own perspective. In this sense, everyone uses rhetoric. A child learns that adding "please" to his request for a cookie gets better results than screaming, "Cookie!" A teenager knows that asking for the family car should involve some mention of her intentions to be home early. Imagine the following exchange between an employee and his boss:

"Hey, I need to leave early today."

"Well, Vick, you can't."

Then notice the added layers of rhetoric in the following:

"Excuse me, Kim. My daughter has an important doctor's appointment, and I was wondering if I could leave early today to be with her."

"Sure, Vick. Can you come in early tomorrow to make up for the lost time?"

Greek philosopher Aristotle.

We might call the second exchange more polite or more respectful. But the layer of respect is also a layer of rhetoric, a strategy for inviting the audience (Kim) into the speaker's perspective. Vick is not being dishonest in the second example—at least, we cannot assume he is. He merely gives some information that helps make his request seem valid. In fact, anytime someone offers information, describes something a particular way, or arranges information in a particular way so that someone else will accept a claim, he or she is making rhetorical decisions.

But the preceding examples are rather basic. The child who says "please" and the worker who nuances his request are not *studying* rhetoric. They are simply using the available means of persuasion. The student of rhetoric explores the ways in which different uses of language impact people in various situations. That is, students of rhetoric ask questions about particular situations:

- What is happening? Why should someone speak out?
- Who is present? Who is the audience?
- What are the audience's values and beliefs?
- What kind of language would best appeal to those beliefs?

When we try to make a point seem reasonable, ethical, or emotional for a particular audience, we are involved in a rhetorical effort. That effort can be dramatic, such as when a lawyer is trying to persuade a jury to see facts in a particular way or when a politician gives an impassioned speech. Sometimes, the rhetorical effort can be subtle. For instance, when scientists arrange information on a laboratory report, they present their findings so that their work appears coherent and logical. The scientists may not make a dramatic point about their own thinking, but the report may still have a rhetorical dimension:

> Results: Overall, beavers showed a preference for certain species of trees, and their preference was based on distance from the central place. Measurements taken at the study site show that beavers avoided oaks and musclewood . . . and show a significant food preference ($x_- = 447.26$, d.f. = 9, P < .05). No avoidance or particular preference was observed for the other tree species. (http://www.ncsu.edu/labwrite/res/labreport/res-sample-labrep.html)

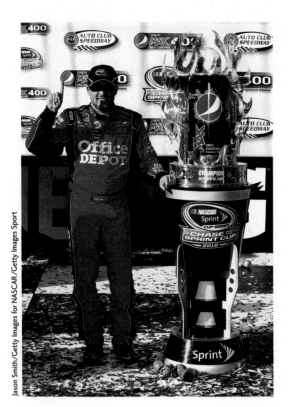

Jason Smith/Getty Images for NASCAR/Getty Images Sport

Driver Tony Stewart in victory lane after winning the NASCAR Sprint Cup Series Pepsi Max 400.

One of the most obvious uses of rhetoric is in advertising. Television, radio, magazine, Internet, and even restroom advertisements use language and graphics to persuade us to buy things. It works. Americans are profoundly influenced by advertising rhetoric—so much so that it has become an art form. Companies spend billions of dollars each year in a rhetorical race for our attention. They shape every sentence and carefully select every image so each ad will have the most dramatic effect on its audience. Rhetoric is a powerful aspect of language, perhaps the most powerful. When used for positive purposes, it can help people share ideas, values, and visions. When used for negative purposes, it can prompt people to waste money on useless trinkets or lead them into treachery.

Rhetoric is more than the selection and arrangement of words. It also is a deeper exploration of thought and language. Students and scholars of rhetoric can ask theoretical questions:

- What is the relationship between thought and language?
- How does a particular type of language influence consciousness?
- How do particular values or beliefs stay in place over time?
- How do some values or beliefs get dismissed or overrun?

The study of rhetoric is still at the heart of writing classes today. Students learn not just about correct grammar but also about the relationship between language and thought, the processes of analyzing and creating *discourse* (language in use). The goal of studying rhetoric is to examine the nuances of persuasive language as they appear in essays, reports, literature, slogans, advertisements, speeches, memos, policies, art, entertainment, and even actions. Rhetoric is key to the study of argument. In a sense, there can be no argument without rhetoric.

The ancient Greek lessons on rhetoric still apply today. In writing, debate, communication, and speech courses, students study the five categories, or canons, of rhetoric passed down from the ancient Greeks:

- **Invention:** the discovery and development of ideas
- **Arrangement:** the organization of ideas in a coherent and engaging fashion

- **Style or voice:** the personal or individualized use of language conventions, with attention to appropriateness, situation, and audience
- **Memory:** the recollection of prepared points
- **Delivery:** the presentation of ideas

These canons are used as intellectual tools for developing, extending, and shaping ideas. Because discovering and developing ideas is so important to academic writing, invention is an extensive part of the process, and it has a primary place in this book. As you will see in Chapters 7–12, arrangement and voice are also important components.

   Rhetorical situation refers to an opportunity to address a particular audience about a disputed or disputable issue. Looking back at the definition of *rhetoric*, we might say that the rhetorical situation is an opportunity to gather and use the available means of persuasion. A rhetorical situation involves an *exigence*—an occasion when something happens or does not happen that results in some uncertainty. The rhetorical situation also involves a speaker/writer, an audience, a method of communication, and the rules of communication (whether directly stated or implied), as well as the text, or message. All elements of the rhetorical situation exist in time and place, which impact what can and should be said. Good rhetoricians (good writers) know how to seize upon all the particular elements of time and place. They build points out of the raw social materials around them.

   Academic essays have their own rhetorical situation. The student is the speaker/writer; the audience is usually defined by a group of peers and an instructor; the rules of communication are explicitly defined (and even evaluated) on a syllabus and assignment prompt; and the assignment itself is the exigence—the opportunity to address the audience, to assert a way of thinking about a topic. (Imagine seeing an

➔ Rhetorical Situation

The rhetorical situation includes the

- tension or "exigence"
- arguer (speaker/writer)
- audience
- method of communication
- rules of communication
- text or message

assignment as a rhetorical opportunity!) In academic settings, writers should assume that their audiences are attentive, informed, and tuned in to all the layers of an argument. Academic readers are constantly thinking about the messages being sent and the way the ideas can be received. As a result, they expect rhetorical moves that are not common in many popular culture arguments:

- **Revelatory rather than familiar points:** While popular culture attempts to make audiences comfortable by repeating familiar phrases and announcing widely held opinions, academic argument attempts to give the audience a new way of seeing the topic. Academic argument attempts to reveal previously unseen layers of ideas.
- **Appeals to logic rather than emotion:** While the goal of much popular culture, from news programs to MTV, is to engage our emotions (such as fear or desire), academic argument appeals more to the audience's ability to reason and think through difficult or complex issues. This is not to say that academic argument avoids emotional appeals, but it uses them sparingly.
- **Analysis rather than packaging:** While popular culture packages ideas into slogans, academic argument seeks to *unpack* ideas, breaking open familiar phrases and concepts.
- **Inclusion rather than exclusion:** Many arguments in popular culture exclude groups of people. Some political talk show hosts, for example, will deride liberals or conservatives, thereby confirming their audience's beliefs. But academic arguments attempt to place less focus on people's individual qualities and instead invite the audience into a way of thinking.

Activities

1. Think of a recent college class. Make a list of all the rhetorical strategies of the instructor and the students. Consider all the subtle and explicit ways that instructors work to bring students into a way of thinking—about the class, the rules, the rewards, the penalties. And consider how students work to persuade instructors of their abilities, their dedication, or even their apathy about the course. Consider particular language, phrasing, words, suggestions.

2. Make a list of situations from history or current events in which rhetoric has been used for good or bad purposes.

3. Describe a situation in the past twenty-four hours in which you made a rhetorical decision.

What Is Invention?

[handwritten: more than brainstorming and clustering · Forming probing questions]

Invention is the discovery and development of ideas. It is the engine of argument: It moves everyone involved (arguer and audience) away from worn-out statements and toward new territory and vital ideas. Without it, arguers end up reasserting tired statements, going around in circles, or simply projecting their initial opinions on a given topic. Invention allows arguers to discover, for themselves and their audiences, something worthy of their attention.

Beginning writers sometimes assume that invention means merely brainstorming for a topic—tricks such as clustering or free writing. Once they have a topic that seems like it might generate lots of ideas, they stop inventing and start drafting. But this strategy is flawed in two important ways. First, invention is not necessarily a chaotic storm in the brain, a mysterious and random array of lightning strikes. (If that's all it were, writing would be a complete disaster.) Invention can be a deliberate process, a challenging journey driven by probing questions and strategic intellectual moves. Second, invention is not something that ends once someone finds a topic and takes a stand. In fact, the real thinking and the most intensive intellectual probing begin once a topic is found: a writer must develop support (evidence, examples, and appeals) that adds dimension and substance to a position.

[handwritten: 1) 2) evidence examples appeals]

A common misconception about argument, and about academic writing in general, is that opinions must be proven with facts based on some form of research. According to this view, the best arguments must be those that have lots of statistics and data to support claims. Because of this, writers may feel inclined to depend on others' words and ideas, and they might have difficulty developing points on their own. But those who know key invention strategies can use research more strategically than those who rely on it to make every point for them. And those who know how to invent can get beyond their initial opinions about a topic and develop thoughts that shed new light on hidden layers. Notice how the following discussion goes from an initial opinion to a more complex insight:

Jack: Old people should stay off the roads.

Linda: Just because they drive slowly?

Jack: No, because they drive slowly and they hold up other people. And because everyone else is in a hurry, the older drivers make driving hazardous.

Diana: So the people in a hurry aren't the hazards?

Jack: Well, of course they are, but the slower drivers just frustrate everyone who wants to go the speed limit.

Diana: Or faster?

Jack: Yes . . . or faster.

Linda: If everyone on the roads had no obstacles and they could speed to where they needed to be, would the roads be safer? Would people drive any better?

Jack: Well, maybe not.

Linda: So is the problem really "old people"?

Jack: The problem is that everyone—those people in a hurry and those who aren't—have to share the roads.

Diana: And most people aren't very good at sharing space.

Jack: In general, people have their own cars, their own homes, their own lawnmowers, their own . . . everything. But suddenly, they pull out into the street, and they're in shared space.

Linda: So you're saying that the problem isn't with only one group of drivers—it's with an attitude that might include all groups?

The conversation develops into something more insightful than Jack's first personal opinion. As the three writers talk, they invent increasingly layered ideas. They ask questions about their own claims and thereby open up intellectual possibilities that they could not previously have imagined. They do not merely express opinions or give answers. Instead, they assert an idea and then interrogate it. In this way, inventive writers learn to see the lurking arguments:

- The real danger on the highways is speed and the belief that speed is an inherent good.
- American roadways are plagued not so much by particular groups of drivers but by the pace of everyday life.
- Americans' prejudices against one another are dramatized on the highway.
- Americans' strong sense of individuality (which centers on their own homes, their own cars, their own lawnmowers, etc.) makes it difficult for them to share anything—even the highways.

In short, invention gets writers past their initial ideas and propels them beyond their personal opinions. It is the genesis of good writing and powerful argumentation. Because the goal of argument is to reveal a new way of seeing a topic (hence persuading people to rethink their positions and beliefs), good invention strategies are the key to success. Invention is such a key part of good writing and good arguing that Chapters 7–12 in this textbook devote several sections to it. These Invention sections offer series of questions that lead writers to increasingly complex and revelatory ideas.

Goal is "to reveal a new way of seeing a topic."

Activities

1. Closely examine the discussion among Jack, Linda, and Diana. Describe the specific points in the conversation that take the ideas beyond Jack's initial opinion. Describe, in specific terms, how Diana and Linda help Jack go from his initial opinion to a more complex insight.

2. With a small group of peers (in class or online), develop an idea from an initial opinion to a more complex insight (as Jack, Linda, and Diana do on page 14). Keep a running record of the conversation. Try to trace the progression of thought. After the discussion, answer the following:
   a. What new ideas (new ways of thinking about the topic) emerged?
   b. What prompted the new way of thinking—a probing question, a provocative statement, a debate about some particular word or phrase?

3. At the beginning of the chapter, we claim that "American history can be seen, and is often taught, as a series of arguments." Consider the following recruitment ad from World War II. How does it, as an artifact of history, make an argument about America, women, gender, or war?

Library of Congress/LC-USZC4-1856

Claims

What Is a Claim?

All arguments have two major parts: claim and support. A **claim** is the main argumentative position (or thesis) being put forward. It is the assertion being made. The **support** gives substance and legitimacy to the claim and comes in various forms, such as facts, statistics, scenarios, appeals to logic, and appeals to emotions. The support is what allows, or convinces, the audience to accept the claim. (Support is discussed in Chapter 3.)

Complex arguments, like the ones expressed in essays, have more than one claim: they have a main claim and supporting claims. These arguments are actually one argument made up of smaller arguments.

Basic Argument	Complex Argument
Claim	Main Claim
Support	Supporting Claim
	Support
	Supporting Claim
	Support
	Supporting Claim
	Support
	Supporting Claim
	Support

A main claim can have any number of supporting claims (not just four, as shown in the preceding illustration). For example, in a discussion about where to take a week's vacation, someone might claim, *We should go to Myrtle Beach.* To support this claim, the person would make other claims, such as *Myrtle Beach has one of the finest beaches on the east coast, Myrtle Beach has over 250 golf courses,* and so on.

Just like main claims can be developed with supporting claims, those supporting claims can be developed with additional supporting claims. For example, to support *Myrtle Beach has one of the finest beaches on the East Coast,* one might claim that *The Myrtle Beach area includes sixty miles of diverse beaches* or that *The beach includes a new boardwalk with amusements, food, and lots of great people-watching.*

Types of Claims

Main claims, which are sometimes called thesis statements, are the primary assertions made about a given topic. Main claims do not merely state what the argument is about; they reveal the arguer's particular stance on a given topic. Some theorists split argumentative claims into three types: fact, value, and policy.

Claims of fact argue that a condition exists, has existed, or will exist. This type of claim may be confusing because we often associate fact with truth (and therefore think it's beyond dispute), but facts themselves are always in dispute. They must be proven.

> The Roman Empire influenced all of Europe.
>
> CO_2 emissions are impacting temperatures globally.
>
> The Packers will win the Super Bowl this year.

Claims of value argue that something possesses or reflects a particular quality (good, bad, just, unreasonable, practical, unfair, etc.). They may assert approval or disapproval. Any claim that argues worth is a claim of value. An adjective, or what is called a predicate of value, usually can be found in the claim. For instance, *good, underhanded,* and *wrong* are all predicates of value in the following:

> The Packers are not a very good team this year.
>
> The governor's strategies for getting elected are underhanded.
>
> Abortion is wrong.

Claims of policy argue that some action should be taken or some change made. Claims of policy call for a particular change in behavior, policy, approach, or even attitude.

The Confederate flag should not be flown above government buildings.

Voluntary prayer should be allowed in public schools.

We should get out of class early today.

Each type of claim can occur in any situation. Notice, for instance, how different types of claims can work in an argument about the past:

Claim of Fact: The failed school levy of 2000 changed the operations of the public schools for the entire decade.

Claim of Value: The voting public was misguided in its decision to vote down the 2000 school levy.

Claim of Policy: The voting public should not have voted against the school levy in 2000, and the community should work to repair the negative impact of that significant year.

The claims correspond to the purpose of an argument and to the intended reaction of the audience. Will the audience be persuaded into taking action, into seeing value, or into understanding a condition? These categories help readers (and writers) to know the nature of the argument and may help you to understand an argument's purpose.

Activity

As a class, consider the following topic: the blurring between news and entertainment. In small groups, develop three argumentative claims (fact, value, and policy) about this topic.

Understanding different claims is vital to good argument. In fact, in our everyday lives, we sometimes work hard to manage the way others hear us. We use a standard formula for dispelling any confusion: I'm not saying _____; I'm saying _____. Often, this move is to make sure others understand the nature of our point:

Dispelling confusion

- *I'm not saying we should do anything; I'm just saying that the guy is a fake!*
- *I'm not saying that Martha's parties are boring; I'm saying that I don't want to go tonight.*
- *I'm not saying that we shouldn't get a dog; I'm saying that it will be hard work.*
- *I'm not arguing whether or not they won; I'm arguing that they didn't win fairly.*

Jerry Seinfeld.

In each case the speaker is clarifying the nature of the claim—saying, in effect, "I am making this type of claim, not one of the others." For *Seinfeld* fans, this potential confusion was played out in an episode in which the main character, Jerry, found himself insisting that he wasn't gay. He said repeatedly, "I'm not gay" (a claim of fact), and then followed each time with "not that there's anything wrong with that" (a claim of value). In other words, he didn't want people to think he was making a value judgment about sexual orientation. He was, instead, making a claim of fact about his own orientation.

Sometimes, the types of claims work in tandem. For instance, a claim of fact may help to launch a claim of policy or value. In Charles Nelson's essay "Investing in Futures" (Chapter 12), he makes a claim of fact about college tuition (that it will likely grow past the worth of some degrees) and then suggests a claim of value about the cultural effects:

> Students are paying the same tuition for different degrees, and some of those degrees will eventually be boxed out of college because students graduating with the degree won't be able to pay back the loans. Unless something gives, when the cost of a college degree hits two or three hundred thousand dollars, colleges may be void of students studying art, poetry, or (in some states) education. If college tuition continues to increase at its present rate (and there's nothing to suggest it will not), higher education might price itself out of teaching literature, humanities, anthropology, sociology, philosophy . . . all the disciplines that explore what it means to be human. From there, it doesn't take a science fiction writer to imagine the ill effects on our little civilization.

Nelson does not make a claim of policy: he does not argue that students shouldn't major in literature and humanities. But imagine if someone were to read this passage and claim, "Nelson thinks people shouldn't major in philosophy!" Such a characterization would distort Nelson's argument beyond the point of recognition.

In sound argument, we should work to understand what people are arguing—not only the topic but the type of claim. Sometimes, people intentionally distort the nature of someone else's claim. For example, notice how the following exchange veers away from Senator Green's original claim:

> Senator Green: "Our state spends twenty million dollars on employee health care."

Senator Gray: "This seems like the right amount to me. We cannot simply go cutting employee health care every time someone mentions the word."

Senator Green originally made a claim of fact. But Senator Gray changed the terms of engagement by pulling the issue into a claim of value (the amount is appropriate) and then a claim of policy (the state should not cut employee health care). When people like Senator Gray thrust the conversation too quickly away from the claim of fact—and into a claim of value or policy—they move the argument prematurely to the realm of judgments and solutions before the audience has a good grasp of the situation.

[handwritten margin note: Example of claim of fact ↓ claim of value and policy]

Characteristics of Claims

Powerful arguments develop *focused, arguable,* and *revelatory* main claims or thesis statements.

Focused claims guide the reader's and writer's attention to a particular aspect of an issue. When a claim is focused, the argument gains depth, while a broad claim generates a shallow or incoherent argument. To check for focus, writers examine the main parts of a sentence, the subject and predicate, to see if they can be more specific. Notice the following unfocused claim:

Today's popular music is bad for children.

The subject is only slightly focused. While *popular music* is more focused than *music, today's popular music* includes a wide variety of genres and styles, from hip-hop to country. The writer would do well to focus on a particular aspect of popular music—a genre, a particular style, a particular medium, or a particular element of the music world:

[handwritten margin note: unfocused claim (linking verb (is) versus action verb)]

fashion trends packaged with today's pop music

lyrics about inflated egos in today's hip-hop music

marketing strategies of today's country music

lack of genuine storytelling in today's rock music

The predicate of the sentence is vague as well. The fact that something *is bad* does not give us any particular insight. The adjective *bad* can be attributed to anything from pneumonia to cookies. Part of the problem stems from the verb *is*, which is a linking verb rather than an action verb. When linking verbs are used as the main verbs in sentences, they work like equal signs:

today's popular music = bad for children

Linking verbs prompt writers to think in vague terms and to use unfocused adjectives such as *bad.* Action verbs can help focus ideas:

> deteriorates children's ability to think critically
>
> directs children to trivial issues
>
> oversimplifies the complexities of urban life
>
> conjures up delusions of self-importance in children

Notice how the verbs *(deteriorates, directs, oversimplifies, conjures)* create focus.

Arguable claims make assertions that could be challenged on various grounds. In other words, they invite or directly address opposition. Some common problems can keep thesis statements from being arguable.

The Question Problem:

A question is not a claim because it offers no stance. People sometimes use questions to imply a stance: *Isn't that the point of democracy? Why can't you be more like your sister?* But this is generally an informal strategy, something done in everyday communication. A formal argumentative stance usually suggests a particular position amid a realm of many others, something that a question does not do.

[handwritten margin note: No stance (position) implied only informal comm. strategy]

The Obvious Fact Problem:

Good arguments often attempt to overturn common beliefs or ideas that people presume to be true. For instance, in opposition to the beliefs of his day, the medieval astronomer Copernicus argued that the Earth was not the center of the universe. In contrast, an argument that simply announces a commonly known condition or a widely held belief is no argument at all. Imagine someone arguing: *Many people go to college for their futures; Americans love cars; space exploration is expensive.* Because they express common beliefs instead of overturning them, such statements function as observations but not argumentative claims.

[handwritten margin note: Overturn common belief or ideas – yes State widely held position No argument]

The Personal Response Problem:

Argument depends upon the presence of multiple perspectives peering at the same topic. When writers proclaim a personal response about their tastes, likes, dislikes, or desires, they merely make public their own state of mind. "I really liked the first *Pirates of the Caribbean*" is not an argumentative stance; it is a statement about a person's tastes. But the statement "Johnny Depp's portrayal of a wayward pirate illustrates his superior range as an actor" invites opposition. It goes beyond a personal response, and other positions can then engage the point critically.

Revelatory claims reveal an unfamiliar topic or a new layer of a familiar one. They challenge something that previously seemed entirely agreeable, or they show a hidden side to an issue. Revelatory claims do more than simply take a stand on an issue; they imply "You may already have an opinion, but . . . have you seen *this* side of the issue?" They tear down the curtains and show who is hiding behind them; they clear away the dirt and reveal the roots.

Notice the difference between the following claims:

- Home schooling is good for families. *opinion*
- Home schooling reconnects home life and formal learning. *keeps going*
- Home schooling reestablishes a key concept that disappeared throughout the twentieth century: that the home is the center of *sit. it in history* learning, development, and intellectual growth.

While the first claim celebrates home schooling, it does not offer a particular insight about its worth. It is an opinion, but nothing more. The second claim goes further and suggests a particular aspect about home schooling. The third claim goes further still by situating the point in history. The reader of the last two claims, especially the third, has been given a novel insight about home schooling. And the reader is bound to encounter a fresh way of thinking about the topic in the argument that develops. Revelatory claims are more than personal opinion; they are particular and persuasive insights. Revelatory argument depends on fresh perspectives that make an audience reconsider topics.

Activities

1. Consider how the following unfocused thesis statements could be more focused. Decide if the problem lies in the subject or in the predicate. Create at least two different subjects and two different predicates for each.

A. People should avoid large corporate retailers.

B. *King Lear* is Shakespeare's best work.

C. The settlers were wrong in driving out the Native Americans.

D. There are many good things about public television.

2. Explain why the following statements are not arguable, and change them to invite opposition:

A. Should people shop at Walmart?

B. Injustice hurts people.

C. The Internet has changed the world.

D. I prefer taking the train to flying.

3. Revelatory claims do not belong exclusively to academic writers. Performers, public figures, and artists often push audiences to reconsider common topics and basic assumptions.

Kevin Winter/Getty Images

JIM LO SCALZO/epa/Corbis

A. How is Lady Gaga's meat dress a revelatory claim? What does it claim?

B. What other public figures have urged audiences to reconsider a particular topic or assumption?

C. Is there a difference between shock and revelation? Or is shock value a part of revelation?

A Community of Cars

RYAN BROWN

Ryan Brown attends Northern Michigan University. In this essay, which he wrote for a college English course, he argues that our overreliance on the automobile diminishes important human needs. And he offers a fresh insight by arguing that fuel-efficient cars actually keep people from seeing the negative effects of an automobile culture.

A small stuffed animal buffalo sits on my bookshelf, a reminder of my childhood and my grandmother. In all her eighty-odd years on this planet my grandmother never once drove a car. Occasionally she would ride the bus, but almost anywhere she went she walked. The sight of her trudging along with her determined nurse's gait in rain, shine, or snow was familiar to many in our town. I remember going shopping with her when she would babysit me. We would walk along tree-lined sidewalks down to the neighborhood grocery store, along the way stopping so I could race sticks and leaves down the creek. The store was worlds removed from modern, antiseptic supermarkets. The old brick building had worn hardwood floors that creaked when you walked across them. The store's specialty was buffalo meat, and the grocer, who knew my grandmother by name, would lift me up on his shoulders so that I could pet the enormous buffalo head mounted on the wall.

The store is gone now, replaced by a modern supermarket outside of town. No doubt business has improved. The new location is more spacious and better lit, with a better selection, and most importantly, much better parking. They even offer a service through which a person can call in their grocery order and simply drive up to have it loaded into their vehicle. All in all, much more convenient. But whenever I see those shelves towering up from the gleaming linoleum floors towards the blinding lights far above I am struck with the thought that eight brands of canned peas are paltry recompense for the loss of the character in that old wood floor. I can't help but feel that an old friend sold his soul for a parking lot.

How ironic it is that one must drive by the location of the old neighborhood store to reach the new one outside of town. Why is the remote new location more convenient than the old centralized one? Because a person can drive there in the time it took to walk to the old store, and the parking is more than ample.

We are increasingly becoming a drivers' society. "Why walk when you can drive?" seems to have become our creed. We ignore the negative impacts to our environment, our communities, and our own health for the sake of convenience.

The greetings and brief, friendly conversations we used to have when passing an acquaintance while walking have been replaced with honks of a car horn. The friendly banter at a lunch counter has given way to a voice crackling through our car window, "Would you like fries with that?" We are a society of drivers, preferring to drive ten miles over walking two blocks. Downtown areas and neighborhood stores have been pushed aside in the wake of urban-sprawl shopping centers. Ever outwards we expand, paving over forest and farmland.

What, in this sprawling world of parking lots, subdivisions, strip malls, and shopping centers, can be defined as a community? A community is a group of interdependent, interrelating people, sharing culture, history, and traditions. Our community is our home. It represents a large part of our identity, who we are, where we came from, what we care about. But in a society built around cars, not the people who drive them, we seem willing to sacrifice *community* for *convenience*.

Along with community, we are also sacrificing the human body, perhaps the most efficient and best-designed mode of transportation known to us. Fueled entirely by a variety of organic, renewable fuels, the human body produces an amount of

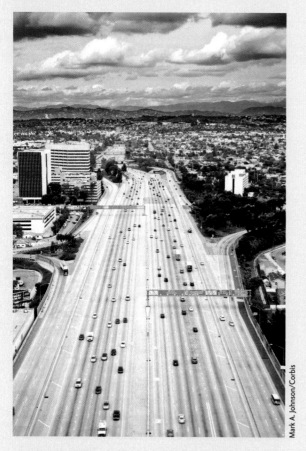

Mark A. Johnson/Corbis

walking five kilometers or cycling twenty kilometers each day (the daily exercise regime recommended by the US Institute of Medicine of the National Academies), carbon dioxide emissions would be reduced by eleven percent and the average weight loss would be "enough to virtually eliminate the obesity epidemic" (qtd. in Cohen).

It seems clear that as our driving increases, our health deteriorates. The driver's culture is a sedentary one. Nearly any conceivable product or service can now be found through a drive-through window, making it no longer necessary to exert even the energy to walk across a parking lot. A person can now tend to all daily errands without ever leaving the comfort of the driver's seat. We are increasingly bereft of natural exercise and exposed to harmful pollution and increased stress, so it is no wonder that our health as a nation is deteriorating. "Post–World War II-style suburban planning assumes everyone has a car and wants to use it. This model, some urban planners assume, is what accounts for the growing epidemic of obesity, heart disease and diabetes" (Ryberg). In her article, "Building Illness," Amanda Spake outlines some statistics:

- Since 1960, the number of people commuting to work out of the county they live in jumped by 200 percent. Residential "sprawl" has meant a 250 percent increase in vehicle miles traveled. The average driver spends 443 hours yearly behind the wheel, the equivalent of 11 workweeks.
- Driving displaces other activities, like exercise. "Being in a car doesn't do anything for you in terms of being thin," says Lawrence Frank of the University of British Columbia. "For every additional hour people spend in the car, there's a six percent increase in the likelihood of being obese" (qtd. in Spake).
- Increased auto traffic is also a key source of ground-level ozone. Asthma rates among

kinetic energy per calorie input unmatched by any technology we have yet developed. In addition, it suffers from a low instance of mechanical failure, is self-maintaining and repairing, produces only ecologically useful emissions, and, unlike the pollutant effects of automobiles, its use is actually beneficial to human health. Walking truly is the most efficient and ecologically friendly mode of transportation, yet we make every effort to minimize this healthful and sensible activity.

University of California, Berkley, Earth systems scientist Paul Higgins touted increasing walking as a solution both to obesity and global warming. Higgins pointed out that if Americans between the ages of ten and sixty-five substituted driving with children, who are believed to be particularly sensitive to ozone, more than doubled between 1980 and 1995.

- Living in the suburbs is linked to eating more higher-calorie fast food. At least 1 in 4 adults now eats fast food on any given day. For children, 1 of every 3 meals is fast food.
- Childhood obesity has more than doubled in three decades. But the number of kids who walk or bike to school has dropped from nearly half in 1960 to about 1 in 10 today, largely because schools are far from homes.

That automobiles are environmentally harmful is unarguable (Harrington and McConnell 6). Emissions from burnt fuel produce greenhouse gases that contribute to global warming, oxides of nitrogen that deplete the ozone layer, sulfides that result in acid rain, and toxic carbon monoxide. Roadways tear up the countryside, destroying wildlife routes and habitats; road and parking lot runoff pollutes watersheds. Increased driving and expansion of vehicle-related infrastructure naturally increases this pollution.

Relatively low fuel prices and high gas mileage keep the cost of driving low, allowing this drivers' society to perpetuate. As fuel economy increases, fuel prices can rise, sprawl can expand further outward, and the consumer can rest easy knowing he is a friend to the environment by virtue of his efficient new vehicle as he shops at the shopping center (formerly pastureland) twenty-five miles from his subdivision home (at one time, forest). Everyone wins, right? Progress at its finest. And never once does the driver of the thirty-six mile-per-gallon ultra-efficient compact car pause to remember how his mother used to walk down to the corner grocery store with her canvas shopping bag for her groceries, or how his grandfather used to drive to town only once a month for whatever supplies were needed on the farm.

We modern Americans think with our wallets. We will take a stand on an issue, if it's not too inconvenient and we can afford it. Perhaps if it costs us a bit more to drive, we would be more conscious of how many miles we drive each day. This is beginning to happen with the rise in gas prices. Government regulations pushing higher fuel efficiency and keeping fuel prices reasonable keep the consumer happy and spending while paying lip service to environmental causes. Perhaps our efforts would be more wisely focused on development of alternative fuel sources and on the strengthening of communities.

New Urbanism and other social reform movements promise to bring back the days of centralized, walkable communities, incorporating features such as wide sidewalks and narrow streets, neighborhood stores and schools. Proponents claim that these planned neighborhoods make for stronger communities, better health, and are more ecologically friendly. Susan Handy, Associate Professor of Environmental Science at the University of California, Davis, writes, "I strongly believe that as planners we have an obligation to give the residents of our communities choices, in particular, choices that are healthier for us as individuals, for the community as a whole, and for the environment." These ideas seem novel only in light of the sidewalk-less subdivisions and strip malls on the outskirts of town.

The notion of walking any significant distance as a necessary means of transportation seems so alien to us, but the drivers' society is a recent phenomenon. A hundred years ago hardly anyone drove. Suburbia did not exist prior to the Second World War. Fast food dates back to the sixties, strip malls to the seventies. Have the developments of these last few decades really been enough for us to cast aside our relationships with our neighbors for the sake of our conveyance?

Ultimately it is individual choice that will determine if our communities are to become mere pit stops on the highway. We can choose the easy route and drive, or exert a little extra effort for the sake of ourselves, each other, and our Earth.

Perhaps we need to take a step back from our highway-paced lives and slow things down to a gentle stroll. The liberalists of the industrial revolution predicted that technology would free our time so that we might live lives of leisure. Running late and stuck in traffic, I often think back to the days when Grandma and I would spend a whole afternoon just getting groceries. Maybe the only difference between *inconvenience* and *leisure* is mindset.

Works Cited

Cohen, Philip. "To Cool the World Eat Less, Walk More." *New Scientist* 18 Dec. 2004: 17. *Academic Search Elite*. Web. 14 Dec. 2006.

Congress for the New Urbanism. *Charter for New Urbanism*. Chicago: Cong. for the New Urbanism, 2001. Print.

Handy, Susan. "Questioning Assumptions 1: Do New Urbanists Walk More?" *Planning* 72.1 (2006): 36–37. *Academic Search Elite*. Web. 14 Dec. 2006.

Harrington, Winston, and Virginia McConnell. *Motor Vehicles and the Environment*. Washington: Resources for the Future, Apr. 2003. Print.

Hutchinson, Harry. "Easy on the Gas." *Mechanical Engineering* 128.7 (2006): 26–33. *Academic Search Elite*. Web. 14 Dec. 2006.

Ryberg, Erica. "Building the New Urbanism." *Smithsonian*. Smithsonian Inst., Aug. 2006. Web. 13 Dec. 2006.

Spake, Amanda. "Building Illness." *U.S. News & World Report* 20 June 2005: 54–55. *Academic Search Elite*. Web. 14 Dec. 2006.

Torma, Tim. "Urban Sprawl and Public Health: Designing, Planning and Building for Healthy Communities." *Journal of the American Planning Association* 72.1 (2006): 123–24. *Academic Search Elite*. Web. 14 Dec. 2006.

United States. Environmental Protection Agency. Office of Transportation and Air Quality. *Towards a Cleaner Future*. 2005. *United States Environmental Protection Agency*. Web. 14 Dec. 2006.

"The US Weighs In." *Tufts University Health & Nutrition Letter* 24.6 (2006): 3. *Academic Search Elite*. Web. 14 Dec. 2006.

Assignments: Identifying and Describing Claims

1. Categorize the following claims from Brown's essay as fact, value, or policy:

A. "[W]henever I see those shelves towering up from the gleaming linoleum floors towards the blinding lights far above I am struck with the thought that eight brands of canned peas are paltry recompense for the loss of the character in that old wood floor."

B. "[I]n a society built around cars, not the people who drive them, we seem willing to sacrifice *community* for *convenience*."

C. "The greetings and brief, friendly conversations we used to have when passing an acquaintance while walking have been replaced with honks of a car horn."

D. "New Urbanism and other social reform movements promise to bring back the days of centralized, walkable communities, incorporating features such as wide sidewalks and narrow streets, neighborhood stores and schools."

E. "Perhaps we as a society need to take a step back from our highway-paced lives and slow things down to a gentle stroll."

2. In a brief passage, state Brown's main claim (or thesis), and identify his main supporting claims.

3. In a small group, write out a simple opinion that is a claim of value (such as *Home schooling is good for families*), and then develop a more revelatory insight (such as *Home schooling reconnects home life and formal learning*). Ask questions about the opinion—about each word in the opinion—until you've opened up new intellectual possibilities. Based on your discussion, write a new claim of value that is more revelatory and focused than the original opinion.

Support

Sometimes called grounds or proofs, support comes in various forms: authorities, testimony, facts, statistics, allusions, anecdotes, illustrations, scenarios, appeals to logic, appeals to character, appeals to emotion, appeals to need, and appeals to value. Scholars have categorized and re-categorized these support strategies for centuries. One long-standing perspective divides them into three main groups:

Evidence: authorities, testimony, facts, statistics

Examples: allusions, anecdotes, illustrations, scenarios

Appeals: to logic, character, emotion, need, value

Certain types of claims may rely more heavily on a particular support category. For instance, a claim of fact may rely more on evidence than appeals. A claim of value may rely on appeals more than evidence. However, most arguments rely on support strategies from all three categories. In everyday life and even in specialized situations, we use a range of appeals, types of evidence, and examples.

Evidence

Evidence is a type of support that already exists, unlike appeals, which are created by a writer. Evidence can be used at any point in an argument: it can support the main claim or a supporting claim. But merely mentioning evidence or providing a fact is not enough. Arguers must explain the relevance of the evidence.

In his essay "Somewhere in the Past" (from Chapter 11), Cameron Johnson refers to facts and authorities and then, at the end of the paragraph, connects the evidence to his main point—that decreased school funding decreases community involvement:

> All across America, local school systems have been facing consistent budget cuts, and as in Clarksville, the cuts impact the delicate layer of social life around the schools: summer school, sports, music, and art programs have consistently been lopped off the agendas. Some districts, such as one in Orange County, Florida, are considering moving back starting times to 10:30 or 11:00 a.m. (Stover). It is easy to see that budget cuts have made schools shrink inward—balling themselves into smaller space and smaller bits of time. And even when communities pass local levies, they are often not enough to turn the tide. Increased taxes have not always kept up with the rate of inflation. According to the League of Education Voters, in the state of Washington, for example, from 1993 to 1999 state funding per student increased $528. Yet because of inflation, there was actually a decrease—of $527. Even in those few years, the system lost money. And when that loss is projected over decades, it is easy to imagine the economic effect: a consistent reduction of programs and a consistent reduction in the role that schools once played in their communities.

The specific evidence about Orange County is not simply presented to the reader. Instead, Johnson invites the reader to imagine "the economic effect" and to see his argument's relevance.

Authorities are experts who offer specialized knowledge. These sources are used in arguments to give credibility to a writer's claims, to illustrate outside or opposing perspectives, to help explain a topic, or to give a sense of popular opinion or historical context. In his essay "Shakespeare and Narcotics" (from Chapter 11), David Pinching uses authority to help support his own claims about the past:

> The mindset behind such an outlook is the really depressing thing. People like to imagine Shakespeare freebasing and rolling up joints because they see him as an establishment figure. As such, portraying him as a junkie causes amusement and indignation because of our modern attitude to substances that allows certain kinds of intoxication but not others. Shakespeare would not have understood our simultaneous and hypocritical prudishness and excess. He was, in his time, a radical, a novelty and far more dangerous to the establishment with his damning indictments of royalty in *King Lear*, *Richard III* and *King John*, among others, than any of our media starlets. The idea that you can be anti-establishment by becoming incapable of thinking properly is pretty out of date anyway. And, as the worst excesses of post-Sixties fiction, music and art have

proved, "mind-altering" does not necessarily mean "art-improving." Ann Donnelly, the curator of the Shakespeare Birthplace Trust, was unimpressed with the evidence from the pipes and claimed that people are always trying to "come up with reasons for saying Shakespeare was not a genius." This may be something of a spoilsport attitude, but it is a fair one.

As Pinching attempts to discredit the claims that Shakespeare used drugs, he brings in a credible voice on the matter, Ann Donnelly. Notice that Pinching states Donnelly's credentials in a phrase (highlighted) directly after he first gives her name. This short phrase, referred to as an *appositive*, helps writers quickly explain their sources' qualifications. Since authorities are a kind of evidence, explaining their qualifications is a way of explaining the relevance of the evidence.

Authorities, or references to outside sources, can be used in a variety of ways, but they are used most often to give an idea credence or believability. In his essay "Lunar Eclipse," Ed Bell follows up the initial point of his paragraph with a quotation:

> Because of light pollution, some people have never seen a dark sky. "In most cities, there's little point in gazing at the sky—unless you're fascinated by the sight of a few stars and some airplanes against a glowing background," says David Tennebaum, a science, health, and environment writer (for ABCNEWS.com, *Technology Review, Bio-Science, Environmental Health Perspectives, American Health,* and other publications). "If you have not seen a truly dark sky, you may not know that the urban glow conceals a network of uncountable stars in intriguing constellations."

Testimony is an eyewitness or firsthand account. An arguer's personal testimony appeals to readers by inviting them into his or her vision of the world. For example, Ed Bell's essay on light pollution strategically opens with his own testimony:

> The moon is gently orange with a thin, star-white bottom; its dark top disappears into the blackness surrounding it. Thirty-seven miles north, in town, it lacked the magically dull glow it has here eleven miles south of the store and gas station and twenty miles north of the next nearest

In court cases and Congressional hearings, testimony and authority often blend together.

Jonathan Ernst/Reuters/Corbis

bright lights. Driving east while it was still light out, I noticed a crescent moon, but knew it was a full-moon night. An eclipse! I watched as the crescent got smaller and smaller; I was hoping to find a dark spot where I could pull off to the side of the road and take in the full beauty of a lunar eclipse. I was approaching town, though.

I grew up in the country, then moved to the city in my early twenties. I must have seen star-filled skies as a child. I don't remember any. After a young adulthood of city lights, I remember the first night I saw the stars again. I was in my mid-thirties, traveling west, and we stopped to camp for the night. The rest of that summer we traveled the West, camping Utah, Oregon, Arizona, pitch-black nights and a billion stars, uncountable, so many that shooting stars were not rare to see and the constellations were so full of other stars I had trouble making them out.

Bell's testimony, a type of evidence, gives a personal angle to the issue. Rather than simply tell the reader "many people are bothered by light pollution," he narrates a personal experience. This testimony establishes Bell's character and helps the reader feel a sense of wonder about the stars.

Facts are agreed-upon bits of knowledge that do not require further support in an argument. As a type of evidence, facts are verified claims. This is not to say that facts cannot be disputed; they often are. But when arguers use a fact, they assume that it carries its own support. Notice how Laura Tangley uses facts in her article "Natural Passions":

Even scientists who are most opposed to the idea of animal passion acknowledge that many creatures experience "primary emotions"— feelings such as aggression and fear that are instinctive and require no conscious thought. Essential to escaping predators and other dangers, fear, in particular—along with predictable freeze, flight or fight responses— seems to be hardwired. A laboratory rat that has never encountered a cat, for example, will still freeze if it is exposed to the smell of this predator.

As readers, we get the sense that Tangley's assertions in this passage can be easily verified, that "primary emotions" in animals are considered a fact among those who study them or observe them casually. This is her starting place. She later goes on to argue that animals feel more than primary emotions, that they experience a complex range of emotions, much like humans. These latter points require other types of evidence beyond a declaration of facts. Like Tangley, many arguers use facts as a starting place and build from what is evident or easily verifiable.

In academic writing, facts that the audience would not otherwise know should be cited, as illustrated in the following excerpt from Charles Nelson's "Investing in Futures: The Cost of College":

> It is widely known that college has been a good investment for students. It has traditionally offered many advantages, the most obvious being that some degrees pay off financially. For example, according to the National Association of Colleges and Employers' 2002 Salary Survey, starting salaries for some majors exceed $50,000—chemical engineering: $50,387; computer science: $50,352; mechanical engineering, management information systems/business data processing, accounting, civil engineering, and economics/finance all start above $40,000 (Geary).

Statistics are figures drawn from surveys, experimentation, and data analysis. In her essay "Higher Education through Discombobulation" (from Chapter 9), Betsy Chitwood explains her own learning experience and then offers statistical research to support the idea:

> This learning process, albeit an extreme example, motivated me to take risks and seek ways to succeed in my chosen career. The impact of the disorientation was in direct proportion to the personal growth brought about by my "education" and it definitely shaped who I am today.
>
> Evidence from academic research supports this theory. In a study by Craig and Graesser at the University of Memphis, college students participated in an introduction to computer literacy by using AutoTutor, an intelligence tutoring system (ITS). The study, which tracked the effect of confusion and other emotions on students' responses, showed that a higher percentage (68%) of learning gains were achieved when the students were met with confusion (4).

Or notice Ellen Goodman's strategic use of statistics in her article "Culture in Need of an Extreme Makeover":

> But even after the ban on silicone, women chose to "enhance" or "augment" their breasts, this time using saline implants. The annual number of breast enlargements actually grew, hugely, from 32,607 in 1992 to 225,818 last year.

Like all forms of evidence, statistics can be used dishonestly. For instance, opinion polls are often used as evidence of a particular trend in society. But those polls may be conducted on an unrepresentative section of the population. If someone were to poll viewers of Fox News, for example, the results would be characterized by the ideological leanings

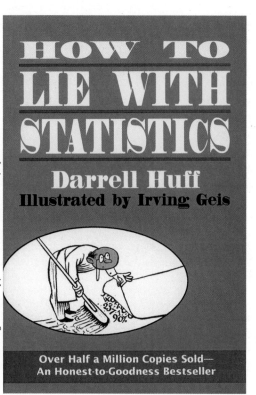

(the unstated beliefs and values) of that audience. So imagine that Fox News (or MSNBC or CNN) reported the following:

> According to a recent national poll, 72% of Americans are not overly concerned about honesty in the stock market. This suggests that revamping the role of the Securities and Exchange Commission should not necessarily be a priority.

While the statistic gives some sense of legitimacy to the statement, we do not know if the poll was taken on a representative sample of the U.S. population. Also, we do not know the nature of the survey questions. Many respondents could have said they were "concerned" but not "highly concerned" (as they might have been about terrorism or job security). Statistics can be valuable and add legitimacy to claims, but their origin should be revealed to the audience so that readers know not just the numbers, but the process that gives them meaning. (For more statistics and persuasion, see Julie Burks's essay, "The Patsy: A Story of a Number," page 398.)

Activities

1. In small groups, discuss how a writer might use authorities, testimony, facts, and statistics to support one of the following claims: *College football is more like a professional than an amateur sport. Reality TV shows help teach viewers some important lessons about life. Employers should provide more incentives for workers to bike to work.*

2. Explain a recent instance from everyday life when you used authorities, testimony, facts, or statistics to support a claim.

Examples

Examples are specific occurrences of a phenomenon. Whenever arguers support a claim with particular versions of a point, they are using examples. For example, in her essay about technological addiction (at the end of this chapter), Lynda Smith gives a range of everyday examples that support her claim about "the desire of instant gratification":

> In this fast-paced society of compacted time restraints, we long for more leisure time. At the same time, we are consumed with the desire for instant gratification. We want immediate access to people, information, and services any time, day or night. We believe that somehow if we do everything faster, we will have more free time. Our lives have become a world filled with services to help us move through life with increased speed. We have drive-thrus for food, banking, even laundry so we don't have to leave our cars. We have u-scan checkouts at grocery stores so we don't have to wait in line. And now, different speeds at which we can choose to move through life. There is high speed, turbo speed, and new elite speeds where you can, without leaving your home, hit speeds up to 6.0 Mbps (AT&T).

Allusions are references to some public knowledge from history, current events, popular culture, religion, or literature. (For more about literature, see page 41.) Allusions add depth and meaning to an argument. By making connections to culturally shared bits of knowledge, allusions link an argument to the world beyond it. In her essay "No Sex Please, We're Middle Class" (from Chapter 8), Camille Paglia alludes to popular culture to develop her argument:

> In the 1980s, commercial music boasted a beguiling host of sexy pop chicks like Deborah Harry, Belinda Carlisle, Pat Benatar, and a charmingly ripe Madonna. Late Madonna, in contrast, went bourgeois and turned scrawny. Madonna's dance-track acolyte, Lady Gaga, with her compulsive overkill, is a high-concept fabrication without an ounce of genuine eroticism.

By using these allusions, Paglia taps into the readers' collective knowledge about popular culture and links her argument to that knowledge, thus adding power to her ideas. Earlier in the essay, she alludes to the "racy lingerie" of Victoria's Secret, the "blazingly raunchy" scenarios of country music, the "Black rhythm and blues" of the Mississippi Delta, and the "hard rock bands of the '60s." When she alludes to the Rolling

Stones' recording of Willie Dixon's "Little Red Rooster," Paglia's *New York Times* readers are likely to hear the Stones' "visceral rawness and seductive sensuality."

Anecdotes are short accounts of a particular event or incident. They often are given in the form of a brief story that supports an arguer's point. While *testimony*, another form of support, comes from an eyewitness ("I saw the train coming around the mountain. . . ."), an anecdote is told by the arguer as though he or she is an objective reporter of events ("The incident on the train tracks started with the train coming around the mountain. . . ."). The details in an anecdote can provide powerful support: Since anecdotes are examples, they help to draw an audience into a specific scene. However, they should always be relevant to the main idea of the argument.

Imagine that a writer is arguing that the small local farmer has a more positive impact on communities than large corporate farms do. Notice the following two possible anecdotes. Which one seems more relevant to the main claim?

> Martin Grove farmed the fields of Northwestern Ohio for decades, and he bought his supplies locally—everything from basic tools to seed. But last summer, he came into Feed & Supply and made his last purchase: materials for packing up his farm so he could sell it off. In a five-year period, four other local farmers did the same thing, and this year, Feed & Supply has begun laying off employees because the corporate farms that have moved in do not rely as heavily on local business for supplies.

> Martin Grove farmed the fields of Northwestern Ohio for decades. He had fields of corn, wheat, and soybeans, and he developed a healthy orchard of apples—the best around, according to locals. In fact, in the summer of '68, Jerry Foster announced at the town jubilee that, next to Grove's apples, his own apples were fit for birds only. (And some say that the old saying "that's for the birds" comes from Foster's proclamation.)

The details in the first anecdote speak directly to the idea that local farmers support communities more than corporate farms do. The second anecdote, while interesting, is not obviously related to this claim. The writer would have to make that connection for the reader.

Illustrations are graphic descriptions or representations of an idea. Writers may illustrate a point with words alone, carefully describing the details of an idea to create an image in the reader's mind. In essence, they are drawing a picture—an example—with words. But illustrations, in the strict sense of the word, use actual graphics. Alone, they can make persuasive points. For instance, Florence Nightingale used graphics to argue about medical conditions. The following commentary, from the Florence Nightingale Museum website, points out significant elements of the illustration:

> The other highly original chart is what I will call the "Lines"—a bar chart showing how soldiers in peacetime, living in their barracks in England, were dying at a faster rate than civilians in the cities around them.
>
> There is a black bar in each of four age ranges, and a longer red bar. The black bar is the number of civilians who die each year, and the red is the number of soldiers. There are a number of curious overtones to this graphic, which may just be a coincidence.
>
> First, the title "Lines" (in ornate script in the original) makes it sound like a poem, as in Lines on the Death of Bismarck. There are four pairs of bars, when actually the message is clear from one pair alone. There seems to be a kind of repetition, as in a chorus. This effect is increased by the words, repeated at the end of each line, English Men, English Soldiers . . . It sounds like a funeral march.
>
> Second, the red bar for the soldiers would certainly make some people think of the "Thin Red Line," which had become famous in the Crimean War when a two-deep row of red-jacketed British infantrymen stopped a Russian heavy cavalry charge, something that was thought to be impossible. The thin red lines on Nightingale's chart represented these same heroic soldiers who were now dying unnecessarily because of bad hygiene in their barracks.

LINES

Representing the Relative Mortality of the Army at Home and of the English Male Population at corresponding Ages

AGES.	Deaths Annually to 1000 living.	DEATHS.	
20-25	8.4		Englishmen.
	17.0		English Soldiers.
25-30	9.2		Englishmen.
	18.3		English Soldiers.
30-35	10.2		Englishmen.
	18.4		English Soldiers.
35-40	11.6		Englishmen.
	19.8		English Soldiers.

Note   The Mortality of the English Male Population, at the above Ages, is taken from the English Life Table (1849-53)

Scenarios are fictional or hypothetical examples. As a persuasive tool, they can support nearly any argumentative claim. For example, imagine a writer, Angela, is arguing about grading policies at her college:

> The problem with the four-point system is that it does not present the true variation among students. Imagine three students all achieve a 4.0 in a class. James's final score was 93%, Tonya's 95%, and Will's 100%. The 4.0 final grade would not reflect the broad range of performance between James and Will. In fact, Will's perfect score is not at all differentiated from a student who balances on the margin of a 4.0 and 3.0.

Although these students are not real people, they put a picture in readers' minds. Scenarios like these help readers to envisage an otherwise abstract point. If the scenario is likely, readers can imagine it actually occurring. If the scenario is detailed enough (and if those details correspond to a possible reality), readers may not make a distinction between what's possible and what has occurred. In Angela's scenario, readers can easily imagine the three students and their grades.

When arguers use scenarios, they should signal the audience that they are in hypothetical territory. This can involve a simple cue such as "Imagine that . . ." or something even subtler, such as verb mood:

> If one student were to score 93%, another 95%, and another 100%, they would all receive a 4.0. However, the final grade would . . .

Or notice Tracy Webster's strategy in his argument, "Big House in the Wilderness. Webster simply asks a set of questions that introduce readers to a possible reality:

> What would happen if Americans could somehow overcome their own selfish and hypocritical desires to overbuild and overdestroy, and instead make *every* effort, not just *some* effort, to peacefully and respectfully co-exist with non-human life? Doing this would require a new sort of vision—seeing all the wildlife that they presently overlook. It would also require a new look at rhetoric, replacing words like "harvest" with "slaughter" and "environment" with "home." What would happen if all new homebuilders saw themselves more as visitors, guests, and newcomers? And better yet, as intruders, conquerors, and imperialists?

Notice that the verb mood often changes in scenarios from the *indicative* ("Americans overcome their own desires") to the *subjunctive* ("Americans could overcome their own desires").

➔ Literary Works

Literary works function uniquely as allusions. Novels, poetry, drama, songs, and short stories speak to broad themes such as government corruption, self-sacrifice for family, institutional oppression of the individual, self-discovery, and so on. Writers often allude to literature because it sheds light on human affairs. In each of the following examples, writers use a literary passage or quotation to give dimension to an idea. Notice how the writers set up the literary work: Before they give the key lines or scene, they first give the author and title. For fiction (novels and short stories), they also give a brief explanation of the overall setting or scene. And they always explain the relevant idea—the point that the reader should take away from the excerpt:

- If we paid attention only to mainstream media and governmental posturing, we might come to see revenge as a simple knee-jerk human response, a reaction that is inherently justified and morally correct. But the path of revenge is difficult, fraught with its own hardships, ambivalences, and self-destruction. Shakespeare's *Hamlet* embodies the uncertainty; he is caught between the desire to strike out against his father's murderer and a web of other, unspeakable, thoughts:

  > To be, or not to be: that is the question:
  > Whether 'tis nobler in the mind to suffer
  > The slings and arrows of outrageous fortune,
  > Or to take arms against a sea of troubles,
  > And by opposing end them. (*Ham.* 3.1.56–60)

- Throughout our history of warfare, there has been one constant: It always exceeds our expectations of horror and confusion. Each new war seems to bring about its own particular type of confusions. In *Legends of the Fall*, Jim Harrison tells of World War I, when American soldiers were caught between an old world of physical contact and a new world of technological horror. The scene is a Parisian hospital. The main character, Tristan, has lost his brother to German mustard gas and has gone on a rampage of revenge by scalping numbers of German soldiers. After being subdued by his commanders, Tristan now stands in the main office of a psychiatric ward:

  > The doctor so doubted his ability to knit up [the soldiers'] souls that he became almost bored with his patients and did all he could to have them shipped home. Thus he was fascinated with the arrival of Tristan when the ambulance driver advised him that a true "crazy" was waiting to be unloaded. The doctor sent attendants and read the report from Tristan's commander. He felt himself oddly unmoved by the scalpings and was surprised at the commander's horror. How could mustard gas be considered normal warfare and not scalping, in the reaction to the death of a brother? (218)

- The sexuality of young women in small towns is far more complex, and even political, than what polite society normally wants to acknowledge. Barbara Kingsolver's narrator in *The Bean Trees* invites the reader into the lives of several young women whose lives illustrate the deep connections among sexuality, social acceptance, reproduction, and motherhood. Almost immediately in the novel, we hear of Jolene, a small-town Appalachian girl who comes into a medical center with a gunshot wound to the shoulder:

> Jolene was a pie-faced, heavy girl and I always thought she looked like the type to have gone and found trouble just to show you didn't have to be a cheerleader to be fast. The trouble with that is it doesn't get you anywhere, no more than a kid on a bicycle going no hands and no feet up and down past his mother hollering his head off for her to look. She's not going to look till he runs into something and busts his head wide open. (8)

• Americans, say many scholars and thinkers, have always been after something that we destroy by pursuing it. F. Scott Fitzgerald's classic *The Great Gatsby* brings us face to face with a narrator who realizes this at the end of the novel, as he peers over the Eastern coastline:

> And as the moon rose higher the inessential houses began to melt away until gradually I became aware of the old island here that flow-ered once for Dutch sailors' eyes—a fresh, green breast of the new world. Its vanished trees, the trees that had made way for Gatsby's house, had once pandered in whispers to the last and greatest of all human dreams; for a transitory enchanted moment man must have held his breath in the presence of this continent, compelled into aesthetic contemplation he neither understood nor desired, face to face for the last time in history with something commensurate to his capacity for wonder. (189)

Religious Texts

To many people, religious texts are paths to the truth. But in public argument, in situations that involve diverse audiences, writers cannot simply hold up a particular religious text *as* truth. Because there are so many religious perspectives (Hinduism, Buddhism, Sikhism, Judaism, Christianity, Islam, Shinto, Confucianism, just to name a few), and so many religious texts (the Vedas, the Bhagavad Gita, the Torah, the New Testament, the Koran, the Guru Granth Sahib, and so on) referring to one as the truth is apt to alienate readers. Because most audiences are diverse and cannot be assumed to hold a consensual belief in one religious text, writers must be cau-tious. (One cannot assume, for instance, that everyone accepts, as fact, that Jesus is the son of God.) But, with that caution in mind, writers can use religious texts. These books have enormous significance in people's minds, whether or not they are follow-ers of a specific faith.

So, how do religious texts function in argument? In the New Testament, Jesus says, "Love your neighbor," and then tells a parable about the Good Samaritan to explain the concept. Whether or not one's reader is a Christian, Jesus's point about love and his supporting parable can be used to develop an argument about personal relationships, national policies, or world affairs. Because the particular religious teaching transcends Christianity, it can be applied to various situations and argu-ments. The ideas of Buddha, Muhammad, Parsvanatha, and others can be used in the same way—not as unquestionable truths, but as appeals to value. At the very least, these appeals can help writers create common ground with their readers.

Appeals

Appeals are a major form of support in argumentation. They call on the reader's sense of logic, character, emotion, need, or value. Because the arguer makes a connection between the topic and the reader's consciousness, appeals call for intellectual commitment, both on the part of the arguer and of the audience.

Appeals differ from forms of evidence (statistics, facts, illustrations, etc.) in an important way: While evidence is already formed for the writer, an appeal must be constructed out of logical steps, shared values, beliefs, or needs. The writer must *create* the bridge between the topic and the audience. For this reason, Aristotle called appeals *artistic proofs* and forms of evidence *inartistic proof.*

Appeals constitute most of what we know as argument; without appeals, other types of support such as statistics, examples, and illustrations have little persuasive power. In the hands of a good writer, appeals make all the difference between a flat argument that does not speak to audiences and an engaging argument that calls out audiences' reasoning power, values, beliefs, and needs. Good writers can use appeals to make a topic come to life and enter the lives of their audience.

Notice how the above leaflets, dropped into Iraq during the first phase of the war in 2003, appeal to values.

Appeals to Logic

In mainstream culture, people believe that something is "true" if it can be substantiated with mounds of data. But in academic writing, it's not the mounds of data but the appeal to logic that matters most. In fact, without a logical framework, statistics and facts can mean nothing—or anything. Writers use an appeal to logic whenever they invite an audience to think through an idea, to walk along an intellectual path. Sometimes, that invitation is direct. Statements like the following show a writer appealing explicitly to readers' logic:

- Let us consider the following reasons . . .
- Because of the stated conditions, we can only conclude that . . .
- Yet another reason to accept the idea . . .
- Given the following rationale, we should dismiss the idea of . . .

Or in the next passage, the writer calls on readers to set aside emotions and investigate the legal issues. This, too, is a direct appeal to logic:

> Gay marriage in America has become a fairly emotional issue. But we should work around the emotions involved and investigate the issue of rights and state law. It has been established that individual states can define marriage. The question, then, lies in the role of other states: Does every state have to honor a marriage licensed in other states? This, it seems, is merely a matter of constitutional law.

But logical appeals are often more indirect. The writer often establishes a subtle line of reasoning: a series of logical steps (or premises) that lead arguer and audience to a main claim. If the path is well crafted—with few missteps or gaps between premises—readers follow along and become more accepting of the overall argument. Sometimes the line of reasoning is easy to see; it has been made explicit. (Writers may even use cues such as "first" or "the first reason.") But the line of reasoning is usually harder to detect. It works quietly behind the progression of supporting ideas. In the following passage from "Somewhere in the Past" (Chapter 11) Cameron Johnson invites the reader to follow his line of reasoning, to see

John Metz

the links among school budgets, school programs, students, and the surrounding community. Once these logical links are established, Johnson makes the final point that less funding equals less community:

> Another example helps illustrate the vital connection between school and community. Many Clarksville citizens grew up in, and have fond memories of, the school's summer recreation program that was cut back steadily each year and finally abandoned in 1996. While this program can be seen as nonessential, it was hardly fluff in the budget. The summer recreation program was an important link between school and community. It not only gave kids something to do, but it helped forge a stronger bond between school and student, and this bond created other bonds: between school and community and between community and student. Because of less funding, schools end up offering less support (for academics) and less attraction (for extracurricular activities). In the long run, schools with less funding become less important to students and less important within the community as a whole. The summer recreation program is just one example of this subtle, or silent, breakdown.

For an argument to be successful, the reader must accept each premise in the line of reasoning—not stumbling, getting off the path, or stopping halfway through. Therefore, the writer has to make certain that each step is supported or made acceptable so the reader can move forward. This is where all the support strategies come into play: personal testimony, allusions, facts, examples, statistics, and primary and secondary sources. Imagine an argument emerging from the following premises:

- Popular culture influences how people think.
- Mainstream popular culture encourages young people to be overly energized and unfocused.
- The lack of focus is one of the main hurdles to educational success—and seems to be increasing in schools and colleges.
- The recent surge in energy drinks increases the problem because they decrease students' ability to maintain focus.
- The energy drink fad adds more twitch to an overly twitchy generation of students.

Each of these premises needs support. For instance, the first premise calls for some examples in the present or past that show a pop culture message influencing the behavior of the masses. The second premise calls for examples of pop culture encouraging people to be unfocused. Specific commercials, messages, products, and fads would illustrate the point. For the third and fourth premises, the writer might search for teachers' testimonies about students. Once all the premises are supported, the final claim can be accepted. (In this way, a line of reasoning can function as the scaffolding of an argument. When a writer thinks through the premises that support the main claim, she can discover a basic structure or support system for the argument.)

Types of Reasoning *Deductive reasoning* builds a conclusion from accepted premises or general principles. Often, this means relying on classes (all dogs, all men, all raincoats, all months beginning in J). For example:

- All birds have beaks. (General statement about the class)
- Polly the parrot is a bird. (Specific statement that puts Polly in the class)
- Therefore, Polly has a beak. (Conclusion built from the premises)

Deduction may also rely on, or build from, a definitional statement—a statement that says what something is:

- Bipeds are animals with two legs.
- Ostriches are two-legged animals.
- Therefore, ostriches are bipeds.

Deductive logic often lurks behind legal or ethical decisions. A general principle or legal definition helps people conclude something about a specific case or situation. In the following passage, the writer makes a deductive case that begins with a constitutional premise and works toward a specific claim about gay rights:

> Under the Constitution, people are endowed with equal rights. Throughout history, we have been prompted to act from that fundamental notion despite public opinion about minorities: women, African Americans, Hispanics, and Japanese Americans. Gay and lesbian couples are no different. Their sexuality does not strip them of citizenship, nor exile them from constitutional rights. They should be given the same rights as heterosexual couples despite public or religious opinions to the contrary.

In everyday life, we often use a form of reasoning called the enthymeme, which is a line of reasoning that contains an unstated premise. The unstated premise is so widely accepted that it goes unmentioned. The audience is left to conclude or assume the point. For example, if someone says, *I've received high marks on every assignment thus far, so I'm going to receive a high grade in the course,* she omits a point: high grades on all the assignments will lead to a high grade in the course. This point is so widely assumed that it can safely be left unsaid.

Inductive reasoning builds from specific premises and leads to a general claim. Here's a basic example: *I found a mouse in the toilet last week. I saw a mouse in the kitchen yesterday. Therefore, mice have found a way into the house!* In other words, anytime we make a conclusion based on several specifics, we are doing induction. Of course, the situation can be more sophisticated. In the following line of reasoning, the preliminary steps are specific, and the more general concluding statement is derived from those specifics:

- The warmest average annual temperatures recorded have occurred since 1991.
- Throughout the world, most high-temperature records have been set in the past three years.
- On the whole, average winter temperatures have increased in the past fifty years.
- While the average temperature of all regions is increasing, no regions have experienced average decreasing temperatures.
- The Earth is warming.

What kind of reasoning is operating in this billboard? What are the premises?

You are probably familiar with inductive logic. It is the primary engine of scientific argument and of many of the arguments that come from scientific study. Much of what we accept about our food, medicine, even our own health comes from inductive reasoning. Researchers line up tests to prove something occurs not just once but many times under certain conditions. Then they draw a general conclusion about such things as eggs, liver, artificial sweeteners, red wine, and so on. But the conclusion does not always account for other variables. Consider this increasingly common scenario: A pharmacology company is studying a particular kind of pill. The company does many studies, testing the pill on a variety of animals and then people. After hundreds or thousands of tests, the researchers conclude that the pill works to increase bone density. Their logic looks something like this:

The pill increased density in test subject A.

The pill increased density in test subject B.

The pill increased density in test subject C. (And so on.)

Therefore, the pill increases bone density.

The many premises seem to support the conclusion. However, the conclusion is not certain. The researchers may later discover that the studies did not account for a particular age range, particular racial variables, even particular genetic predispositions. Therefore, the company will qualify its conclusion: The pill increases bone density in Caucasian women over 60 with a particular bone loss disease. As this example shows, induction always works against the variability of life—all the possibilities that might challenge the conclusion.

Analogical reasoning depends on comparisons (or analogies). The arguer moves from one particular to another particular, instead of from general to specific (deductive) or specific to general (inductive). Comparisons, metaphors, allegories, parables, and examples all have an analogous quality: they argue that if two things are alike in certain respects, they are also alike in other respects. Analogies shed light on something by comparing or contrasting it with something familiar. For example, an analogy can be historical, explaining a present situation by comparing it to a similar situation from the past. Some people have compared the U.S. involvement in Afghanistan to the Vietnam War. Drawing attention to similarities between the two situations (an elusive enemy halfway around the world, a divided nation, a questionable cause, and so on) sheds light on the Iraq war and makes a case for pulling troops out. The line of reasoning is that since key circumstances are similar, the results are likely to be similar.

Good logic is critical to sound argument. The tighter the logic, the better the argument. But poor logic often sounds good. Politicians use nice-sounding phrases and reasonable-sounding premises to hide poor logic. If we had no tools for figuring out good versus bad logic, we might simply accept all those nice-sounding arguments. That is why readers and writers of argument study *logical fallacies:* flaws in the structure of an argument that make a claim invalid. A fallacy is a falsehood, so a logical fallacy is a logical falsehood that makes no sense within a given situation. Some of the most common fallacy types are discussed next, but many more types exist.

Ad hominem (Latin for *to the person)* fallacies are personal attacks. Instead of responding to the *ideas* someone has put forth, the arguer attacks the *person* or some quality of the person. In politics, these personal attacks draw attention away from important policy debates and focus instead on character. For example, if one group does not believe in the science that supports global warming, they might make fun of Al Gore, a leading voice on global warming, for having a big house. (The size of Gore's house has nothing to do with the evidence about global warming.) Concerns about someone's character can be relevant to an issue. However, ad hominem attacks focus on character at the expense of the issue at hand.

Strawperson fallacies involve misrepresenting a position and then dismissing it as wrong. In this type of fallacy, an arguer sets up an opposing position (called a *strawperson* or *scarecrow)* that is easy to knock over or beat up. For example, imagine that Molly opposes leash laws. But Tom argues that dogs should be kept on leashes when they are walked through town. Rather than engage Tom's position in a fair manner, Molly responds by saying, "Tom isn't a dog person. He thinks they should always be tied up and *never* allowed to run free." Molly has distorted Tom's position. She has made him seem unreasonable, even mean-spirited, which unfairly bolsters her position.

Post hoc, ergo propter hoc (or faulty cause-effect) fallacies claim that if one thing happened before another, then the first thing must have caused the second. *Post hoc, ergo propter hoc* is Latin for "after this, therefore because of this" (and is often shortened to *post hoc).* Such arguments are false because they confuse sequence with cause. If a rooster crows just before sunrise, that rooster didn't cause daylight. That's easy to conclude. But in public life, things can be more complex. For instance, if a new governor takes office just before the state's economy goes into a recession, the cause might involve a range of complex financial dynamics—and *not* the new governor.

Either/or fallacies oversimplify an issue by claiming that only two options exist when there are more options to choose from. The old slogan "love it or leave it" suggests only two choices. A third (unmentioned) alternative is to stay and work toward changes that will improve the situation. Either/or thinking can transcend particular arguments and seep into the collective state of mind—the national consciousness. For example, in the United States we tend to label political positions as either conservative or liberal.

Hasty generalizations draw conclusions based on too little evidence. For example, generalizing about a city because you drove through it on a Sunday morning can be dangerous because cities are quieter and have less traffic on Sunday mornings. Claiming that Santa Rosa is a sleepy little town, based on one Sunday morning, ignores many other dimensions and possibilities about the town. A generalization based on so little evidence is considered *hasty* or *broad*. This intellectual habit often surfaces in arguments about gender, race, age, sexual orientation, and even vocation—for example, *lawyers are not to be trusted.*

Non sequitur (Latin for *it does not follow)* skips or confuses logical steps. The conclusion cannot logically be arrived at through the premises. Any argument in which the conclusion doesn't follow logically from the premise can be considered a non sequitur. Each of the following conclusions may be true, but they do not follow logically from their premise: Because Bob is smart, he will get a good job. Alphie is honest; therefore, he will lead a happy life. The buildup of nuclear arms in the past twenty-five years was the only thing that kept the United States out of war.

Slippery slope fallacies claim that a certain way of thinking or acting will necessarily lead to more of the same—that once you begin sliding down a slippery slope, you will keep sliding. While one action may in fact lead to similar actions, the slippery slope fallacy appeals to fear by claiming that taking a certain moderate action will lead to more extreme actions: *If we put limitations on the sale of semi-automatic guns, it won't be long until shotguns are illegal, then steak knives.*

Begging the Question (also called *circular reasoning* and, in Latin, *petitio principii)* involves supporting a claim by restating (in different words) the claim itself. No support is provided; the arguer simply repeats the claim. *Tim would be a good president because he is presidential material* is circular reasoning. It is like a dog chasing its own tail. A student who argues that he should not receive a C because he is an *A* student is caught up in circular reasoning. Instead, the student must argue that he deserves an *A* because of his quality of work.

Red herring fallacies are deliberate attempts to change the subject. Instead of dealing with the actual argument, the arguer introduces irrelevant points to distract the audience. A red herring is like rattling keys in front of a crying baby: the baby's attention becomes focused on something else—the keys. If a supervisor confronts an employee about being late for work again, and the employee responds that tech support still hasn't solved his computer problem, he is using a red herring to shift attention away from the supervisor's charge.

Bandwagon fallacies claim that because everyone else is doing it, you should, too. They invite people to accept something because it is popular. This is also referred to as *herd mentality.* If a child argues for her right to get a tattoo by pleading, "All of my friends already have one," she is relying on the bandwagon fallacy. Or if a cell phone company urges people to buy its product by proclaiming, "Everyone's coming over to our plan," it is relying on bandwagon logic, which—by the way—tends to work on consumers.

Association fallacies claim that two people or things share a quality just because they are somehow associated, connected, or related. One type of association argument is guilt by association, in which the arguer claims that one person or thing has the same negative characteristics as another because the two are somehow associated. Honor by association is also possible, and can be just as fallacious. A particular type of association fallacy is *reductio ad Hitlerum.* This type of fallacy claims that anything Adolf Hitler (or the Nazi party) did or thought must be evil. (The same false logic could be applied to anything: Republicans, Democrats, the ACLU, Osama bin Laden, and so on.) The logic is that something is evil because it is associated with Hitler. But genocide, for example, is evil on its own merits, not because of Hitler. And Hitler was a vegetarian, but that doesn't make vegetarianism evil.

Golden age fallacies characterize the past as broadly and inherently better. Arguments based on a golden age perspective prompt us to imagine some bygone era as though no crime, no immodesty, no illicit behaviors existed before the present. In the mainstream media and in popular political rhetoric, people often associate the 1950s with purity, simplicity, and easy living. They rely on Hollywood versions of the past and on sanitized memories while ignoring the violence, war, and rampant racism of the era. Certainly, life may have been more innocent or more peaceful for some people at some point in the past. But only lazy arguers imagine that all parts of their civilization were inherently better "back in the day." Such a perspective yields some other fallacies such as appeals to antiquity or appeals to tradition, in which arguers imagine that any values from the past are good simply because they are "tried and true."

Activities

1. Take one of the fallacies listed in this section. In a small group, generate at least two statements that illustrate the particular fallacy. Share the two statements with the rest of the class and explain how they are flawed.

2. Do a Google search for logical fallacies. Find one not listed in this section and report it to others in your class. As you describe the fallacy, invent your own statement that demonstrates the flawed logic. If possible, use a timely political or cultural issue.

Appeals to Character

Appeals to character draw attention to the arguer's (writer/speaker's) personal nature, integrity, experience, wisdom, or personality. They are used to fend off any doubts about the arguer's credibility. Appeals to character are usually a small part of a bigger argument and are used to make the audience comfortable and more apt to accept other claims. They are an explicit strategy for building trust or confidence in the arguer. For instance, imagine that a writer is arguing against increasing standardized testing in elementary education. To create credibility, she draws attention to her own experience:

> In my fifteen years as an elementary school teacher, I have watched students' learning time diminish and their test-taking time greatly increase. I have seen first-hand how students leave behind their curiosity and wonder—essential for the development of young minds—and fix their attention on the little circles and blanks on standardized tests.

Politicians often use appeals to character, either to suggest something positive about their own credibility or to make voters doubt the credibility of their opponents. For instance, a presidential candidate may discuss his military duty to show his own patriotism and then point to his opponent's lack of military duty. Even campaign photos of political candidates work as appeals to character.

Appeals to character can be used dishonestly, as a way to avoid focusing on other issues. For instance, if someone asked a politician about the logic of a policy decision and she replied, "Don't question what's in my heart," she would have side-stepped the question and drawn attention to something the audience cannot possibly know anyway: her "heart." Such dishonest rhetorical moves are common in political debate. In the following passage from George Orwell's *Animal Farm*, Squealer, the pig, appeals to character:

> We pigs are brainworkers. The whole management and operation of this farm depend on us. Day and night we are watching over your welfare. It is for your sake that we drink that milk and eat those apples.

Squealer focuses on the pigs' intentions, something his audience cannot possibly know or dispute. The move distracts the animals from asking other questions about the pigs' behavior.

In formal argument, appeals to character should be used with caution. While they can help an arguer create credibility, they should not replace a strong logical argument. Some voters may be swayed by good looks, charismatic gestures, or even a good movie career, but academic readers look for sophisticated logic as the primary attribute of an argument.

Appeals to Emotion

Appeals to emotion draw on the emotions (fears, hopes, sympathies, yearnings) of the audience. In her essay "More Than Cherries" (from Chapter 8), Samantha Tengelitsch appeals to her readers' emotions by describing the illness and death of a local woman:

> Last spring an article ran in the local paper about a young woman running for the prestigious title of National Cherry Queen. It told the story of Lauren Hemming, a twenty-year-old college student, who was raised on a Peninsula Township cherry farm and who was battling non-Hodgkin's lymphoma (a cancer of the lymphatic system) while running for the prestigious title. A photograph included with the article captured Lauren sitting cross-legged in a hammock in front of her home. It was spring and sun shown brightly. At the time of the photograph, Lauren was undergoing chemotherapy for the lymphoma and had lost her hair, but this in no way detracted from her beauty. Her story was inspirational and touched me as I'm sure it touched others.
>
> Unfortunately, Lauren was not able to continue with her bid for Cherry Queen. Instead, she fought bravely to save her own life and the following winter died from the cancer, which had spread to her brain.

Tengelitsch even points to her own emotional state—and attempts to draw readers into a sense of loss. As her argument about cause continues, it depends heavily on forms of evidence, so this initial emotional appeal helps to create an important human element.

Appeals to emotion are sometimes used dishonestly. For instance, notice another set of appeals from George Orwell's *Animal Farm*, in which Squealer tries to convince the other animals that only the pigs should eat the milk and apples:

> "Comrades!" he cried. "You do not imagine, I hope, that we pigs are doing this in a spirit of selfishness and privilege? Many of us actually dislike milk and apples. I dislike them myself. Our sole object in taking these things is to preserve our health. Milk and apples (this has been proven by science, comrades) contain substances absolutely necessary to the well-being of a pig. We pigs are brainworkers. The whole management and operation of this farm depend on us. Day and night we are watching over your welfare. It is for your sake that we drink that milk and eat those apples. Do you know what would happen if we pigs failed in our duty? Jones would come back! Yes, Jones would come back! Surely, comrades," cried Squealer almost pleadingly, skipping from side to side and whisking his tail, "surely there is no one among you who wants to see Jones come back."

Squealer appeals to his audience's sense of fear. Rather than appeal to their logic, which might prompt the other animals to think in more reasonable ways, Squealer blurs the issue with panic. In this case, the dishonest Squealer knows that the other animals' fears will allow him to justify an unreasonable claim.

Appeals to Need

Appeals to need make a connection between the subject and a basic human need (such as food, shelter, belonging, intimacy, self-realization, etc.). Like appeals to value, appeals to need tap into a broad spectrum of human affairs. They try to reach inside an audience, into people's essential requirements for living.

Appeals to need can be highly effective. For instance, if many people are living in poverty, a politician may attempt to connect their basic human needs (food, work, security) to his or her particular goals. The Bolshevik revolution in Imperial Russia, which overthrew the czar and established communist rule for most of the twentieth century, gained momentum by appeals to need. Because so many people were poor and lacked basic elements of survival, the Bolsheviks were able to convince them to join their cause and overthrow the aristocracy. In more recent times, we know that terrorism is bred at least in part out of poverty, out of conditions that leave people in need. When people's basic needs are not met, they are vulnerable; others can appeal to the void in their lives and draw them into behavior they would not otherwise consider.

But appeals to need are not exclusively used for destructive ends. They can be used to make valuable arguments. For instance, political leaders may argue for universal health care as a basic human need, against those who place more importance on profit. In American politics, basic human needs often are pitted against profit or economic growth: basic individual needs versus broader economic goals.

Notice how Samantha Tengelitsch distinguishes between hospital policies and women's needs during the birthing process:

> Women actually experience less pain at home. During labor, oxytocin, the hormone that causes contractions and helps the baby to be born, works in harmony with endorphins—the body's own pain-relieving hormone. During a homebirth, the woman's body will release these hormones according to her needs and she will usually cope well with the sensation of labor.

Appeals to Value

Appeals to value make a connection between the topic and a shared value or principle (such as fairness, equality, honor, kindness, selflessness, duty, responsibility, profit, or practicality). For example, in her essay "In Defense of Darkness" (from Chapter 5), Holly Wren Spaulding links her topic, nighttime darkness, to values such as mystery, enchantment, release, and calm. She even nudges readers to treasure these values, to find them precious in our busy everyday lives:

> It's like this: darkness bleeds the boundaries between myself and that which is just beyond my physical form. It contains unknown depths (the lake is hard to make out as its surface melts into the rest of night), enchantment, and a release from the manners and mannerisms of daytime, circumscribed as it is with routine and work and propriety. Nighttime darkness also bears the prospect of sleep and dreams (increasingly precious in this age of insomnia and sleep disorders), and an unbridling of inhibitions by way a kind of anonymity, if not invisibility. In the dark one finds light-footed walking and slowness; a sense that there is enough time and that rushing is no longer necessary.

Like Spaulding, all good arguers understand that people are moved by their sense of value. Good arguers know how to bring a particular value to the foreground and make it seem pressing. For example, notice how Justin James in "Standardized Testing vs. Education" (from Chapter 7), highlights the value of curiosity over high test scores:

> The [No Child Left Behind] act has placed an emphasis on accountability, which is being determined by student test results. Test scores might rise. But does that really mean the schools are doing a better job or students are getting a better education? The current emphasis on testing can have harmful results. What's more, the method used to find out the scores teaches students a dangerous definition of *education.*
>
> The emphasis placed on standardized testing teaches students that *education* means getting content from a teacher or getting good at a skill. They come to think *education* means getting a grade on a test, accumulating points, and arriving at an average grade based on those points. But students will benefit more in all aspects of life if they can experience education differently—as having to do more with exploring, discovery, being curious. Standardized testing deprives students from the opportunity to experience an education that values curiosity, and is more valuable than an education consumed with standardized tests.

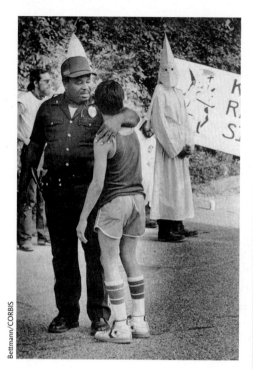

Bettmann/CORBIS

Some situations contain a range of competing values.

Appeals to value may be the most intense and abundant appeals in popular arguments. Whenever someone says, "It's not fair!" he or she is appealing to a value (fairness). In fact, any argument based on equality, justice, duty, responsibility, security, or honesty probably relies on an appeal to value. When arguers can connect a particular point to a broader value, they tap into something beyond their particular argument and call on the belief system of both their audience and the broader public.

Activities

1. For one of the following claims, develop a line of reasoning with at least three steps. Explain what support strategies could be used to develop each premise.

- Facebook should be used in college classes because it engages students in course material and helps them stay actively involved.
- Because it is harmful to the environment and consumers, holiday shopping must be reduced.
- Elementary school classrooms should rely less on computers.
- Colleges and universities should offer more women's sports.

2. Develop an inductive line of reasoning that supports a claim about the students in one of your classes.

3. As a class, choose a popular political, social, or cultural topic. Then list the appeals to value that are used in the arguments about the topic. (Make sure to explore all the positions toward the topic.)

4. Carefully examine an advertisement and describe how it uses an appeal to character, emotion, need, or value.

Disconnected

LYNDA SMITH

Lynda Smith wrote the following essay for her second-semester college English course. Originally, she used the Arguing Crisis chapter of this book (see Chapter 10) to reveal a critical part of everyday life that people normally take for granted or ignore entirely. In the argument, she uses a wide range of rhetorical strategies.

A jogger runs down the Leelanau Trail talking on a cell phone. A student text-messages while in class. High-speed. Real-time. BlackBerry, Razr, and Firefly. Like it or not, technologically advanced communication devices have taken over our lives. Rapidly reaching epidemic proportions, we have come to accept and rely on them as if our very lives depended on it. But have we slowed down long enough to ask ourselves, is "faster" giving us more time? Are more ways to connect making us more connected? Have we compromised our values for mass produced values?

I admit it! I am a technophobe. Or in technospeak, a P.O.N.A. (acronym for *person of no account).* Yes, I have exercised my right to choose what communication devices I will allow in my world. But, it's hard. Every day, I am bombarded with catchy commercials, communication catalogs, and people who are trying to convince me all of this techno stuff is inevitable, a sign of the times, the way of the world. That "faster" will give me more time and being hyper-connected will fulfill my needs for connecting with friends and loved ones. While I do own a cell phone (it's in my car somewhere) and a computer, I resent the fact that the outside world attempts to persuade me to compromise my values for mass-produced values. I treasure the choice to talk to whom I choose when I choose, time to enjoy a lazy walk in the woods where the only sound is nature, real-time, face-to-face conversations with close friends over a nice dinner and a bottle of wine. Call me old-fashioned, but I'm not convinced all this technology is giving us more time or making us more connected.

Communication technology has been around for a long time. "In point of fact, humans have been creating ways to transmit, store and manipulate information and messages for centuries—if not millennia" (Thurlo, Lengel, and Tomic 37). Inventions such as the printing press, telegraph, and telephone were exciting, important innovations that for the first time allowed us to "reach out and touch" family and friends in ways that were previously not available. But, with the rapid advancement of present-day technologies, it has become an obsession to be connected with the latest devices.

Advertising for these communication devices is big business. Appealing to our desires for connectedness and more leisure time, communication conglomerates spend billions of dollars on advertising campaigns. Their ads are bigger and more prevalent than ever before. Every day we hear about new inventions that make it easier to stay connected. We are bombarded with catchy commercials and sophisticated ads for high-speed Internet, long-distance calling plans, and cell phones. Infectious phrases such as "Can you hear me now?" saturate our subconscious, silently reinforcing our need for connection. High-speed Internet surfing caters to the rampant desire for instant gratification while quietly leading us to believe faster will give us more time. Visual images lure us in using color, strategically placed props, and text to appeal to our emotions. The omnipresent repetition of these persuasive messages is seducing us into a state of intellectual numbness, making us immune to logical thinking so we will buy their products. In the United States, there are now 194,479,364 cell phone users and 203,824,428 Internet users (US, Central Intelligence Agency). We can't go anywhere these days without seeing a cell phone attached to someone's ear or pocket. Ask anyone on the street and he or she will tell you they have a cell phone "just in case" someone needs to contact them, or they are "handy to have" because they can do so many things. According to a report by the United States Department of Transportation, cell phone subscriptions rose from 340,213 in 1985 to a whopping 117,000,000 in 2001. These numbers clearly indicate that this subliminal invasion has taken hold.

But are technologically advanced communication devices inevitable, or are we allowing huge corporations to lead us blindly from being real-time human beings to virtual puppets?

Human beings are social by nature. We desire heartfelt connections with our families and friends. This desire is exactly what communication conglomerates use in their advertising campaigns to convince us that we need cell phones. This is how it works. First, they fill their ads with lots of pictures. Photos of smiling people talking on cell phones and pictures of the endless variety of wireless devices we can fill our lives with. Next, they bombard us with catchy phrases and text, phrases like "spread the word" and text such as "be connected" and "let's talk." In other words, they use a need to create a need.

Take my friend Randy, for example. When I first met him, his cell phone was his constant companion. He felt that he needed to be available for his family and friends any time day or night. And he was. Barely a minute went by that he was not talking on his phone. After a while, he started to realize the constant connection was taking up more and more of his time and the amount of stress in his life was increasing. What had initially started

out as an innocent need to connect had turned into a self-perpetuating cycle. The more time he spent talking on the phone, the less connected he felt to his family and friends. That in turn triggered the need to feel connected, and the cycle would repeat. He came to realize that the phone was preventing him from spending quality face-to-face time with loved ones as well as himself. He has since learned to use his phone in moderation.

Being connected is easier than ever before, but it has allowed us to become "hyper-connected." The time we spend keeping "in touch" is on the rise. Cell phone customers used 1.5 trillion MOU's (minutes of use) in 2005, up 36% from 1.1 trillion in 2004 ("Wireless"). This obsession with our cell phones has become a type of cultural addiction. The *Encyclopedia of Psychology* describes an addiction as an "overpowering desire or need for an . . . action or interaction . . . that produces a psychophysical 'high.' This desire or need is repetitive, impulsive, and compulsive in nature" (Hatterer 16). Our obsession with cell phones is not unlike other addictions that consume our lives—addictions such as working too much, buying too much useless stuff, or even taking drugs.

And the more an addiction takes over, the more our true needs are not being met. While many would insist that talking on their cell phones is synonymous to face-to-face communication, the fact remains that talking on a cell phone can't replace real-time human connection with its eye-to-eye contact, physical touches, and emotional responses.

In this fast-paced society of compacted time restraints, we long for more leisure time. At the same time, we are consumed with the desire for instant gratification. We want immediate access to people, information, and services any time, day or night. We believe that somehow if we do everything faster, we will have more free time. Our lives have become a world filled with services to help us move through life with increased speed. We have drive-thrus for food, banking, even laundry so we don't have to leave our cars. We have u-scan checkouts at grocery stores so we don't have to wait in line. And now, different speeds at which we can choose to move through life. There is high speed, turbo speed, and new elite speeds where you can, without leaving your home, hit speeds up to 6.0 Mbps (AT&T). This desire for speed is just one more way that big communication companies can use to draw us in. They appeal to our desire for more time by supplying us with increasingly faster services.

Even though we can connect with the world at faster rates, our whole sense of time gets warped. We get mesmerized by the speed and actually end up with less time. It becomes a self-perpetuating cycle. The faster we go, the more time spent, the less time we have, the greater our needs, the more we crave, and the faster we want to go. AT&T's new slogan promises, "Your world delivered." But is all that speed really giving us the time and connections we desire? Mark Slouka's example in his book *War of the Worlds* says it well:

> As everyone knows, unreality increases with speed. Walking across a landscape at six miles an hour, we experience the particular reality of place: its smells, sounds, colors, textures, and so on. Driving at seventy miles an hour, the experience is very different. The car isolates us, distances us; the world beyond the windshield—whether desert mesa or rolling farmland—seems vaguely unreal. At supersonic speeds, the divorce is complete. A landscape at 30,000 feet is an abstraction, as unlike real life as a painting. (3)

In other words, the further we move away from our basic needs, the more separated from our lives we become.

Technologically advanced communication devices are the guiding force leading us into our own virtual worlds. For example, look at the recent advancements in cell phones. Besides talking on them, we can e-mail, text-message, watch TV, play games, and take pictures. The Samsung Company is now working on developing a cell phone that can "feel, think, evolve, and reproduce" (Maney). That's scary. We already use computers for information, entertainment, companionship, and even love. "Our home computers . . . will soon come with a face capable of responding to our expressions, understanding our gestures, even reading our lips. Its eyes will follow us around the room. We'll be able to talk with it, argue with it, flirt with it. . . . Will it have emotions? You bet" (Slouka 8). That's even scarier!

The acceptance of these technological advances into our lives has propelled us toward a virtual society. What does this mean?

> A culture once based exclusively on physical contact is in the process of being transformed into one where goods and services are accessible without the need for face-to-face contact with other people. Technology has enabled this transformation toward virtual societies. Technology is the glue that makes virtual societies plausible, but technology alone does not guarantee the viability of the virtual society, for the technical power must be used intelligently and deliberately by an informed population. (qtd. in Agres, Edberg, and Igbaria)

With all this talk about cell phone addiction, high-speed Internet surfing, and virtual societies one might believe that I am totally against computers and cell phones. Although I am a self-proclaimed technophobe, I do recognize there are benefits to having both. Having a computer has enabled me to write this paper, and it allows me to keep in contact with friends and family who live far away. And while I have never had to use a cell phone for an emergency, I do believe it is an important reason to have one. More than 224,000 9-1-1 calls are placed each day and many lives have been saved ("Wireless"). But I am still not convinced that all this technology stuff has given me more time or has made me feel more connected. Mark Burch says it best:

> To the degree that we cultivate the capacity to enter deeply into the experience of the moment, we also cultivate the experience of joy, plentitude, and well-being in our lives. This requires few things, but the capacity to know and enjoy them with profound intensity. It is a process, finally, of cultivating oneself and one's relationships with others. . . . Mainstream society consists of the exact opposite—ever-briefer and more superficial encounters with ever-larger quantities of goods, services, and people. There is no pleasure or contact, only the giddy adrenaline-fueled whirl of changing experience without substance, touch without intimacy, information without meaning, company without community. (qtd. in Pierce 305)

Computers and cell phones can benefit our lives, but spending too much time with them can lure us away from real-time experiences, face-to-face interactions, and isolate us from our surroundings. We need to ask ourselves: Are we going to accept these devices as inevitable, a sign of the times, the way of the world? Are we so busy connecting with the outer world that we have forgotten what it feels like to connect with our inner worlds? Have we moved away from our most basic needs? "Within the universe created by Isaac Asimov [a science fiction writer], people slipped unconsciously into a virtual society. The pendulum swung from a physical to a virtual society without any examination or recognition of the changes . . ." (Agres, Edberg, and Igbaria). What will your choice be?

Lynda Smith, "Disconnected." Reprinted with the permission of the author.

Works Cited

Agres, Carole, Dana Edberg, and Magid Igbaria. "Transformation to Virtual Societies: Forces and Issues." *Information Society* 14.2 (1998): 71–82. *Academic Search Elite.* Web. 6 Apr. 2006.

AT&T. *Why Just Surf When You Can Fly?* N.p.: AT&T, 2006. Print.

Hatterer, L. J. "Addictive Process." *Encyclopedia of Psychology.* Ed. Raymond J. Corsini. New York: Wiley, 1994. Print.

Maney, Kevin. "Top Popped on What Cell Phone Technology Can Do for Us." *USA Today* 1 Mar. 2006: n. pag. *Academic Search Elite.* Web. 5 Apr. 2006.

Pierce, Linda Breen. *Choosing Simplicity.* Carmel: Gallagher, 2000. Print.

Slouka, Mark. *War of the Worlds.* New York: Basic, 1995. Print.

Thurlo, Crispin, Laura Lengel, and Alice Tomic. *Computer Mediated Communication: Social Interaction and the Net.* Thousand Oaks: Sage, 2004. Print.

United States. Central Intelligence Agency. *The World Factbook.* 2006. Central Intelligence Agency. Web. 14 Apr. 2006.

United States. Dept. of Transportation. Research and Innovative Technology Administration. Bureau of Transportation Statistics. "Cell Phone Service Subscriptions: 1985–July 2001." *Transportation Statistics Annual Report.* 2001. Bureau of Transportation Statistics. Web. 6 Apr. 2006.

"Wireless Quick Facts." *CTIA.* CTIA, n.d. Web. 6 Apr. 2006.

Assignment: Summarizing Arguments

Summary is a process of abbreviating and rewording the main ideas of a text. If that text is an argument, the main ideas can often be identified by focusing on the line of reasoning. For instance, if we were to identify Ryan Brown's line of reasoning (pp. 25–28), we would work through the essay and find the main statements that lead us to accept his argument about cars.

¶1–2 Intro/background/description.

¶4–5 We are a society of drivers, preferring to drive ten miles over walking two blocks.

¶6 But in a society built around cars, not the people who drive them, we seem willing to sacrifice community for convenience.

¶7 Along with community, we also are sacrificing the human body, perhaps the most efficient and best-designed mode of transportation known to us. Walking truly is the most efficient and ecologically friendly mode of transportation, yet we make every effort to minimize this healthful and sensible activity.

¶9 It seems that as our driving increases, our health deteriorates.

¶10 That automobiles are environmentally unfriendly is unarguable.

¶11 Relatively low fuel prices and high gas mileage keep the cost of driving low, allowing this drivers' society to perpetuate.

¶12 We modern Americans think with our wallets.

¶13 New Urbanism and other social reform movements promise to bring back the days of centralized, walkable communities, incorporating features such as wide sidewalks and narrow streets, neighborhood stores and schools.

¶14 The notion of walking any significant distance as a necessary means of transportation seems so alien to us, but the drivers' society is a recent phenomenon.

¶15 Ultimately it is individual choice that will determine if our communities are to become mere pit stops on the highway.

¶16 Perhaps we as a society need to take a step back from our highway-paced lives and slow things down to a gentle stroll.

Identifying Brown's line of reasoning helps us to see the scaffolding—the basic structure—of his argument. Now, we can develop a thorough and accurate summary by putting Brown's premises into our own words:

In his essay, "A Community of Cars," Ryan Brown argues that society's reliance on driving instead of walking has sacrificed community, our bodies, and the environment. Our reliance on driving has replaced human interaction such as friendly conversation with less personal interaction such as honking horns and drive-thru transactions.

According to Brown, we have sacrificed community for the convenience of driving—of zooming across town to grab everything at once in one big store.

We have also, he explains, sacrificed our bodies, which are well designed for transportation. They run on organic and renewable fuels, are durable, self-maintaining and self-repairing, and they produce only ecologically useful emissions. Walking is efficient and ecologically friendly, yet we avoid it. And as our driving increases, our health deteriorates. The Post–World War II suburban model has contributed to obesity, heart disease, and diabetes.

Brown also contends that driving harms the environment. Auto emissions produce harmful greenhouse gases, oxides of nitrogen, sulfides, and toxic carbon monoxide. And roads hurt the environment because they destroy wildlife habitat and contribute to runoff that pollutes the water.

Low fuel prices and good gas mileage encourage driving, but even if people drive a vehicle that gets good gas mileage, they are still driving instead of walking. Reform movements like New Urbanism encourage walking, but walking a significant distance is foreign to us now, even though driving is a recent phenomenon.

Whether we drive or walk is a matter of personal choice. And since driving has not provided us with the leisure that was predicted, Brown suggests that we step back and examine the pace of our lives.

This summary follows some basic conventions:

- The title and author of the essay are given in the first paragraph.
- Brown's essay is discussed in present tense ("Brown also contends" rather than "Brown also contended").
- The main points are separated in paragraphs.

Now, try your own summary. In a 250–300 word passage, summarize Lynda Smith's argument in "Disconnected." Start by identifying the premises in the line of reasoning. Then, put those premises in your own words. Make the summary flow. To do this, you may decide to combine sentences, add connecting or transitional words (and, but, on the other hand, etc.), or make other changes in word choice and sentence structure. As you do this, be accurate! Your summary must accurately reflect the meaning of the original. (For more specifics on writing summaries, see p. 403 in the Research Guide.)

Opposition

A rgument is not a monologue. It is not one person expressing a solitary, personal opinion. Instead, argument is about
engagement, tension, and friction among claims. In academic
writing, that engagement is crucial. It must be dramatized and
highlighted. Projecting one's opinion is not enough. Writers cannot simply assert a claim and offer support. Instead, they must directly engage
other and opposing ideas. They must deal with the friction or overlap
between their own claims and those of others. In fact, the most successful arguments are those that deeply engage opposition—that enter into
intensive dialogue with other claims and values. Counterargument, concession, and qualifiers bring opposing ideas into contact.

Counterargument

Counterarguments refute claims or positions opposed to those that
the writer or speaker is forwarding. Good arguers *counterargue*. They
explain how other positions opposed to their own are somehow wrong.
Perhaps other positions are unethical, unreasonable, logically flawed,
or impractical. Whatever their shortcomings, opposing viewpoints must
be addressed head-on. Notice how C.S. Lewis in "The Law of Human
Nature" responds to an opposing claim:

> I know that some people say the idea of a Law of Nature or decent behav-
> ior known to all men is unsound, because different civilizations and dif-
> ferent ages have had quite different moralities.

But this is not true. There have been differences between their moralities, but these have never amounted to anything like a total difference. If anyone will take the trouble to compare the moral teaching of, say, the ancient Egyptians, Babylonians, Hindus, Chinese, Greeks and Romans, what will really strike him will be how very like they are to each other and to our own.

Lewis begins the first paragraph with what "some people say" and then responds to that claim in the next paragraph. He has anticipated the logic of the opposition. Notice, also, that his acknowledgment is not drawn out. He quickly mentions the opposing perspective and then responds with his own reasoning. In other cases, the writer may choose to explain the opposing perspective in more detail, especially if it is complex. Writers may dedicate several paragraphs to an opposing perspective so that they can respond to particular ideas, assumptions, or phrases.

Writers use counterarguments to help the audience understand and possibly accept a claim. But counterargument also generates ideas. In other words, counterargument is an important invention strategy. Before they communicate their thinking, good arguers examine others' positions and try to imagine contrary points. This helps them draw clear boundaries between their positions and others'. Imagine, for instance, a writer asserting a definition of education:

Education is an exploration of what is possible in any given field.

By imagining how other people might define education (*Education is a process of learning what experts know. Education is the accumulation of knowledge. Education is the process of becoming socialized into a way of thinking and behaving.*), the writer might realize that *an exploration* is starkly different from *an accumulation*—that her way of thinking is, in fact, very different from other ways of thinking. And she might then come to a more intensive position:

Education is a process of exploring new ground and struggling against conventional modes of thinking.

When counterarguing, writers should be cautious of tossing aside the opposition too quickly. Dismissing opposing positions too easily can strangle or short circuit an argument. Imagine a writer, Sam, is arguing that U.S. corporations should not freely take their operations out of the country. He begins a paragraph by explaining an opposing position:

> The Center for Applied Business argues that American corporations need to take their operations overseas because labor in the United States is too expensive. However, this is just silly. Americans should be paid well because they do a great job.

Sam counterargues by taking on the opposing position of the Center for Applied Business. However, his counterargument misses the mark because it moves too quickly in saying that the center's claim is "just silly." (See "Personal Response Problem" on page 22.) If Sam wants his readers to share his judgment, he should further analyze that claim. That is, he should more closely examine the layers of the claim and unearth the values beneath it:

> The Center for Applied Business argues that American corporations need to take their operations overseas because labor in the United States is too expensive. This position obviously values the bottom line of business rather than the life of business. The claim comes from a desire to maximize profit at the expense of the people in and of the company itself—and the communities that first gave them their start. The emphasis on cutting labor costs also assumes that the money is simply saved, that moving operations to another country somehow alleviates the strain caused by higher wages demanded in American industry. However, the desire to maximize profit by shrinking labor costs is a never-ending, and often self-defeating, battle.

Sam could then go on to develop his logic and show the specific nature of that self-defeating battle. He not only would make better use of the opposing claim but also would develop a more layered argument.

Activity

Write down your position (claim and support) on the following issues, and then for each issue, imagine at least two claims that oppose your own.

1. The government has a right to know what a citizen is smoking.

2. Spam e-mail should be illegal.

3. Spammers should pay a fine and spend at least one year in prison.

4. The school cafeteria should not use Styrofoam plates and cups.

MIGUEL MEDINA/AFP/Getty Images

Concession

While counterargument looks to others and says, "I'm afraid not, and here's why," concession looks to others and says, "Okay. Good point." In short, concession acknowledges or grants value to an opposing claim. Arguers who simply ignore, dismiss, or explain away ideas that challenge their own are simplifying arguments instead of dealing with complexities. Not all opposing positions or accounts should be (or can be) explained away. Conceding certain points and qualifying others are important strategies for strengthening an argument. Some opposing points have value, and good arguers acknowledge those points by conceding them. In a letter to the department store Kohl's, K. T. Glency argues that the store deceives customers into applying for credit cards. However, he does concede several points:

> **I agree with you that people should be able to figure some things out.** Some people will be able to figure out more than others. And some people will be able to figure out very little.

> **Of course Kohl's employees cannot spell out every detail of a situation,** but they should not take any action to purposely deceive. Society has a responsibility to educate people enough so that they can figure things out on their own. And influential executives such as you have a responsibility to *not* purposely deceive the public.

Glency anticipates an opposing claim and concedes to it so that he can make an important distinction between inadvertently misleading people and purposely deceiving them. His concessions do not undermine his argument; instead, they acknowledge common ground and show that he has a reasonable understanding of the situation.

It is easy to become fixated on our own opinions and draw firm boundaries between our perspective and others'. Concessions allow writers to cling less tightly to their own perspectives and invent more nuanced points. This does not mean that *conciliatory* arguments (those that concede points) are wishy-washy. It means that they are engaged with the opinions swirling around in the rhetorical situation. Consider, for instance, how Glency's argument gains important nuance (or dimension) when he concedes that Kohl's cannot "spell out every detail" for its customers. This concession allows him to dig further into the issue—into the kinds of details that retail stores *should* spell out. Because Glency understands an opposing viewpoint, his own argument becomes more sophisticated.

In mainstream political debates, arguers rarely concede. In fact, concessions are often seen as weakness. Even when political candidates are shown to be wrong, they might not acknowledge the value of opposing positions or even undeniable evidence! Consequently, their own arguments become overly simplistic. Public issues like the economy, health care, the environment, immigration, and military deployment are complex, and that complexity demands a certain degree of concession. Without it, arguments turn into boxing matches wherein each side tries to outpunch, rather than out-think, the opposition. Mature debate, the kind that we hope to nurture in academic writing, embraces the real complexity of issues, and concession is one of its key tools.

Activities

1. Choose an argument you strongly disagree with, and then make an important concession to that argument. Explain how your concession makes your response to the argument more persuasive.

2. Watch an interview about a controversial issue—national health care, global warming, deep sea drilling, etc. What concession does the person being interviewed make, or what concession should the person have made? How does the concession strengthen the interviewee's position? If it doesn't, why?

Qualifiers

Qualifiers are closely related to concessions, but while concessions focus on others' ideas, qualifiers focus on the arguer's ideas, acknowledging their limitations. We often use qualifiers in everyday conversation: "I'm not saying that all politicians are bad, but many of them seem to distort the truth." "Granted, some country music is good, but a lot of it just rubs me the wrong way." We do this to make our opinions more acceptable.

Imagine a day without qualifiers. We would go around spouting hasty generalizations: *College students are too immature to manage their time. Television is evil. Professors don't care about their students. Teenagers are rotten drivers.* While such claims might work in a small crowd of like-minded friends, they would quickly draw fire from others.

Qualifiers make such claims more reasonable and potentially worthy of public attention: *When distracted by cell phones and stereos, even the most attentive teenager can become a rotten driver.*

In more formal argument, qualifiers prevent arguers from making claims that are too extreme. Tracy Webster uses a qualification in this passage from "Big House in the Wilderness" (in Chapter 10):

> I began by thinking out loud how it seems odd that men come here to hunt deer that you have to try not to hit with your car. The deer aren't hard to find, and when they see you they just stand there, motionless, staring. Of course, you can't shoot the ones standing on the road. You have to drive out a ways, then walk a bit farther, and then shoot one. Back there, in the woods, the deer might have a better chance, by blending in with the trees and hearing or smelling or seeing you before you see them.
>
> But this is not an anti-hunting essay or an anti house-in-the-wilderness essay. It is an anti big-house-in-the-wilderness essay. The big house in the wilderness is more dangerous than any hunter is. It's the big house, the too-big house, that is unjustifiable.

In the second paragraph, Webster qualifies his ideas by making clear that he is not condemning hunters or all houses in the wilderness.

Qualifiers also show up as words that make statements seem less extreme. By qualifying claims, words such as *perhaps, seems, often, some, sometimes, most, certain, occasionally, probably, might* and so on can make an argument appear more careful. Notice the qualifiers John Adams uses in "Evaluation of 'The Education of Ms. Groves'" (from Chapter 9):

> Many people will realize that *Dateline NBC* turned a complex issue into a TV drama like *Desperate Housewives* or *Grey's Anatomy.* It had an attractive leading character, some good drama (even a fight!), and an emotional (uplifting) ending. Unfortunately, though it will entertain, this show will disappoint a curious mind because it reduces a serious issue to a Hallmark card. A lot of dedicated, loving, trick-savvy teachers are probably laughing (though with frustration) at the TV-style docu-drama of American education. While it showed the father in prison, the homeless family, and so on, according to *Dateline NBC,* it can all be overcome (all of American culture can be overcome) if our teachers just know to count backwards. *Supernanny* and *Wife Swap* deal with complexity more than this.

The qualifiers (highlighted) temper Adams's position. While Adams makes some bold claims (*it had an attractive leading character; it reduces a serious issue to a Hallmark card; it can all be overcome; Supernanny and*

Wife Swap *deal with complexity more than this*), he tempers other claims with qualifiers (*many* [not all] *people will realize; it had some* [not a lot of] *good drama; teachers are probably* [not definitely] *laughing*). Arguers must decide what ideas to qualify, what ideas not to qualify, and what type of qualifier to use. An unqualified argument can be effective, but such force and certainty requires an argument that makes the readers equally certain. Unless an argument will create certainty for readers, it should allow space for caution, and qualifiers allow that space. While qualifiers are valuable tools for argument, they must be used judiciously. If points are overqualified, arguments lose their intensity and arguers end up backing out of their positions inadvertently.

Activities

1. In groups, generate a list of ways to qualify an idea. Write down words and phrases and any other ideas your group comes up with.

2. As a class, discuss the following: What qualifiers operate in our everyday lives? Consider claims of the college, counselors, professors, government officials, and students. (For instance, what qualifying statements are operating in your course syllabus or textbook?) How do those qualifiers affect your thinking?

3. Consider the following image. How is the flower emerging from the woman's hijab a response to some other position? Does it seem like a counterargument, concession, or qualifier?

Alain Keler/Sygma/Corbis

Learning, Styles, Freedom, and Oppression

SIMON BENLOW

In the following essay, Simon Benlow takes on a popular educational trend: learning styles. The trend asserts that every student can be categorized into a particular group according to his or her supposed style of learning. Benlow takes on the trend and the thinking that drives teachers to accept it. Notice how he counters, concedes, and qualifies his claims.

During the Cold War, when people conjured nightmarish visions of life in Soviet Russia, they imagined long lines of comrades waiting to be told their lot in life. If the communist rulers told Alexi to be a plumber, then plumber he was. If Nikoli was good at jumping, then he would be deemed long jumper for the Soviet Olympic team; if Marta was good with her fingers, she'd be a filing clerk at the Kremlin. Americans, on the other side of the world, shuddered at the idea of limiting the range of possibility for individual human growth. Based on enlightenment philosophy, the American belief in human potential stood opposed to the nightmarish cookie-cutter identity politics of the Soviets. But since the Cold War, American education has done a fine job of making Soviet identity protocols a reality.

In the United States, we have not had absurd degrees of control foisted upon us from our rulers; instead, we have run willingly toward oppression, control, and reductionism. In an increasingly disorienting and saturated society, we have become enamored with the ring of truth that *seems* to accompany simplicity. We have given increasingly younger children (as young as twelve) battery tests that recommend careers—hence education tracks. And in college, we are moving away from intellectual potential and toward direct career paths that correspond to particular *learning styles*.

Today, as the post–Cold War generation comes to college, students are not told exactly *what* they should be. It's far creepier than that: After taking long multiple-choice surveys, students are told *how* they think—and presumably how they have always thought and how they will always think. After one survey, they are categorized as one of only three types: visual, auditory, or kinesthetic. These categories, or "modalities," say the researchers, define the three basic ways that people learn. Increasingly, on campuses, instructors and students alike are proclaiming, "I'm an auditory learner, so. . .," "I'm kinesthetic," etc.—people proudly announcing their intellectual labels as though they were characters in Aldous Huxley's horrific futuristic tale *Brave New World*. (But even Huxley's genius for imagining reductionist horrors could not compare to the learning styles perspective. Huxley, after all, could whittle down humanity to *five* human categories. Learning styles fans trumped him with *three*.) And amazingly, the learning styles movement has not been drummed off campuses; it's been embraced by an alarming number of administrators, counselors, and academic departments around the country.

Beyond its wild reductionism, there are many deep logical flaws with the research that grounds the learning styles movement. It dismisses years of research that shows a significant (if not dramatic and direct) cause/effect relationship between socioeconomic factors and education. It rests on a set of non sequiturs and indirect measures. (For instance, if a student says, through a battery of test questions, that she likes to study at home in a chair, this, say the researchers, helps them to determine how she learns. But there is no direct correlation between *liking* something and *learning from* it. In fact, the opposite could be entirely true, but the surveys do not acknowledge the correlation either way.) The surveys ignore the huge impact of situational contingencies on learning,[1] and, like most battery tests of their kind, assume that when someone chooses option A (out of possible options A or B), that A

---

1. The test asks many questions about situational contingencies, but only as a means to discover something internal and presumably permanent in the individual, so that environmental factors in an educational situation are not seen as influential but as elements in the bigger profile of a coherent, self-enclosed, and consistently systematic individual consciousness.

is inherently true. Of course, much research has been done to show that even if people could choose among A, B, C, D, E, F, G, H, I, J, K, L, M, N, O, P, Q, R, S, T, U, V, W, X, Y, Z, their choice is not necessarily related to the truth of their behavior or personality or thought processes or anything outside of the specific language of survey question itself.

But this argument is not necessarily about invalidity. If the logical holes of the theory do not prompt educators to shun the fad outright, then the implications for students should. Imagine a student, Jennifer. She didn't do well in her K–12 education. She hated the town she lived in; she suffered constantly from a chaotic home life, and spent much of her time with friends—outside of the home and away from school. When she goes to a local community college, someone gives her a learning styles survey, which asks where she is comfortable learning, what kinds of environments most help her to feel energized, etc. After the test, she is told that she is a kinesthetic learner. The test, which ignores the relationship between academic learning and Jennifer's lived experiences, prompts her to internalize a reductive label. So rather than evaluate her education (analyze the system itself or the pedagogy which introduced her to literature or calculus or chemistry), Jennifer learns that she is a particular *type*. She has been given a tool for limiting herself, a terminology for pigeon-holing her entire intellectual constitution. If she takes the new category seriously, she will learn to permanently close off certain intellectual pathways that were, perhaps because of her prior experiences (and not her innate learning style), hardly ever opened. If she's a dutiful student and listens to the results of the impressive-looking survey, she will come to believe that she does not have the intellectual wherewithal to do physics or read *Moby-Dick*.

People steeped in learning styles discourse ask questions, such as "How do we teach philosophy to concrete thinkers?" We should reveal the absurdity of such a question, which is based on a false binary. Thinking is not simply concrete or abstract. How could thinking be only concrete? It's thought. Thought

is abstract. An idea is abstract. Certainly, there are layers to thought—ranging from basic comprehension to meta-theory, but to say that thinking is *either* concrete *or* abstract not only reduces the complexity of thinking; it totally misrepresents what thinking *is*. To ask people if they are concrete or abstract thinkers is tantamount to asking them if they use their skin or bodies more. Imagine someone asking, "Do you use your skin or body more when you run? How about when you write? How about when you take a shower?" The questions are absurd because the skin is an organ of the body. It is not a separate entity. Similarly, theoretical thought processes are not separate from comprehension. Students who aren't good at "abstraction" are simply not good at juggling various abstractions at once. But, despite the discourse of the learning styles movement, they can learn. Given close attention, guidance, and thoughtful pedagogy, students who have become their own worst learning enemies can, in fact, be more than one of three types.

Absurd categorizations (e.g., concrete/abstract, visual/auditory/kinesthetic) defeat students. Such monstrosities rarely, if ever (and I would argue strongly for *if ever)*, benefit students. Most often, students get pinned beneath such contraptions. When given labels for their personalities or intellectual habits, they think of the hardships they have had in their education, pin themselves beneath one of those labels, and dismiss any future association with the others. And rather than diffuse this intellectual self-abuse, the learning styles movement enables it. Rather than free students from self-defeating categories or helping them to crawl out from under bad experiences, the movement trains students to limit themselves, to defeat themselves, to adopt a harmful language about their own potential.

Some have argued that the movement has had one good outcome: It's prompted teachers to rethink the habit of lecture. Of course, this is a positive effect. But we did not need the learning styles movement to teach us that students learn better when they participate actively in building ideas. John Dewey argued this point, without the fallacies, distortions and pseudo-science, early in the 20th century. Many scholars before and since have developed theories of participant knowledge-making without reducing human identity into silly categories.

Certainly, learning styles advocates are not evil-minded people. They want to help students. But the grounding assumptions of the movement emerge from some dubious intellectual traditions—from the tendencies of 19th and 20th century pop psychologists, phrenologists, Nazi regimes, and Cold War propagandists to codify human identity—to see behavior as the consequence of human types rather than a complex web of forces (biological, sociological, political, and spiritual). In some ways, it is an echo of a scientifically aggressive but naïve time—a time when people believed they could, quickly and easily, determine *who you are.*

Contrary to the learning styles movement and its ghastly scientific cousins of the past, neurologists are recently uncovering the wild complexity of learning. In the past few years, neurologists have been substantiating what philosophers have thought for millennia: that humans are *not* hard-wired for a particular type of learning; rather, the processes of learning change the person—the wiring of the brain. In a variety of studies, neurologists have shown that the adult brain (not only the brains of children and infants) actually reorganizes with new experiences ("A New Window"). Synapses, the connections between neurons, actually form and reform according to experience. That is, experiences prompt the brain to reorganize how it processes information—and in the world of the brain, that amounts to reconstitution. Such a revelation has huge implications for education. James Zull, a biology professor at Case Western Reserve University, describes teaching as "The Art of Changing the Brain," also the title of his latest book. "What the title says is that learning is a physical change in the brain. This is one thing neuroscience has shown us, and if it is true, then it must be that successful teachers produce change in the learner's brain" (Zull). And the more neurologists learn, the more they shun fads like learning styles as oversimplified

A phrenological chart of presumed character traits and their locations in the brain. Phrenology was popular in the early 19th century but is now considered a pseudoscience.

Bettmann/CORBIS

"folk psychology" that poisons the educational climate for students (Geake 130–32).

As science on learning gets more sophisticated and as we reconnect with the powerful insights of past philosophers, we should continue to evaluate the habits of education. And we should be careful enough to teach students out of their habits as well. We should help them to be free of oppressive categories. If we are truly interested in teaching "lifelong learning," a commonly celebrated phrase in higher education, we should give students tools for intellectual transformation—not stagnation and pigeon-holing. Rather than helping students to remain entrenched in their intellectual habits, we ought to give them tools for digging out of the past, out of the present, and out from under any bizarre categories that get dropped on them in the future.

Works Cited

Geake, John. "Neuromythologies in Education." *Educational Research* 50.2 (2008): 123–133. *Academic Search Elite.* EBSCO. Web. 17 May 2010.

"A New Window to View How Experiences Rewire the Brain." *Howard Hughes Medical Institute.* Howard Hughes Medical Inst., 19 Dec. 2002. Web. 17 May 2010.

Zull, James E. "What Is 'The Art of Changing the Brain?'" *New Horizons for Learning.* New Horizons for Learning, May 2003. Web. 15 May 2010.

Assignment: Identifying and Summarizing Opposition

Arguments do not exist alone. They exist in a world of other arguments. They emerge from opposing ideas, and they are developed through an ongoing process of examining other, contrary positions. In a brief essay, describe Benlow's (pp. 72–74), Brown's, (pp. 25–28) or Smith's (pp. 57–61) argument and focus specifically on counterarguments, concessions, and qualifiers. Use the following questions to help guide your thinking:

1. What is the purpose of the argument? How does the arguer want the audience to think and act differently?

2. What prompted the argument? Why has the author bothered to make it?

3. To what other argument is the author responding? How does the writer analyze opposing or popular positions on the topic?

4. What counterarguments are made? How do they help the audience understand and possibly accept the writer's main claim?

5. What concessions are made? How do they impact the overall argument?

6. What points are qualified? Which qualifiers are most important and why?

Caution: As you develop the essay, avoid getting pulled into the argument. If you agree or disagree with the writer (Benlow, Brown, or Smith), try to remain outside of the fray. Don't attack, defend, or celebrate the writer's position. Instead, imagine that your job is to describe how the writer deals with opposition. Also, concentrate your focus on the essay itself—on the writer's rhetorical moves rather than the writer. In other words, describe the argument, not the arguer.

Hidden Layers

elow the surface of New York City lies a hidden layer that includes thousands of miles of electrical cable, fiber-optic and coaxial cable for telecommunications, water pipes (carrying a billion gallons of water a day), a central steam heating system, gas pipes, air ducts, the subway, sewer pipes, parking garages, and underground foundations. Most people are unaware of what lies beneath the surface of a city—and of what lies beneath the surface of an argument. To read and understand an argument, one must be aware of its *hidden* layers. While some people see only the surface, others are communicating about the hidden layers, where the force of argument lives.

Assumptions

An assumption is a logical connection between a claim and its support. Every argument contains an assumption that is crucial to its validity. Assumptions are sometimes stated and sometimes unstated, or hidden. Unstated assumptions can rest so deeply and quietly in the arguer's mind that he or she may not even recognize it. The following argument contains an unstated assumption:

> You should dress nicely for your interview because you want to make a good impression on the employer.

Broken down into claim and support, this is the argument:

> **Claim:** You should dress nicely for your interview.
>
> **Support:** You want to make a good impression on the employer.

And inside the argument lies an unstated assumption so obvious that it need not be stated:

> **Assumption:** Dressing nicely makes a good impression on potential employers.

The assumption lurks between the claim and support, connecting the two. This assumption is beyond debate, as most people in most situations would not dispute it. However, assumptions are often debatable, even highly questionable, as in the following example:

> **Claim:** We should invade Vietnam before the communists take it over.

> **Support:** The communists will threaten the American way of life.

Inside this argument lies a debatable assumption: *If the communists take over Vietnam, the American way of life will be threatened.* This was the logic that drove the United States into a long and tragic war; when we reveal the assumption, we can see why so many people protested in the late 1960s and '70s. Many Americans could not accept the assumption that a communist takeover in a small Southeast Asian country would ultimately threaten their own way of life. The Johnson and Nixon administrations were hard-pressed to maintain the argument.

British philosopher Stephen Toulmin (1922–2009) developed a system for digging up and evaluating hidden assumptions—or what he called *warranting assumptions.* Toulmin's system involves six primary components: main claim, grounds (or support), warranting assumptions, backing, modal qualifier, and rebuttal.

> **Claim:** a conclusion whose merit must be established (an assertion about something)

> **Support:** appeals, evidence, and examples that help the reader accept the claim

> **Warranting Assumption:** a statement (expressed or implied) that connects the claim and support in a logical and acceptable way, allowing the audience to accept the claim

> **Backing:** the evidence that supports a warranting assumption

> **Modal Qualifier:** words and phrases that limit the scope of a claim

> **Rebuttal:** a statement that refutes an opposing, or other, claim

In Toulmin's approach, the warranting assumption connects a claim and its support. In other words, every supporting statement carries an assumption with it.

Discovering warranting assumptions can serve arguers in two primary ways. First, we can point out others' questionable warranting assumptions and, second, we can analyze our own arguments and then explain why the assumptions are acceptable or valuable. Consider, for example, the following claim and supporting reason:

> Drug tests are essential for maintaining a safe workplace. They allow employers grounds to dismiss anyone impaired by drugs.

A writer might respond not simply by arguing with the claim but by digging up and refuting the warranting assumption:

> Advocates of drug tests believe that they ensure a safe working environment—that drug tests screen out those people whose drug use creates dangerous situations. This argument assumes that drugs are a significant cause of workplace accidents. However, the attention on drugs is misplaced. Recreational drug use is not responsible for reckless managerial policies, lax safety codes, and overworked laborers—the dominant causes of workplace insecurity.

Sometimes, writers bring their own assumptions to the surface and argue for them directly. This depends on the situation—the writer's purpose, the audience, the nature of the assumption. For instance, if the writer believes an assumption is shared among readers, she may leave it unstated and simply move on through her argument. However, if she imagines that the audience may question an assumption, she may argue at length. In each case, the arguer's understanding of the specific audience is key.

Assumption stated and argued for at length	The arguer believes the audience will not easily accept the assumption, so he or she makes an argument to persuade the audience to accept it.
Assumption stated and argued for to some extent	Arguing for an assumption can take many pages or a sentence or two.
Assumption stated and not argued for	The arguer says what the assumption is in order to be clear, but doesn't feel that he or she needs to explain it any further.
Assumption unstated	The arguer determines that the assumption will be obvious to the audience and that the audience will not challenge it. Or, the arguer has overlooked the assumption.

We can add an important layer to arguments by calling attention to and backing up our assumptions with the same support strategies that are to support claims: evidence, examples, and appeals. Notice how Tracy Webster reaches into his own argument and pulls out an assumption, which he calls a premise:

> One question is: Can't individual Americans simply build differently? (Are moratoriums necessary?) Of course, to pursue this question (this line of thinking), the reader must accept the premise that Americans are over-building, and that by overbuilding, Americans are foolishly and unnecessarily overdestroying nature, the environment, wildlife. They have to accept the premise that current building practices are somehow harmful. Some Americans, to be certain, don't accept this premise. Here's why they should:

This passage, Webster goes on to support the premise (or a stated warranting assumption) that "current building practices are somehow harmful." That is, he backs up his own assumption—and argues for it at length. (See the Webster argument in Chapter 10.)

In academic argument, readers look carefully at assumptions before accepting an arguer's claim. They ask the following questions:

- What assumption(s) lurk(s) between a particular claim and its support?
- Does the assumption (whether stated or unstated) make a sound logical connection between claim and support? Is the assumption logically flawed?
- On what grounds can the assumption be legitimately challenged, and how does that affect the overall argument?

Activity

For each of the following, discover the assumption and then decide if it is acceptable or questionable. Explain your decision for each.

Claim: Retirement accounts should be in the hands of private companies and not the federal government.

Support: Private companies can generate more money than government-controlled accounts can.

Claim: Light pollution is a crisis that should be addressed.

Support: Most people cannot see the stars anymore.

Claim: Power companies should not be regulated by the federal government.

Support: Power companies can self-regulate more efficiently.

Underlying Values

We are constantly encountering subtle strategies designed to nudge
our thinking in a particular direction. Businesses, activists, government
offices, and everyday citizens choose language that corresponds to what
we value and what we hope for. Many common terms have been carefully
selected to replace old terms that did not have the desired effect on the
audience. *Anti-abortion* became *pro-life; in favor of lawful abortion* became
pro-choice; global warming is now *climate change;* and *tax cuts* are called *tax
relief.* While businesses, politicians, and activist organizations select words
to elicit a particular response, regular people do the same thing, often
quite naturally. For example, instead of asking someone out on a "date,"
a person might ask someone if he or she would like to "get some coffee." Such moves are not necessarily meant to deceive. Instead, they may
simply reveal the underlying values between arguers, between arguer and
audience, or between two people standing on a sidewalk.

Arguments emerge from value systems, from the collective group of
ideals that people quietly cherish. In mainstream modern America, the
following values are generally, and automatically, seen as good:

Achievement	Adventure	Affection	Art
Change	Community	Competition	Cooperation
Country	Creativity	Democracy	Efficiency
Excellence	Excitement	Fame	Freedom
Friendships	Harmony	Hard work	Independence
Integrity	Intellect	Honesty	Leadership
Location	Loyalty	Knowledge	Nature
Order	Physicality	Money	Power
Privacy	Public service	Pleasure	Relationships
Religion	Responsibility	Quality	Self-respect
Stability	Status	Security	Wealth
Wisdom	Work	Truth	Youth

For the most part, people do not walk into a room and argue for the
worth of friendship, integrity, or wisdom. There are probably very few,
if any, *anti-wisdom* groups. Wisdom is simply one of those ideals that
most Americans, and others, believe in as an inherent good. And while
it may not count as a hot argumentative issue, it underlies—quietly sits
beneath—other topics. For instance, when people make an argument
that United States presidential candidates should be at least thirty-five
years old, they may rely on or tap into that shared belief in wisdom.

Understanding underlying values helps writers invent more convincing
arguments. If we know the shared values in a rhetorical situation, we can

create better appeals. We can tap into something the audience deeply cherishes. In "Standardized Testing vs. Education" (from Chapter 7), Justin James argues against educational trends that value memorization and rote skills. To move his readers beyond those trends, he taps into the shared value of curiosity. James begins with a reference to a child's sense of discovery:

> It is no wonder my niece says school is boring. When she was younger, she loved it. It was all about discovery; now it's all about tests. Tests can be valuable in education, of course. But they can be hazardous, too. They can hinder learning and teach students and society at large a false definition of education. Standardized tests teach students to *practice and perform*, but education is more about *developing a sense of curiosity*. [. . .]

This reference helps to root James's argument in the underlying shared value—in the belief that curiosity and discovery are inherently good and worth nurturing.

Activities

1. Consider each of the following claims and what value it suggests.
   a. People should not litter.
   b. When you come across other people's litter, you should pick it up.
   c. You should not litter, but you shouldn't feel obligated to pick up other people's litter.
   d. It is wrong to make money off other people's hardship.
   e. It is wrong to make money off other people's ignorance.
   f. It is fair to make money off other people's ignorance.

2. Decide what values are lurking in these bumper stickers.

InternetBumperStickers.com

In Defense of Darkness

HOLLY WREN SPAULDING

In this essay, Holly Wren Spaulding shows how quiet ideals, unstated assumptions, learned associations, and unquestioned values impact people's lives and the natural world around us. Spaulding, a poet, essayist, and activist who lives in northwestern Michigan, nudges readers to confront an entire unexamined belief system.

There was the time we climbed atop Sentinel Rock, a massive quartzite granite formation in Joshua Tree National Monument, and looking at the dark sky and the moving lights above us, we wondered about the top secret tests that the military is said to conduct at nearby Area 51. Or the time, in my late teens, when I arrived in Florence in the middle of the night and rather than spend scarce resources on a hostel, camped out in a city park for the final hours of that summer night. My travel companion and I laid our heads on our backpacks when we noticed the many figures murmuring in the shadows. Night travelers—loners, junkies, lovers, and the homeless—were busy living and moving about

in the darkness, bursting with what is never imagined during the day.

Or, the June I drifted through layers of warm and cool air as my friend, a composer, sampled lake and air sounds for a piece of electronic music he was writing. I paddled, always aware not to knock the side of the boat for the sake of the recording, and eventually found a rhythm with one stroke for every four or so heartbeats. The sky and shore and water were all one inky darkness though stars sparkled on the watery surface. We were soaked from all directions in night and sky and when the moon rose, full and brilliant, I leaned back against the boat while we coasted, our eyes adjusting so that we could see the shapes of bats, profiles of cedars on the far shore, a single boulder rising out of the lake. I remember how my senses seemed suddenly more alert. Loons yodeled anciently. Cricket hums and owl calls carried across Eagle Lake as we made our way from one side to the other. We were quiet adventurers, rapt and attentive to each ordinary and remarkable thing we encountered. The Milky Way draped itself over our heads like a cosmic veil threaded through with a hundred billion sparkling

Credit Data courtesy Marc Imhoff of NASA GSFC and Christopher Elvidge of NOAA NGDC. Image by Craig Mayhew and Robert Simmon, NASA GSFC.

gems until it disappeared in the fog and we were soon almost invisible to one another, uncertain of where we were on the lake. We barely moved, smitten as we were with the perfection of everything: the lake was ours, the night was ours, and no one knew where we were. We would likely always remember this journey.

* * *

Meanwhile, darkness is a habitat and it's dwindling. My city friends respond with childlike delight when they visit me at my rural homestead. They stand in the yard pointing and ahhing as if at a performance. Where they live it's never dark, and the stars are actually satellites. Here, the sky is like a museum exhibit, and it's novel and compelling because it stands apart from the familiarity of their usual experience. I enjoy their enthusiasm and their giddiness at seeing something this rare and, indeed, rather magical. As far as I can tell, they accept that urban living means they won't see many stars and instead they enjoy the other amenities of the city and, as any forward thinking urban planner will explain, high density living is in fact the greenest lifestyle choice. So I'm not trying to talk anyone into giving up the city. And yet, I am thinking about the dark; what it might mean to ignore it or lose it or live entirely without the spaces, the habitats—both physical and mental—that it helps to shape; how to make sense of a value that seems otherwise underappreciated by so many others around me.

Darkness can feel like nothing—like no place, like Nothingness. But it is not nothing. It is alive with insect hum, wind in the trees, warm air rising off the surface of the water. It is one of the places we encounter ourselves in right proportion, or in a more reasonable proportion, to the world around us. Among its many qualities is a spiritual dimension. Beyond what we know about the environmental impacts of light pollution, the carbon footprint, the trouble it makes for astronomers, migrating birds, and nocturnal animals, and beyond the fact

that it wastes huge amounts of public and private money, I remain focused on this other, less tangible quality that is lost when our lives are lit from every angle at all times.

We modern, industrial, technological Homo sapiens favor light; it is one of the ways we control our environments, both natural and built. Our lives are well lit and we've gotten used to the way things look and feel from this side of darkness. That which is illuminated is regarded as safe, and evidence of progress; it represents human achievement and development. So-called security lights, billboards, communications towers, and decorative lighting (have you been to Las Vegas lately?) are ubiquitous to the point that we mostly take all of it for granted. The infrastructure goes largely unchallenged and so we tacitly accept things as they are. But what is that infrastructure? What are the systems, structures, attitudes and modes of living that result in such a widespread decline of the dark?

Consumer capitalism quietly brands our daily lives with reminder after reminder (made more obvious by spotlights) that *the action is here, this is the thing* to buy, that *we are open for business*, that *this is the way.* All of this light strikes me as a kind of cultural inertia if not outright hostility toward the dark. Whether or not we take action against the creep of light pollution in its many guises, or simply accept all as it is, our indifference is destroying darkness, by which I mean not only those remarkable night skies, but the realm within our minds and the experiences that go with all of it, that are layered with texture and meaning of a darker variety.

Perhaps it seems ungenerous or even paranoid to regard the physical, bright-lit world in such a way. I know that it is more common to be surrounded by a gazillion watts of light at night than to spend more than a few minutes in any kind of real darkness each day. In this country, most of us would have to make a considerable effort if we wanted to get anywhere that was not bathed in perpetual light. But why not bask in our remarkable achievement? I can imagine

John Metz

all manner of push-back, devil's advocacy, disagreement or shoulder shrugging dismissal of the idea that darkness matters. Who cares? says the voice. With all of the other things to worry about, speak out for, and take action against, why defend darkness? The answer is fairly straightforward: When we are estranged from the dark, we lose access to vital human emotions and sensual experiences including wonder and awe and humility.

It's like this: darkness bleeds the boundaries between myself and that which is just beyond my physical form. It contains unknown depths (the lake is hard to make out as its surface melts into the rest of night), enchantment, and a release from the manners and mannerisms of daytime, circumscribed as it is with routine and work and propriety. Nighttime darkness also bears the prospect of sleep and dreams (increasingly precious in this age of insomnia and sleep disorders), and an unbridling of inhibitions by way of a kind of anonymity, if not invisibility. In the dark one finds light-footed walking and slowness; a sense that there is enough time and that rushing is no longer necessary. Is there anything about our daylight existence that does all of this? No, because our values have evolved such

that speed, availability, exposure and outward interaction are the flavor of the moment. It is harder and harder to come by the circumstances which permit anything but a full-blown light-show in which attention is drawn to our every action, thought or location on the planet (witness the rise of social media and reality television).

This is not a manifesto against light, per se, or against the daytime, which is its own and necessary habitat. I am not an anachronist, though it is poignant to note how "of another time" my values suddenly seem. But what is at the heart of our neglect, if not disdain, for darkness and the dark? We quickly recognize the ways in which it is associated with crime, danger, clandestinity, and revolt. We freely employ it as a metaphor for the "unknown" and "uncertainty," even as a synonym for ignorance ("he was totally in the dark on the issue"). We have other negative associations as well: dark secrets, going over to the dark side, the dark underbelly; it represents that which is marginal and Other, but also pleasure and vice (women of the night, libertines). We fear it and yet some of us are simultaneously attracted to it, perhaps precisely because we are not entirely at home there.

The dominant religions of the world preach a dualism that pits light against dark, and man against nature; at the heart, or so it seems to me, is a presumed separation between ourselves and the Other (whether that is nature, the divine, each other). It is a deeply entrenched paradigm, a default setting of sorts, and so we go about without realizing some of our prejudices. If I transgress those boundaries and distinctions, even just in my imagination, I already sense a shift in my perception of the world and people and phenomena around me.

So that I am clear: my point is not exclusively about the dark; after all, there are many ideas, sensations, and realms of awareness that we humans veer away from, not wanting to know or to feel what is potentially foreign, other, uncomfortable. Our deep anxiety about our own mortality must be part of that instinct to withdraw; why penetrate that veil any sooner than necessary? Let's close the lid, let's cover the evidence. The prevailing sentiment seems to be that the best possible life is the one in which we proceed with a broad smile and full of hope into the bright day before us.

I recently found myself among a group of writers, discussing a new work of fiction by one of those assembled and in which a character's experience of childhood abuse by a family member is implied, but not explained directly. The reader senses the dark history, but it is a faint mention, and we don't know for certain what happened. And yet we know. One of our group said, "I thought maybe that had happened but I didn't want to go there." In her mind, she was not committing to that interpretation of the story because she "hated to think of it." Another reader said, "I was afraid to ask." Because we were discussing the story with its author, our suspicions were confirmed: indeed, bad things had happened to the character in the story. Initially, and due to an aversion to that side of experience, an essential part of that character's past was being denied by certain readers. It may be a stretch to suggest that those readers were bent on preserving a happier, less flawed view of the world, but I do wonder: is denial of darkness—in this case, the metaphorical version—not at the heart of our history as a nation? At the core of so many of our psychological ailments? Perhaps even an explanation for the kind of distance that can separate people from one another as soon as their differences become evident or suggest anything but an impeccable resume? I think of the soldiers who are returning from the Iraq and Afghan wars these days, the reports of P.T.S.D., and the supreme loneliness that they must feel when it becomes clear that few of us can possibly understand what they've been through, and worse, don't actually want to "go there" in conversation or in our imaginations.

Am I stretching too far? Are fear of the actual dark and our apprehension of the metaphorical dark related?

But of course, there really are dangers that lurk in dark places. During my first year of college in Ann Arbor, female students were cautioned over and over to never to go anywhere alone after dark. A serial rapist had been terrorizing the area and so we got accustomed to carrying mace, walking in pairs, and prevailing upon our male friends to walk us home from the library at night. I was grateful that in general, the streets near my apartment were well lit. Indeed, it is useful and suitable to light our public spaces to ensure safety. But this is not the bone I am trying to pick. There is a difference between light that is useful, suitable, even aesthetic, but must there be light all of the time?

Franz Kafka wrote that we must read the books that are "an ax to the frozen sea inside us" (qt. in Cixous). The poet Emily Dickinson said that she knew she was reading a great poem when it felt as if her head had been blown off. It is a commonplace that great art of all kinds can be profound and affecting, and I have found that the same happens to be true of my encounters with darkness. Sitting on a midnight lake surrounded by mountains and the sky can trigger a similar sense of being transported to awe, and confronted with beauty and strangeness. Faced with an uncompromised night sky, I immerse myself in vastness and take stock of the space around me; I re-situate myself in relation to the other beings and phenomena with which I share the space. A sort of elegant contraction occurs: I shrink in size but in so doing, something in me is enlarged because the ego recedes, as do some of my more mundane discontents, cravings, petty aspirations. I'd like to think I am more fully human at these moments because it is a time when I do feel that I am among (as opposed to "apart from") the multitudes (as Whitman would have said) or as the Buddhists say, interconnected with all beings. "By acknowledging such links between the inner psychological world and the perceptual terrain that surrounds us, we begin to turn inside-out, loosening the psyche from its confinement within a strictly human sphere . . ." says David Abram, a philosopher, cultural ecologist and

performance artist. It seems true to my experience.
Or as the German poet Rainer Maria Rilke wrote:

> Ah, not to be cut off,
> not through the slightest partition
> shut out from the law of the stars.
> The inner—what is it?
> if not intensified sky,
> hurled through
> with birds and deep
> with the winds of homecoming.

Works Consulted

Abram, David. *The Spell of the Sensuous: Perception and Language in a More-Than-Human World*. New York: Vintage Books, 1997.

Cixous, Helene. *Three Steps on the Ladder of Writing*. Trans. Susan Sellers and Sarah Cornell. New York: Columbia University Press, 1994.

Kafka, Franz. *Letters to Friends, Family and Editors*. Trans. Richard and Clara Winston. New York: Schocken, 1978.

Palmer, Bryan D. *Cultures of Darkness: Night Travels in the Histories of Transgression from Medieval to Modern*. New York: Monthly Review Press, 2000.

Rilke, Rainer Maria. "ah, not to be cut off." *Ahead of All Parting: The Selected Poetry and Prose of Rainer Maria Rilke*. Ed. and Trans. Stephen Mitchell. New York: Modern Library, 1995. 191. Print.

Suzuki, David T. "Forward: Thoughts on Extinction." *Left Bank #2: Extinction*. Hillsboro, Oregon: Blue Heron Publishing, Inc., Summer 1992.

Works Cited

Abram, David. *The Spell of the Sensuous: Perception and Language in a More-Than-Human World*. New York: Vintage Books, 1997.

Cixous, Helene. *Three Steps on the Ladder of Writing*. Trans. Susan Sellers and Sarah Cornell. New York: Columbia University Press, 1994.

Kafka, Franz. *Letters to Friends, Family and Editors*. Trans. Richard and Clara Winston. New York: Schocken, 1978.

Rilke, Rainer Maria. "ah, not to be cut off." *Ahead of All Parting: The Selected Poetry and Prose of Rainer Maria Rilke*. Ed. and Trans. Stephen Mitchell. New York: Modern Library, 1995. 191. Print.

Activities

1. In a brief essay, describe how Holly Wren Spaulding argues at the layer of assumptions and values. Point out specific passages and statements. Explain how each takes the reader beyond the surface claims about light pollution, light, darkness, and so on. Describe how Spaulding's line of reasoning delves into the unstated assumptions about the topic.

2. Find an advertisement and identify the value to which it appeals. Explain how the appeal would sway the audience. Why does the appeal seem legitimate or disingenuous?

Arguments in Disguise

Often, the most persuasive arguments are those in disguise, those that seem like reports, histories, songs, advertisements, or harmless statements. Their persuasive power lies in their silent appeal, their quiet movement into our consciousness. Arguments disguised as something else are hidden. Although indirect and subtle, their claims, appeals, and assumptions still affect audiences. While our intellectual backs are turned, we can be persuaded into consuming a particular view of the world. However, we can raise our awareness and pick out the disguises of argument. We can learn to see through the emotional appeals, to recognize a selective portrayal of facts, and to recognize persuasion even when it is hidden.

The Objectivity Disguise

The objectivity disguise fools the audience into thinking that the presented information is entirely unbiased. An objective statement or text lacks personal opinion or bias; it solely presents facts. However, facts do not appear out of thin air. They exist within a rhetorical situation: someone chose these facts over those, to start with A and not B, to ignore C, to minimize D. All of these decisions or reflexes help to create a particular version of the truth. A news report, for instance, may exclude important facts, oversimplify a complicated situation, or minimize a detail important to another perspective. Consider the following news report:

Chet Huntley (left) and David Brinkley anchor NBC's television coverage of the 1968 Republican National Convention.

Bettmann/CORBIS

Today in Florida, protesters blocked sidewalks and caused undue congestion in downtown Miami. The protesters were demanding a change in voting statewide. When reached for comment, the Miami chief of police said that two people were arrested for blocking the free flow of traffic, and that everything was back to normal by 6:00 p.m.

This report seems like an objective statement of facts; however, it persuades an audience to think a particular way.

- Immediately, we learn about "protesters"—not "concerned citizens" or "voters' rights supporters."
- The first sentence of the report characterizes the protesters as a nuisance. They "blocked" sidewalks and caused "undue congestion."
- The story focuses on (is about) the congestion, not about the political issue that sparked the protest.
- The second sentence characterizes the protesters as insistent and threatening, by describing them as "demanding" change.
- The third sentence reinforces the idea that the protesters are criminals, as the chief of police (a strong symbol of government authority) says "two people were arrested."
- The report ends with everything getting "back to normal" (no protesting).

Such a report subtly urges the audience to see protests as offensive, inherently wrong, and against the best interests of society. It encourages audiences to see quiet streets and unblocked sidewalks as important American values.

How else might the protest be characterized? Consider the following account of the same event:

> Today in Florida, over five thousand protesters assembled in front of the courthouse in Miami to draw attention to the inequity in voting technology across the state. According to organizers, wealthier counties have more updated voting technologies than poorer ones, and officials have yet to address the disparity. Said Martha Krug, a voting rights advocate, "It's un-American, and against the basic principles of democracy."

Instead of characterizing the protesters as dangerous or threatening, this report explains their message. Instead of casting them as criminals, it humanizes them by including, and ending with, a particular person's words. That person is referred to not as a "protester," but as an "advocate." Both reports present facts. And neither report distorted the facts (or lied about them). But the selection and placement of information forwards a particular way of thinking. By characterizing the issue as it does, the second report prompts the audience to see equality and citizen action as American values.

There are too many facts to mention for any given situation. News organizations and anyone else who makes an argument must choose which facts to include (and where to place them) and which facts to leave out. The arguer's values and beliefs play a major role in determining which facts get mentioned and how. To find arguments disguised as objective information, readers ask, *How might the selection and placement of facts, or apparently objective information, make an argument? What might the selection and placement of facts reveal about the arguer?*

The Personal Taste Disguise

This disguise camouflages an argument in an appeal to the audience's personal tastes and desires. While speaking directly to the audience's passion for color, interest in sex, or longing for family fun, for example, the text *conceals* a hidden argument. The argument nestles up against us, makes us feel comfortable, and then delivers a way of thinking about ourselves, others, and the world around us.

The disguise can come in any genre (an essay, song, speech, etc.), but it often comes in the form of advertising. Most ads try to make us believe that they are addressing us personally, that they are reaching out to something we enjoy or desire. They lure us in with colors, images, and words that sit well with our tastes. At the same time, they make arguments about what we should value, what we should long for, what we should eventually possess, whom we should admire, and even whom we should dislike.

Sometimes the appeal to personal taste is obvious. Someone may ask, "Wouldn't you like a greener lawn?" Such a question goes directly to a personal desire, but it may also bring along assumptions and values: a green lawn is good; lawns should be well-manicured, not wild-looking; it is worth a homeowner's time and money to keep a yard (and home) looking a certain way; neighbors may think negatively of the homeowner who doesn't maintain his or her yard; the wildness of nature must be tamed (kill the weeds). The simple question about "a greener lawn" makes sense only because of the assumptions and values that it implies. Whenever someone appeals to our personal desires, we should be aware of the unstated assumptions and values behind the appeal.

It might be easy to dismiss hidden arguments, saying, for instance, that an ad does not make people think a particular way. That is true: a single advertisement (or any one argument) does not *make* an audience behave a certain way or accept a certain value system. However, arguments (including hidden arguments) do help to create a reality that we all inhabit. Through sheer repetition and allure, arguments with the personal taste disguise reinforce beliefs and values. They help to shape what we like and dislike, what we find acceptable and unacceptable, and what we tolerate and dismiss. They eventually can become so pervasive that they become part of our *ideology:* our way of seeing and valuing the world.

Consider images of women's bodies. Eroticized women are used to sell everything, including insurance and bank loans. What's sexy about a bank? Nothing. But when an attractive woman nestles up to the camera and pitches herself to the audience, many viewers are ready to listen. At the most obvious level, such an ad pulls readers in by their attraction to a particular female body. A subtle message is that the bank is available. But such advertising strategies also project an argument about women—that they should be erotic and presented as a service. When ads like this are shown by the thousands every day, they make a powerful argument that women should look and act a particular way. Even if the ads (the arguments) don't persuade you, they persuade others. And when other people adopt particular beliefs, those beliefs create an aspect of the world in which *you* live. You are affected too. To uncover the personal taste disguise, readers ask, *How does this text appeal to the audience's personal tastes or desires? Is the appeal easy or difficult to notice? What argument does it disguise?*

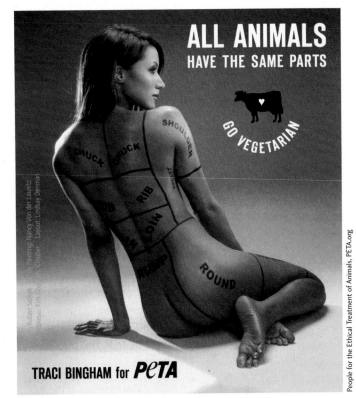

This PETA (People for the Ethical Treatment of Animals) ad featuring Traci Bingham appeared in the July 2002 issue of *Gear* magazine. What is the hidden argument? What particular values, perspectives, or claims are hiding in the text and image?

Spin

Spin is a heavily biased portrayal of information. *Spinning* an event or statement involves turning its obvious or apparent meaning into something else—a meaning that is more favorable to the spinner's cause or position. The term *spin* is most often associated with political discourse, but it is not exclusive to politics. Anyone can spin situations to his or her advantage by making an argument that changes the meaning of an event or statement.

Anyone who pays attention to the arguments of politicians, their advisors, and partisan political analysts is familiar with spin. For example, if a president's approval rating drops significantly, his or her supporters are likely to spin the situation, turning an obviously negative situation into something positive. Spin is an effort to distract people from the real meaning:

> The approval rating actually is higher than it has been at this point in the term for many presidents. We see the slight drop as a sign that the president's policies are taking root and making people's lives significantly better in the long run.

This statement puts a positive spin on a negative situation. But spin involves more than just being positive. Spin is often dishonest and harmful. When public speakers spin every event or statement, public discourse suffers. People must sift through the spin to discover the truth. Instead of argument being a tool for the exploration and discovery of ideas, it becomes a tool for the advancement of a particular ideology at the expense of everything else.

One way spin works to shift meaning is by focusing the audience's attention away from one aspect (the broader picture) and toward a particular aspect the arguer deems worthy. In the following passage from George Orwell's *Animal Farm*, notice how the speaker creates *selective attention*. Here, Squealer the pig is spinning, trying to convince the other animals that the pigs did not break a commandment by sleeping in the house:

> "You have heard then, comrades," he said, "that we pigs now sleep in the beds of the farmhouse? And why not? You did not suppose, surely, that there was ever a ruling against beds? A bed merely means a place to sleep in. A pile of straw in a stall is a bed, properly regarded. The rule was against sheets, which are a human invention. We have removed the sheets from the farmhouse beds, and sleep between blankets. And very comfortable beds they are too! But not more comfortable than we need, I can tell you, comrades, with all the brainwork we have to do nowadays. You would not rob us of our repose, would you, comrades? You would not have us too tired to carry out our duties? Surely none of you wishes to see Jones back?"

Although the commandment says nothing about sheets, Squealer has created a diversion. He also turns the question (Did the pigs break a commandment?) back onto the other animals: *You would not rob us of our repose, would you?* With such a question, Squealer makes the other animals into potential villains who want to rob the pigs of sleep. And he even adds an appeal to emotion (fear) at the end in mentioning Jones, the farmer who had previously owned them.

Orwell's animals illustrate how humans dishonestly use arguments to make one thing mean something else. Orwell's pigs make spin and all other types of argumentative disguises easy to see (unless you are one of the animals in the book). But in everyday life (politics, work, popular culture, schools, etc.), these tactics are often more subtle. To recognize spin, readers ask, *How does the text move attention away from an obvious or apparent meaning and into something else, favorable to the arguer's position? Is the shift in meaning legitimate or deceptive?*

Propaganda

Propaganda is a complex set of strategies used to drive audiences into a uniform way of thinking and feeling (often called a *doctrine*). Propaganda serves to crush differences in thinking, minimize nuances, and squash potential reflection. It works to unite many people into a simple intellectual habit. Propaganda may depend on the objectivity disguise and/or the personal taste disguise to achieve its goal. It may also use any of the following devices:

- Vague or ill-defined words and phrases
- Repetition of simple words and phrases (or slogans)
- Strong appeals to emotions (fear, anger, happiness, regret, etc.)
- Strong appeals to human need (belonging, sexual intimacy, food, safety), etc.
- Strong appeals to character
- Intellectual and moral certainty
- Conflation of groups (Us versus Them)
- Fallacies (hasty generalization, faulty cause-effect, either/or reasoning, etc.)

Notice that the tools of propaganda run counter to sound reasoning. Propaganda deliberately saturates the consciousness with appeals to value, need, emotion, and character *and* with persistent slogans so that sound logic is drowned out. When people are victims of propaganda, they accept a doctrine as unquestionable truth. They are immune to curiosity. And when their doctrines come into question (because of someone else's views), the victims of propaganda defend with intensity what they accept as truth.

Imagine the propaganda necessary to make millions of people buy the same style of jeans. Imagine the language necessary to make millions of people hate millions of other people they have never met. Imagine the repetitive and consistent messages required to make millions of people follow the words of one man. Imagine the disguised argument necessary to make hundreds of millions of people feel like a single team against the rest of the world. Such intellectual obedience requires training—training that is invisible to the uncritical eye and ear. Readers looking for propaganda ask, *How does the text use the tools of propaganda to crush differences in thinking, minimize nuances, and squash potential reflection (to drive all readers into a uniform way of thinking and/or feeling)?*

Activities

1. Examine a news report that appears to be objective, and explain how the selection and placement of information makes an argument.

2. Imagine that you work for a political campaign and that you hope to protect your candidate's character above all else—above honesty, the public good, democratic principles. It's been discovered that your candidate accepts funds from a racist organization. In a small group, write a passage that would spin public attention away from the issue. Use as much subtlety as possible. After all groups have presented their spin, discuss the following: How does spin impact your understanding of national events?

3. Businesses often use spin to fool customers. Describe how you, as an employee, used spin on customers, or how a business used spin on you. How effective was the spin, and why?

4. As a class, discuss the following: Is spin dishonest?

5. What propaganda strategies or devices are used to sell a Big Mac? What strategies are used to sell (or to influence people to think a predetermined way about) a particular fast food chain, a political candidate, a clothing brand, a type of music, a sport or game, a celebrity, a policy, or a way of life? Provide specific examples of the strategies or devices.

Assignment: Identifying and Summarizing Hidden Layers

As you examine the rhetoric of an argument, you will begin to see beneath the surface layer. For this project, read either Ryan Brown's "A Community of Cars" (pp. 25–28) or Lynda Smith's "Disconnected" (pp. 57–61) and summarize the argument's hidden layers. To explore hidden layers as much as possible, use the following questions:

1. How does the writer engage readers' unstated assumptions (about driving, spending money, walking, connecting with others, and so on)?

2. What assumptions are operating in the argument? Are those assumptions acceptable or questionable? If the writer makes a questionable assumption, how does this damage the argument?

3. What values exist beneath the explicit claims and support? How do they create or fail to create a connection between argument and audience?

4. What arguments are in disguise, and how might these hidden arguments influence the audience? (Look for the objectivity disguise, personal taste disguise, spin, and propaganda.) Caution: Do not confuse a strong argument with propaganda. If a writer is calling for change in thinking, that doesn't mean he or she is trying to blur away complexity and establish doctrine.

5. What appeals are disguised, and how might they influence the audience? (Look for appeals to character, emotion, logic, need, and value.)

Analyzing Argument

nalysis is the act of investigating how something works. It involves seeing how individual parts add up to the whole, how specific aspects figure into the overall operation. If we were to analyze a car engine, we would try to figure out how individual components—the pistons, carburetor, battery, air filter—contribute to the working machine. If we were to analyze a novel, we would ask how characters, plot, setting, and narrative style figure into the whole aesthetic experience. The same goes with analyzing argument. We can ask how specific rhetorical moves work in the overall piece, how the line of reasoning proceeds, how examples support the main claim, how opposition is countered, how underlying values give way to appeals, or how the writer engages the intended audience.

The Analytical Posture

Analyzing an argument requires reading with a specific goal: to understand how the argument works. Reading analytically calls for a particular posture, one that is different from some of our most basic intellectual reflexes. When we are reading an argument, we may feel the reflex to respond—to seek out points of agreement or disagreement. We might ask ourselves, *Do I agree or disagree? Do I like the point being made or not? Do I like this author or not?* But in analysis, such questions must be put aside. Even if we find ourselves outraged by or in total agreement with the argument, we have to think in analytical terms. Sometimes, it's difficult to put aside the basic reflex to agree or disagree, especially if the argument itself is heated. For example, consider the following argumentative passage from Cameron Johnson:

> Facebook is fun. It connects people to old friends and, many would say, it even generates new friendships. But here's a question that's not often asked: so what? Even if we accept the idea that friends confirmed on FB are anything close to real friendship (and only the most giddy among us would), we might ask ourselves if another corporate controlled friend-making device should be so celebrated. While America is well known as a civilization absolutely turned in on itself, unaware of its own history, ignorant of the grisly business just outside its borders, millions of otherwise savvy thinkers are spending countless hours learning what their e-friends are drinking or feeling after drinking whatever they drank. Certainly, FB fans would say that many users trade important views about war, poverty, history, religion, and so on. But there's nothing about FB itself that urges hard reflection on such matters. In fact, the medium works, primarily, to thrust quick blurby opinions back and forth. From what I've seen in my admittedly limited experience, FB is yet another bourgeois tool for celebrating *me,* my personal thoughts, and my closed bubble of acquaintances. Like an electronic junior high clique, it reinforces a pre-adolescent take on the world. Like *Fox News,* like most morning news programs, like most talk radio, like mainstream sports, FB bolsters the everything-I-like-about-my-life mentality that civilizations, at some point, must evolve beyond.

We might have a range of responses to the passage: *Hell, yes! It's totally true! No way! I love Facebook! What if Facebook has made my life bigger, not smaller? I hate Cameron Johnson!* But such responses are argumentative rather than analytical. When we ask these questions, we're being pulled into the argument about Facebook rather than remaining outside of the argument on analytical ground. To be an analytical reader, we have to ask how the passage works. We have to ask what premises the passage puts forward, how it seeks to convince us of each premise, how it appeals to shared values, how it relies on examples to create a convincing reality.

Analyzing an argument is commonly called *rhetorical analysis* because we are trying to discover the basic rhetorical strategies—those discussed in the previous chapters: Claims, Appeals, Examples, Evidence, Counterarguments, Concessions, Qualifiers, and Assumptions. If we can point to these argumentative moves and understand the intended audience, we are well on the way to analysis. It can be tricky business because these moves are not evident. (Writers do not go out of their way to tell us what they're up to!) But if we can, for example, identify an appeal to value amid a range of other moves, we begin to understand how the argument functions. Here's how we might begin to identify the moves in Johnson's passage about Facebook:

Allusions:	To *Fox News*, talk radio, mainstream sports
Appeals to Value:	To the value of world knowledge, history, maturity
Appeal to Logic:	"Even if we accept the idea that friends confirmed on FB are anything close to real friendship (and only the most giddy among us would), we might ask ourselves if another corporate mediated friend-making device should be so celebrated."
Concession:	"Facebook is fun."
Counterargument:	"But there's nothing about FB itself that urges hard reflection on such matters. In fact, the medium works, primarily, to thrust quick blurby opinions back and forth."
Qualifier:	"From what I've seen in my admittedly limited experience, . . ."

Once we've identified these basic rhetorical ingredients, we are on an analytical path. But analysis goes far beyond labeling the parts. Good analysis involves explaining *how* something works, how each part functions in the whole. It is not enough to simply call something an appeal to value and then move on. The following example not only identifies an appeal but also explains *how the appeal works* in Johnson's passage:

> Johnson's argument against Facebook relies on several appeals to value—especially to the concept of world knowledge. Johnson calls on readers to condemn Facebook primarily because it fixes users' concentration on personal, even petty, rather than global issues. The worst parts of American culture, he argues, are those that turn people's attention inward away from a world of difference. The passage suggests that global consciousness is inherently good while self-involvement is a form of arrested development, a reflex that keeps people and entire civilizations from maturing. The appeal is most apparent in the description of FB users as junior high children who disregard the bigger world beyond their own small social network.

Staying on the analytical path is difficult. But the path does lead to new insights. In fact, the goal of analysis is just that: to discover something about a text—to see some complexity, some underlying connections, some underlying principle. Analysis should lead us to some better, richer understanding of the thing itself. All three sample analyses in this chapter achieve that richer understanding. They each identify rhetorical moves, explain how the moves work, and then articulate some insight about the text being analyzed.

In his analysis of Chief Seattle's speech (pp. 100–111), Andrew Buchner discovers an important layer—something that a quick glance might not reveal. After carefully walking through specific rhetorical strategies in the speech, Buchner finds an interesting and subtle tension within Seattle's concession:

> So, while Seattle's speech can be broadly viewed as a concession, it is a concession *on his own terms*. He hasn't assented to the superiority of the white way of living. He hasn't conceded that he has been beaten by the better opponent. He only concedes to the fact that his wave has crested and spilled onto the shore, whereas the white man's wave may simply be further out at sea.

In her analysis of a Benetton clothing ad, Megan Ward discovers something about the interplay between the ad and its broader context. The ad itself (p. 115) says very little. But through careful analysis, Ward shows that its complexity is bound to the cultural arguments it quietly engages:

> Benetton engages its audience on an "immediate, emotional level" with the bare images of meat so starkly presented. But when we acknowledge the ad's context—all the cultural debates about race, difference and equality—we can see how it argues on a "much broader stage."

And in his analysis of *Avatar* (pp. 120–122), Benjamin Wetherbee discovers a powerful tension in the movie's implied values:

> Here, however, enters *Avatar's* logical contradiction. The movie's explosively violent final act implies what most action films do (e.g., the *Rambo* and *Lethal Weapon* franchises): real results, ultimately, come only from manning up and settling matters through armed conflict. This macho, right-wing truism, popular among American film audiences, appears most transparently in the climactic final battle, wherein Sully expresses unequivocal joy at the chance to fight and kill the merciless colonel who had been his superior officer. The movie glorifies this moment, even as it gainsays the Na'vi wisdom that killing should be only an affair of sad necessity. In its finale, *Avatar* does not bemoan the violence it presents. The violence is meant to be fun. As audiences uncritically tag along on this final explosive ride, they accept its logic; they accept the "git-'er-done" attitude that values decisive, violent action, and rebukes diplomacy and dialogue.

All of these discoveries are the result of powerful analysis—close inspection of the argumentative parts. Each writer (Buchner, Ward, Wetherbee) comes to a new understanding about the original argument.

Summary and Analysis

To understand how an argument works (analysis), we must understand what it is arguing (summary). The *how* depends upon the *what*. Usually, rhetorical analysis relies on an initial, brief summary. For instance, if we were conducting an analysis of Holly Wren Spaulding's essay, "In Defense of Darkness" (from Chapter 5), we first would need to understand it to accurately portray its claims:

> In her argument, Holly Wren Spaulding celebrates the power of darkness, genuine darkness that is not injured by artificial light. She explains how nighttime gives birth to vital dimensions of life: connectivity to others, an ability to wonder, the reflex to extend outward and feel something other than fear. Part of this celebration involves condemning the increasing drive to illuminate the world. She denounces the uncritical and deeply engrained habit of keeping on the lights.

After we get a good sense of the argument, we can begin to understand how it works, how Spaulding urges readers to believe in something that is different from, even contrary to, mainstream assumptions. Without that initial basic understanding, analysis is nearly impossible.

And even after we summarize, when we enter analytical territory, we still need summary. For instance, notice how the following passage begins with a brief summary statement and then moves to analysis. In this case, summary and analysis work together. The power of the analysis depends upon a close and accurate summary:

> Spaulding begins her fifth paragraph with a general point about modern industrial society. She says that we, in this current age, favor electrical light—that it defines our lives. This characterization puts her argument, and her readers, in time—in the long epic narrative of the human species. She describes herself and readers as "We modern, industrial, technological Homo sapiens," which puts us in proportion within the bigger human story. And this desire for proportion—for understanding ourselves in proper relation with the rest of the world—is a major component of Spaulding's argument.

Summary versus Analysis

While summary is important to good analysis, it can also become a problem. It can overshadow the analytical moves. If we are doing analysis (if analysis is the goal), then we must be careful to keep summary from taking over—from eclipsing our explanation of how the argument works. This can be a difficult path. In the following passages, a writer examines Ryan Brown's essay (from Chapter 2). In the first, the writer strictly summarizes. In the second, the writer identifies Brown's appeal to value but then shifts into summary, merely restating the argument rather than analyzing the appeal. And in the third, the writer genuinely analyzes Brown's argumentative move:

> **Summary:** In his third paragraph, Brown says that we have lost the intimate dialogue that comes from walking in our everyday lives. He goes on to blame cars for pulling us away from downtown communities and to suburban shopping centers.

> **Almost-Analysis:** In Brown's sixth paragraph, he appeals to value. He argues that our communities are our homes. But, he says, we don't treat them as such. Instead, we drive quickly through them for the sake of convenience.

> **Analysis:** In Brown's sixth paragraph, he appeals to value by connecting the over-reliance on cars and the breakdown of community. Brown draws our attention to the inherent good in familiarity, location, and social connectedness. He then shows how car culture undermines those principles—those ideals that people seem to cherish but also ignore on their way to the shopping plaza on the other side of town.

In the following examples, we see the writer summarizing, almost-analyzing, and finally analyzing Holly Wren Spaulding's argument. Notice the critical difference between almost-analysis and analysis:

> **Summary:** In her third paragraph, Spaulding tells about her city friends' awe at the dark skies above her home. She explains that they can hardly believe the beauty of all the stars.

> **Almost-Analysis:** Spaulding appeals to our yearning for calm. She says that our cultural reflex is to brighten up the landscape, to turn away from darkness and watch only what is easily visible. This, she explains, is a result of consumer capitalism.

Analysis: Spaulding appeals to our yearning for calm. In her testimony about the silent canoe ride across the lake, she describes, in lush detail, moments of reflection and discovery. These moments are contrasted by descriptions of fast-paced mainstream life that is lit up, overly bright, and "insomnia-producing." In her personal testimony, the darkness is characterized as inspiring and even curative while everyday mainstream life is characterized by isolation and petty consumer fulfillment.

To accomplish genuine analysis, the writer has to both identify the argumentative move (such as an appeal to value) and then *explain how it works*. If we discover an appeal to value, we have to describe what value, what cherished ideal, the writer appeals to and how that drives the argument forward or how it supports the main claim.

Four Common Pitfalls

Rhetorical analysis comes with a few unique dangers—four traps to avoid. First, some writers get lured inside the points of the argument they are analyzing, and rather than remain outside of that argument, on solid analytical ground, they begin **making a case** for the argument. In the first passage below, the writer further develops—makes a case for—Brown's idea. It's as if the writer has suddenly been possessed by Brown. In the second passage, the writer analyzes Brown's argument:

> **Making a Case for Brown:** Brown shows why communities in our modern civilization are breaking down. We elect the car over our own feet. And when we get into cars, roll up the windows, turn on the tunes, and drive away, we have little interaction with the people around us. We learn to see the world around us as a blurry landscape on the road to our singular destination.

> **Analyzing Brown:** Brown shows why communities in our modern civilization are breaking down. Through a series of connected premises, he describes a cause/effect relationship between consumer habits, driving patterns, and urban planning. The cause/effect relationship is developed over several paragraphs that detail everyday life for mainstream Americans in typical towns like Brown's.

The second pitfall involves **describing the effect** of the original argument. In this situation, the writer describes how the argument (or a part of it) might affect an audience. This is not inherently wrong. After all, rhetorical analysis does involve an understanding of the argument's impact. But, as you will see, dealing with effect can be tricky. In the

Summary vs analysis

"lured by points" vs analysis of them

following passage, the writer examines Lynda Smith's essay (from Chapter 3) and *appropriately* considers the effect on readers:

> Lynda Smith likens technological dependence to drug dependence. She walks through the harmful effects of chemical addiction and compares them to the quieter, but equally ruinous, effects of technological craving. This comparison appeals to readers' knowledge of drug addiction—its peril, its obvious harm to individuals and communities. It taps into the emotional baggage associated with drugs.

But imagining the effect quickly gets dangerous. After all, we don't know exactly how an audience will respond. We cannot assume that readers or viewers will automatically laugh, think, cry, or get angry. But we can examine how a specific argumentative move corresponds to an audience's characteristics. This is a fine line. The danger is that the original argument (the text being analyzed) gets left behind while the focus shifts to imagined audience responses. The following passage crosses into dangerous territory because it begins to move away from Smith's argument and emphasizes particular audience responses:

> Lynda Smith's argument strikes at the core for many readers who are already leery about the latest cell phone technology. Her claims make us realize that *we are surrounded by a growing and alarmingly powerful wave of technological progress.* Because we cannot, alone, stave off the power of corporate America, *we feel her argument at an emotional level. We become afraid for our own ability to live an independent life.*

While the previous pitfall focuses too much on an imagined audience, the third pitfall involves **describing the author's intent.** This strategy is fraught with problems. Because we cannot genuinely know a writer, advertising agency, or movie director's thoughts, we must be careful not to conjure them based on one argument. In the following example, the writer examines Simon Benlow's essay (from Chapter 4) and begins imagining the interior life of the author. In this case, analysis of the argument gets abandoned for a guess at the author's hopes:

> Benlow was hoping to force teachers out of categorizing their students too quickly. Because he sees the learning styles fad as scientifically and logically flawed, he thinks that it should not be applied to unknowing students. This is why he uses the scenario about Jennifer, the student who doesn't even understand why she's had bad educational experiences. He wanted everyone to feel angry for her.

Evaluation is the fourth pitfall. In evaluation, we make and defend judgments about the worth of an argument. We condemn it, celebrate it, or explain that it's okay but not great. Analysis does none of that. It avoids judging the success, the worth, the soundness, the acceptability of any of its claims. Analysis avoids taking a side for or against the argument. In the first of the following lists, the statements judge the worth of Brown's, Smith's, or Johnson's argument. They are evaluative statements. The second list makes analytical points.

Evaluative:

Brown does a good job of supporting his main idea.

Smith's ideas are right on target.

Brown convinces me that we definitely are reliant on automobile culture.

I don't accept these claims.

I am suspicious of Johnson's ideas because they seem ungrounded.

Analytical:

Brown relies on personal testimony to set up his main idea.

Smith develops an appeal to need with several paragraphs.

Brown directly addresses opposing assumptions about transportation.

Johnson immediately appeals to emotion by connecting the topic, telemarketers, to a predatory economic climate—to the fear and quiet anger associated with corporate power.

Now, let's look at the difference between evaluation and analysis in a full paragraph. In the first passage, the writer openly condemns Johnson's passage about Facebook (p. 98). This passage is clearly evaluative because it judges the soundness of Johnson's points. The second passage is clearly analytical. It avoids judging Johnson's argument and, instead, explains its rhetorical strategies.

Evaluative: Johnson's argument mischaracterizes Facebook users. He suggests that users think primarily about themselves and their own small social circles. But users have lives beyond the website. They heal, govern, administrate, build, preach, sell, and even teach in their everyday lives. While Johnson's claims against the broader popular culture might hold some water, his insistence that all Facebook users think like adolescents ignores their real non-Facebook lives and caricaturizes the reality.

Analytical: Johnson's argument against Facebook relies on several appeals to value—especially to the concept of world knowledge. Johnson calls on readers to condemn Facebook primarily because it fixes users' concentration on personal, even petty, rather than global issues. The worst parts of American culture, he argues, are those that turn people's attention inward, away from a world of difference. The passage suggests that global consciousness is inherently good while self-involvement is a form of arrested development, a reflex that keeps people and entire civilizations from maturing. The appeal is most apparent in the description of FB users as junior high children who disregard the bigger world beyond their own small social network.

Activities

1. Write a short analysis paragraph of the Cameron Johnson argument on page 98. Try to avoid evaluating, agreeing, or disagreeing. Instead, explain how a particular rhetorical strategy works.

2. Read the following passage from Holly Wren Spaulding's essay, "In Defense of Darkness" (pp. 83–87). Identify the primary rhetorical moves in the passage. In other words, what is the main argumentative strategy here? Then, explain how that move works in Spaulding's overall argument. How does the move work to make her main claim acceptable?

> Perhaps it seems ungenerous or even paranoid to regard the physical, bright-lit world in such a way. I know that it is more common to be surrounded by a gazillion watts of light at night than to spend more than a few minutes in any kind of real darkness each day. In this country, most of us would have to make a considerable effort if we wanted to get anywhere that was not bathed in perpetual light. But why not bask in our remarkable achievement? I can imagine all manner of push-back, devil's advocacy, disagreement or shoulder shrugging dismissal of the idea that darkness matters. *Who cares?* says the voice. With all of the other things to worry about, speak out for, and take action against, why defend darkness? The answer is fairly straightforward: When we are estranged from the dark, we lose access to vital human emotions and sensual experiences including wonder and awe and humility.

3. Read Chief Seattle's speech on the land (pp. 107–109). Decide on his main claim. What is Seattle's main assertion about the land? And what is the main line of reasoning? In other words, what individual statements (premises) build up to his main claim?

4. After reading Chief Seattle, read Andrew Buchner's analysis (pp. 110–111). Buchner identifies Seattle's line of reasoning, a counterargument, a concession, and at least one major appeal to value. Beyond those strategies Buchner identifies, what other important rhetorical strategies does Seattle use?

Chief Seattle's Speech

Chief Seattle (c. 1786–1866) was leader of the Suquamish and Duwamish Native American tribes, in what is now the state of Washington. During treaty negotiations in 1854, he gave a now-famous speech about Native American rights and environmental values. Different versions of his speech exist—all secondhand accounts. This version appeared in the *Seattle Sunday Star* on October 29, 1887, more than thirty years after Chief Seattle gave the speech. It was reconstructed by pioneer Dr. Henry Smith, based on Smith's notes.

Yonder sky that has wept tears of compassion on our fathers for centuries untold, and which, to us, looks eternal, may change. Today it is fair, tomorrow it may be overcast with clouds. My words are like the stars that never set. What Seattle says, the great chief, Washington . . . can rely upon, with as much certainty as our pale-face brothers can rely upon the return of the seasons.

The son [a reference to Terr. Gov. Stevens] of the White Chief says his father sends us greetings of friendship and good will. This is kind, for we know he has little need of our friendship in return, because his people are many. They are like the grass that covers the vast prairies, while my people are few, and resemble the scattering trees of a storm-swept plain.

The great, and I presume also good, white chief sends us word that he wants to buy our lands but is willing to allow us to reserve enough to live on comfortably. This indeed appears generous, for the red man no longer has rights that he need respect, and the offer may be wise, also, for we are no longer in need of a great country.

There was a time when our people covered the whole land, as the waves of a wind-ruffled sea cover its shell-paved floor. But that time has long since passed away with the greatness of tribes now almost forgotten. I will not mourn over our untimely decay, nor reproach my pale-face brothers for hastening it, for we, too, may have been somewhat to blame.

George Rose/Getty Images

Chief Seattle statue in downtown Seattle, Washington.

When our young men grow angry at some real or imaginary wrong, and disfigure their faces with black paint, their hearts, also, are disfigured and turn black, and then their cruelty is relentless and knows no bounds, and our old men are not able to restrain them.

But let us hope that hostilities between the red-man and his pale-face brothers may never return. We would have everything to lose and nothing to gain.

True it is, that revenge, with our young braves, is considered gain, even at the cost of their own lives, but old men who stay at home in times of war, and old women, who have sons to lose, know better.

Our great father Washington, for I presume he is now our father, as well as yours, since George [a reference to King George III, i.e., Great Britain] has moved his boundaries to the north; our great and good father, I say, sends us word by his son, who, no doubt, is a great chief among his people, that if we do as he desires, he will protect us. His brave armies will be to us a bristling wall of strength, and his great ships of war will fill our harbors so that our ancient enemies far to the northward, the Simsiams [Tsimshian] and Hydas [Haidas], will no longer frighten our women and old men. Then he will be our father and we will be his children.

But can this ever be? Your God loves your people and hates mine; he folds his strong arms lovingly around the white man and leads him as a father leads his infant son, but he has forsaken his red children; he makes your people wax strong every day, and soon they will fill the land; while my people are ebbing away like a fast-receding tide, that will never flow again. The white man's God cannot love his red children or he would protect them. They seem to be orphans who can look nowhere for help. How then can we become brothers? How can your father become our father and bring us prosperity and awaken in us dreams of returning greatness?

Your God seems to us to be partial. He came to the white man. We never saw Him; never even heard His voice; He gave the white man laws but He had no word for His red children whose teeming millions filled this vast continent as the stars fill the firmament. No, we are two distinct races and must remain ever so. There is little in common between us. The ashes of our ancestors are sacred and their final resting place is hallowed ground, while you wander away from the tombs of your fathers seemingly without regret.

Your religion was written on tables of stone by the iron finger of an angry God, lest you might forget it. The red man could never remember nor comprehend it.

Our religion is the traditions of our ancestors, the dreams of our old men, given them by the great Spirit, and the visions of our sachems, and is written in the hearts of our people.

Your dead cease to love you and the homes of their nativity as soon as they pass the portals of the tomb. They wander far off beyond the stars, are soon forgotten, and never return. Our dead never forget the beautiful world that gave them being. They still love its winding rivers, its great mountains and its sequestered vales, and they ever yearn in tenderest affection over the lonely hearted living and often return to visit and comfort them.

Day and night cannot dwell together. The red man has ever fled the approach of the white man, as the changing mists on the mountain side flee before the blazing morning sun.

However, your proposition seems a just one, and I think my folks will accept it and will retire to the reservation you offer them, and we will dwell apart and in peace, for the words of the great white chief seem to be the voice of nature speaking to my people out of the thick darkness that is fast gathering around them like a dense fog floating inward from a midnight sea.

It matters but little where we pass the remainder of our days.

They are not many. The Indian's night promises to be dark. No bright star hovers above the horizon. Sad-voiced winds moan in the distance. Some grim Nemesis of our race is on the red man's trail, and wherever he goes he will still hear the sure approaching footsteps of the fell destroyer and prepare to meet his doom, as does the wounded doe that hears the approaching footsteps of the hunter. A few more moons, a few more winters, and not one of all the mighty hosts that once filled this broad land or that now roam in fragmentary bands through these vast solitudes will remain to weep over the tombs of a people once as powerful and as hopeful as your own.

But why should we repine? Why should I murmur at the fate of my people? Tribes are made up of individuals and are no better than they. Men come and go like the waves of a sea. A tear, a *tamanawus,* a dirge, and they are gone from our longing eyes forever. Even the white man, whose God walked and talked with him, as friend to friend, is not exempt from the common destiny. We *may* be brothers after all. We shall see.

We will ponder your proposition, and when we have decided we will tell you. But should we accept it, I here and now make this the first condition: That we will not be denied the privilege, without molestation, of visiting at will the graves of our ancestors and friends. Every part of this country is sacred to my people. Every hill-side, every valley, every plain and grove has been hallowed by some fond memory or some sad experience of my tribe.

Even the rocks that seem to lie dumb as they swelter in the sun along the silent seashore in solemn grandeur thrill with memories of past events connected with the fate of my people, and the very dust under your feet responds more lovingly to our footsteps than to yours, because it is the ashes of our ancestors, and our bare feet are conscious of the sympathetic touch, for the soil is rich with the life of our kindred.

The sable braves, and fond mothers, and glad-hearted maidens, and the little children who lived and rejoiced here, and whose very names are now forgotten, still love these solitudes, and their deep fastnesses at eventide grow shadowy with the presence of dusky spirits. And when the last red man shall have perished from the earth and his memory among white men shall have become a myth, these shores shall swarm with the invisible dead of my tribe, and when your children's children shall think themselves alone in the field, the store, the shop, upon the highway or in the silence of the woods they will not be alone. In all the earth there is no place dedicated to solitude. At night, when the streets of your cities and villages shall be silent, and you think them deserted, they will throng with the returning hosts that once filled and still love this beautiful land. The white man will never be alone. Let him be just and deal kindly with my people, for the dead are not altogether powerless.

Seattle's Rhetoric

ANDREW BUCHNER

Chief Seattle's speech on the land is read widely. There are many interesting layers to consider. Andrew Buchner focuses on Seattle's main line of reasoning—and a consistent tension between Seattle's religion and the religion of white man. Andrew Buchner has a BA in English from Western Michigan University. He is now a graduate student in rhetoric.

In his speech on the land, Seattle opens with a major premise in his line of reasoning: that which seems eternal will change according to the dictates of nature. He contrasts this state of change with the strength of his words, which, he claims, are as reliable as the stars in the sky. With these introductory statements, Seattle situates himself as a reliable person and puts the weight of his character behind the speech itself. He also establishes that his claims will remain true and accurate regardless of the passage of time.

In the third paragraph, Seattle acknowledges the American president's good will in allowing the Native-Americans to retain some land. Then, he provides personal testimony about the decline of his people. He openly accepts this fate, and his acceptance echoes the reasoning of his speech. He views his people's passing as analogous to the changing weather or other natural phenomena indifferent to the will of anyone under their power.

He then contrasts his own stoicism with that of the young people in his tribe, who are enraged at the present state, and who, against the advice of the elders, go to war against the white man. This contrast between stoicism and rage borrows a shared assumption—one that may even transcend the divide between Native American and European American cultures: that older men are wiser than younger men because younger men tend to be rash and foolhardy.

Seattle then offers a scenario wherein his people accept the American government's offer and are protected from their enemies by the American navy and army. But the next paragraph begins a strong counterargument to this proposed scenario. This counterargument takes the form of an appeal to authority. Seattle argues that while the American government may promise to provide protection to his people, the white man's god will not offer the same protection. He is essentially going over the US government's head and arguing that a higher power will prevent it from keeping its promise.

Seattle uses an allusion to the Ten Commandments to further highlight the irreconcilable differences between the whites' god and the religion of the indigenous people: Christianity, he suggests, primarily stresses the afterlife and an escape from this world, while his religious beliefs are tied to this world. In Seattle's belief system, his people will not end up in Heaven but will, instead, choose to remain with the world they love. Seattle frames these differences within the main line of reasoning. He notes that "the red man has ever fled the approach of the white man, as the changing mists on the mountainside flee before the blazing morning sun." This comparison echoes the opening lines of the speech where he shows the indifferent and Protean character of the natural world, a comparison which again highlights the fact that everyone is subject to the dictates of nature.

This main line of reasoning also contains an unstated premise—one that haunts the argument and acts as a counterargument. He does not accept the white man's religious worldview, nor does he believe that white dominance is proof of an inherent superiority. Instead, he explains the current state of white dominion as one more caprice of nature. As he puts it, "men come and go like the waves of the sea." This leads to an inevitable, but unstated, point: the fate of his people will be the fate of white men, and so one day "they may be brothers after all." Such a statement reads like an expression of Seattle's spiritualism. But it is also an intense counter to the white man's belief in himself, in his rightful place as the dominant force on the continent. If white men are bound to the same destiny as the native population, then his god will have failed him. The impending doom of the white man would mean he was subject to the same principles of nature as anyone else and that his god does not offer him any special protection. It would also mean that Seattle's conception of the world is the correct one.

So, while Seattle's speech can be viewed as a concession, it is a concession *on his own terms.* He has not assented to the superiority of the white way of living. He has not conceded that he has been beaten by the better opponent. He only concedes to the fact that his wave has crested and spilled onto the shore, whereas the white man's wave may simply be further out at sea. The one qualifier Seattle adds further cements this position. Seattle claims he will only agree to the terms set forth if the American government allows his people to visit the graves of their ancestors. This qualification confirms Seattle's commitment to uphold the underlying values of his people, even in the face of his tribe's destruction.

The two closing paragraphs further affirm this commitment and bring the main line of reasoning to its conclusion. In these final paragraphs, Seattle reaffirms his people's special connection with the land. He argues that this connection will keep them residing on this earth even after they are dead, even after their lives are but myths on the tongues of the whites. Finally, he explains that white man's children will never be truly alone, that they will also be surrounded by the native dead. Thus, even if Seattle's people are destroyed in their material form, their spiritual form will eventually, again, take sole possession of the land that was once theirs.

"So, while Seattle's speech can be viewed as a concession, it is a concession on his own terms."

Analyzing Visual Arguments

Written language is not the only argumentative force in our lives. We are surrounded by arguments. Films, images, photographs, songs, and art of all genres make arguments. They make claims and appeals, they use examples, they employ evidence, they engage opposition, and they even tap into cultural assumptions and values. Consider this historically important painting, *George Washington Crossing the Delaware* by Emanuel Leutze:

Bettmann/Corbis

Many details in the painting make a point about Washington's—and America's—strength. Consider the placement of Washington in the boat, his height, his posture, the lighting, the colors, the position of his boat in comparison to others. These details add up to a claim. While they may not make a direct line of reasoning, they still function inductively. They accumulate visually and lead the viewer to a conclusion about General Washington.

Or consider the following two pictures of President Obama. Both were taken by professional photographers and selected for the White House gallery. In other words, like in the painting of Washington, the elements are not accidental. The composition, lighting, angle, and overall tone of each picture were considered—and they all add up to different claims about the president's character.

Official White House Photo by Pete Souza

Official White House Photo by Pete Souza

Of course, not every image is an argument. Alone, and without some context or language, an image may not make a focused and readily apparent argument—one that can be experienced or discussed publicly. Consider the following image of the Grand Canyon. Does it, alone, make an argument? Maybe. But the possibilities are so broad, so varied, so vague, that it would be difficult to decide. People would first have to answer some basic questions and come to shared conclusions. Is the argument about beauty, nature, the West, serenity, unity? It's hard to say. Nothing in the image itself dictates the focus of the would-be argument.

GRAND CANYON N.P. NPS PHOTO

But if a few words are added, everything changes. With a short statement, the image suddenly takes on argumentative force. Now, the image functions as a kind of appeal. The grandeur and magnitude of the land supports an unstated claim about the magnitude of a country. The image can be seen as a premise in a line of reasoning about America.

GRAND CANYON N.P. NPS PHOTO

God Bless America!

Advertising

In advertising, images and words are meticulously crafted to form intensive arguments. The lines of reasoning are simple and usually lead to some form of the claim: *buy this product!* But the support strategies can be wildly complex and subtle. Sometimes they involve a list of the product's attributes: it will get your toughest stains out! Sometimes they involve appeals to values, such as cleanliness: it will keep grime out of your life for good! Or they may go beyond the product and argue something about the consumer: You don't want to be a disorganized mess, right?

As many historians have explained, advertising took a dramatic turn in the latter half of the twentieth century. The majority of ad makers realized that arguments about the consumer's values, fears, and hopes were far more powerful than arguments about the product. For example, which of the following passages, A or B, would have more impact on someone's behavior?

> A. Our Super Round tires are very strong, with steel-belted reinforcements. They have complex and tested traction patterns for maximum stopping power. Make sure you consider Super Rounds.

> B. Your family puts their trust in you. When you drive, their well-being—their collective future—is entirely in your hands. Your driving ability depends on the quality of your tires. Make sure you consider Super Rounds, the best choice for your family's future.

As it turns out, the appeals to family, responsibility, safety, duty, honor, attractiveness (indeed, the whole range of human needs and hopes) are far more powerful than facts about the product. When advertisers link their brands with shared principles, values, hopes, and fears, the buying public responds. In short, version B works. And as the last several decades prove, it works really well. Millions of perfectly intelligent and reasonable people respond immediately to advertising campaigns that appeal to values, character, need, and emotion. (For more on appeals, see pages 43–63.)

And as imaging software has evolved, those appeals have become more visually layered. Words and images are married to create the maximum effect. In this ad for a GMC truck, the image and words function together. The main text simply states, "Makes the most dangerous maneuvers seem routine." But the statement takes on more meaning because of the photograph: As the bikers closely watch the woman pull around their motorcycles, the GMC truck appears huge. It is a wall of steel that surrounds the lone woman and separates her from the two men. (Notice that she is outnumbered.) The photograph gives particular meaning to the broader term *dangerous,* and it even establishes an unstated premise, which is something like, *The GMC truck will protect you from dangerous people.* And we could go even further. Together, the image and the words distinguish between the types of people who are dangerous and the types of people who are worth protecting. In other words, *the type of woman who drives this truck should be protected from the type of people who drive motorcycles.*

This magazine ad, part of a national advertising campaign, appeared in 2004. What is the hidden argument? What particular values, perspectives, or claims are hiding in the text and image?

The Hearts of Argument: Benetton's Advertising Appeal

MEGAN WARD

Advertising taps into broader cultural conversations. The images and words are often chosen specifically to echo present debates, jokes, concerns, crises, even other ad campaigns. So doing rhetorical analysis of an ad involves some awareness of the social context. In this analysis, Megan Ward explains how the broader social context can figure into one ad's persuasive elements. Ward is the Writing Center Director at Northwestern Michigan College.

In 1996, United Colors of Benetton, a clothing company based in Italy, created an advertisement that shows three human hearts with the labels: *white, black,* and *yellow,* respectively. The type is bold and black on a stark white background. The only colors present within the ad are the vivid, wet, fleshy browns and reds of the hearts and a green box on the right side that reads "United Colors of Benetton." With that, the ad is complete. However, beneath the surface, an entire argument takes place, one that engages shared assumptions and cultural values.

With the visual interplay of the hearts and the three labels, the ad asserts a claim of fact about human identity: when stripped of superficial identifiers, we are all the same. And with the hearts, as opposed to lungs or livers or kidneys (which also could have been used), the ad's argument goes further than same-ness. The heart represents humanity. It is a symbol of love, caring, generosity, and spirituality. Art, cinema, literature, and everyday mainstream language consistently celebrate the heart as the center of human life. When we are devastated, our hearts are broken; when we forgive, we have heart; when we love, we give our hearts away; when we have found truth, we are at the heart of it all. Such common phrases illustrate how much we use the heart as a representation of who we are and what we assume about identity. Benetton uses this powerful symbol, and what it means within culture, to say that we share a basic "human-ness" beneath visible, political, ethnic differences.

While the ad asserts a singular claim of fact, it is also participating in a broader conversation about race. In a sense, it is a counterargument. It speaks back to common assertions about difference—to claims about heritage and descent. One common argument about race is that we can take difference and make it into something positive. Difference, say many, is real. It should not be ignored but embraced and used for better understanding. However, the Benetton ad obliterates the idea of difference. The visual impact of three human hearts pushes against the words, the labels, the very notion of Caucasian (white), African (black), and Asian (yellow) descent. In this sense, Benetton uses the more striking feature (extracted human organs) to trump the less striking feature (plain black words). In Benetton's argument, identifiers are useless—not worthy of attention. There is no acknowledgment of historical complexity, political oppression, slavery, or genocide. These are conspicuously absent.

Benetton's ad was featured on billboards in France and other countries as part of World Anti-Racism Day ("United Colors"). As in many fashion ads, Benetton does not outwardly define its products, but expects the audience to fill in the details about the product and the company. These billboards were in European cities, where the public would likely be aware of United Colors of Benetton and its usual risqué advertising moves, which draw attention to the brand's character or attitude rather than its product. The ad does not argue that people should buy Benetton's clothing. Instead, it implies a broader point about the company's character—that it cares about social issues, that it is in touch with the things that matter. And beyond that, the ad suggests something about the character of Benetton's consumers: people who buy from Benetton are people who care deeply about important issues.

As a visual argument, especially one placed on such a large scale, the ad's complexity cannot be overlooked. Benetton uses shock value, acting on the audience's visceral, and perhaps emotional, response at seeing internal organs. The startling image calls on audiences to pay attention, to feel something intense, and may even draw on people's beliefs about "acceptable" material for a billboard. Benetton then uses the emotional effect to push its assertion about human identity, equality and homogeny.

J. Francis Davis says, in an article discussing images and their power, "Pictures have become tools used to elicit specific and planned emotional reactions in the people who see them." Benetton made a specific choice in using such imagery in its advertisement. Davis points out two main ways that images are utilized today: "First there is the immediate, emotional level on which we recognize the flag or the sexy body and react in a way that taps our inner stories or emotions. But second, there is a much broader stage on which we can step back and look at one image in context with hundreds of others." Benetton engages its audience on an "immediate, emotional level" with the bare images of meat so starkly presented. But when we acknowledge the ad's context—all the cultural debates about race, difference and equality—we can see how it argues on a "much broader stage."

Works Cited

Davis, J. Francis. "Power of Images: Creating the Myths of Our Time." *Center for Media Literacy.* Center for Media Literacy, 1992. Web. 3 June 2010.

"United Colors of Benetton Celebrates World Anti-Racism Day with MTV and Liberation." *Press Area: Press Releases – 1996.* United Colors of Benetton, 1996. Web. 3 June 2010.

Image courtesy of The Advertising Archives

Film

Popular movies often make arguments about love, war, government, freedom, history, crime, and religion—just to name a few. The *Da Vinci Code*, for example, makes a heated argument about the Catholic Church's control over history. It makes its point through a wide range of rhetorical moves: the protagonist himself appeals to viewers' beliefs in honesty and truth. He also appeals to viewers' emotional comfort. Tom Hanks, after all, has a familiar, common face for mainstream white viewers. The antagonists (enemies) reinforce the opposite. The menacing albino monk functions as an opposing force, an opposing ethos. In this way, popular movies often assert arguments—about who or what is good, who or what is bad. And these arguments often correspond to mainstream biases and assumptions. For instance, Arabic men are often cast as villains in modern American movies. Fat or obese people are often cast as bumbling fools—comic relief characters who have little sense of right and wrong. The government is often drawn as quietly evil, plotting, dangerous. The single hero (usually thin and muscular) saves the day, the world, or the universe.

Mainstream movies often use these biases and assumptions. Because they are so widely and quietly accepted as normal, they support the movie's claims about good and bad, right and wrong. Some movies, however, challenge mainstream assumptions. The hero, for instance, may be a very pregnant folksy sheriff—as in the movie *Fargo*.

Consider how your favorite movie ends. Who wins? Who doesn't? What does the plot invite you to dread, believe in, and hope for? What kind of person gets celebrated? What kind of person gets demonized? What behavior has consequences? What behaviors have none? Answers to these questions reveal the subtle (sometimes not-so-subtle) arguments of that movie. If a character wins in the end, we might conclude that the movie makes an argument for that person's behaviors and worldview. When Luke Skywalker finally defeats Darth Vader, *Star Wars* concludes its argument: the allure of power and domination can, in fact, be denied. The prevailing question recurs throughout the six episodes: Can people resist the drive to rule the universe? Or is the lust for power really too overwhelming? As viewers, we are made to sympathize with Luke. We don't want him to become his father. Of course, the opposition lines up against us: Darth Vader, the Emperor, Count Dooku, Jabba the Hutt, and so on. All these characters embody the lust for absolute power. They are the opposition. On our side are Luke, Leia, Yoda, Obi Wan.

They make the film's primary argument. As it turns out, Darth Vader was wrong: the dark side isn't all that powerful.

But figuring out a movie's primary argument is not as simple as describing the characters' fates. Often, sympathetic characters (those with whom we are supposed to share hopes) die in the end. When Thelma and Louise drive off the cliff, viewers do not cheer. Thelma and Louise are, after all, not the villains of the movie. Their apparent suicide makes a point about the overwhelming power of men's rules. When Jack dies in *Brokeback Mountain,* we understand this as mainstream society's condemnation of gay men. And as Ben Wetherbee explains, the death of the Na'vi chief (in *Avatar)* makes a point about imperialism.

Analyzing movies can quickly become perilous work. It's easy to drift into movie review territory—a form that blends analysis and evaluation. The goal of a review is to share judgments about the movie's worth. But a movie analysis focuses strictly on how the movie works. And specifically, for our purposes, such an analysis focuses on how its elements work together to make a claim about the world and support it.

Activities

1. Find an image that doesn't already have text attached to it. Add a single statement that gives the image argumentative force. Share your image and statement with the class and explain the relationship between the image and the statement. How do they relate? Does the image suggest a claim? Or does the image function as some kind of support? Or maybe even a counterargument?

2. Choose an online or print ad. Closely examine the images and text. What is the main claim in the ad? (It's likely related to the product or service.) How does the ad support its claim? To what common values does the ad appeal? What common assumptions (about identity, happiness, technology, progress, superiority, exclusion, freedom) does the ad rely on? Is there a subtle line of reasoning? What premises (stated or unstated) would the audience have to accept before accepting the main claim?

3. In a small group, focus on a popular movie—one that all members have seen. Consider the following questions: In the end, who wins? Who doesn't? What does the plot invite you to dread, believe in, and hope for? What kind of person gets celebrated? What kind of person gets demonized? What behavior has consequences? What behaviors have none? How might all of these elements lead to some overall claim? What is that claim?

Progressive Profiteering: The Appeal and Argumentation of *Avatar*

BEN WETHERBEE

As Ben Wetherbee shows, mainstream films often make overt arguments. And if a claim about the world is asserted and supported, it can be analyzed. In this concise essay, Wetherbee avoids arguing for the film's worth and, instead, shows how it makes and supports a particular claim. Wetherbee is completing a master's in English, specializing in the rhetoric of film.

In December 2009, director/screenwriter James Cameron's sci-fi epic *Avatar* swept American cineplexes like a gale. Amid vast critical praise, the film grossed nearly 749 million dollars, a record in the United States, besting *Titanic, The Dark Knight* and *Star Wars* on the list of the nation's all-time top box-office draws ("All-Time"). Clearly, the film struck a certain chord with American audiences, but to what, exactly, do we owe the monolithic financial and critical success of *Avatar?* One might highlight Cameron's Hollywood savvy, the spectacular CGI jungle serving as the film's setting, the steady action, the familiar storyline, or any number of other facets. Most scholars of film or rhetoric, though, would quickly rebuke the oversimplification. *Avatar's* appeal comes from its fusion of standard Hollywood action movie features and the specific time of its release.

One avenue worth exploring is the movie's social-political consciousness. I recall a friend of mine who loved *Avatar.* "It's the perfect movie for a liberal," he said, a claim that is perhaps problematic but also understandable. It isn't difficult to imagine why *Avatar* might fare better among moderates and left-wingers than conservatives. Entwined in no subtle terms into the film's plot is a message of environmentalism and anti-imperialism that seems particularly deliberate and timely—coming off the heels of George W. Bush's administration. Contrary to most other sci-fi films dealing with extraterrestrial life (including Cameron's own *Aliens), Avatar* vilifies humankind, illustrating a scenario wherein the technologically superior humans seek to exploit and devastate the home of the Na'vi, a race of 12-foot blue-skinned humanoids with feline lineaments, for its natural resources. Moreover, the film evinces a distinct allusion to contemporary American politics; as critic J. Hoberman points out, "The rampaging Sky People are heavy-handedly associated with the Bush administration. They chortle over the failure of diplomacy, wage what is referred to as 'some sort of shock-and-awe campaign' against the Na'vis, and goad each other with Cheney one-liners. . . ." Cameron's screenplay, then, succeeds in landing immediate appeal by grounding its fantastic story in the actual. Viewers who might have dismissed *Avatar* as a fine-looking fairy tale are invited to consider the film as something weightier. Whether this consideration takes the form of applause or indignation might very well depend on the political ideology the viewer takes into the theater, but either way, the movie assumes an air of importance.

Social relevance alone, however, cannot guarantee box-office success. *Avatar* would have had meager success were the viewer unable to establish an emotional bond with the characters. In asking American audiences to identify with the Na'vi, Cameron pulls a textbook Hollywood maneuver that echoes the likes of *Dances with Wolves, Last of the Mohicans* and *The Last Samurai.* In each of these titles, the "good guys" are not, as they are in most Hollywood fare, the Anglo-Saxon Americans. These films employ white males—the characters of Kevin Costner, Daniel Day-Lewis and Tom Cruise, respectively—as conduits into the "foreign" cultures with which the audience is meant to identify. The main character is not Native American or Japanese, but white. In *Avatar,* Sam Worthington's character, the paraplegic marine Jake Sully, fills the same role; he is the white male whose consciousness is inserted into a Na'vi body—his "avatar." The movie thus establishes a small chain of emotional appeals: viewers identify with Jake Sully, the archetypal white, male American hero (and wounded veteran, to boot), and, then, after Sully has assimilated into the Na'vi, "learned their ways," and fallen in love with a Na'vi woman, *Avatar* invites viewers to emotionally invest themselves in and cheer for the blue alien "good guys." Cameron, one might infer, concluded before writing his screenplay that American audiences are unready to identify with a group of non-white (indeed, non-*human*, here) "others" without a "normal" protagonist to introduce the group.

While technically non-human, though, the Na'vi are hardly unfamiliar to American audiences. Their culture comprises a cliché-heavy amalgam of Native American philosophies and religious tenets—or simplistic pop-cultural perversions thereof—that abound in other Hollywood films, *Dances with Wolves* and *Last of the Mohicans* included, that attempt to treat Native Americans sympathetically. The artificial culture Hollywood concocts for these natives incorporates such teachings and assumptions as, one should only kill out of need, one finds happiness in simplicity, God—or The Great Spirit—is found in nature, and happiness, harmony and truth lie in oneness with nature. The common Hollywood representation is that of a simple, self-sustaining and naïve people who are, barring the azure skin and catlike features, the spitting image of the Na'vi. Such beliefs are those exactly of the Na'vi, and these alien natives speak and dress just like stereotypical Hollywood Native Americans. Their chief, to cap off the comparison, is played and voiced by Wes Studi, a full-blooded Cherokee.

Such Native American pseudo-culture and its assumed wisdom becomes the scaffold upon which Cameron hangs his environmentalist argument. It is interesting to note, here, the lack of a renowned star—a Tom Cruise or Daniel Day-Lewis—to fill *Avatar's* primary role. Worthington, like most of the film's actors, is a B-list Hollywood name; Sigourney Weaver is the only exception, playing an important but decidedly secondary role. *Avatar's* "star," then, its true selling point, is not the cast but the CGI world, Pandora—complete with sky-eclipsing foliage, trees 40 stories high, phosphorescent airborne jellyfish, dragons and floating rocks. Drowning in this ceaseless computer-rendered spectacle, the viewer is meant to develop an awe-induced emotional connection to Pandora, whose beauty towers above and beyond the run-of-the-mill screenplay and performances. The logic that the movie creates, furthermore, reaffirms that true power comes from oneness with nature. Only by praying to Eywa, the Na'vi's equivalent of "The Great Spirit," is Sully able to harness Pandora's natural power on behalf of the Na'vi and defeat the rampaging humans. Nature trumps technology, the argument goes.

Here, however, enters *Avatar's* logical contradiction. The movie's explosively violent final act implies what most action films do (e.g., the *Rambo* and *Lethal Weapon* franchises): real results, ultimately, come only from manning up and settling matters through armed conflict. This macho, right-wing truism, popular among American film audiences, appears most transparently in the climactic final battle, wherein Sully expresses unequivocal joy at the chance to fight and kill the merciless colonel who had been his superior officer. The movie glorifies this moment, even as it gainsays the Na'vi wisdom that killing should be only an affair of sad necessity. In its finale, *Avatar* does not bemoan the violence it presents. The violence is meant to be fun. As audiences uncritically tag along on this final explosive ride, they accept its logic; they accept the "git-'er-done" attitude that values decisive, violent action, and rebukes diplomacy and dialogue.

The movie exploits its conflicting arguments for several purposes: the cultural teachings that Hollywood fabricates for its Native Americans and the Na'vi, on one hand, serves the purpose of making *Avatar* a "serious" film with "something to say" about the real-world issues of environmental destruction and the American propensity to meddle with cultures it doesn't understand. The second set of arguments—the "any means necessary" attitude of valorized militarism—satisfies the simple expectation of fighting, explosions and a decisively happy ending that American audiences bring to a sci-fi epic. Logically, these arguments do *not* add up, but a quick glance toward *Avatar's* box-office numbers, and toward the enthusiasm that buzzed around its theatrical and DVD releases, indicates that they do financially.

Works Cited

"All-Time Box Office: USA." *The Internet Movie Database.* 25 May 2010. Web. 27 May 2010.

Avatar. Dir. James Cameron. Perf. Sam Worthington, Sigourney Weaver. Twentieth Century Fox, 2009. Film.

Hoberman, J. "*Avatar's* Sticker Shock (and Awe)." *The Village Voice.* 15 Dec. 2009. Web. 1 June 2010.

"In its finale, *Avatar* does not bemoan the violence it presents. The violence is meant to be fun."

Assignment: Inventing a Rhetorical Analysis

As the essays in this chapter show, nearly any text, image, or artifact from popular culture can be analyzed. If it works to address or attract an audience, if it appeals to people's sensibilities, if it makes an argument (for itself or about anything in the world), then it has rhetorical dimensions. As writers and thinkers, we are free to explore how those dimensions work. For your own analysis, take on one of the following: a written essay (from this book or elsewhere, such as a magazine or blog), an image, an advertisement, or even a film. Examine the text closely—with a particular posture toward analysis. Consider the main argumentative moves and apply the following questions:

1. **Audience/Rhetorical Situation:** Who is the audience? Can you tell? If it's not clear by the language and nature of the argument, consider the publication. Where was it published? What organization wrote, supports, or sponsors the publication?

2. **Claim:** What is the main claim (or thesis)? What type of claim is it? In other words, what is the argument working toward? Does it seek to make the audience evaluate the worth of something (claim of value); believe in a past, present, or future condition (fact); or want to do something (claim of policy)?

3. **Line of Reasoning:** Every argument has some line of reasoning—premises that walk the audience toward the main claim. What individual premises are asserted? How do they lead to the main claim? What premises are unstated? What points does the reader fill in?

4. **Other Appeals:** How does the argument tap into shared values (courage, peace, honor, trust, personal responsibility, knowledge)? How does the argument prompt a certain feeling (fear, anger, hope, regret)? How does the argument call on basic human needs (safety, belonging, actualization)? How does the argument refer directly to the writer's own experience or wisdom?

5. **Examples and Evidence:** How does the argument rely on allusions, scenarios, illustrations, anecdotes, personal testimony, facts, or statistics? How do the specific forms of example or evidence function in the overall argument? How do they support the main claim or serve within an appeal?

6. **Opposition:** In what ways does the argument engage opposition? Or how does opposition shape the premises of the argument? Does the argument engage one major opposing position or does it take on several? Does the argument dismantle the assumptions or values operating in an opposing position? Or does it just refute some factual claim? Does the argument grant value to another position? Does it qualify its own claims?

7. **Hidden Layers:** What assumptions do you detect? What does the argument assume, but not necessarily state, about the topic—or about people, institutions, life, social norms, and so on? Do those assumptions point to any underlying values? Does the argument, for instance, rest on the notion that progress, or freedom, or creativity, or responsibility, or equality, is inherently good? (For more shared ideals, see page 81.)

How Should I Arrange the Analysis?

There are two common structures for arranging a rhetorical analysis: rhetorical and sequential. In *rhetorical arrangement,* the writer focuses on individual elements separately. For instance, you might begin by describing the type of claim, and then move to supporting appeals, and then to supporting examples, and then to forms of evidence, and then to counterargument, and so on. The idea here is to thoroughly describe each major rhetorical move before moving to the next:

- Brief, one paragraph summary of the argument or argumentative situation
- Analysis of the line of reasoning
- Analysis of other appeals
- Analysis of evidence and example
- Analysis of counterargument, concession, qualifiers
- Analysis of unstated or hidden layers
- Articulation of new insights gained from analysis

In *sequential arrangement,* the writer simply walks through the original text passage by passage, or element by element. The writer uses the structure of that text to organize the analysis.

- Analysis of the introductory rhetorical moves
- Separate analytical paragraph for each segment (paragraph, feature, or image)
- Articulation of new insights gained from analysis

As you can see in the sample analyses, the writers in this chapter illustrate the two general strategies detailed here. Andrew Buchner's analysis of Chief Seattle proceeds sequentially. He walks through the main sections of the speech and explains the major rhetorical moves. Notice that he does not describe each individual sentence—or even each individual paragraph. Instead, as he proceeds through the speech, he finds the major moves (which may involve two or more paragraphs).

Wetherbee's analysis uses rhetorical arrangement. Rather than walking through the movie chronologically, he deals with rhetorical issues separately. In each paragraph, Wetherbee focuses attention on distinct dimensions—regardless of when/where they show up in the movie:

¶1 Description of the rhetorical situation

¶2 Explanation of the hidden political argument

¶3 Analysis of appeals

¶4 Analysis of allusions

¶5 Analysis of the movie's logic

¶6–7 Analysis of the logical tension and the new insight

Ward's analysis also uses rhetorical arrangement:

¶1 Summary of the ad

¶2 Analysis of the hidden argument

¶3 Analysis of the opposition (on the broader cultural stage)

¶4 Analysis of value and logical appeals

¶5 Analysis of emotional appeals

¶6 Analysis of the rhetorical situation and the new insight

Of course, these strategies can be combined, parsed out, and re-mixed. But generally, the writer benefits from having a general plan for arranging ideas.

The willingness to
genuinely explore
nuances creates an
engaging argument.

Part Two

INVENTING ARGUMENT

Arguing Definitions

What Is It?

When you think of the term *argument,* you might imagine people debating an issue that has already been defined: *Should abortion be legal? Should the death penalty be eliminated? Should the drinking age be lowered? Should states legalize gay marriage?* Such arguments usually play out according to preestablished positions, with people lining up on one side or the other. But beneath such typical arguments lurks a layer of questions (and possible arguments) such as *What is guilt? What is innocence? What is responsibility? What is marriage? What is love?* Such questions get to our basic assumptions. They prompt us to examine and defend definitions that operate undetected beneath everyday life. Consider, for instance, the various ways we might define *love:* a chemical attraction, a social declaration, an interpersonal commitment, an emotional feeling, a gift from God, a state of selflessness, a highly evolved psychological attribute. Each definition has profound significance for how one might live and think—and how one might argue about issues like marriage.

In short, definitions have power. This is not to suggest that definitions make everyone think in a particular way, but they do suggest a mental framework, and once that framework is in place, ignoring it becomes difficult. Consider this: If a forested area is called *undeveloped,* people may imagine it as empty space to build on; if it is called *virgin timber,* people may think of it as wood; if it is called *wildlife habitat,* people are apt to imagine it as a place already occupied. And once people imagine the forest in a particular way, they respond to it accordingly. An *undeveloped* piece of land is apt to be built on, whereas a *wildlife habitat* is more likely to be preserved. A similar debate reached fevered pitch when Congress debated the nature of the Alaskan Natural Wildlife Arctic Refuge (ANWAR). While some insisted that the acres are merely wasteland, others argued that they are vital ecological terrain.

In short, what we call something matters. And definitions enable us to make other arguments. For instance, in the ANWAR debates, those who characterized the terrain as a wasteland hoped to conjure a picture of useless space. Those who characterized it as a vital ecology hoped to create the idea of its worth within a larger environmental cycle. Or consider how one might define *patriotism*. If we argue that patriotism involves supporting all the policies of one's country, right or wrong, then we can say that the Nazis were good patriots and Martin Luther King Jr. was not. If we argue that patriotism involves guiding and correcting the policies of one's country, then we would say the opposite about Nazis and King.

Unclear or slippery definitions can drive arguments. Debates might arise because of competing definitions of an unclear term or phrase. For example, a professor might explain that a student's project illustrates "good writing." But when the student receives the final grade, he is surprised to see a *B* rather than an *A*. The student and professor then debate the grade, but beneath their debate is a slippery concept: *good writing*. If the phrase had not been defined formally in the course, the professor and student may each carry their own definitions, which are associated with different grades. Not until they reach a shared understanding of *good writing* will the professor and student come to an understanding about the grade.

Often, a particular situation will prompt an argument over definitions. Someone may ask if a particular event or thing fits into a broader category. This is the case in court trials, when the jury must decide if a particular event fits into a definition that has already been outlined. Was it murder or manslaughter? Was the driver reckless or merely careless? Was the bar patron disorderly or annoying? Is this copyright infringement or artistic license? In such cases, the definition already exists and the lawyers debate the specifics, trying to contrast or compare them with the definition. But this type of argument doesn't belong solely to court proceedings. Consider some important political debates from recent history: Is oral sex "real" sex? Is hooding a prisoner and shocking him with electrodes a form of torture? Is bailing out the nation's big banks a form of socialism or federalism? Is a lone terrorist truly a terrorist?

Arguments over definitions may arise because a subject has so many dimensions. Words like *science, God, love, marriage, economy, war,* and *peace* evoke a huge number of possible definitions. And people across nations, cultures, towns, or even within a single classroom are likely to hold different definitions. *Science* to one group of people might be *mythology* to another. *War* to one group might be *terrorism* to another. In all these cases, people debate a word that seems obvious or self-evident to someone else.

It may be easy to disregard all this potential diversity of thought, to simply announce, "One person's trash is another person's treasure," but people who share a world, a democracy, an environment, a community, a workplace, or a classroom must have some shared definitions. They must have a common understanding of certain concepts; otherwise, decisions about public affairs are nearly impossible. Arguing definitions is more than wordplay. Those who define terms in any situation define the intellectual landscape. Those who know how to argue definitions are those who define the starting points of other debates—and even shape policy in the long run. As you read the essays and images for this chapter, notice how the authors forward a narrow definition of their topics. Either directly or subtly, they make a case for a particular way of seeing.

Much of the argument in academic disciplines focuses on definitions:

- Each discipline defines *human* in a particular way: as a tool-using animal, as a symbol user, as a spiritually motivated being, as a conscious dreamer, and so on.
- Each discipline debates the definition of its own work: Geographers always redefine the nature of their field; psychologists constantly reshape the boundaries of their study; historians take on increasingly more diverse questions about human affairs.
- Higher education itself wrestles with its identity: an institution that creates new knowledge, a tradition that dispenses what is already known, a community of scholars that questions what is already known, or even a service that enables people to enter the workforce.

Activity

In small groups, write a definition for *love*. Share your definitions with the class, and then answer the following questions:

1. Which definitions are most similar? What particular concepts do they share?

2. Which definitions are most dissimilar? Try to specify exactly where and how they differ.

3. What does each definition assume about human emotions, about people's wants or needs? How do the groups' assumptions differ or relate?

What's the Economy for, Anyway?

JOHN DE GRAAF

A definitional argument might involve a basic question of purpose: *What is X for?* In this essay, de Graaf argues that we should ask this basic question about the economy—that the question itself would reveal something critical about our collective situation. John de Graaf is the national coordinator of the Take Back Your Time campaign, coauthor of *Affluenza: The All-Consuming Epidemic* (2002), and editor of *Take Back Your Time: Fighting Overwork and Time Poverty in America* (2003). He is also a filmmaker and recently coproduced *The Motherhood Manifesto* (2006).

> "If they can get you asking the wrong question, they don't have to worry about the answers."
>
> —Thomas Pynchon, *Gravity's Rainbow*

Suggest any alternative to the status quo these days—greater environmental protection, for example, or shorter working hours—and the first question reporters are likely to ask is, "But what will that do to the economy?" Immediately, advocates must try to prove that their suggestions will not adversely affect economic growth or the Dow Jones industrial average.

It's long past time for a new framing offensive, one that turns the obligatory question on its head and shifts the burden of proof to those who resist change. Imagine bumper stickers, posters, Internet messages, a thousand inquiries visible everywhere, asking a different question:

"What's the Economy for, Anyway?"

It's time to demand that champions of the status quo defend their implicit answer to that question. Do they actually believe that the purpose of the economy is to achieve the grossest domestic product and allow the richest among us to multiply their treasures without limits?

For in practice, that really is their answer.

But what if we answer the question differently, perhaps as Gifford Pinchot, the first Chief of the U.S. Forest Service, did a century ago? His answer was, "The greatest good for the greatest number over the long run."

In that light, economic success cannot be measured by Gross Domestic Product (GDP) or stock prices alone. It must take into account the other values that constitute the greatest good—health, happiness, knowledge, kindness—for the greatest number—equality, access to opportunity—over the long run—in a healthy democracy and sustainable environment.

Historical Background

It's time to set America back on course.

After increasing social equality and greatly improving health and other quality-of-life measures (including major increases in leisure time) from World War II until the mid-1970s, the United States abruptly changed its economic trajectory.

"It will be a hard pill for many Americans to swallow," *Business Week* predicted in October, 1974, "—the idea of doing with less so that big business can have more. Nothing that this nation or any other nation has done in modern history compares in difficulty with the selling job that must now be done to make people accept the new reality."

Emboldened by Richard Nixon's landslide 1972 victory, extreme conservatives moved to reduce the responsibilities (and increase the wealth) of wealthy Americans, while cutting back on public services for the poor and average working Americans.

These policies accelerated during the 1980s and early 1990s and are now enshrined in the "you're on your ownership" attitude of the present federal policies.

Meanwhile, Western European nations took a different course, maintaining their social contracts and at least modestly improving their safety nets for the poor. Their provision of more public goods—healthcare, education, transportation, common space, etc.—supported by higher and more progressive taxation measures than in the United States—reduced the need (or desire) of individuals to maximize their own incomes.

So What Happened?

First, in terms of productivity per worker hour, Western Europeans nearly closed the gap with the United States. They were producing, on average, 65 percent as much as Americans produced per hour in 1970. By 2000, their productivity was 95 percent that of Americans.

But on the other hand, their consumption of goods and services, measured in GDP per capita, remained where it was in 1970—roughly 70 percent that of Americans.

There is a simple explanation for this seeming anomaly: European working hours, which in 1970 were slightly longer than those of Americans, dropped to about 80 percent of U.S. hours.

We could say that Europeans traded major portions of their productivity increases for free time instead of money, while Americans—consciously or otherwise—put all their gains into increasing their per capita GDP.

Pose the question, "What did that do to the economy?" and the answer appears clear—Americans, with a much bigger GDP, are the obvious winners.

But ask instead, "What is the economy for, anyway?" and a different answer emerges.

For most of the final quarter of the 20th century, Europeans improved their quality of life relative to Americans in almost every measure.

Health

While American health has improved in absolute terms since the 1970s, the United States once ranked near the top in terms of overall health. It now rates below that of every other industrial country, despite spending by far the highest percentage of GDP on health care.

Equality

If one looks at equality, a similar pattern emerges. America, which was about at the median among industrial countries in terms of economic equality in 1974, now has the widest gap between rich and poor.

Savings

Savings are a key indicator of security for many people. While American personal savings rates (10 percent) were slightly higher than those of Europeans in 1970, they have dropped to negative numbers (-1.6 percent last year), while EU citizens now save an average of 12 percent of their incomes.

Sustainability

European progress has also come at a lower cost to the environment. While EU nations were choosing more leisure time rather than working harder to close the consumer gap with Americans, they also took greater steps toward sustainability.

The result is that EU countries require only half the energy consumption per capita as that of Americans, while producing 70 percent as many goods and services. The average American has an ecological footprint (the productive land and water necessary to produce his or her lifestyle) of 24 acres; for Europeans, the average is 12 acres.

One can find similar results in many other areas of quality of life, including: levels of trust, crime, incarceration, family breakdown, literacy, happiness indicators, preschool education, and even access to information technologies.

Tellingly, the Genuine Progress Indicator—an alternative to the GDP developed by Redefining Progress that measures 24 quality-of-life indices—shows a fairly consistent decline in well-being in the United States since a peak in 1973. Similar indices for Europe show consistent improvement in most areas of life, even if increases are sometimes slow or spotty.

Meeting Our Needs

One model for judging the success of the economy is to see how well it allows citizens to meet their needs as outlined by psychologist Abraham Maslow. In his often-cited hierarchy of needs theory, Maslow suggested that humans must first adequately satisfy such basic needs as food, shelter, health and safety, and "belongingness" before moving on to what he called "higher" or "meta" needs.

In the early 1970s, Maslow suggested that as a society the United States had met nearly all its citizens' physiological and safety needs and was moving to satisfy higher needs as well. Ironically, by such a standard, we have lost ground rather than gaining it—we have more citizens living in poverty and a much greater overall sense of insecurity today than we did then, despite more than a 60 percent increase in real per capita GDP.

Most Americans know intrinsically that increases in GDP do not mean economic success if health outcomes and social connections continue to decline relative to other countries.

This is why we must raise the question "What is the economy for, anyway?" to a crescendo that cannot be ignored by the media or our political leaders. Only when we begin to ask the right question can we hope to find answers that can improve our quality of life.

We must then ask, "What roles do the market, the state, nongovernmental organizations, and our common wealth respectively have to play in achieving the greatest good for the greatest number over the long run?"

Inevitably, even sympathetic reporters and others will ask us, "Can we change the economy in the ways the Europeans have and still compete in the global economy?"

The answer, quite simply, is yes.

According to the World Economic Forum, the United States ranks second in world economic competitiveness. So it's possible to do things our way—reducing government, slashing taxes, cutting the safety net, and widening the divide between rich and poor—and be competitive.

But is it necessary? Consider that the other four most competitive nations are Finland (ranked first), Sweden, Denmark, and Norway. In fact, European nations make up most of the top 10. All these nations are far more globalized and far more subject to international competitive pressures than we are and have been for many years.

And all of them are far more egalitarian than the United States. Finland has, in fact, the smallest gap between rich and poor of any nation. The Finnish social safety net is a generous one and workers enjoy a great deal of leisure time—an average of 30 days of paid vacation. The story is similar in other European countries. Clearly, it is possible to have a more just and people-friendly economy and compete globally.

Imagine seeing our simple question: "What's the economy for, anyway?" everywhere—in print, posters, on bumper stickers, on websites—or hearing it asked over and over on TV, radio, and in forums and debates. It might be seen as a Trojan horse, seemingly innocent, but remarkably subversive.

The point of all this is not simply to change this or that specific policy, but to create a different thought context by which we might begin to change the entire trend toward privatization and inequality. The point is to show that current "common sense" about economics is "non-sense" if our goal is a better quality of life that is sustainable over the long run.

When we forget to ask, "What is the economy for, anyway?" we leave ourselves open to the GDP worship of so many of our leaders. When we ask the question over and over and demand answers, we open possibilities for a new and better world.

Analyzing Argument

1. What claim or position is de Graaf countering? What passages best illustrate his counterargument?

2. According to de Graaf, what is wrong with the current frame we have for looking at the economy, and how should the issue be reframed?

3. How does de Graaf support his claim that "Europeans improved their quality of life relative to Americans"? Why is or isn't his support persuasive?

4. What competing assumptions and values are at the root of de Graaf's argument?

5. Why do so many Americans accept the "common sense" about economics without question?

Warfare: An Invention— Not a Biological Necessity

MARGARET MEAD

Margaret Mead (1901–78) was a highly acclaimed, and sometimes controversial, anthropologist and writer. In her long career, she served as president of various organizations, including the American Anthropological Association, and she counseled several U.S. presidents on ecological and domestic affairs. Her studies of world cultures and shrewd insights on contemporary issues prompted *Time* magazine to call her "Mother of the World" in 1969. In the following argument, published in 1940, before the United States entered World War II, she illustrates her well-known strategy: discovering and debunking a widely held assumption.

Is war a biological necessity, a sociological inevitability, or just a bad invention? Those who argue for the first view endow man with such pugnacious instincts that some outlet in aggressive behavior is necessary if man is to reach full human stature. It was this point of view which lay back of William James's famous essay, "The Moral Equivalent of War," in which he tried to retain the warlike virtues and channel them in new directions. A similar point of view has lain behind the Soviet Union's attempt to make competition between groups rather than between individuals. A basic, competitive, aggressive, warring human nature is assumed, and those who wish to outlaw war or outlaw competitiveness merely try to find new and less socially destructive ways in which these biologically given aspects of man's nature can find expression. Then there are those who take the second view: warfare is the inevitable concomitant of the development of the state, the struggle for land and natural resources, of class societies springing not from the nature of man, but, from the nature of history. War is nevertheless inevitable unless we change our social system and outlaw classes, the struggle for power, and possessions; and

in the event of our success warfare would disappear, as a symptom vanishes when the disease is cured.

One may hold a sort of compromise position between these two extremes; one may claim that all aggression springs from the frustration of man's biologically determined drives and that, since all forms of culture are frustrating, it is certain each new generation will be aggressive and the aggression will find its natural and inevitable expression in race war, class war, nationalistic war, and so on. All three of these positions are very popular today among those who think seriously about the problems of war and its possible prevention, but I wish to urge another point of view, less defeatist, perhaps, than the first and third and more accurate than the second: that is, that warfare, by which I mean recognized conflict between two groups as groups, in which each group puts an army (even if the army is only fifteen pygmies) into the field to fight and kill, if possible, some of the members of the army of the other group—that warfare of this sort is an invention like any other of the inventions in terms of which we order our lives, such as writing, marriage, cooking our food instead of eating it raw, trial by jury, or burial of the dead, and so on. Some of this list anyone will grant are inventions: trial by jury is confined to very limited portions of the globe; we know that there are tribes that do not bury their dead but instead expose or cremate them; and we know that only part of the human race has had the knowledge of writing as its cultural inheritance. But, whenever a way of doing things is found universally, such as the use of fire or the practice of some form of marriage, we tend to think at once that it is not an invention at all but an attribute of humanity itself. And yet even such universals as marriage and the use of fire are inventions like the rest, very basic ones, inventions which were, perhaps, necessary if human history was to take the turn that it has taken, but nevertheless inventions. At some point in his social development man was undoubtedly without the institution of marriage or the knowledge of the use of fire.

The case for warfare is much clearer because there are peoples even today who have no warfare. Of these the Eskimos are perhaps the most conspicuous examples, but the Lepchas of Sikkim described by Geoffrey Gorer in *Himalayan Village* are as good. Neither of these peoples understands war, not even defensive warfare. The idea of warfare is lacking, and this idea is as essential to really carrying on war as an alphabet or a syllabary is to writing. But, whereas the Lepchas are a gentle, unquarrelsome people, and the advocates of other points of view might argue that they are not full human beings or that they had never been frustrated and so had no aggression to expand in warfare, the Eskimo case gives no such possibility of interpretation. The Eskimos are not a mild and meek people; many of them are turbulent and troublesome. Fights, theft of wives, murder, cannibalism occur among them—all outbursts of passionate men goaded by desire or intolerable circumstance. Here are men faced with hunger, men faced with loss of their wives, men faced with the threat of extermination by other men, and here are orphan children, growing up miserably with no one to care for them, mocked and neglected by those about them. The personality necessary for war, the circumstances necessary to goad men to desperation are present, but there is no war. When a traveling Eskimo entered a settlement, he might have to fight the strongest man in the settlement to establish his position among them, but this was a test of strength and bravery, not war. The idea of warfare, of one group organizing against another group to maim and wound and kill them was absent. And, without that idea, passions might rage but there was no war.

But, it may be argued, is not this because the Eskimos have such a low and undeveloped form of social organization? They own no land, they move from place to place, camping, it is true, season after season on the same site, but this is not something to fight for as the modern nations of the world fight for land and raw materials. They have no permanent possessions that can be looted, no towns that can be burned. They have no social classes to produce stress and strains within the society which might force it to go to war outside. Does not the absence of war among the Eskimos, while disproving the biological necessity of war, just go to confirm the point that it is the state of development of the society which accounts for war and nothing else?

We find the answer among the pygmy peoples of the Andaman Islands in the Bay of Bengal. The Andamans also represent an exceedingly low level of society; they are a hunting and food-gathering people; they live in tiny hordes without any class stratification; their houses are simpler than the snow houses of the Eskimo. But they knew about warfare. The army might contain only fifteen determined pygmies marching in a straight line, but it was the real thing none the less. Tiny army met tiny army in open battle, blows were exchanged, casualties suffered, and the state of warfare could only be concluded by a peacemaking ceremony.

Similarly, among the Australian aborigines, who built no permanent dwellings but wandered from water hole to water hole over their almost desert country, warfare—and rules of "international law"—were highly developed. The student of social evolution will seek in vain for his obvious causes of war, struggle for lands, struggle for power of one group over another, expansion of population, need to divert the minds of a populace restive under tyranny, or even the ambition of a successful leader to enhance his own prestige. All are absent, but warfare as a practice remained, and men engaged in it and killed one another in the course of a war because killing is what is done in wars.

From instances like these it becomes apparent that an inquiry into the causes of war misses the fundamental point as completely as does an

AP Photo/Steve Ruark

insistence upon the biological necessity of war. If a people have an idea of going to war and the idea that war is the way in which certain situations, defined within their society, are to be handled, they will sometimes go to war. If they are a mild and unaggressive people, like the Pueblo Indians, they may limit themselves to defensive warfare, but they will be forced to think in terms of war because there are peoples near them who have warfare as a pattern, and offensive, raiding, pillaging warfare at that. When the pattern of warfare is known, people like the Pueblo Indians will defend themselves, taking advantage of their natural defences, the mesa village site, and people like the Lepchas, having no natural defences and no idea of warfare, will merely submit to the invader. But the essential point remains the same. There is a way of behaving which is known to a given people and labeled as an appropriate form of behavior; a bold and warlike people like the Sioux or the Maori may label warfare as desirable as well as possible, a mild people like the Pueblo Indians may label warfare as undesirable, but to the minds of both peoples the possibility of warfare is present. Their thoughts, their hopes, their plans are oriented about this idea—that warfare may be selected as the way to meet some situation.

So simple peoples and civilized peoples, mild peoples and violent, assertive peoples, will all go to war if they have the invention, just as those peoples who have the custom of dueling will have duels and peoples who have the pattern of vendetta will indulge in vendetta. And, conversely, peoples who do not know of dueling will not fight duels, even though their wives are seduced and their daughters ravished; they may on occasion commit murder but they will not fight duels. Cultures which lack the idea of the vendetta will not meet every quarrel in this way. A people can use only the forms it has. So the Balinese have their special way of dealing with a quarrel between two individuals: if the two feel that the causes of quarrel are heavy, they may go and register their quarrel in the temple before the gods, and, making offerings, they may swear never to have anything to do with each other again. . . . But in other societies, although individuals might feel as full of animosity and as unwilling to have any further contact as do the Balinese, they cannot register their quarrel with the gods and go on quietly about their business because registering quarrels with the gods is not an invention of which they know.

Yet, if it be granted that warfare is, after all, an invention, it may nevertheless be an invention that lends itself to certain types of personality, to the exigent needs of autocrats, to the expansionist desires of crowded peoples, to the desire for plunder and rape and loot which is engendered by a dull and frustrating life. What, then, can we say of this congruence between warfare and its uses? If it is a form which fits so well, is not this congruence the essential point? But even here the primitive material causes us to wonder, because there are tribes who go to war merely for glory, having no quarrel with the enemy, suffering from no tyrant within their boundaries, anxious neither for land nor loot nor women, but merely anxious to win prestige which within that tribe has been declared obtainable only by war and without which no young man can hope to win his sweetheart's smile of approval. But if, as was the case with the Bush Negroes of Dutch Guiana, it is artistic ability which is necessary to win a girl's approval, the same young man would have to be carving rather than going out on a war party.

In many parts of the world, war is a game in which the individual can win counters—counters which bring him prestige in the eyes of his own sex or of the opposite sex; he plays for these counters as he might, in our society, strive for a tennis championship. Warfare is a frame for such prestige-seeking merely because it calls for the display of certain skills and certain virtues; all of these skills—riding straight, shooting straight, dodging the missiles of the enemy and sending one's own straight to the mark—can be equally well exercised in some other framework and, equally, the virtues endurance, bravery, loyalty, steadfastness can be displayed in other contexts. The tie-up between proving oneself a man and proving this by a success in organized killing is due to a definition which many societies have made of manliness. And often, even in those societies which counted success in warfare a proof of human worth, strange turns were given to the idea, as when the plains Indians gave their highest awards to the man who touched a live enemy rather than to the man who brought in a scalp—from a dead enemy—because the latter was less risky. Warfare is just an invention known to the majority of human societies by which they permit their young men either to accumulate prestige or avenge their honor or acquire loot or wives or slaves or sago lands or cattle or appease the blood lust of their gods or the restless souls of the recently dead. It is just an invention, older and more widespread than the jury system, but none the less an invention.

But, once we have said this, have we said anything at all? Despite a few stances, dear to the instances of controversialist, of the loss of the useful arts, once an invention is made which proves congruent with human needs or social forms, it tends to persist. Grant that war is an invention, that it is not a biological necessity nor the outcome of certain special types of social forms, still once the invention is made, what are we to do about it? The Indian who had been subsisting on the buffalo for generations because with his primitive weapons he could slaughter only a limited number of buffalo did not return to his primitive weapons when he saw that the white man's more efficient weapons were exterminating the buffalo. A desire for the white man's cloth may mortgage the South Sea Islander to the white man's plantation, but he does not return to making bark cloth, which would have left him free. Once an invention is known and accepted, men do not easily relinquish it. The skilled workers may smash the first steam looms which they feel are to be their undoing, but they accept them in the end, and no movement which has insisted upon the mere abandonment of usable inventions has ever had much success. Warfare is here, as part of our thought; the deeds of warriors are immortalized in the words of our poets, the toys of our children are modeled upon the weapons of the soldier, the frame of reference within which our statesmen and our diplomats work always contains war. If we know that it is not inevitable, that it is due to historical accident that warfare is one of the ways in which we think of behaving, are we given any hope by that? What hope is there of persuading nations to abandon war, nations so thoroughly imbued with the idea that resort to war is, if not actually desirable and noble, at least inevitable whenever certain defined circumstances arise?

In answer to this question I think we might turn to the history of other social inventions, and inventions which must once have seemed as finally entrenched as warfare. Take the methods of trial which preceded the jury system: ordeal and trial by combat. Unfair, capricious, alien as they are to our feeling today, they were once the only methods open to individuals accused of some offense. The invention of trial by jury gradually replaced these methods until only witches, and finally not even witches, had to resort to the ordeal. And for a long time the jury system seemed the best and finest method of settling legal disputes, but today new inventions, trial before judges only or before commissions, are replacing the jury system. In each case the old method was replaced by a new social invention. The ordeal did not go out because people thought it unjust or wrong; it went out because a method more congruent with the institutions and feelings of the period was invented. And, if we despair over the way in which war seems such an ingrained habit of most of the human race, we can take comfort from the fact that a poor invention will usually give place to a better invention.

For this, two conditions, at least, are necessary. The people must recognize the defects of the old invention, and someone must make a new one. Propaganda against warfare, documentation of its terrible cost in human suffering and social waste, these prepare the ground by teaching people to feel that warfare is a defective social institution. There is further needed a belief that social invention is possible and the invention of new methods which will render warfare as out of date as the tractor is making the plough, or the motor car the horse and buggy. A form of behavior becomes out of date only when something else takes its place, and, in order to invent forms of behavior which will make war obsolete, it is a first requirement to believe that an invention is possible.

Analyzing Argument

1. In Mead's view, what is wrong with the three most popular conceptions of warfare?

2. As Chapter 3 explains, analogical reasoning depends on comparisons (or analogies). The arguer moves from one particular to another particular, instead of from general to specific (deductive) or specific to general (inductive). Comparisons, metaphors, allegories, parables, and examples all have an analogous quality: they argue that if two things are alike in certain respects, they are also alike in other respects. Analogies shed light on something by comparing or contrasting it with something familiar. Examine the logic in paragraph two and write out the line of reasoning. (Be especially mindful of the analogous reasoning.)

3. How does Mead deal with the opposing claim outlined in paragraph four? In what passages does she counterargue this claim?

4. Examine the logic in paragraph ten and write out the line of reasoning. How important is this paragraph to the overall argument?

5. Although the argument primarily focuses on redefining warfare, Mead also urges readers to see a purpose for a new definition. In your words, what is the reason she offers? Why should we begin to imagine warfare as invention?

The Fashion Punk Paradox

ANDREW HYDE

For years, Andrew Hyde was interested in punk, and a college English assignment was an opportunity to explore the idea. Hyde saw a problem with the way punk was being defined in mainstream fashion, and so developed the following argument. Although mainstream fashion was not deliberately or explicitly defining punk, Hyde saw the quiet suggestions (the unstated definitions) being asserted in advertising. His argument is a response to those unstated definitions.

When most folks consider the word "punk," two ideas come to mind: a troublesome youngster with funny hair, or the dry and crumbly innards of an old log. Probably more accurate is an anonymous submission to Urbandictionary.com. The writer explains punk with an anecdote: "A guy walks up to me and asks, 'What's Punk?' So I kick over a garbage can and say, 'That's punk!' So he kicks over the garbage can and says, 'That's Punk?' and I say, 'No, that's trendy!'" Nonconformity has always been key in the punk subculture, and yet conformity is taking over in the form of fashion. Now, the real punks and fashion punks battle over the term itself.

The connotation of punk as a musical genre and fashion style has roughly a thirty-year history. There is much debate over when and where it began. Some would say punk began with the Rolling Stones, the Beatles, or Iggy Pop and the Stooges. A few would even proclaim that the attitude was born with stars such as Johnny Cash or Bob Dylan. Although these artists earned large sums of money, they still had a hatred for the popular music industry. The songs were written for personal satisfaction, and money was a bonus. Regardless of attitude, punk music made a definitive entrance to popular culture in 1976. This occurred with the nearly simultaneous introduction of the Ramones in New York and the Sex Pistols in Great Britain. Punk music was defined by simple and fast-paced

Andrew Holbrooke/Corbis

chord progressions, and the lyrics were rebellious and often had a political theme.

Fashion styles also began to differ drastically in the punk scene from disco and the leftover hippies. Clothing became dark, ragged, and often brandished hand-sewn patches and safety pins. Facial piercing and wild hairstyles came about. Dick Hebdige's *Style in Revolt: Revolting Style* describes punk fashion as correlating with the artistic Dada movement of the 1910s and '20s, and specifically Marcel Duchamp's "ready-mades." Hebdige explains how punks used similar items for the same purpose: "The most unremarkable and inappropriate items— a pin, a plastic clothes peg, a television component, a razor blade, a tampon—could be brought within the province of punk (un)fashion." Not only did punks draw fashion ideas from Dada, but political and social views as well. The Dada movement was a response to the Great War. Artists were disgusted with the events of the time, and made a statement by proclaiming insignificance. Dadaists describe themselves as nihilists, as believers in nothing:

> Dada knows everything. Dada spits on everything. Dada says "knowthing." Dada has no fixed ideas. Dada does not catch flies. Dada is bitterness laughing at everything that has been accomplished, sanctified. . . . Like everything in life, Dada is useless, everything happens in a completely idiotic way. . . . We are incapable of treating seriously any subject whatsoever, let alone this subject: ourselves. (Kleiner 754–55)

Although the punks have not directly attributed much to Dada, the connection is almost lucid. Punk is not simply a subculture of rebellious kids with nothing better to do than dress up in costumes and listen to loud music. Anarchy became more effective than nihilism, but the intent remained the same as Dada: to ridicule government policy and attack the flaws of society.

Through the 1980s, punk became even more political. With bands like T.S.O.L., Social Distortion, and Operation Ivy, the movement focused on social issues that were not being acknowledged by the Reagan administration. Tax codes were changed in a way to benefit the rich, while social policy moved away from helping the poor. And punk bands responded with a litany of album titles, song titles, and lyrics, for example, the Dead Kennedys released "Kill the Poor" in 1980 on the album *Fresh Fruit for Rotting Vegetables*. Punk became a mindset rather than a statement. The increasingly thoughtful political awareness continued into the 1990s, until a series of events significantly changed punk. Bands like Green Day, the Offspring, and Rancid were getting attention. Songs were heard on the radio, and videos seen on MTV. Punk went pop. My middle school years put me right in the

middle of this musical transformation. Specifically, in seventh grade, Katie (one of the popular girls in my class) asked what I was listening to on my Walkman. I took out the dirty, overplayed cassette tape to show her Green Day's 1994 release of *Dookie*. Of course I was teased for my musical taste that differed from the Gin Blossoms, or whatever was popular at the time. Less than a few weeks later, I saw Katie listening to the compact disc version of *Dookie*, singing along to "When I Come Around." The song had become a hit on Rick Dees's weekly top 40.

Through the late '90s and the first few years of the new millennium, many have said that punk is officially dead. While the movement may not be entirely dead, thirty years since the beginning, punk ideologies have changed. Clothing styles of modern-day punk still embrace the roots of the movement, but have become a target for fashion companies to market as a popular trend. The music is still fast and simple. Unfortunately, it has almost completely lost the political aspect it once had. Both bands and fans reject being labeled as "punks" yet hold

With bands like T.S.O.L., Social Distortion, and Operation Ivy, the movement focused on social issues that were not being acknowledged by the Reagan administration.

onto many of the characteristics that have been around since the 1970s. This fashion-based genre known as "emo" is becoming increasingly popular. Teens relate with bands through lyrics describing failed relationships, depression, and lack of attention from parents. Personal-identity politics and clothing are the foci rather than current political issues, with kids spending large amounts of money in order to separate themselves from other styles in pop culture. In this sense, punk has transformed— from kicking over the can to dressing it in particular clothes.

One aspect of online teen culture closely associated with emo is the Internet fad called MySpace. The site allows anyone to build a simple Web page, which allows the user to easily connect with any of the 50 million other users (McDermott). A website for teens to chat may not seem like such a bad thing. It allows them to meet new people, hear about other parts of the country and world, and maybe even discuss political issues. The original intent of MySpace was to allow up-and-coming bands to stream music, allowing more people to hear them. This should allow for a diverse music collection among teens, right? Spend just a few minutes surfing the site, and you will see that almost all bands sound very similar. Of course, they focus on emo points of view in order to attract more listeners. Instead of discussing socio-political issues, users spend time rating the attractiveness of fellow members' photographs. Many schools have banned students from accessing MySpace from school computers, as well as many similar sites such as Xanga or Facebook (McDermott). This banning apparently hasn't fazed teens, as MySpace is expected to make over $200 million this year.

MySpace is not the only company capitalizing on the emo fad. The chain store Hot Topic is rapidly spreading through the malls of the United States. Hot Topic markets the punk fashion trend to the kids who resist (but ironically promote) conformity, and is making money hand over fist. Not only does Hot Topic market this trend, it attempts to create a new image of punk rock, with no respect for the values that punk originally created. Hot Topic encourages anyone interested in the punk scene to spend money on its products. Unfortunately the company is putting a fashion mask over the face of punk, and not only hiding but also obliterating the defining quality of punk. By creating a slickly manufactured image of punk, Hot Topic takes a movement that previously rejected conformity, and twists it into a fashion trend. Just when true punk was beginning to scratch the surface of the mainstream, it was buried by the music that goes along with this fashionably slanted image of punk. Hot Topic and similar corporations seem to enjoy keeping America's youth in check in order to further manipulate fashion trends and make another buck. It would seem that punks would rise up and simply boycott the store, putting them out of business. However, the punks who would be willing to boycott the store already avoid it at all costs. Luckily for Hot Topic, the target market consists of kids who have no interest in punk's deeply rooted anti-capitalist ideals.

> It would seem that punks would rise up and simply boycott the store, putting them out of business. However, the punks who would be willing to boycott the store already avoid it at all costs.

Punks would gladly put many corporations under by means of boycott if they existed in a large enough population. Unfortunately, punks make up a rather small part of America's youth. Even smaller yet is the portion of punks that aren't infatuated with tight clothing and makeup. What about the rest of the youth in America? Regardless of choice in music, teens are losing interest in important issues across the country. What was once the politically active pop music of Creedence Clearwater Revival, Neil Young, or even the Grateful Dead has become Ashlee Simpson and Kelly Clarkson. Country was once very socially minded with the lyrics of Johnny Cash and Willie Nelson, but is now interested in beer and women. Hip-hop used to consist of NWA and the Beastie Boys, who both spoke up for civil rights. Rap has now become obsessed with money, demonstrated by 50 Cent's new movie, *Get Rich or Die Tryin'.*

I spent a year living in Midland, Texas, during the 2004 presidential election. At the same time, Green Day's new album *American Idiot* was released. While riding my motorcycle on a hot summer day, I was stopped at a traffic light next to a man in his early twenties. For the next 40 seconds, all I heard was his voice over a radio blaring "American Idiot."

For a moment I was relieved. As I listened to the lyrics questioning and rejecting dominant political, cultural, and consumerist messages, I thought that maybe people were catching on to current issues and possibly even thinking for themselves. My moment was over as I realized the context of the situation. The young man was sitting in a jacked-up two-wheel-drive truck, wearing a cowboy hat. The truck brandished stickers and magnets pledging allegiance to President Bush, and promising to support our troops. More stickers explained that marriage belongs between only a man and a woman, and that abortion is a mortal sin. The vehicle and driver seemed to be a rolling contradiction.

This is not to say that people cannot listen to Green Day if they do not agree with the message. In fact, it is a wonderful feeling to continue to enjoy something that conflicts with your own beliefs. This is also by no means to say that all music must be politically minded. In fact, not all "real" punk music is politically minded. Punk makes a simple statement by questioning authority and not accepting the status quo. And even with that consistent principle, punk is always changing. According to John Goshert:

> The call for an absolutely correct definition of punk will always miss the point, for the stable form of genre or fashion is always subject either to appropriation by the flattening forces of the entertainment industry, or to transformation by punks themselves. Instead, punk is better seen as a series of performative traces [that] will never serve as hardened constraints of its definition.[1]

As popular culture changes, punk consciousness will also transform. Large companies will move away from punk to support something else—or the watered-down version of something else—with the intent of making a few dollars and keeping America's youth brainwashed enough to purchase overpriced items. And beneath the fashion parades, the real punks will be chafing against and kicking over whatever is hailed as lovely, admirable, and attractive. And maybe there is one thing we can say for sure: whatever punk is or will be, it sure as hell won't be pretty.

---

[1]Goshert, John. "Punk after the Pistols: American Music, Economics, and Politics in the 1980s and 1990s." *Popular Music and Society* 24.1 (2000): 85. *Academic Search Elite.* Web. 28 Apr. 2006.

Works Cited

Goshert, John. "Punk after the Pistols: American Music, Economics, and Politics in the 1980s and 1990s." *Popular Music and Society* 24.1 (2000): 85. *Academic Search Elite.* Web. 28 Apr. 2006.

Hansell, Saul. "New MySpace Goal: Profit, Not Just Friends." *New York Times.* New York Times, 26 Apr. 2006. Web. 28 Apr. 2006.

Hebdige, Dick. "Style in Revolt; Revolting Style." *Subculture: The Meaning of Style.* New York: Routledge, 1981. 106–12. Rpt. in *Reading Culture: Contexts for Critical Reading and Writing.* Ed. Dianna George and John Trimbur. New York: Longman, 1999. 232–35. Print.

Heisel, Scott. "Your Antidote for Apathy." *Alternative Press.* Alternative Press, 15 Oct. 2005. Web. 28 Apr. 2006.

Kleiner, Fred, and Christin Mamiya. *Gardner's Art through the Ages: The Western Perspective.* Belmont: Thomson, 2006. Print.

McDermott, Irene. "I Need MySpace." *Searcher* 14 (2006): 22–25. *Academic Search Elite.* Web. 28 Apr. 2006.

Operation Ivy. "Unity." *Energy.* Lookout! 1989. CD.

"Punk." *Urban Dictionary.* Urban Dictionary, n.d. Web. 27 Apr. 2006.

Analyzing Argument

1. How is Hyde's notion of punk fundamentally opposed to mainstream messages about punk? Why is that difference important?

2. Allusions are a key part of Hyde's argument. Choose one cultural allusion, and explain how it functions in the overall line of reasoning.

3. What values lurk beneath the explicit claims about original punk culture? (In other words, what principles or qualities must a reader value to accept Hyde's argument?)

4. Describe Hyde's use of counterargument. Point to a particular passage and explain how it works as counterargument—and how it helps to develop Hyde's overall point.

5. Take a close look at Hyde's Works Cited list. Based on this list and Hyde's use of song lyrics, how would you define "authority" in academic argument?

Standardized Testing vs. Education

JUSTIN JAMES

James wrote the following essay for a college English assignment. His goal was to argue a definition of education as it applies to today's schools. While standardized testing was the starting place for James's argument, he discovers an underlying tension—one of competing definitions.

In three sentences, a personal example introduces the main issue.

The introduction provides an overview of the problem with standardized testing.

Appeal to logic (deductive): Students, like humans in any situation, respond to cues they are given.

Reference to the No Child Left Behind Act helps to emphasize the relevance of the argument.

The first two sentences explain how education comes to be defined a certain way.

Beginning with "But," James provides an alternative definition of education.

It is no wonder my niece says school is boring. When she was younger, she loved it. It was all about discovery; now it's all about tests. Tests can be valuable in education, of course. But they can be hazardous, too. They can hinder learning and teach students and society at large a false definition of education. Standardized tests teach students to *practice and perform,* but education is more about *developing a sense of curiosity.* Practice and perform actually discourages curiosity: All the practicing and performing takes time, which takes time away from activities that might encourage a more curious mind. Standardized testing ends up sending a wrong message: It tells students and society that *education* is a quantity to be consumed and measured.

Students, like humans in any situation, respond to cues they are given. If they are not taught to be curious, if they are prompted toward other modes of thought and behavior, they will act accordingly. In short, standardized testing takes the curiosity out of students. Standardized tests don't engage students' sense of curiosity. Instead, school becomes drudgery. And now more than ever, despite these effects, standardized tests are being touted as the saving grace to failing schools. The No Child Left Behind Act of 2001 was well intended, perhaps. Signed by President George W. Bush on January 8, 2001, the act "gives our schools and our country groundbreaking educational reform, based on the following ideals: stronger accountability for results, more freedom for states and communities, encouraging proven education methods, more choice for parents" (No Child Left Behind). The act has placed an emphasis on accountability, which is being determined by student test results. Test scores might rise. But does that really mean the schools are doing a better job or students are getting a better education? The current emphasis on testing can have harmful results. What's more, the method used to find out the scores teaches students a dangerous definition of *education.*

The emphasis placed on standardized testing teaches students that *education* means getting content from a teacher or getting good at a skill. They come to think *education* means getting a grade on a test, accumulating points, and arriving at an average grade based on those points. But students will benefit more in all aspects of life if they can experience education differently—as having to do more with exploring, discovery, being curious.

Standardized testing deprives students of the opportunity to experience an education that values curiosity, and is more valuable than an education consumed with standardized tests.

In 2001, Donald Perl, a middle school teacher in Greeley, Colorado, refused to administer a standardized test. Perl, who said he "anguished" over the decision, believed "the test cultivates competition instead of cooperation and test-taking skills over 'true stimulation of our children's curiosity'" (qtd. in Ednalino). Many teachers, like Perl, have doubts about the side effects of standardized testing. Ann Lahrson Fisher, in "Side Effects of Standardized Testing," compiles an interesting list of more than thirty side effects. She argues that tests teach students, in subtle ways, ideas such as:

- Someone else knows what you should know better than you do.
- Learning is an absolute that can be measured.
- Your interests are not important.
- The subject areas being evaluated on the test are the only things that are important to know.
- Thinking is not valued; getting the "right" answer is the only goal.
- The answer (to any question) is readily available, indisputable, and it's one of these four or five answers here; there's no need to look deeper or dwell on the question.

Fisher's long list of side effects suggest it is at least possible that standardized tests define education for students: "Reliance on standardized test scores reduces initiative, independence, creativity, and willingness to take risks in learning situations." Fisher explains that "test scores become the goal of student work (extrinsic reward) rather than the sense of satisfaction and wonder that naturally follows discovery of something new (intrinsic reward)." Should the goal of education be test scores, or should students experience a sense of satisfaction and wonder? Should students discover something new, or prep for tests?

As students in American public schools get older, they don't necessarily encounter increasingly intense opportunities to explore intellectually. But they should. If they don't get this opportunity, they'll get bored—not because education is boring, but because what students have been exposed to as *education* is an absence of *education,* and that is boring. If students aren't having fun, it's because they're not encouraged to be curious. When we focus so much on standardized tests, we ask students to leave their curiosity behind and start down the practice-and-perform path. Like a magician, the tests misdirect everyone's attention, and students, based on their educational experiences, develop a false belief. For example, a student who is taught to explore the meaning of revolutions, to imagine the connection between the Revolutionary War and the Civil War, will ultimately have a deeper understanding of history than the student who is asked to

---

When quoting, James provides name (Donald Perl), context (who Perl is), and only as much quoted material as necessary.

Support from an authority is introduced and listed.

James shows how Fisher's points support his argument.

Fisher, an authority, is quoted briefly and with purpose.

James explains the negative consequences of a false definition of education: Students will think education is boring.

Appeal to value: Exploring motivations and discovering connections is more educationally valuable than memorizing facts.

memorize the dates of the decisive battles in each war. When a student is asked "Why did people in both wars want to free themselves from another government?" she is given an opportunity to think about the motivations of real people and to discover connections. But under the yoke of standardized tests, teachers are obliged to pump students full of facts and then move to test-taking (performance) strategies. The students, then, reach the easy conclusion that *education* equals memorize and then test.

The concluding paragraph qualifies an important point: Opponents of standardized testing are not for throwing standards out the window; they don't think all testing is bad. This clarifies the writer's position and strengthens the argument by pointing out common ground with those who might disagree. (This point was also qualified in the opening paragraph.)

Today's No Child Left Behind testing is redefining *education*. This new definition is harmful. People are coming to believe that education is primarily about practicing and performing on exams—not about developing curiosity and exploring vast possibilities. But in an environment (a definition) where they can explore, students thrive; teachers thrive; learning thrives. Standardized tests squelch all that. They should be used modestly. It is not that opponents of standardized testing are for throwing standards out the window. And it's not that they think all testing is bad. They simply believe the more valuable definition of *education* promotes curiosity, not practice and perform.

Works Cited

Ednalino, Percy. "Teacher Won't Administer CSAP Tests." *Denver Post.* 27 Jan. 2001: A1. Print.

Fisher, Ann Lahrson. "Side Effects of Standardized Testing." *National Home Education Network.* Natl. Home Educ. Network, 2004. Web. 8 July 2004.

No Child Left Behind Act of 2001. Pub. L. 107–10. 115 Stat. 1425. 8 Jan. 2002. Print.

Analyzing Argument

1. According to James, how does standardized testing define education?

2. What is James's line of reasoning? What basic premises must you follow before you accept his main claim? (Are any of those premises unstated in James's essay?)

3. Discuss how the following sentence makes an appeal to values:

   Standardized testing ends up sending a wrong message: It tells students and society that education is a quantity to be consumed and measured (paragraph 1).

   Then find another sentence in the essay and explain how it appeals to a value.

4. Explain how the testimony from teachers works in the argument. What premise do they help to support?

5. How do counterarguments and concessions function in the argument? What additional counterarguments or concessions could have been helpful?

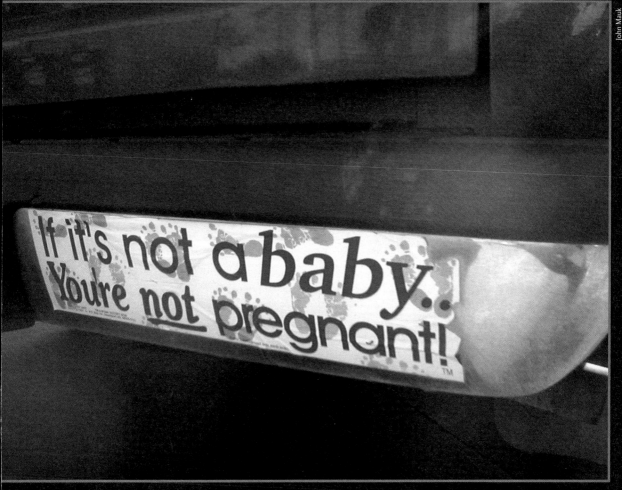

This bumper sticker was on a truck in Livingston, Montana.

1. What does the bumper sticker argue?

2. Explain the logic behind the bumper sticker. Is it sound or flawed logic?

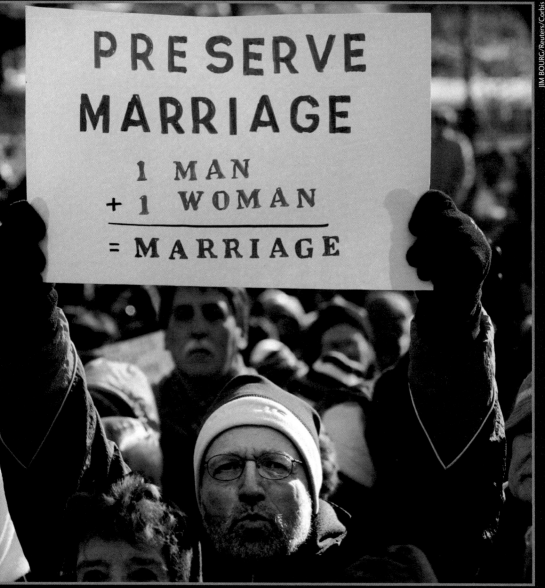

PRESERVE
MARRIAGE

1 MAN
+ 1 WOMAN
———————
= MARRIAGE

Exploring for Topics

In this chapter, you will argue for a particular definition. The goal is to draw clear boundaries—to argue for what a thing *is* and *is not.* As you consider possible topics, dig into common situations. Any situation, an everyday occurrence or a special event, can help us to rethink the very essence of things. Imagine a World Wrestling Entertainment match: If we are watching a 300-pound man in a yellow leotard stomp around a wrestling ring, we might think about the nature of entertainment. We might ask ourselves, "What exactly *is* entertainment?" Once the question is asked, it can be answered in a number of ways. Every situation holds potential for digging up basic definitions. But we must be willing to ask questions that normally do not get asked. Following are possible starting places for an argument about a definition:

Focus on a specific situation or thing—and ask whether it falls within or outside of a particular definition.

- **Popular culture:** Is *American Idol* a reality show or something else? Is *Dateline* a news program? Is the "No Spin Zone" really a no spin zone? Is your local news program really *news,* or is there a more accurate word? Is *Adult Swim* really for adults? Can WWE competitions be defined as *wrestling,* or are they some kind of muscle-bound ballet?
- **Politics:** Is the United States government really a democracy? Is the current administration liberal? Is the Tea Party really conservative?
- **School:** Is business an academic discipline? Are you a college student in the traditional sense? How would you define your instructors? Are they professors, instructors, teachers, or lecturers?
- **Work:** Do you have a job or a career? In what sense are you a laborer? Could someone say that you're part of a team? (Or is it a team only in name?)
- **Choose a reading or image from this chapter:** Enter the argument by raising a new way of seeing the disputed term.

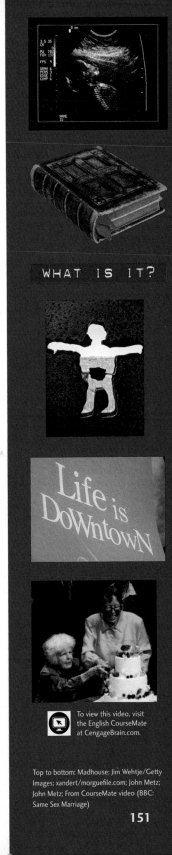

WHAT IS IT?

Life is DoWntowN

To view this video, visit the English CourseMate at CengageBrain.com.

Top to bottom: Madhouse; Jim Wehtje/Getty Images; xandert/morguefile.com; John Metz; John Metz; From CourseMate video (BBC: Same Sex Marriage)

Focus on a term—and argue for a specific definition.
- What term do people misunderstand or misapply?
- In your eyes, what is the most important debate currently being waged in your community? What definition is at the root of the debate? (Even though people might not label the debate as one about definitions, what word are they disagreeing about?) For example, a debate about which farmers have the right to sell their produce at the local farmer's market might ultimately hinge on the definition of "local" (or even "produce").
- Focus on an important cultural or national debate. At the heart of the debate, beneath all the fervor, what word seems undefined or misunderstood? For example, what is liberalism? What is fascism? What is conservative? Fundamentalism?

Focus on an unstated definitional argument that lurks in a common practice.
- Justin James argues that standardized tests teach students to define *education* as practice and perform. What other common academic practices make subtle definitional arguments? How does the standard classroom arrangement define *education*? How does a syllabus define *education*?

Focus on the visual.
- How does the appearance and design of a course textbook define *college?* How does your campus geography or architecture define *college?*
- How does a particular fashion trend define *woman* or *man?*
- How does your current hairstyle define your gender?
- Look for visual arguments about definitions where you work. Even landscaping or the interior of a building could be arguing a definition.

Invention Workshop

For each category on the previous page, develop more questions. Consider both cultural situations, such as the Super Bowl or Christmas, and professional situations, such as a business meeting. Then generate questions to highlight potential arguments of definition. Generate as many examples as possible—and consider even the most eccentric or seemingly insignificant ideas.

There are two general approaches to arguing definitions: (1) examining a specific subject and arguing that it fits or does not fit into a category, and (2) examining a term and arguing for or against an accepted definition. If you start with a specific subject (for example, a classroom, a television program, an image), then it will be helpful to inspect its particulars. For instance, imagine that a writer is examining *American Idol*. She wonders if it fits into the reality show category. First, she might list qualities of the show itself:

- The contestants are ordinary people, not professional actors.
- Judges and producers whittle down the contestants according to their own tastes and understanding of the audience.
- As the judges eliminate contestants, a select few are given air time, mini-biographies, that showcase their stories.
- The mini-bios are heavily produced and characterize the contestants in a particular way.
- As the competition progresses, the finalists perform in Hollywood for the judges, a live audience, and the television viewers.
- The viewers vote on winners—but only after the judges give official commentary.

The writer could go on listing qualities or elements of the show: advertisers, stage production, contestant guidelines, and so on. Then she might find a definition of *reality show* and compare the definition with her specific notes. In this early phase, she might find that some of the show's qualities match that definition while others seem to oppose it.

If you begin with a specific subject, consider the following invention questions:

▶ What are the particular qualities of the situation or thing?

▶ How do those qualities match up with an agreed-upon definition?

▶ How do those qualities oppose or stretch an agreed-upon definition?

If you begin with a general term (such as education or entertainment), consider the following invention questions:

▶ What specific behaviors, attitudes, values, policies, or qualities does the term involve?

▶ What specific qualities differentiate it from other like things?

▶ What is its opposite? (Does it have an opposite?)

▶ Under what conditions does it thrive or suffer?

Inventing a Claim

Because any argument exists within a context of public opinion, good arguers plan how they will engage other positions and insights. To engage those other positions, research common understanding about your subject. Consider conducting an informal survey about your subject (see pages 372–373) or exploring your library's periodical databases, which contain journal and magazine articles that can help uncover many layers of a topic. Scholarly, or peer-reviewed, journal articles can be especially helpful in an argument about definitions because much academic research seeks to define terms. Scholars are constantly making arguments about the nature of things: *psychology is . . . ; life is . . . ; American currency is . . . ; the human mind is. . . .* Even a basic Internet search can reveal some common thinking about the topic—everything from informal rants to official government studies. Using the same noun strings as you used in the periodical databases, search Google or another major search engine. As you search, be open to opinions and associations. The goal is not to find sources that agree with your initial position but to explore *what's out there,* to see what has been said.

Answers to the following questions will help you to craft a specific position in relation to others.

What Do Others Claim?	**What Do I Claim?**
▶ What do people normally think of when they hear the word?	▶ What important aspect or layer do others overlook?
▶ What do specific sources say about the subject or the word itself?	▶ Why is it important that the topic be defined correctly?
▶ Why might reasonable people disagree about or argue over the word?	▶ What specific notion or understanding can you correct or clarify?

If you can answer the last question, you are well on your way to developing a main argumentative claim. Your argument might do one of the following:

- Argue that a particular (situation, event, show, etc.) does or does not match a definition:
  —Because a few powerful corporations, rather than civic groups and people, make policy in America, we are closer to an oligarchy than a democracy.

—Although *American Idol* often gets lumped in with other reality shows, the tightly controlled contestant selection makes it more of a slick national talent show.

—The standard classroom layout and overreliance on big-screen technology suggest propaganda rather than education.

- Argue that a common term is often misapplied or entirely misunderstood:

—Higher education is not about job training or occupational retrenchment; it's about the development of intellectual possibilities beyond any particular job.

—Punk is not about a particular fashion but the constant denial of the mainstream, manufactured aesthetic.

—Despite the successful propaganda of the Right, liberalism is not hell-bent on killing God, disbanding the military, and putting white men at the bottom of the food chain. Instead, liberalism hopes for the democratization of knowledge and power, which a good many people still fear.

Such finely tuned statements do not fall from the sky; they must undergo some tinkering and shaping. Notice how Justin James's claim evolved. The first statement is merely a broad response to a situation. His final claim is more than just a position—and it is more than a simple definition. It is a statement that promotes a new way of thinking about education.

- Standardized tests are ruining education.
- Education is about discovery, not performance.
- While standardized tests teach students that education is a practice-and-perform process, education is actually a discovery process.
- While standardized tests teach students to practice and perform, education is actually about developing a sense of discovery in each subject.

More Sample Claims

Popular Culture

- Popular culture in mainstream America is actually popular *anti*-culture.
- The product sold on television is the viewing audience.

Politics

- While nations are defined by borders, a nation can also be defined as a group of people engaged in argument about common issues.

- A strong economy cannot be determined by the stock market, new housing starts, or automobile sales; instead, one must examine the financial circumstances of middle- and lower-class citizens.
- Although characterizing terrorists as evil can have short-term motivational effects in the war on terror, terrorists can only be dealt with in the long run if their motives are explored and understood, not oversimplified and distorted.
- Despite the Democratic Party's stated principles, it can easily be defined as the slightly less corporate wing of the Republican Party.

School

- While training is the process of acquiring skills, it should not be confused with education, which is the active process of uncovering ideas.
- Education is the process of personal intellectual restructuring.
- Education is the deliberate escape from boredom.
- Education is the process of building new concepts and destroying old ones.
- Dental hygiene is not an academic major and should not be under the control of community colleges or universities.

Work

- Comfort is an illusion unless it is achieved through perseverance and struggle.
- Work should be considered a spiritual dimension of one's life, not merely an economic necessity.
- Teaching is not part of the new "service industry"; if anything, it resembles politics because of its role in maintaining, or vitalizing, popular consciousness.
- Psychologists are the new pioneers, seeking out the most uncharted spaces of the living world.

Activity

In small groups, share your main claims. Evaluate the claim of each group member and help each to evolve in the same way as James's did. Apply the following questions:

- Is the claim arguable? Could it be more arguable by referring to an opposing idea?
- How could the claim be more focused? What words could be more precise?
- How could the claim be more revelatory? How could the definition suggest something unique or surprising?

Inventing Support

While many other support strategies can be applied to this project, the following forms of evidence and appeal are commonly used. (For a more complete explanation of the support strategies listed in this section, see Chapter 3.)

Lines of Reasoning call on the audience to make logical connections between points or ideas. In an argument of definition, the arguer hopes to lead readers to a particular definition—to believe that a particular definition is the most correct or most applicable to a situation. This involves more than simply stating the definition. Often, the arguer has to convince the audience that several premises are true. For example, consider the following definitions of education:

A. Education is the process of making people better thinkers.

B. Education is the process of changing the brain.

Readers are not likely to accept each definition without some reasoning or premises that lead to the idea. Therefore, the arguers would need to walk readers through a line of reasoning:

A. Education is the process of making people better thinkers.
- Humans are natural thinkers.
- Humans are naturally *bad* thinkers (predisposed to prejudice, egocentrism, superficiality, vagueness, etc.).
- No occupation or discipline values bad (egocentric, superficial, vague, narrow-minded, prejudicial, imprecise) thinking.
- We must train people in explicit ways to become better thinkers.
- **Therefore, education is the process of making people better thinkers.**

B. Education is the process of changing the brain.
- Learning prompts the brain to take on increasingly challenging stimuli.
- The brain changes to accommodate new stimuli.
- The act of learning actually changes the brain's structure—how the brain works.
- **Therefore, education is the process of changing the brain.**

Each premise may require support of its own, such as examples, analogies, statistics, scenarios, and so on. The arguments, then, would move slowly, treating each premise as a mini-argument. Without some development of these premises, the arguments would likely fail. Readers wouldn't see the rationale for accepting the definitions.

Analogical Reasoning allows writers to compare two things, to argue that if those two things are alike in certain respects, they are also alike in other respects. In his essay, Andrew Hyde works to define punk. In the following passage, he borrows some analogical reasoning from a source:

> Dick Hebdige's *Style in Revolt: Revolting Style* describes punk fashion as correlating with the artistic Dada movement of the 1910s and '20s, and specifically Marcel Duchamp's "ready-mades." Hebdige explains how punks used similar items for the same purpose: "The most unremarkable and inappropriate items—a pin, a plastic clothes peg, a television component, a razor blade, a tampon—could be brought within the province of punk (un)fashion." Not only did punks draw fashion ideas from Dada, but political and social views as well. The Dada movement was a response to the Great War. Artists were disgusted with the events of the time, and made a statement by proclaiming insignificance.

This is an important move in Hyde's essay. The comparison to Dadaism allows him to articulate the political dimension of punk. Even though the Dadaist movement occurred decades before punk rock, it shares a number of social and aesthetic qualities. Hyde goes on to make the case that understanding Dadaism is a key to understanding punk.

Appeals to Value make a connection between the topic and a value such as fairness, equality, duty, or responsibility. Although the appeal to value is more often used in arguments of value or crisis, it can promote or give urgency to a definition; it can prompt people to see why a particular definition *should* be accepted. For example, Margaret Mead's argument urges readers to see the moral benefits to accepting her definition of warfare:

> There is further needed a belief that social invention is possible and the invention of new methods which will render warfare as out of date as the tractor is making the plough, or the motor car the horse and buggy. A form of behavior becomes out of date only when something else takes its place, and, in order to invent forms of behavior which will make war obsolete, it is a first requirement to believe that an invention is possible.

Mead attaches an important value to her definition. Likewise, Andrew Hyde attaches a positive value to the original notion of punk and a negative value to its corporate-sponsored notions. For Hyde, the corporate-sponsored version of punk misses an important social quality: the denial of manipulation and conformity:

> By creating a slickly manufactured image of punk, Hot Topic takes a movement that previously rejected conformity, and twists it into a fashion trend. Just when true punk was beginning to scratch the surface of the mainstream, it was buried by the music that goes along with this fashionably slanted image of punk. Hot Topic and similar corporations seem to enjoy keeping America's youth in check in order to further manipulate fashion trends and make another buck. It would seem that punks would rise up and simply boycott the store, putting them out of business. However, the punks who would be willing to boycott the store already avoid it at all costs. Luckily for Hot Topic, the target market consists of kids who have no interest in punk's deeply rooted anti-capitalist ideals.

Examples, specific cases or illustrations of phenomena, may be the most valuable support strategy in this project. Directing attention to particular examples can help show important aspects of your definition. Margaret Mead, for instance, relies on two particular examples:

> The case for warfare is much clearer because there are peoples even today who have no warfare. Of these the Eskimos are perhaps the most conspicuous examples, but the Lepchas of Sikkim . . . are as good. Neither of these peoples understands war, not even defensive warfare.

Mead then goes on to detail the Eskimo and Lepcha cultures, further explaining how they support the idea that war is a human invention, not a universal trait.

Scenarios, hypothetical or fictional accounts, can help illustrate important layers of your definition. Writers often invite readers to imagine situations that focus attention on particularly relevant information. For instance, notice how James constructs a scenario to support his take on *education:*

> For example, a student who is taught to explore the meaning of revolutions, to imagine the connection between the Revolutionary War and the Civil War, will ultimately have a deeper understanding of history than the student who is asked to memorize the dates of the decisive battles in each war. When a student is asked "Why did people in both wars want to free themselves from another government?" she is given an opportunity to think about the motivations of real people and to discover connections. But under the yoke of standardized tests, teachers are obliged to pump students full of facts and then move to test-taking (performance) strategies.

Notice that James does more than describe the scenario; he also relates it to the standardized test problem, which gives his argument some context. Because scenarios are entirely created by the writer, they can be very persuasive. With a scenario, a writer can focus readers' attention on a particular situation that illustrates the exact nature of the point.

Allusions are references to bits of public knowledge (from history, current events, popular culture, religion, or literature). They invite an audience to consider a commonly known reference and see its relevance to the argument. Allusions are persuasive because audiences feel like they are reminded of something that they have held in the backs of their minds; when an arguer makes a connection to a familiar point in history, a line in a song, or a scene from a movie, the audience is apt to follow along with the thinking. In his essay on punk, Andrew Hyde relies heavily on pop culture allusions:

> Regardless of choice in music, teens are losing interest in important issues across the country. What was once the politically active pop music of Creedence Clearwater Revival, Neil Young, or even the Grateful Dead has become Ashlee Simpson and Kelly Clarkson. Country was once very socially minded with the lyrics of Johnny Cash and Willie Nelson, but is now interested in beer and women. Hip-hop used to consist of NWA and the Beastie Boys, who both spoke up for civil rights. Rap has now become obsessed with money, demonstrated by 50 Cent's new movie, *Get Rich or Die Tryin'.*

Hyde assumes his readers know the difference between Neil Young and Ashlee Simpson—between a politically outspoken songwriter and a mainstream pop singer. He assumes that readers understand how Young represents one way of thinking and Simpson another, so he does not give details about their songs.

Literary Works are a particular type of allusion. Writers often borrow the words of poets, songwriters, playwrights, and fiction writers to lend heft and credibility to their own ideas. Sometimes, the words are directly related to the writer's argument as in Andrew Hyde's essay. The song lyrics he gives directly support his main claim about the nature of punk. Notice how Hyde first sets up the lyrics by explaining their significance:

> Through the 1980s, punk became even more political. With bands like T.S.O.L., Social Distortion, and Operation Ivy, the movement focused on social issues that were not being acknowledged by the Reagan administration. Tax codes were changed in a way to benefit the rich, while social

policy moved away from helping the poor. This hate for Republican conservatism may have been expressed best by the Dead Kennedys:

> The sun beams down on a brand new day
> No more welfare tax to pay
> Unsightly slums gone up in flashing light
> Jobless millions whisked away
> At last we have more room to play
> All systems go to kill the poor tonight

Most often literary works are used more indirectly—not to show the particular sentiments of a decade but to orient the reader's thoughts. And one of the common applications is the epigraph: a short quoted passage that occurs before an essay. The epigraph floats above the argument and functions like a sign to readers: before entering the argument, consider this broader point. For example, in his essay about the economy, John de Graaf begins with an epigraph from a contemporary novel:

> "If they can get you asking the wrong question, they don't have to worry about the answers." —Thomas Pynchon, *Gravity's Rainbow*

The quotation from *Gravity's Rainbow* says nothing directly about de Graaf's topic. But it helps to establish a broader point in de Graaf's argument: that most people have been duped into thinking the wrong thing about the economy.

As you consider your topic, use the following questions to help create support:

▶ What line of reasoning must people follow to accept this definition?

▶ What examples best illustrate my understanding of the topic?

▶ What hypothetical situations can I create to illustrate my point?

▶ What other real situations might make useful comparisons to my topic? What references to history, literature, nature, current events, or popular culture help to illustrate something important about the topic?

▶ How might a literary passage illustrate the point or function as an epigraph to orient the reader's thinking?

▶ Why is it important (good, fair, practical, fulfilling, honest, moral) to accept this definition?

Arrangement

Where Should I Give My Definition? Your definition might appear early and then get developed throughout the rest of your argument. This direct approach can help the reader more easily understand the support that comes later. But the direct approach is not always preferable. Some situations might call for the new definition to come later, after the reader has been introduced to some key ideas or even an entire line of reasoning. For instance, Andrew Hyde uses most of his argument to explain the seemingly inexplicable nature of punk. He details the differences between the past political movements and the recent fashion trends. He even argues that the nature of punk cannot be packaged and easily consumed. And toward the end of his argument, only after he has complicated the readers' thinking, he firms up the idea:

> Punk makes a simple statement by questioning authority and not accepting the status quo.

And in his final paragraph, he goes one step further toward concretizing the abstraction:

> And beneath the fashion parades, the real punks will be chafing against and kicking over whatever is hailed as lovely, admirable, and attractive. And maybe there is one thing we can say for sure: whatever punk is or will be, it sure as hell won't be pretty.

Hyde's essay illustrates the point that a main claim—in this case, a definition—should come only when readers are ready for it.

How Should I Counter Opposing Definitions? Any term can be defined in various ways, and a sound argument will counter(argue) or refute opposing definitions. As in most arguments, the opposition can be dealt with in a number of ways, even at the beginning of the essay. For example, Margaret Mead begins her essay with three views of warfare. Her first two paragraphs detail the logic of those views, and then she offers a counter:

> All three of these positions are very popular today among those who think seriously about the problems of war and its possible prevention, but I wish to urge another point of view, less defeatist, perhaps, than the first and third and more accurate than the second. . . .

Mead then goes on to develop her definition against others' logic. She pushes off against them into her own argument. This is a standard, and powerful, move in all forms of argument.

Does a Concession or Qualifier Have to Go in Every Argument? Conceding and qualifying are valuable argumentative strategies: they show readers that a writer is listening and dealing with the complexities of an issue instead of oversimplifying it. Most credible arguments acknowledge their own weaknesses as well as the validity of certain opposing views. As Andrew Hyde shows, even an essay about punk can concede points. Although Hyde laments the loss of political edge in popular music, he concedes some ground:

> This is not to say that people cannot listen to Green Day if they do not agree with the message. In fact, it is a wonderful feeling to continue to enjoy something that conflicts with your own beliefs. This is also by no means to say that all music must be politically minded. In fact, not all "real" punk music is politically minded. Punk makes a simple statement by questioning authority and not accepting the status quo. And even with that consistent principle, punk is always changing.

Concessions (and counterarguments) reveal a writer who is engaging other points of view and therefore interacting with readers, not just speaking at them. While concessions are not always required, and making unimportant concessions can be a harmful distraction, writers should explore what concessions they might make in order to strengthen their argument. Not conceding points that should be conceded weakens an argument.

How Many Other Definitions Should I Include? You may include just one or several other definitions in your argument. To decide, reflect on your reason for writing. If you are arguing for a particular definition, then you are responding to some other definition(s). Mead, for example, sees a need to push against three popular definitions, or "positions," for the basis of warfare. As you develop your own argument, consider other, perhaps flawed, definitions or ways of thinking, and address them in your argument. While you might respond only to one main definition, you might respond to several other definitions as well. For your own topic, ask the following questions:

- ▶ What do readers need to know before getting my definition?

- ▶ Do readers need to hear about a particular situation before they understand the nature of my argument?

- ▶ If I start with someone else's definition (or way of thinking about the topic), what will that show? Good thinking? Bad thinking?

Audience and Voice

Unless it's a part of some daring writing strategy, be careful not to offend the reader. The way you say it is as important as what you say. Identify words, phrases, and sentences that may sound rude or insulting. Be confident but not overbearing. Remember, you are arguing to persuade, to influence the reader's way of thinking. Readers nearly always tune out a harsh or insensitive voice, and they are less likely to be influenced by an insecure or wishy-washy one.

The language you choose can influence how your readers feel as they move through your argument. Imagine your audience—specific people, with particular beliefs and opinions. And imagine how they might come to your argument: bored, uninterested, focused, unfocused, skeptical, hopeful. Following are a few strategies to consider:

Formality Depending on your readers and their relationship with the topic, formality can elevate the reading experience and make the topic itself feel important and worthy of serious attention. Formality can be created by careful word choice. Notice the difference between these two sentences:

> For this, two things have to happen.

> For this, two conditions, at least, are necessary. (Margaret Mead)

The difference between the words themselves can create a subtle shift in formality. However, more formal writing does not always depend on sophisticated vocabulary. Ornate language can over-formalize a text and render it weak. Imagine a comparison to clothing: A suit and tie are more formal than blue jeans and a T-shirt. But a suit and tie, with a sparkling silver top hat, a golden cape, and a jewel-studded walking cane is, in most situations, overly dramatic, and therefore less appropriate. Like a person, language can be overdressed, even gaudy.

Formal writing avoids slang or excessive figurative language—phrases that draw attention to themselves or go beyond literal meaning:

> After emerging from the primordial goo, humans were probably not marrying each other or singing songs around a fire.

> At some point in his social development man was undoubtedly without the institution of marriage or the knowledge of the use of fire. (Margaret Mead)

The first sentence uses a particularly vivid image, "primordial goo," to communicate an idea. The phrase itself lends a kind of informality to the point. The second sentence, from Mead's essay, makes a similar point but does so with more restrained and formal language.

Informality As you might infer from the preceding passages, informal writing may employ street language, slang, and everyday figurative language. Informality can also be created with attention to the writer and to the writer's own thinking, as in this passage from Andrew Hyde's essay:

> I spent a year living in Midland, Texas, during the 2004 presidential election. At the same time, Green Day's new album *American Idiot* was released. While riding my motorcycle on a hot summer day, I was stopped at a traffic light next to a man in his early twenties. For the next 40 seconds, all I heard was his voice over a radio blaring Green Day's title track from the most recent album: . . .
>
> For a moment I was relieved. I thought that maybe people were catching on to current issues and possibly even thinking for themselves. My moment was over as I realized the context of the situation. The young man was sitting in a jacked-up two-wheel-drive truck, wearing a cowboy hat. The truck brandished stickers and magnets pledging allegiance to President Bush, and promising to support our troops. More stickers explained that marriage belongs between only a man and a woman, and that abortion is a mortal sin. The vehicle and driver seemed to be a rolling contradiction.

The personal testimony helps support Hyde's premise about punk, but it also establishes an informal voice, which works with the nature of Hyde's topic and position.

Informality/Formality Writers are always creating voices; they tweak word choice, sentence structure, and figurative language to account for the particular situation. Even the most zany writer can (and should!) heed formal expectations when the situation calls for it. Most academic writers walk a middle road between formal and informal. They want to keep important ideas elevated with formal moves, but also keep readers awake with subtle cues and nudges. Justin James's essay walks this fine line. He maintains a sober and serious tone; he keeps metaphors to a minimum; and he draws little attention to his own presence. But he also keeps sentences varied and lively:

> Today's No Child Left Behind testing is redefining *education.* This new definition is harmful. People are coming to believe that education is primarily about practicing and performing on exams—not about developing curiosity and exploring vast possibilities. But in an environment (a definition) where they can explore, students thrive; teachers thrive; learning thrives. Standardized tests squelch all that. They should be used modestly. It is not that opponents of standardized testing are for throwing standards out the window. And it's not that they think all testing is bad. They simply believe the more valuable definition of *education* promotes curiosity, not practice and perform.

Revision

Inventing claims and support involves hard mental work. As you prepare your draft for Peer Review, return to the Invention questions and respond more fully. This can be a valuable way to fill in gaps, or to see some aspect of your thinking in a different way. Remember, as you responded to these questions earlier, you were thinking about them for the first time. Now that you have developed your thinking, you can return to those same questions and explore them from a different, more informed, point of view.

Research and Revision: If you used outside sources, consider the following questions. As you revise, refer to the corresponding pages in The Research Guide:

- Have you used research as means of discovery? (pp. 432–434)
- Have you evaluated sources for ideology, reliability, relevance, timeliness, and diversity? (pp. 464–471)
- Are the ideas from outside sources integrated smoothly into your ideas? (pp. 472–488)
- Are the sources documented appropriately (with in-text and end citations)? (pp. 489–518)

Peer Review

Exchange drafts with at least one other writer. (If time allows, exchange with two or three writers to gather a range of perspectives or comments.) Use the following questions to generate specific constructive comments about others' drafts:

1. Does the argument focus on a definition? Does it get to the defining characteristics of the topic—and avoid slipping into an argument about its value?

2. Identify the writer's claim. Can it be further narrowed and more revelatory? Does it offer a clear way of seeing the topic?

3. What is the most supportive passage in the argument? Describe why it works well in the argument.

4. Examine the logic of the argument. A successful argument will establish distinct qualities or defining characteristics for the topic (for example, education is X, Y, Z—not Q, R, S). These characteristics will then be illustrated in some particular fashion. Does the writer give specific qualities or defining characteristics that support the claim?

5. Look out for vague or overly general passages. Where could the writer use more allusions, examples, scenarios, or testimony to illustrate specific points? For example, rather than a broad phrase ("reality shows are about uncertainty"), could the writer describe how uncertainty plays into the specific components of a show?

6. The writer should have already engaged opposing perspectives, other opinions about the definition. But what other opposing points could the writer address? Can you imagine further objections to the argument?

7. Should the writer concede or qualify any points? Do you sense any passages that make the writer's argument seem too unwavering and narrow-minded? How would a concession or qualifier help that passage?

8. Rewrite the introduction to the argument. Even if the present introduction seems appropriate, write a totally new paragraph that demands attention while also bringing the reader into the argument's particular logic. (This rewrite may then prompt the writer to try something equally engaging and fresh.)

9. Check for paragraph coherence: Identify any paragraphs that seem to shift focus or take on too many separate points without a clear line of reasoning.

10. Are sources integrated smoothly, rather than being forced into passages? Explain any gaps between the writer's line of reasoning and the ideas from an outside source. (See pp. 472–488.)

Arguing Causes

Why Did This Happen?

A major fire in 2006, started in the wake of Hurricane Katrina.

n the early 1990s, a popular beverage company promoted its drink with the question: *Why ask why?* It was catchy—and probably helped to sell plenty of beer. It tapped into a popular culture attitude, a sense that people shouldn't think too hard about their decisions, their lives, or their situations. They just should consume and enjoy. Meanwhile, educators shook their heads and claimed that the slogan was yet another blow to the intellectual power of mainstream consciousness. What educators feared (and continue to fear) is that the average citizen might abandon his or her ability to ask *Why?* and to understand sophisticated causal arguments.

Asking *Why?* is fundamental to human existence. Why does lightning strike? Why do hurricanes hit during a particular time of year? Why do bad things happen to good people? Answers to these questions are a form of argument. They are assertions about causes, and different perspectives will generate different answers to the question *Why did this happen?*

We can look back through history and see a range of interesting causal arguments:

- Lightning strikes because God is angry.
- Women aren't as educated as men because they have smaller brains.
- People get sick because their humors are out of balance.
- The crops failed because a witch lives among the villagers.

Today, we realize the deeply flawed logic in such claims. But even contemporary arguments about causes can be suspicious. What caused the attacks on 9/11? Consider some of the following answers: God was punishing our culture for promoting feminism and homosexuality; the terrorists hate freedom; the U.S. government wanted a reason to increase its military presence in the Middle East. Political commentators, religious figures, bloggers, and even politicians have forwarded these arguments. Of course, the real causes are far more complex—and we have probably not yet heard all the political and cultural factors that led to the attacks.

In any career, probing for causes is critical to success. People at the top of business organizations constantly make causal arguments: they try to discover the cause of decreased sales, increased sales, increased competition, consumer behavior, and so on. And then they have to persuade others that X, not Y, caused sales to shoot downward. In short, the executive is paid to find out why things happen, to persuade others of certain causes, and to direct his or her organization to benefit from those causes. Arguments about causes constitute the everyday work across career fields and academic disciplines:

- Business executives meet at the beginning of the quarter and ask: *Why are we suddenly losing market share?*
- A group of political scientists probe the reasons behind the rise of the Tea Party movement.
- Environmental scientists pile up evidence showing that fossil fuel emissions and deforestation are the primary causes of global warming.
- Cultural theorists and sociologists ask, *Why do so many Americans dismiss or ignore the claims of science?*
- A pharmacology company works to find the cause of serious side effects related to its latest arthritis drug.

Sometimes, the most obvious causal arguments are the most flawed: The student failed because she didn't work hard enough; the candidate lost because people didn't like his policies; the company failed because it lacked focus. While such statements have a ring of truth, they may conceal more important causes. The student may have failed because she didn't know *how* to work hard; the candidate may have lost because voters were distracted by mischaracterizations and phony appeals; the company may have failed because it miscalculated the power of transnational competitors. In any organization, academic discipline, or public situation, the most valuable contributions often come from those who can look beyond the obvious causes and make a case for some lurking cause, some factor that others might overlook. Such contributions take inventive thinking and well-wrought arguments.

No Sex Please, We're Middle Class

CAMILLE PAGLIA

We may have a range of gut reactions to a product like Viagra for women. We might judge its worth, necessity, potential effectiveness. But Camille Paglia goes causal. She inspects the reasons for decreased female libido. Rather than think in medical terms, Paglia explores the material conditions, the everyday lives, of middle-class women. She builds up a forceful argument about the real causes—those that are beyond the reach of medical science.

Will women soon have a Viagra of their own? Although a Food and Drug Administration advisory panel recently rejected an application to market the drug flibanserin in the United States for women with low libido, it endorsed the potential benefits and urged further research. Several pharmaceutical companies are reported to be well along in the search for such a drug.

The implication is that a new pill, despite its unforeseen side effects, is necessary to cure the sexual malaise that appears to have sunk over the country. But to what extent do these complaints about sexual apathy reflect a medical reality, and how much do they actually emanate from the anxious, overachieving, white upper middle class?

In the 1950s, female "frigidity" was attributed to social conformism and religious puritanism. But since the sexual revolution of the 1960s, American society has become increasingly secular, with a media environment drenched in sex.

The real culprit, originating in the 19th century, is bourgeois propriety. As respectability became the central middle-class value, censorship and repression became the norm. Victorian prudery ended the humorous sexual candor of both men and women during the agrarian era, a ribaldry chronicled from Shakespeare's plays to the 18th-century novel. The priggish 1950s, which erased the liberated flappers of the Jazz Age from cultural memory, were simply a return to the norm.

Only the diffuse New Age movement, inspired by nature-keyed Asian practices, has preserved the radical vision of the modern sexual revolution. But concrete power resides in America's careerist technocracy, for which the elite schools, with their ideological view of gender as a social construct, are feeder cells.

In the discreet white-collar realm, men and women are interchangeable, doing the same, mind-based work. Physicality is suppressed; voices are lowered and gestures curtailed in sanitized office space. Men must neuter themselves, while ambitious women postpone procreation. Androgyny is bewitching in art, but in real life it can lead to stagnation and boredom, which no pill can cure.

Meanwhile, family life has put middle-class men in a bind; they are simply cogs in a domestic machine commanded by women. Contemporary moms have become virtuoso super-managers of a complex operation focused on the care and transport of children. But it's not so easy to snap over from Apollonian control to Dionysian delirium.

Nor are husbands offering much stimulation in the male display department: visually, American men remain perpetual boys, as shown by the bulky T-shirts, loose shorts and sneakers they wear from preschool through midlife. The sexes, which used to occupy intriguingly separate worlds, are suffering from over-familiarity, a curse of the mundane. There's no mystery left.

The elemental power of sexuality has also waned in American popular culture. Under the much-maligned studio production code, Hollywood made movies sizzling with flirtation and romance. But from the early '70s on, nudity was in, and steamy build-up was out. A generation of filmmakers lost the skill of sophisticated innuendo. The situation worsened in the '90s, when Hollywood pirated video games to turn women into cartoonishly pneumatic superheroines and sci-fi androids, fantasy figures without psychological complexity or the erotic needs of real women.

Furthermore, thanks to a bourgeois white culture that values efficient bodies over voluptuous ones, American actresses have desexualized themselves, confusing sterile athleticism with female power. Their current Pilates-honed look is taut and tense—a boy's thin limbs and narrow hips combined with amplified breasts. Contrast that with Latino and African-American taste, which runs toward the healthy silhouette of the bootylicious Beyoncé.

A class issue in sexual energy may be suggested by the apparent striking popularity of Victoria's Secret and its racy lingerie among multiracial lower-middle-class and working-class patrons, even in suburban shopping malls, which otherwise trend toward the white middle class. Country music, with its history in the rural South and Southwest, is still filled with blazingly raunchy scenarios, where the sexes remain dynamically polarized in the old-fashioned way.

On the other hand, rock music, once sexually pioneering, is in the dumps. Black rhythm and blues, born in the Mississippi Delta, was the driving force behind the great hard rock bands of the '60s, whose cover versions of blues songs were filled with electrifying sexual imagery. The Rolling Stones' hypnotic recording of Willie Dixon's "Little Red Rooster," with its titillating phallic exhibitionism, throbs and shimmers with sultry heat.

But with the huge commercial success of rock, the blues receded as a direct influence on young musicians, who simply imitated the white guitar gods without exploring their roots. Step by step, rock lost its visceral rawness and seductive sensuality. Big-ticket rock, with its well-heeled middle-class audience, is now all superego and no id.

In the 1980s, commercial music boasted a beguiling host of sexy pop chicks like Deborah Harry, Belinda Carlisle, Pat Benatar, and a charmingly ripe Madonna. Late Madonna, in contrast, went bourgeois and turned scrawny. Madonna's dance-track acolyte, Lady Gaga, with her compulsive overkill, is a high-concept fabrication without an ounce of genuine eroticism.

Pharmaceutical companies will never find the holy grail of a female Viagra—not in this culture driven and drained by middle-class values. Inhibitions are stubbornly internal. And lust is too fiery to be left to the pharmacist.

Analyzing Argument

1. What is Paglia's main claim? And how does her line of reasoning support that claim?

2. How is Paglia doing more than arguing cause? How is she making subtle judgments (claims of value) about the cause of women's decreased libido? Point to a particular passage where she condemns, even in subtle terms, the lives of middle-class women.

3. How do the allusions to rock music figure into Paglia's argument? What is their purpose? What point (premise) do they support?

4. How does Paglia engage opposition? To answer this, you might first decide on the opposition. What perspective or claims does Paglia seem to be opposing? How does she counter or concede or qualify?

5. What does Paglia mean by a "culture drained by middle-class values," and why is such a phrase important to her argument?

Disparities Demystified

PEDRO A. NOGUERA
AND ANTWI AKOM

The following argument first appeared in *The Nation*, a political magazine, in June of 2000. As Noguera and Akom explain, their argument emerged from an ongoing set of events: Standardized tests consistently revealed an achievement gap between ethnic groups, despite national programs to address this gap. In a time of heated debates about affirmative action and college enrollment policies, the authors try to cut through the argumentative fog and explain the causes behind the persistent achievement gap.

Once again national attention is focused on the racial gap in academic achievement, thanks in part to the high-stakes tests now in vogue across the nation. The appearance of this racial gap is by no means a new development. For years, African-American, Latino, and Native American students have lagged far behind their white and Asian peers on most standardized tests. The gap is also present in graduation and dropout rates, grades, and most other measures of student performance. The consistency of such patterns in almost every school and district in the country has the effect of reinforcing well-established assumptions regarding the relationship between race, academic ability, and intelligence.

More often than not, explanations for the achievement gap focus on deficiencies among parents and students. Dysfunctional families, lazy and unmotivated students, and the "culture of poverty" in inner-city neighborhoods are all frequently cited as causes of the gap. Left overlooked and unaddressed are the conditions under which children are educated and the quality of schools they attend. Since popular explanations often determine the types of remedies that are pursued, it is not surprising that the renewed attention directed toward the racial gap in academic achievement has not led to calls to address the real problem: inequality in education.

First, it's important to recognize that achievement test results reflect more than just racial disparities. An analysis of test scores also reveals a close correspondence between the scores children obtain and broader patterns of social inequality. With few exceptions, children of the affluent outperform children of the poor. Explaining why poor children of color perform comparatively less well in school is relatively easy: Consistently, such children are educated in schools that are woefully inadequate on most measures of quality and funding. This is particularly true in economically depressed urban areas, where bad schools are just one of many obstacles with which poor people must contend. Parents often perceive inner-city public schools as hopeless and unresponsive to their needs, prompting those who can to opt for private schools. Many have also actively sought alternatives through vouchers and various privatization schemes.

Yet what makes the racial gap uniquely paradoxical is the fact that the benefits typically associated with middle-class status don't accrue to African-American and, in many cases, Latino students. In many school districts, children of color from middle-class, college-educated families lag significantly behind white students in most achievement measures. The performance of these relatively privileged students has brought renewed attention to the relationship between race and educational performance. This is the issue that has prompted fifteen racially integrated, affluent school districts to form a consortium called the Minority Student Achievement Network. With the support of researchers assembled by the College Board, the network, comprising districts in such communities as White Plains, New York, Ann Arbor, Michigan, and Berkeley, California, seeks to understand the causes of the racial achievement gap and to devise solutions for reversing it.

Reprinted with permission from the June 15, 2000, issue of *The Nation*. For subscription information, call 1-800-333-8536. Portions of each week's *Nation* magazine can be accessed at http://www.thenation.com.

On the face of it, the potential for success in reducing the gap in these districts would seem high. All fifteen school districts in the network have a track record of sending large numbers of affluent white students to the best colleges and universities in the country. Additionally, unlike schools in high-poverty areas, funding is largely not a major obstacle to reform. Each district is located in an affluent community with a highly educated population known for its commitment to liberal political and social values. Yet in all fifteen districts there is a persistent, deeply ingrained sense that even this ambitious and well-intentioned effort will fail to alter student outcomes.

The pessimism in these districts, and in others that have launched efforts to overcome the racial achievement gap, must be understood in historical context. In many areas greater emphasis has been placed on how to achieve racial integration in schools than on how to serve the educational needs of a diverse student population. Even in the liberal districts in the Minority Student Achievement Network, some of which were among the first in the nation to voluntarily desegregate, the arrival of significant numbers of students of color in the late sixties and early seventies met with considerable opposition. From the very beginning, the presence of African-American children, especially those from low-income families, was perceived as an intrusion, and because the children were perceived as disadvantaged and deficient in comparison with their white schoolmates, educating them has always been regarded as a challenge. Since students of color were framed as "problems" and "challenges" from the very start, it is hardly surprising that they would continue to be treated as a problem requiring special intervention years later.

Moreover, educational practices often have the effect of favoring white students and hindering the educational opportunities of African-Americans and Latinos. This is particularly true when it comes to tracking and sorting students on the basis of

Cengage Learning

ability. A large body of research has shown that students of color are more likely to be excluded from classes for those deemed gifted in primary school, and from honors and Advanced Placement (AP) courses in high school. The Education Trust has shown, through its research on science and math education, that even students of color who meet the criteria for access to advanced courses are more likely to be turned away based on the recommendation of a counselor or teacher. They are also more likely to be placed in remedial and special-education classes, and to be subject to varying forms of school discipline.

A close examination of access to AP courses in California reveals how certain educational practices contribute to the maintenance of the racial achievement gap. Since the mid-eighties, the number of AP courses available to students at high schools in California has tripled. This increase has been attributed to a 1984 decision by the University of California to give greater weight to the grades earned by students who enroll in AP courses. However, AP courses are not uniformly available to students. At some inner-city and rural schools, few if any such courses are offered, while at private and affluent suburban schools, it is not uncommon for students to have access to fifteen or more AP courses. Moreover, our own research at Berkeley High School has shown that even when minority students are enrolled at schools that do offer a large number of AP courses, they are more likely to be actively discouraged from taking them by teachers and counselors.

Beyond the policies and practices that contribute to the achievement gap, a number of complex cultural factors are also important. Missing from the research and policy debates is an understanding of the ways in which children come to perceive the relationship between their racial identity and what they believe they can do academically. For many children, schools play an important role in shaping their racial identities because they are one of the few social settings where kids interact with people from different backgrounds. To the extent that a school's sorting processes disproportionately relegate black and brown children to spaces within schools that are perceived as negative and marginal, it is likely that children of color will come to perceive certain activities and courses as either suitable or off-limits for them.

In schools where few minority students are enrolled in AP courses, even students who meet the criteria for enrollment may refuse to take such courses out of concern that they will become isolated from their peers. The same is true for the school band, newspaper, debating team, or honor society. When these activities are seen as the domain of white students, nonwhite students are less likely to join. Peer groups play a large role in determining the academic orientation of students, not to mention their style of clothes, manner of speech, and future career aspirations. For middle-class African-American and Latino students, this means that despite receiving encouragement from their parents to do well in school, the peer group with whom they identify may push them in a different direction.

There are also cultural factors related to the attitudes and behaviors of students and the childrearing practices of parents that influence student performance. Several studies, for example, have indicated that middle-class African-American and Latino students spend less time on homework and study in less effective ways than middle-class white and Asian students. Also, despite the visibility of African-American students in sports such as football and basketball, research shows that these students are less likely to be involved in other extracurricular activities (which are shown to positively influence achievement), and in their responses to surveys they are more likely to emphasize the importance of being popular among friends than doing well in school.

Finally, images rooted in racial stereotypes that permeate American society limit the aspirations of African-American and Latino students. Despite the daunting odds of success in professional sports and entertainment, many young people of color believe they have a greater chance of becoming a highly paid athlete or hip-hop artist than an engineer, doctor, or software programmer. And with the rollback of affirmative action at colleges and universities, there is little doubt that students who possess entertainment value to universities, who can slam-dunk or score touchdowns, will be admitted regardless of their academic performance, even as aspiring doctors and lawyers are turned away.

When placed within the broader context of race relations in American society, the causes of the racial achievement gap appear less complex and mysterious; the gap is merely another reflection of the disparities in experience and life chances for individuals from different racial groups. In fact, given the history of racism in the United States and the ongoing reality of racial discrimination, it would be more surprising if an achievement gap did not exist. If the children of those who are most likely to be incarcerated, denied housing and employment, passed over for promotions, or harassed by the police did just as well in school as those whose lives are largely free of such encumbrances, that would truly be remarkable news.

Lest recognition of the racial achievement gap drive us into greater despair about the prospects for eliminating racial inequality in America, we must also recognize that to the extent change is possible, it is more likely to occur in education than in any other sector. This is because despite its faults, public education remains the most democratic and accessible institution in the country. In fact, in the post–welfare reform period, it is virtually all that remains of the social safety net for poor children.

Moreover, there are schools where no achievement gap exists, and there are students who achieve at high levels despite the incredible odds facing them. These bright spots of success reveal what might be possible if we lived in a society that truly valued children and was genuinely committed to equity and high-quality education for all.

Realizing such an ideal would require a comprehensive effort to reverse the effects of racial and economic inequality in the classroom, but it might begin with a few basic, though costly, measures: (1) significantly raising salaries so that teaching would be an attractive career for the best college graduates; (2) ensuring that poor children have access to well-qualified teachers from diverse racial and ethnic backgrounds, and to schools with adequate resources; and (3) providing parents in low-income areas with the means to exert greater influence over the schools their children attend. These are not radical measures. Indeed, they are already features of schools in most middle-class suburban communities. But bringing them to low-income areas would require states to address the huge disparities in funding that arise from the way schools are financed throughout the country. Since the electoral defeat of former New Jersey governor Jim Florio in 1993—the last major elected official to make a serious attempt to address such inequities—few have been willing to take on this critical issue.

Despite the defeats such measures have suffered in the courts and at the polls, politicians do recognize that the public is deeply concerned about improving the quality of education, and as they clamor to position themselves as friends and supporters of education we must demand that they address questions of equity. For those of us who believe that public education can serve as a source of hope and opportunity, the time is ripe for making our voices heard so this historic opportunity is not missed.

Analyzing Argument

1. What is Noguera and Akom's main claim?

2. How do Noguera and Akom address other perspectives and claims on this topic? Choose two passages in which they directly take on other views and describe their strategy. In the face of opposition, are they counterarguing, conceding, or qualifying their own claims?

3. How does Noguera and Akom's assertion relate to mainstream views on this topic? How do they address any differences or gaps between their assertions and mainstream views?

4. What is the most persuasive support strategy in the argument? Why? (Consider different appeals, different forms of evidence and examples.)

5. Examine paragraphs three through six. What is the line of reasoning in those paragraphs? Try to summarize each paragraph in a single sentence and then detect how the logic builds from paragraph to paragraph.

More Than Cherries

SAMANTHA TENGELITSCH

Samantha Tengelitsch lives in the top cherry-producing region in the United States. As an ecologically minded writer, mother, and community member, she wondered about the connection between agricultural chemicals and human health. After a local woman was diagnosed with cancer, Tengelitsch began researching that connection. She originally wrote this essay for her college English class. The following semester, the project won first place in the Michigan Liberal Arts Network for Development (LAND) essay contest. A year after researching and writing this project, Tengelitsch herself was diagnosed with non-Hodgkin's lymphoma. After intensive treatments, she is doing well.

> I must find a man who still loves the soil
> Walk by his side unseen, pour in his mind
> What I loved when I lived until he builds
> Sows, reaps, and covers these hill pastures here
> With sheep and cattle, mows the meadowland
> Grafts the old orchard again, makes it bear again
> Knowing that we are lost if the land does not yield.
>
> —*Jeanne Robert Foster*

Each year, an estimated 500,000 people pass through Traverse City, Michigan, for the annual National Cherry Festival. They come here for the pristine national lakeshore, to explore and hike the sand dunes, to taste wine at the local vineyards, and to see our native wildlife. They come for the serenity of a region tucked away in the northern Lower Peninsula, to escape the rigor of their daily lives. And in July they come for the world's largest celebration of cherries, the National Cherry Festival.

What began in the 1920s as a "Blessing of the Blossoms" has grown into a multimillion-dollar event. Last year alone, the National Cherry Festival is said to have contributed over 26 million dollars to the area's revenue (Rodgers). According to Susan Olson, Media Relations Director for the National Cherry Festival, over 40,000 pounds of cherries are sold during the week-long festival and local growers account for 75% of tart cherries grown around the world, just a few of many reasons Traverse City is known as the "Cherry Capital of the World." However, three of the last twelve festivals have not sold local products (Olson). The festival is held the first week of July, to coincide with 4th of July weekend and local cherries are not always ready in time. In those years when there is a delay in production, the cherries must be imported from Washington state and other regions.

While on the surface the cherry festival is about cherries, it was once about something more: the families who worked to produce these cherries and the community where the cherries are grown. Some feel our local festival has outgrown the area. A recent editorial that ran in the Traverse City *Record Eagle* points out: "[L]ots of people have advocated returning to a smaller, less grandiose effort that more closely reflects the festivals they remember. . . ." The festival no longer caters to local residents and growers, but instead focuses on larger crowds and higher revenues. And with this, the demand on farmers for cherries is great. This increase in demand has fostered an environment where farmers have grown dependent on chemical pesticides and fertilizers. And an increase in the use of pesticides and other toxic chemicals has left our once small farming community vulnerable to the dangers of exposure to these harsh chemicals.

It was the cherry festival that highlighted for me, not the pride we might feel in being well known for our cherry production, but the unrealistic expectations we have placed on local farmers. I began to look beyond revenue at the impacts of agriculture, and in particular cherry farming, on our region.

Last spring an article ran in the local paper about a young woman running for the prestigious title of National Cherry Queen. It told the story of Lauren Hemming, a twenty-year-old college student, who was raised on a Peninsula Township cherry farm and who was battling non-Hodgkin's lymphoma (a cancer of the lymphatic system) while running for the prestigious title. A photograph included with the article captured Lauren sitting cross-legged in a hammock in front of her home. It was spring and sun shown brightly. At the time of the photograph, Lauren was undergoing chemotherapy for the lymphoma and had lost her hair, but this in no way detracted from her beauty. Her story was inspirational and touched me as I'm sure it touched others.

Unfortunately, Lauren was not able to continue with her bid for Cherry Queen. Instead, she fought bravely to save her own life and the following winter died from the cancer, which had spread to her brain. I read her obituary and felt a deep sense of loss, not just for the young woman and her family, but also for our community. I questioned the origin of her illness and I began to wonder whether or not it was possible Lauren's illness might have been impacted by the use of chemical pesticides and fertilizers on and around her family farm. I decided to run a query of medical journals and websites to see whether a link existed between the lymphatic cancer and pesticides and was surprised at what I found.

According to the Pesticide Education Center website, non-Hodgkin's lymphoma is the cancer "most frequently associated with pesticide exposure and is now one of the most studied cancers in agriculture" (Moses). The Lymphoma Research Foundation says people exposed to chemicals such as pesticides or fertilizers are at higher risk for non-Hodgkin's lymphoma, or NHL. Over the last twenty-five years, the foundation reports, "new cases of NHL seen each year escalated almost 83%, among the highest increases of any cancer." Twenty years earlier, agricultural communities like ours saw a parallel increase in the use of chemical pesticides and fertilizers. This corresponding increase

caught the attention of researchers who began to question whether or not there existed a significant association between NHL and agricultural families.

A population-based, incidence case-control study which evaluated pesticide product use and the risk of non-Hodgkin's lymphoma in women addresses this correlation: "NHL has received research attention because the recent rapid increase in its incidence parallels an exponential growth in pesticide use with a few decades of lag" (Kato et al.). Researchers investigated other "high-risk" groups as well and found some correlation between these groups and NHL, but the most significant association was found in agricultural families. As one study reports:

> With increasing cumulative number of hours exposed to pesticides at these jobs other than farming, there was a marginal increasing trend in risk of NHL. When farming and other jobs associated with pesticide exposure were combined, the total duration at any of these jobs was significantly positively associated with the risk of NHL (Kato et al.).

While pesticides sold in the United States must first be registered with the Environmental Protection Agency (EPA) and additionally in the states where they are being distributed for use, an EPA label does not in any way imply the product is safe for human exposure. The label discloses vital information about how the user might limit his or her exposure to the chemicals, directions for physicians treating people who have had significant exposure, and warnings of the environmental impact of each product. All pesticides must be labeled for legal sale disclosing the level of toxicity for humans (Smith), but the EPA does not require that pesticide manufacturers list the re-entry periods, or the amount of time that must pass before people can re-enter a treated area (Rindels).

Children, as a result, may be more vulnerable to exposure as they may unwittingly enter a treated

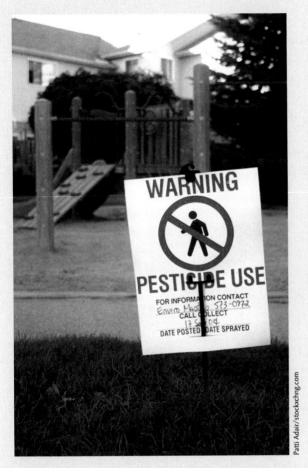

Patti Adair/stockxchng.com

"Metabolites of organophosphates pesticides used only in agriculture were detectable in the urine of two out of every three children of agricultural workers and in four out of every ten children who simply live in an agricultural region."

The Hemmings live in the heart of cherry country, Peninsula Township. The township was home to the region's first cherry farm one hundred and fifty years earlier, but with an increase in demand for cherries, farming techniques have changed since then. The land is weakening with this increase in demand and nutrients must be supplemented with chemical fertilizers. Pests are not controlled, but rather eliminated with insecticides that are harmful to people and to the environment. And while the orchard is an enticing place in the springtime for children, a time when the trees are in bloom and when workers are getting ready for the upcoming summer harvest, it can also present danger of exposure to these toxic compounds. Children playing outside the orchards may still be exposed to the residue of pesticides that may have drifted into their play area.

Organophosphates may vary in toxicity relative to exposure, but children exposed to organophosphates are at a particularly high risk as their livers are immature and unable to detoxify the poisonous compounds. Dr. Michael Collins of the Grand Traverse Health Department explains: "Since the child's liver will [detoxify] less effectively than an adult's, the result is that the chemical will stay in the body, in unaltered form, for a longer time than would be true for an adult. Thus whatever type of damage the chemical may do, it has more opportunity to do it." Most testing done today assesses the risk for adults, so little is known about long-term pesticide exposure in children.

In addition to chemical pesticides, orchards have become increasingly reliant on chemical fertilizers. These chemical fertilizers combined with run-off wastes from livestock and septic systems all contribute to higher levels of nitrogen in the

area too early or because the residue of sprays may be present on the clothing or boots of family members. This factor may make children one of the most pesticide-exposed subgroups in the United States ("Trouble"). The National Institutes of Health (NIH), a government agency, conducted a study to evaluate risk factors for cancer in children exposed to pesticides. They released their findings last year, cautioning: "Identification of excess lymphoma risk suggests that farm exposures including pesticides may play a role in the etiology of childhood cancers" (Flower).

Organophosphates are found in pesticides commonly used by farmers today (Elsner). The Natural Resources Defense Council website reports:

ground. Nitrogen converts into nitrates, which pass through our permeable soil into the water table. An executive summary posted on the EPA website addressing nitrate pollution in groundwater reveals, "EPA found that nitrate is the most widespread agricultural contaminant in drinking water wells, and estimates that 4.5 million people are exposed to elevated nitrate levels from drinking water wells" ("Consumer Factsheet").

While some nitrates are naturally occurring and may be harmless, elevated levels may make people sick. As Leah Halfon writes, "Numerous epidemiological studies have shown higher nitrate concentrations to be associated with hyperthyroidism, non-Hodgkin's lymphoma, reproductive and developmental disorders, gastric cancer, neuropathy, and morbidity and mortality due to several other cancers."

Nitrate levels that exceed the United States Environmental Protection Agency's 10 milligrams per liter may result in illness ("Consumer Factsheet"). Recently, a study was released from the Department of Environmental Quality (DEQ) to the (Grand Traverse) County Health Department that contained historical nitrate data for Grand Traverse County taken from between 1983 and 2003. According to Tom Buss, head of the Environmental Health Division for Grand Traverse County, "Our county equalization department printed a map of the county showing areas of nitrates in 'ranges.' The map does show the highest concentrations of nitrates in Peninsula Township, which has been heavily agricultural throughout the years." In more than one area on the peninsula, nitrate levels not only reached the EPA's warning level of 10 milligrams per liter, but in multiple areas levels exceeded 20 mg/L.

Non-Hodgkin's lymphoma is one of many adverse health conditions associated with exposure to dangerous compounds like the ones mentioned previously. Various forms of cancer, neurological disorders, reproductive problems, birth defects,

and spontaneous abortions have all been linked to long-term pesticide exposure (Moses) and elevated nitrate levels in groundwater. I chose to research non-Hodgkin's lymphoma and its link to agriculture because of a photograph of a Cherry Festival contestant; a young woman who grew up on a cherry farm in the heart of cherry country who died last winter from cancer. Did Lauren Hemming die from high nitrate levels or pesticide exposure in her youth? It is impossible for me to say with any certainty. Yet her story was the catalyst for my research; it inspired me to look further and in doing so, I discovered the true irony of her death.

A new look at the local festival that has "blossomed" into a multimillion-dollar mega-event complete with corporate sponsors will reveal the real problem. We have created a large demand on local growers to produce a flawless product at a relatively low cost to consumers. In doing so, we have overused the land and weakened our soil and, in trying to supplement nutrients naturally found in healthy soil, we have poisoned our water and indirectly we may be poisoning ourselves.

Bill McKibben, in his book *The Age of Missing Information*, writes that while it is said we are living in the Information Age, "we also live at a moment of deep ignorance, when vital knowledge that humans have always possessed about who we are and where we live seems beyond our reach. An Unenlightenment" (9). This "unenlightenment" has spilled over into our agricultural practices. Farms today are so heavily reliant on chemical pesticides and fertilizers that a basic knowledge of farming techniques comes second to a good understanding of the periodic table. Sarcasm aside, farmers today probably know less about traditional farming methods than they did a century ago. And that ignorance has come at a great cost to our health and well-being.

Yet, all hope is not lost. Many farmers are aware of the negative impact that chemical pesticides and fertilizers have had and will have on our environment and, with help from the federal government, are moving to techniques that reduce the usage of these chemicals, according to the Natural Resources Conservation Service website. These techniques include reducing human exposure through groundwater contamination by building Agrichemical Containment Facilities, known as ACFs, designed with an impervious floor and a sump pump to collect run-off. While the use of ACFs is not required, they are growing in popularity among local growers.

I spoke with Tom Adams of the National Resources Defense Council office in Traverse City, who said there is a "huge interest in moving from organophosphates to softer chemicals or pesticides." EQIP aids farmers in identifying and targeting specific pests present in their orchards, resulting in the use of more timely, specific pesticide applications. Some of the newer sprayers even utilize "smart spray" technology, in which the sprayers detect the branches of fruit trees and spray only within a certain distance of the tree, reducing pesticide "drift" to other parts of the orchard. This results in fewer contaminants making their way into our drinking water.

A few farmers in the Grand Traverse region have done away with chemical pesticides altogether. Alan and Cheryl Kobernik own and operate North Star Organics, one of the region's first organic cherry farms. The Koberniks were once conventional farmers who utilized the same farming techniques other area farmers have employed over the last half-century, but the farm was not economically viable.

Their first motivation to making the switch to organic farming practices, they admit, was money. On forty acres, it was difficult for the Koberniks to compete with so many area farms already producing sweet and tart cherries. Over time, however, their attitude toward organic growing has shifted. They have seen their land in the last seven years flourish. In a phone interview, Cheryl expressed her enthusiasm about the change in the soil. She explained

that in place of traditional herbicides used to keep the weeds at bay between trees, they now use mulch and shredded newspaper. In the early days of their transition, the ground was dead—the result of years of poisons and chemical fertilizers. But today the ground is alive with microorganisms that now devour this material in the course of a few days. These microorganisms are vital to the sustainability of the orchard. They are part of a food chain, or a nutrient cycle that exists normally uninhibited in nature. With the orchard chemical-free, Cheryl's children can now lie in the grass between rows, and in fun she warns them not to stay in the orchard too long, or the ground may absorb them as well.

American poet Wendell Berry wrote, "To cherish what remains of the Earth and to foster its renewal is our only legitimate hope of survival." This community is about something more than cherries. Farmers today are rethinking what goes into producing their product. A handful, like the Koberniks, have traded pesticides for peace of mind and gone organic. Others are participating in government subsidies to reduce their dependence on toxic chemicals. And in recent years, efforts like Community Supported Agriculture (CSA) have grown in popularity among local farmers.

A CSA connects farmers with the public, who pay a membership fee in exchange for produce. Some CSAs employ community members and encourage a lasting relationship between the farm and the consumer. CSAs may be one way to reconnect community members with the farmers who sustain them.

I asked Duke Elsner of the MSU Extension Office in Traverse City whether or not he believed farmers were making a switch to less dangerous pesticides because they care and want to or because of EPA regulations banning the more dangerous chemicals. He said he thought it was a mix of both. For some, it's about production and profit to preserve the farm. For others, who look beyond the boundaries of their own farmland, it's about farming today, tomorrow and well into the future; a preservation of thought that the land is not something we own, but rather something we are borrowing from the future.

Works Cited

Berry, Wendell. *Gift of Good Land.* New York: North Point, 1982. Print.

Flower, Kori, et al. "Cancer Risk and Parental Pesticide Application in Children of Agriculture Health Study Participants." *Environmental Health Perspectives* 112.5 (2004): 631–35. *USA.gov.* Web. 23 Feb. 2005.

Halton, Leah. "Ground Water." *Virginia Environmental Quality Index.* Center for Environmental Studies, Virginia Commonwealth U, 2000. Web. 7 Mar. 2005.

Kato, Ikuko, et al. "Pesticide Product Use and Risk of Non-Hodgkin Lymphoma in Women." *Environmental Health Perspectives* 112.13 (2004): 1275–81. *USA.gov.* Web. 4 Apr. 2005.

McKibben, Bill. *Age of Missing Information.* New York: Penguin, 1993. Print.

Moses, Marion. "Cancer in Adults and Pesticide Exposure." *Pesticide Education Center.* Pesticide Educ. Center, Nov. 2002. Web. 21 Feb. 2005.

Quintana, Penelope, et al. "Adipose Tissue Levels of Organochlorine Pesticides and Polychlorinated Biphenyls and Risk of Non-Hodgkin's Lymphoma." *Environmental Health Perspectives* 112.18 (2004): 854–61. *USA.gov.* Web. 4 Apr. 2005.

Rindels, Sherry. "Understanding Pesticides." *Integrated Pest Management at Iowa State University.* Dept. of Horticulture, Iowa State U, 17 June 1997. Web. 7 Mar. 2005.

Rogers, W. Bruce. "Festival Is Vital to Community." *Record-Eagle.* Community Newspaper Holdings, 27 Feb. 2005. Web. 8 Mar. 2005.

Smith, William. "Pesticide Labels." *Pesticide Management Education Program.* Pesticide Management Educ. Program, Cornell U, 10 Dec. 2004. Web. 7 Mar. 2005.

"Trouble on the Farm." *National Resources Defense Council.* Natl. Resources Defense Council, n.d. Web. 4 Feb. 2005.

United States. Dept. of Agriculture. Natural Resources Conservation Service. *Environmental Quality Incentives Program.* N.d. *Natural Resources Conservation Service.* Web. 25 Mar. 2005.

———. Environmental Protection Agency. "Consumer Factsheet on: Nitrates/Nitrites." *Ground Water and Drinking Water.* 14 Feb. 2005. *Environmental Protection Agency.* Web. 7 Mar. 2005.

———.———. "Feedlots Point Source Category Study: Preliminary Data Summary." *Effluent Guidelines.* 31 Dec. 1998. *Environmental Protection Agency.* Web. 15 Mar. 2005.

Analyzing Argument

1. Summarize the series of causes in Tengelitsch's argument.

2. Describe the use of appeals in the essay. Point out particular passages in which Tengelitsch relies on logic, value, character, emotion, or need.

3. How does the author's presence (the "I") function in this argument? While the "I" could have been omitted from the essay, Tengelitsch includes it at key points. What is the effect?

4. Compared to other essays in this chapter, Tengelitsch's topic seems uncommon. Tengelitsch does not have to contend directly with many opposing claims. Nevertheless, she does have to consider mainstream values and assumptions about farming, chemicals, and cancer. Describe how she deals with common ways of thinking about these issues. How do common values and assumptions figure into her argument?

5. What is the most persuasive passage in this argument? Why?

All for a Virtual Cause: The Reasons Behind MMORPG Success

J. NOEL TRAPP

J. Noel Trapp, a poet and barista, became an online gamer in his late 20s. Shortly after discovering City of Heroes, he realized the immense popularity and lurking appeal of the game. He asked an important question: *Why is this game such a huge success?* He developed the following argument by using the prompts in this chapter. He goes beyond more obvious reasons (that the game itself is exciting, that the graphics pull people in, and so on) and discovers a set of causes in the real world—the one outside of virtual reality.

In the 1970s, we played Pong where one pixilated ball was bounced between two bars. In the 1980s, we evolved into Atari. We one-upped with Mario and the generation of Nintendo. By the mid 1990s, gaming consoles such as Nintendo and Sega had become a strong cultural component of middle-class America. Recently, the gaming world leapt ahead, leaving the isolated, individual Nintendo player a century behind. Rather than bonk a ball back and forth or run perpetually across the screen dodging barrels and angry pixilated snakes, gamers now live out elaborate, collective schemes. The advent and growth of MMORPGs (Massive Multiplayer Online Role-Playing Games) has drastically shaped the landscape of the gaming world, and reshaped our cultural roles within such a world. Though the initial success of these games was founded on revolutionary technological qualities, something else is behind their continued and extraordinary success. Something beyond the technological wonders of the games themselves drives thousands of players to their computers and into virtual space.

> The cultural allusions help place the reader within the world of gaming. And they make MMORPGs part of a history rather than an isolated phenomenon.

> Mentions a more obvious cause but suggests a lurking, more hidden, cause.

Psychologically, the impacts and effects of video games have been quite easy to observe. In the original role-playing games of the late 1990s, people were allowed into a virtual realm, no longer as spectators, but as active participants making decisions in realities they could not achieve (or were not possible) in the physical world around them. Fantasy, imagination, and escapist tendencies were all fueled by the increasing number of games, whether a player was the star quarterback of a famous football team, or a mage fighting off the demons of some unknown underworld. This diversity was one cause of initial successes, while another rested on better technologies which allowed these alternate video-based realities to become more lifelike, colorful, and revolve around new engines, which would support worldly (and otherworldly) physics and animations.

> Explains one cause of the early fantasy games' success.

Gamers could escape much more completely into their fantasies, immersed by better graphics, audio, and options among games. Yet, for all the media hype and increasing number, the gamers were still, essentially, isolated in their individual fantasies, communicating with only the artificial intelligence (A.I.) of the game, which, despite great strides, always became predictable.

The updates and continuing improvements of the Internet and wider bandwidths allowed the video game industry an entirely new frontier. Until fast enough access to centralized gaming servers, computer games themselves were no different than video games; both were escapist hobbies allowing the user to interact only with A.I. Once fast and sophisticated enough, centralized gaming servers allowed gamers to face each other in a digital world, where they would be able to interact with both A.I. and H.I. (human intelligence). The results were fantastic. By allowing users the freedoms found in the past along with the infinite new number of variables supplied by other human players, the gaming industry flourished in its new online environment, and the gamers, in turn, began to reap more rewards beyond mere escapism.

Currently, one of the most successful MMORPGs on the market is City of Heroes, by NCsoft. On its website, the company invites users to "live the story" in an "online world that's home to an entire universe of heroes, where you and thousands of other players take on the roles of super-powered heroes." The question of why a user may want to do such a thing is answered with the simple statement: "You are a hero." With hundreds of character options and an advanced graphics component, City of Heroes has won numerous awards in its several years on the market. Players can form supergroups with other members, fight side by side or against each other, hunt for badges (a hobby within a hobby), or simply use the game as a glorified chat room for casual or serious discussion. In addition to simple escapism, this online environment allows people to feel real senses of accomplishment, through feats in the game, in both their own eyes and the eyes of their peers.

In their non-virtual lives, many players are involved in business and the military. They are often separated from loved ones or just insulated within their own busy-ness. Other players are stricken with one illness or another that makes "normal" face-to-face interactions difficult. But in their virtual lives, where no one is ever ill, where everyone has more than human strengths, players share collective achievements, victories, and struggles.

More and more people are finding themselves in this collective space, where they fulfill basic psychological needs. The Hamidon Raid, in City of Heroes, illustrates the desire for collective achievement. The

---

Sidebar annotations:

Explains a drawback to those early games: isolation.

The detailed analysis of the gaming experience may be the best support strategy in this argument.

Creates a careful line of reasoning from previous paragraphs: from escapism to something more . . . .

Now we get a sense of that lurking cause—summed up in this statement.

The line of reasoning is reinforced: The success of MMORPGs is not about mere escapism but a more complex social need.

Another step in the line of reasoning: many players' non-virtual lives keep them from collective action.

"Collective achievement" is tied to the success of the games.

raid is an event scheduled by players, in which over eighty heroes battle a large beast, simply for the satisfaction of beating it together, as well as the game rewards that come with it. Teams are drawn up simply to heal, others to do damage, while a primary "targeter" hero calls out where everyone needs to aim. It is an exercise in teamwork, orchestrated and carried out by huge groups—sometimes over 100 different players simultaneously. The accomplishment and gratification in this case is immediate and shared.

In addition to such collective gaming moments, relationships can develop online, resulting in at least one publicly observed virtual wedding, in which two people were wedded by an actual preacher in a digital world. Other events are much more somber, such as when a player died in real life, and a memorial service was held in a central location in the game. The more active the player, the higher the social and emotional stakes, and simple actions result in all the normal psychological ways: heartbreak, joy, grief, and so on. From friendships to funerals, badges to high-level heroes, the impacts of this online community are far reaching and have implications in the real world as well as the digital one.

The aims of the gaming industry to entice people into using their product have never been so successful as with MMORPGs such as City of Heroes. In addition to the initial forty-dollar cost of the game, users pay a monthly subscription fee of fifteen dollars per account. Some of the avid gamers may hold up to ten accounts at a time in order to have room to create more and more heroes on any particular server. This means that every year, single players are spending at least $180 in subscription fees alone for a single account, and in return, they are given access to a world where their superhuman characteristics can be employed, their valor unleashed, and their needs for gratification, interaction, and accomplishment sated by an invented reality that often supersedes the reality of the actual physical world around them.

Without the incredible and increasing depersonalization of the workplace, the decentralization and dismissal of local communities, such games may not enjoy the kind of success that they have, and remain relegated to the fringes of an industry. However, they have become a financial staple of the gaming industry, as well as a social staple for the lives of many of their players. Regardless of the state of the actual physical world a player experiences, the virtual world meets some basic psychological needs: for intense social interaction, visible and collective accomplishment, and the recognition of individual accomplishment.

MMORPGs have allowed an incredible avenue for such needs to be fulfilled, not necessarily in the healthiest of fashions, but an outlet nonetheless. These games, which once relied solely on better technology and

Specific details of the game reinforce the point about collectivity and belonging.

Examples of deeper human connections among the gamers further reinforce the point.

Articulates all the qualities (human needs) associated with MMORPG success.

Reinforces the driving force behind the games' success.

The conclusion briefly encapsulates the line of reasoning in the argument (and the evolution of the games).

inventive storylines, have become more and more reliant on the social aspects of gaming to ensure their continued success. Having been in existence for at least a decade, the continued success of MMORPGs rests on their rhetoric more than their creativity—on their appeals to fundamental psychology. By offering a virtual world in which a true community can exist, they offer more than a virtual challenge, but rather a full ensemble of potentially sated human needs.

Work Cited

City of Heroes. NCsoft, 28 Apr. 2004. Web. 16 Mar. 2006.

Analyzing Argument

1. What is behind MMORPGs' success? Point out particular passages in Trapp's argument that support your answer.

2. What is the most persuasive support for Trapp's argument? Consider specific appeals, examples, and forms of evidence.

3. Try to summarize Trapp's line of reasoning. What premises must we believe before we accept his claim about the cause of MMORPGs' success?

4. In his conclusion, Trapp argues, "Having been in existence for at least a decade, the continued success of MMORPGs rests on their rhetoric more than their creativity. . . ." How does this distinction (rhetoric versus creativity) support Trapp's overall argument about the causes of MMORPGs' success?

5. Toward the end of his essay, Trapp argues, "Without the incredible and increasing depersonalization of the workplace, the decentralization and dismissal of local communities, such games may not enjoy the kind of success that they have, and remain relegated to the fringes of an industry." How does this point support his argument?

Protesters in Pakistan Chant Anti-American Slogans during a Protest in Islamabad, September 17, 2001.

1. How is this image a counterargument?

2. How is this image an argument about cause?

Exploring for Topics

Why do people argue about causes? Why not simply react or respond to each situation as it arises? Why all the debate? Most public situations worth responding to (from school shootings to forest fires, from grade inflation to political upheaval) are worth careful analysis. History shows that responding to the wrong cause is often more dangerous than not responding at all. So discovering the real cause of a phenomenon—and convincing others of that cause—is often vital.

Good writers often recognize a rhetorical need: Something is misunderstood; something has happened and needs careful analysis; people keep forwarding the wrong set of causes and someone needs to help clarify the situation. Or perhaps some phenomenon keeps occurring despite attempts to address it. For instance, school violence continues to escalate despite "zero tolerance" policies. In this case, a writer may seek to get beyond the conventional responses—the public hand-wringing and political noise. Good writers see an intellectual gap that needs to be filled with new insights. They seek out those topics that seem incomplete, ignored, or entirely misunderstood. As you search for possible topics, consider the following situations:

- **A local event or situation:** Something has happened, and the cause needs to be figured out: Why did the community vote down the recent school levy? Why are there still deep racial divisions between the downtown neighborhoods and the city police force?
- **A particular behavior or trend in college life:** What are the real reasons that students drop out of classes after the semester has begun? Why do students binge drink? What is the cause of procrastination? (Why don't students start their English assignments sooner?!)
- **A particular political phenomenon:** What's behind the upswing in religiously motivated voters? What caused the Tea Party movement? Why didn't it happen ten years earlier?
- **A social phenomenon:** Despite all the public outcries and open forums, why do school shootings continue? What's the real cause behind teenage marijuana use? Despite some attempts to address gender disparity, why do more males than females go into the sciences?

- **A popular culture phenomenon:** Despite a mountain of arguments against super-thin models, why do models continue to resemble wire hangers? Why the huge success of food-related television shows? Why the success of online video games? Why isn't PBS more popular? If PCs are so prone to viruses, why has Mac not converted more PC users? Despite all the arguments against Walmart, Best Buy, and other big box stores, why do shoppers continue to support them at the expense of smaller, local stores?
- **A situation in your academic discipline or career field:** Consider major changes in your discipline or career field. What has caused recent layoffs or upswings in employment?

Remember that any phenomenon—whether a social event, a cultural trend, or a physical occurrence—has many possible causes. Beyond the most obvious cause are a number of situational or environmental factors that give rise to the phenomenon. For instance, if a writer is researching school violence and trying to understand the cause of recent shootings across the country, she might begin by listing all the possible factors:

- **Personal:** The perpetrators of school shootings often carry around feelings of isolation, loneliness, fear, anxiety.
- **Social:** School violence often comes as a result of bullying. Weaker students feel victimized and long to lash out. In high school, the popular cliques learn to perform hostile actions toward or publicly humiliate those who don't fit the popularized norm. And college culture can be lonely and alienating.
- **Cultural:** Movies, video games, and prime-time television dramas feature and glorify violence. A long list of prime-time, crime-based dramas make a consistent point about shooting, blasting, or forcing your way to a victorious conclusion. That's the thesis of every single night on television.
- **Political:** War. We cannot deny the big political message of our day: Getting things done in the world requires a gun. If our politicians make that point on a daily basis—if they constantly justify the need to shoot other people—we have to acknowledge the presence of that logic in kids' lives.

Some of these factors are more abstract or indirect than others. Bullying, for instance, is more direct, more immediate than the political climate. Still, at this early phase, a writer benefits from such expansive and open thinking. Even if she doesn't argue for all of these causes, she has broadened her understanding of the situation.

Use the following invention questions to explore the less obvious causes of your topic:

▶ What are the most direct causes?

▶ What economic or business conditions may have figured in?

▶ What attitudes, fears, or values may have initiated it or indirectly supported it?

▶ What people, organizations, or institutions were directly or indirectly involved?

▶ Might some basic human need or fundamental physical principle have played a part?

Invention Workshop

In a small group, share topic ideas and then walk through the following steps:

1. Apply at least three of the preceding invention questions to each topic. Focus on one topic at a time and collectively try to dig up a range of causal factors for each topic—not simply the obvious physical factors but also the quieter cultural factors.

2. Before moving to the next writer's topic, decide what factors the writer might explore through secondary research. What theories, facts, or statistics might the writer want to know?

3. If the writer should conduct secondary research for the topic, suggest a particular type of source; for example, academic journals, popular magazines, a particular government website. (See more about secondary research on pages 374–383, and web searches on page 383.)

➤ Deeply Rooted Cause or Just an Excuse?

In popular culture, good analysis sometimes is short-circuited by the simplistic statement, "That sounds like an excuse!" People might stop thinking about causes because they imagine that discovering a deeply rooted cause somehow excuses behavior. For example, someone might say, "Blaming prime-time television for school shootings excuses the act." However, rigorous analysis of bad behavior doesn't mean an acceptance of that behavior. Academic writers can try to discover why something happens, beyond the quick reflexes of popular culture. Discovering a deeply rooted cause does not justify or excuse an act or behavior. It does, however, help us to understand why things happen.

Inventing a Claim

Some topics are highly debated: Some people argue X while others argue Y, and both groups try to disprove the other. For example, some high school administrators, parent groups, and school boards blame pop culture influences (like rock music, movies, Goth apparel, unconventional hairstyles) for school shootings. To address these supposed causes, they have enacted "no tolerance" policies that disallow for any visible signs of tension in the student body. Others argue that music and fashion, no matter what type, do not contribute to school shootings. Instead, they claim that teens feel increasingly isolated in their everyday lives— shunned by mainstream high school culture, isolated from neighbors, distanced from their own families. If a writer were researching this topic, she would likely find heated debates. These debates, then, are part of her rhetorical situation. They impact what she will claim—what she will argue.

Other topics are not so heated. But less heated topics are not less interesting. In fact, a topic that has not already been over-analyzed, mis-analyzed, and screamed to death can be a writer's opportunity. The argument may focus on revealing a new insight about a cause, as if to say, "I bet no one realized the cause of this!" Either way, it is essential to understand what others have said or not even imagined about your topic.

What Do Others Claim?

▶ What main causes do other writers put forward?

▶ What causes have other writers not considered?

▶ If you have a particular source, what does the author assume (but not necessarily state) about the topic?

What Do I Claim?

▶ How do my assumptions differ from or overlap with others'?

▶ What cause or set of causes do I think is most critical?

Answers to these questions might shed light on the way people think about your topic—which can make all the difference in determining an argumentative strategy. Because any argument exists within a context of public opinion, because it rests up against a landscape of other positions and insights, good arguers plan how they will engage those other positions and insights.

As you consider your topic and all the possible causes, look back over your notes, especially at your responses to the invention questions, and generate a focused claim. Your project might do one of the following:

Claim a Single Cause Almost every phenomenon has many preconditions—many physical, cultural, political, or natural factors that play an indirect part. But writers may still want to clear the air of those preconditions and point to a single cause:

- The levy failed because the town's population is aging and those who don't have children at home feel no attachment to the schools.
- Students procrastinate because the traditional school assignment has taught them to.

The benefit of the single-cause claim is that the argument gains focus and intensity. The difficulty, however, is that a writer must hold that particular factor well above the list of preconditions. The writer must make a clear and strong connection between that one factor and the phenomenon itself—and explain why other factors are inconsequential.

Claim Multiple Causes Some arguments have too many influencing factors to argue for only one. Claiming that various factors figure into a phenomenon is not necessarily copping out. Pointing to several causes, instead of one, can make for a sophisticated argument:

- More voters are religiously motivated because of several recent religious-themed movies and political rhetoric that frames all cultural issues in Judeo-Christian metaphors.
- Teenagers smoke marijuana because it fits into their socioeconomic structure: it's relatively cheap, easy to obtain, and easy to transport.

The benefit of the multiple-causes claim is that the argument may gain some interesting layers and sophistication. The danger is that the argument could lose intensity and could even become a laundry list of factors. In short, it could turn into no argument at all. To offset this danger, consider forming a counterargument (pages 65–67).

Transcend Common Wisdom Most topics have a common understanding or a widely held view. People generally don't question or argue about why kids hate homework, why people like dogs, why Americans are getting fatter. But the lack of debate doesn't mean lack of opportunity—just the opposite. An uninspected topic can make for the most exciting argument because the writer can open up new logic:

- The loathing for homework comes from popular and wrong-headed notions about *home,* not from the general dislike of *work.*
- People want dogs not for companionship but for routine. Since dogs are highly routinized creatures, they provide flesh-and-blood regularity to increasingly chaotic lifestyles.

These two examples show how a writer can dig up common wisdom and then assert a contrary point. The benefit of an uncommon or anti-conventional claim is that the argument has a built-in sense of revelation: it invites the readers (and writer!) to rethink an issue from the start. The difficulty is that the writer is pretty much on his or her own and must build an argument from unlikely sources and support. (But—as with most writing projects—the difficulty also becomes an opportunity.)

More Sample Claims

Local Situations

- The growth and development issues affecting Crawford City are not the fault of the city manager, but of individual citizens vying for their own financial gain.
- Racial tension in the city lingers because no public official has acknowledged the string of aggressive police actions in recent years.

College Trends or Situations

- The increasing social imperative to attend college is diminishing the intensity of the college experience.
- While many students find that their religious faith is challenged in college, coursework in rhetoric can help students further develop their faith by understanding the ways in which ancient and modern religious texts communicate profound spiritual ideas.

Political Phenomena

- Presidential candidates are not elected by voters on Election Day, but by financial contributors more than a year before Election Day.
- Exaggerated claims from both the right and left wing dissuade young voters from engaging in politics.
- Once the government has lost the support of the people, the war is ultimately lost as well.

Social Phenomena

- Car insurance makes people drive recklessly.
- Many Americans struggle financially not because of poor education or low income but because financial institutions have loaned them money they cannot afford to pay back.
- While many factors, such as international crises and weather events, contribute to the increase in gasoline prices, the underlying factor is Americans' continual and excessive use of gasoline.
- People consider traditional news sources to be either liberal or conservative based not simply on the bias of the news source but on their own biases.
- Focusing on personal satisfaction over community good makes people less, not more, individualistic because they are less able to resist the dominant trends marketed to them by impersonal corporations.

Professional or Career Trends

- The influx of women into the medical field has helped to shift focus onto patients' understanding of their own health.
- More and more companies are shifting to virtual offices because technology continues to make working off-site easier and more economical.

Activities

1. In groups, narrow and intensify the following broad claims:
   - Ignorance is the cause of racism.
   - Lack of governmental planning led to the Hurricane Katrina disaster.
   - School dropout rates increase because of poverty.
   - Higher grades lead to better jobs.

   Share your revised claims with the class, and then discuss exactly how your group proceeded through the task. That is, what phrases or words did you target as you approached the claims?

2. In small groups, choose one claim from this sample list, and describe the opposing positions that the writer would have to address in an argument.

Inventing Support

Line of Reasoning When developing a causal argument, writers need to make a clear connection between potential causes and their effects, especially if those factors are indirectly related. In her argument, Samantha Tengelitsch sets up a complex, but tightly knitted, line of causes:

> While on the surface the cherry festival is about cherries, it was once about something more: the families who worked to produce these cherries and the community where the cherries are grown. Some feel our local festival has outgrown the area. A recent editorial that ran in the Traverse City *Record Eagle* points out: "[L]ots of people have advocated returning to a smaller, less grandiose effort that more closely reflects the festivals they remember. . . ." The festival no longer caters to local residents and growers, but instead focuses on larger crowds and higher revenues. And with this, the demand on farmers for cherries is great. This increase in demand has fostered an environment where farmers have grown dependent on chemical pesticides and fertilizers. And an increase in the use of pesticides and other toxic chemicals has left our once small farming community vulnerable to the dangers of exposure to these harsh chemicals.

After Tengelitsch links the heavy demand for cherries to a change in farming strategies, she links particular pesticides and fertilizers to a deadly form of cancer. Her line of reasoning, which takes up most of her essay, develops according to these steps:

- Over the years, the cherry festival has created a higher demand for cherries.
- That demand has prompted heavy use of dangerous pesticides and fertilizers.
- Those chemicals significantly increase the risk of cancer, especially in children.
- Because a young woman grew up in this area of heavy chemical use, she developed non-Hodgkin's lymphoma.

Tengelitsch devotes several paragraphs to the third step (the connection between chemicals and the risk of cancer). Because it is the most unexpected, and most important, premise of her argument, she carefully builds up evidence (statistics and scientific authorities) to support it.

Local Authorities We should not assume authorities must be distant, published voices that we find on a database or in a book. Often, the most authoritative voices live in our own communities—those who are deeply involved with an issue. Tengelitsch strategically integrates insights from local farmers:

> In a phone interview, Cheryl expressed her enthusiasm about the change in the soil. She explained that in place of traditional herbicides used to keep the weeds at bay between trees, they now use mulch and shredded newspaper. In the early days of their transition, the ground was dead—the result of years of poisons and chemical fertilizers. But today the ground is alive with microorganisms that now devour this material in the course of a few days.

Hidden Layers Academic readers value new understanding. They want to be given a new perspective. Therefore, successful academic writers try to reveal the unseen layers of a topic. They go beneath the surface or most direct and obvious points. Camille Paglia's entire argument emerges from an insight about the hidden layers of the topic. If the effect is decreased libido, then she explores the quiet realm of diligence, decorum, and propriety that have defined mainstream Western life for centuries:

> The real culprit, originating in the 19th century, is bourgeois propriety. As respectability became the central middle-class value, censorship and repression became the norm. Victorian prudery ended the humorous sexual candor of both men and women during the agrarian era, a ribaldry chronicled from Shakespeare's plays to the 18th-century novel. The priggish 1950s, which erased the liberated flappers of the Jazz Age from cultural memory, were simply a return to the norm.

Paglia digs deep. But she cannot merely toss out these broad historical statements. She has to give specifics throughout her argument and let them build persuasively throughout. She describes office life, domestic life, popular movies, and popular music all as a way to illustrate an undeniable force of desexualization.

And in the following passage, Noguera and Akom point to the surface—the most obvious assumption people may have about the topic—and then reveal a less obvious layer:

> On the face of it, the potential for success in reducing the gap in these districts would seem high. All fifteen school districts in the network have a track record of sending large numbers of affluent white students to the best colleges and universities in the country. Additionally, unlike schools in high-poverty areas, funding is largely not a major obstacle to reform. Each district is located in an affluent community with a highly educated population known for its commitment to liberal political and social values. Yet in

all fifteen districts there is a persistent, deeply ingrained sense that even this ambitious and well-intentioned effort will fail to alter student outcomes.

The final sentence of the paragraph suggests that the causes of the achievement gap lurk in a complex set of forces. As their argument continues, the writers explain those forces more specifically.

Literary Works Poems, novels, plays, songs and short stories are often included in arguments to connect the specific topic to a broader human condition, hope, tension, or principle. In her essay, Samantha Tengelitsch uses a Wendell Berry line to connect contemporary farming techniques and the broader hope for human survival:

> American poet Wendell Berry wrote, "To cherish what remains of the Earth and to foster its renewal is our only legitimate hope of survival." This community is about something more than cherries. Farmers today are rethinking what goes into producing their product. A handful, like the Koberniks, have traded pesticides for peace of mind and gone organic. Others are participating in government subsidies to reduce their dependence on toxic chemicals. And in recent years, efforts like Community Supported Agriculture (CSA) have grown in popularity among local farmers.

As you consider your own argument, use the following questions to develop both evidence and appeals.

- ▶ What line of reasoning must I establish? How can I support each premise?

- ▶ What historical or current events or figures illustrate something about my topic?

- ▶ What local authority might help reveal something about the topic?

- ▶ What are the logical causes (direct and indirect) of the topic on a surrounding community—or the broader society?

- ▶ What hidden, or indirect, factors can I describe?

- ▶ How might a literary passage help to illustrate a broader point or principle?

Invention Workshop

Form a group with two or three other writers. After sharing main claims, help each writer develop possible support strategies by collectively answering at least two of the preceding invention questions.

Arrangement

Where Should I Include My Main Claim? A main claim or thesis can be *implied* (suggested by the details of the essay but not directly stated) or *explicit* (directly stated). There is no universal rule for placement of an explicit main claim. Contrary to some high school teaching, the main claim (or thesis statement) of an essay does not have to go at the end of the first paragraph. In fact, the first paragraph in many academic and professional essays is reserved for introducing the reader to the complexities of the issue or getting beyond some common assumptions. In his introduction, J. Noel Trapp gives some basic history about technological development in video games, but he ends the first paragraph by setting up the main argument, the "something else" that he will develop as the essay rolls along:

> The advent and growth of MMORPGs (Massive Multiplayer Online Role-Playing Games) has drastically shaped the landscape of the gaming world, and reshaped our cultural roles within such a world. Though the initial success of these games was founded on revolutionary technological qualities, something else is behind their continued and extraordinary success. Something beyond the technological wonders of the games themselves drives thousands of players to their computers and into virtual space.

Trapp, then, fully describes that "something else" throughout his essay. In his conclusion, we get a complete sense of the idea:

> Having been in existence for at least a decade, the continued success of MMORPGs rests on their rhetoric more than their creativity—on their appeals to fundamental psychology. By offering a virtual world in which a true community can exist, they offer more than a virtual challenge, but rather a full ensemble of potentially sated human needs.

Noguera and Akom's main claim comes toward the end of their essay, after several causes have been explained:

> When placed within the broader context of race relations in American society, the causes of the racial achievement gap appear less complex and mysterious; the gap is merely another reflection of the disparities in experience and life chances for individuals from different racial groups.

Where Should I Deal with Opposition? This depends on the number and intensity of opposing claims. When writers have one primary opposing force, they often begin their argument there—explaining what others believe and detailing the logic of that belief. Then, they begin their argument against that belief. In this sense, the opposition acts as a springboard into the writer's main claim and line of reasoning. In the following example, the writer uses opposition as a springboard to start her essay:

> Political leaders often claim that school shootings are caused by an infection in teenage culture, specifically first-person shooter video games and hard core music. They see a direct cause/effect relationship between entertainment and horrifying outbursts of violence. They imagine that the way teenagers escape from reality directly impacts how they deal with the frustrations of everyday life. Such a simplistic understanding of cause/effect ignores the more complex, but far more powerful, factors that surround teenagers and incite them toward violence. As it turns out, the most direct factors are not at all part of some adolescent sub-culture. They are core parts of mainstream American life.

How Should I Work Scientific Research into the Argument?

Scientific research can provide powerful support, but it comes with a potential hazard: Readers can easily become overwhelmed by unfamiliar terms or too much jargon. Therefore, good writers briefly explain (or set up) scientific findings or conclusions before they give data or dense quotations. In her essay, which relies heavily on scientific conclusions, Samantha Tengelitsch works to set up those conclusions for the reader. In the following passage, she gives two quotations, and before each she explains the significance of the point:

> A population-based, incidence case-control study which evaluated pesticide product use and the risk of non-Hodgkin's lymphoma in women addresses this correlation: "NHL has received research attention because the recent rapid increase in its incidence parallels an exponential growth in pesticide use with a few decades of lag" (Kato et al.). Researchers investigated other "high-risk" groups as well and found some correlation between these groups and NHL, but the most significant association was found in agricultural families. As one study reports:
>
> > With increasing cumulative number of hours exposed to pesticides at these jobs other than farming, there was a marginal increasing trend in risk of NHL. When farming and other jobs associated with pesticide exposure were combined, the total duration at any of these jobs was significantly positively associated with the risk of NHL (Kato et al.).

How Should I Deal with Multiple Causes?

If you are developing a multiple-cause argument, you can use paragraphs to separate and detail each cause. Pedro A. Noguera and Antwi Akom use paragraphs to separate the causes of the achievement gap. In the following, they begin a new paragraph to shift from more direct to less direct (or cultural) factors:

> Beyond the policies and practices that contribute to the achievement gap, a number of complex cultural factors are also important. Missing from the research and policy debates is an understanding of the ways in which children come to perceive the relationship between their racial identity and what they believe they can do academically. For many children, schools play an important role in shaping their racial identities because they are one of the few social settings where kids interact with people from different backgrounds. To the extent that a school's sorting processes disproportionately relegate black and brown children to spaces within schools that are perceived as negative and marginal, it is likely that children of color will come to perceive certain activities and courses as either suitable or off-limits for them.

Similarly, Tengelitsch shifts paragraphs to move from one type of hazard (pesticides) to another (fertilizer):

> In addition to chemical pesticides, orchards have become increasingly reliant on chemical fertilizers. These chemical fertilizers combined with run-off wastes from livestock and septic systems all contribute to higher levels of nitrogen in the ground. Nitrogen converts into nitrates, which pass through our permeable soil into the water table.

The idea here is to use paragraphs as basic organizational units. Even though your argument may grow in complexity—dealing with multiple causes, various hidden layers, different appeals, opposing positions, and several support strategies—the paragraphs can keep those elements from getting too entangled.

Audience and Voice

Voice is key to academic argument. Even when the writing is highly formal, it has a voice. And the writer controls the nature of that voice with each sentence, phrase, and word. Although voice involves a broad range of issues and strategies, this section offers advice on two key issues: sentence variety and pronoun use.

Voice and Sentence Variety Since writers cannot use volume, they must rely on other means to make their voices lively. Sentence length is equivalent to pitch and volume in writing. When sentences are generally the same length, the voice seems flat and monotonous, but when sentences are varied in length (moving from long to short), the voice breaks out of flatness, and readers experience a tug and pull on their minds. In short, sentence length matters. (Big time.) In her essay, Camille Paglia pulls the reader into complex ideas (with complex sentences) and then punctuates the intellectual experience with a short, powerful assertion:

> Nor are husbands offering much stimulation in the male display department: visually, American men remain perpetual boys, as shown by the bulky T-shirts, loose shorts and sneakers they wear from preschool through midlife. The sexes, which used to occupy intriguingly separate worlds, are suffering from over-familiarity, a curse of the mundane. There's no mystery left.

Like Paglia, all good writers try to accent or emphasize ideas with shorter sentences—especially after longer, more nuanced, sentences. Noguera and Akom apply the same strategy:

> A close examination of access to AP courses in California reveals how certain educational practices contribute to the maintenance of the racial achievement gap. Since the mid-eighties, the number of AP courses available to students at high schools in California has tripled. This increase has been attributed to a 1984 decision by the University of California to give greater weight to the grades earned by students who enroll in AP courses. However, AP courses are not uniformly available to students. At some inner-city and rural schools, few if any such courses are offered, while at private and affluent suburban schools, it is not uncommon for students to have access to fifteen or more AP courses (see Alan Jenkins, "Leveling the Playing Field," March 6).

Voice and Pronouns Pronouns are tricky business in academic writing. Particularly, the first-person pronoun "I" raises concerns for many readers because it draws attention to the writer rather than the subject under consideration. Notice the difference between the following statements:

- It is my opinion that the elemental power of sexuality has also waned in American popular culture.
- The elemental power of sexuality has also waned in American popular culture.

The first statement draws attention, first, to the writer's opinion. The power of sexuality is, literally, subordinated to the writer. But in the second sentence (taken from Paglia's essay), the subject matter (sex) is at the front of the sentence. It's the first thing the reader sees. In other words, the second sentence is more intense, more direct.

The point here is a caution about phrases such as "I think that" or "In my opinion." They are unnecessary unless the writer needs to make a distinction between his or her own ideas and those of an outside source.

However, even in the most formal essays, writers sometimes draw attention to their own thinking, to their own experience, to their presence in the text. They do this intentionally to shift attention to their own thinking or writing process—and even to humanize part of an argument. For example, in her essay, Samantha Tengelitsch uses "I" in the middle of a lengthy scientific explanation of pesticides:

> Various forms of cancer, neurological disorders, reproductive problems, birth defects, and spontaneous abortions have all been linked to long-term pesticide exposure (Moses) and elevated nitrate levels in groundwater. I chose to research non-Hodgkin's lymphoma and its link to agriculture because of a photograph of a Cherry Festival contestant; a young woman who grew up on a cherry farm in the heart of cherry country who died last winter from cancer. Did Lauren Hemming die from high nitrate levels or pesticide exposure in her youth? It is impossible for me to say with any certainty. Yet her story was the catalyst for my research; it inspired me to look further and in doing so, I discovered the true irony of her death.

Second-person pronouns *(you, your)* address the reader directly. Such pronouns can be rhetorically effective. But just as using the first person can draw attention away from the subject and to the writer, using the second person can draw it away from the subject and to the reader. Consistent use of third person *(they, he, she, it)* helps focus attention on the subject of the writing, not the writer or the reader.

Another problem with second-person pronouns is that they can actually be third-person references in disguise. This pronoun confusion can be cleared up by changing the second-person references to third-person. Consider the following examples:

- Psychologically, the impacts and effects of video games have been quite easy to observe. In the original role-playing games of the late 1990s, you were allowed into a virtual realm, no longer as a spectator, but as an active participant making decisions in realities you could not achieve (or were not possible) in the physical world around you.
- Psychologically, the impacts and effects of video games have been quite easy to observe. In the original role-playing games of the late 1990s, people were allowed into a virtual realm, no longer as spectators, but as active participants making decisions in realities they could not achieve (or were not possible) in the physical world around them.

The first example unnecessarily involves the reader: The writer doesn't mean when *the reader* was allowed into a virtual realm. The pronoun reference, although understandable, is not accurate. Such unfocused references can draw the reader's attention away from the subject matter and even make inaccurate (and unintentional) statements about the reader. The second sentence, from J. Noel Trapp's essay, maintains focus on gamers—and does not suggest that the reader (*you*) is part of that group. Trapp's strategy represents most academic and professional writing.

↱ Using "I" in Your Writing

Writing instructors sometimes require students to avoid the first-person pronoun in writing. This is to help students develop a more academic writing style. But as you can see, many academic writers use the first-person pronoun even in very formal situations. The prohibition of the first-person often emerges from the hope that students will not rely on—or hide behind—the "I" when pressed to make intensive claims. As you consider your own writing, discuss the issue with your instructor.

Revision

Revision requires both distance and proximity. A writer must pull away from the text and imagine its qualities from a reader's perspective, but also get up close enough to inspect particular claims, sentences, and word choice. Perhaps the biggest mistake that writers make is focusing only on editing at the sentence level. (The harder part, of course, is backing up and asking questions about the project's overall worth.)

Above all else, academic readers value *revelation*—arguments that reveal something beyond common thinking. The argument should argue for a cause that readers might not consider, or a cause that readers may have dismissed.

Ask yourself the following questions:
- In what way is this argument revelatory? (How does it help readers to re-see the topic or discover something?)
- If the argument focuses on a common topic, does it offer some new complexity?
- Does the main claim rely on a variety of support strategies (appeals, examples, and evidence)?
- Does the argument genuinely address opposition—and concede when appropriate?

Research and Revision: If you used outside sources, consider the following questions. As you revise, refer to the corresponding pages in The Research Guide:

- Have you used research as means of discovery? (pages 360–383)
- Have you evaluated sources for ideology, reliability, relevance, timeliness, and diversity? (pages 384–394)
- Are the ideas from the outside sources integrated smoothly into your ideas? (pages 395–410)
- Are the sources documented appropriately (with in-text and end citation)? (pages 411–438)

Peer Review

Exchange drafts with at least one other writer. (If time allows, exchange with two or three writers to gather a range of perspectives or comments.) Use the following questions to generate specific constructive comments about others' drafts:

1. Does the argument answer the basic question: Why did this happen?

2. Identify the writer's main claim. How can it be more focused on a particular cause?

3. What is the most supportive passage? Describe why it works well in the argument.

4. How is this argument revelatory? (What genuinely new perspective does it offer? How does it help us to re-see the topic?)

5. How could the writer use more allusions, examples, scenarios, or testimony to illustrate specific points?

6. The writer should have engaged opposing perspectives. What additional opposing points could the writer address? Can you imagine other objections to the argument? What points might the writer concede or qualify?

7. What phrases or passages could be more focused, more specific? Comment on any phrases, sentences, or passages that speak broadly about the topic and lack specific explanation or a detailed support strategy.

8. Check for paragraph coherence: Identify any paragraphs that seem to shift focus or take on too many separate points without a clear line of reasoning.

9. Are sources integrated smoothly, and not forced into passages? Explain any gaps between the writer's line of reasoning and the ideas from an outside source. (See pages 395–410.)

Arguing Value

What Good Is This?

Master Jeweler Henry Phillips cleaning the Imperial State Crown.

We are often told to avoid judging others. But the advice to "judge not" can easily turn into a kind of avoidance—a perspective that sees no distinctions between that which is harmful and that which is helpful. It would be reckless, and probably impossible, to live without judging the world around us, without making distinctions between the dangerous and the valuable. We must engage in complex judgments; we must think actively and speak publicly about people, policies, behaviors, laws, products, and even attitudes: Is the new policy on overtime hurtful to the staff? Is the local curfew good for teenagers? In these situations, we do more than react at a gut level. We weigh arguments, analyze the layers of the issue, and ultimately act—for instance, by protesting a new overtime policy or voting against a local proposal. We make reasoned decisions about how to act on a personal level.

In academic, civic, and professional settings, evaluations are not personal. They are important to a larger situation—and it is the individual's job to convince others of a particular way of seeing:

- A scientist must convince her colleagues that a proposed research program is unfocused.
- The faculty at an elementary school must convince the principal and ultimately the school board that a testing program is unsuccessful and counterproductive.
- A magazine publisher must persuade two major advertisers that the cover story of a particular issue is not potentially offensive to a politically conservative audience.
- A basketball coaching staff argues about the value of a potential player: to justify the player's potential salary, the coaches must convince team owners of the player's worth.

In these situations, the topic is in plain view. However, in other cases, people have to argue about the *hidden* value of something. Imagine a doctor who has detected a flaw not only in a surgical procedure but also in the broader approach to diagnosing potential surgery patients. Or a citizen who sees the harm caused by a long-standing tradition in her community. People are often in such situations, noticing aspects of something that others do not see, and so they must do more than argue an opinion; they must use argument to reveal the issue.

Whenever writers argue value, they are in difficult territory. They are not merely expressing a personal opinion: they are working to shape others' responses to something—to make others see the same qualities or dimensions as they do. This is no small task, especially in America, where we generally believe that people have their "own opinions." The writer has several big jobs: to understand the topic itself, to detect what readers value in relation to that topic, to change what readers value so they see the topic differently, to address resistance to change. In rhetorical terms, the writer has to research the topic, understand the rhetorical situation, assert and support a way of seeing, and counterargue. Counterarguing is especially difficult with arguments of value because people keep their values protected. They defend any hint of a challenge with learned phrases: "Everyone's entitled to his opinion," "Beauty is in the eye of the beholder," "I like what I like," and so on. So writers must work around or through those intellectual walls.

The readings in this chapter reveal something new to readers and then call on some shared values, inviting readers into a way of thinking and evaluating. They go far beyond saying that something is simply bad, good, evil, wrong; they seek to show their readers *how* something harms or helps people. As with all academic writing, the goal is to reveal something (some new point, some layer of meaning, some hidden element) so that readers rethink the topic.

Activities

1. Generate a list of prevailing attitudes or behaviors that cause harm to a community or people. Try to focus on widespread attitudes or behaviors that seem totally acceptable to most people. For each, explain the harm it causes and why people tend to ignore or overlook the harm.

2. In small groups, take a stance on this question: *What is the value of the automobile to American culture?* Share responses with other groups in the class:
   - Which groups have the most similar stances?
   - Which groups have the most competing or different stances?
   - What basic values and beliefs underlie the stances in each group?
   - Beneath the groups' stated positions, what values and beliefs do they share? What values and beliefs collide?

Evaluations

Evaluation is another term for an argument of value. But it usually refers to a particular type of text—a particular situation or convention. Evaluations come in many guises, ranging in levels of formality: movie reviews, music reviews, book reviews, restaurant reviews, employee evaluations, teacher evaluations, and so on. Each of these categories has a set of stated or unstated rules. Readers of movie reviews, for instance, expect to see a brief summary of the movie, a description of its genre (comedy, horror, action), a list of key actors, a statement about expectations, and a judgment about the movie's ability to meet those expectations.

The particular context (an institution, a media outlet, a company) helps to define expectations. For example, a positive movie review on Rotten Tomatoes.com is marked with a fresh, red tomato icon, and a bad review with a smashed, rotten tomato icon. Evaluations are very much defined by particular institutional or audience expectations. The argument emerges from a prescribed, established situation (an assignment, an annual program review, a new fiscal year, an entertainment section in a magazine) rather than an unscripted social situation.

For this chapter, we use the phrase "argument of value" to cast a category that is broader than any particular type of evaluation. With this phrase, we hope to promote the idea that people often begin arguing outside of prescripted situations. They see something in the world around them—within or beyond specific institutional situations—and recognize a need to call it out, make people aware of it, ring the alarm bell, or defend it . . . whatever the case may be. But every evaluation—whether it closely follows certain conventions or not—consistently addresses the following two questions, either explicitly or implicitly:

- What are the criteria for judgment? In other words, what does a good example of this (teacher, comedic movie, novel, budget, etc.) do or possess?

- How well does the subject under consideration fulfill those criteria?

If you are asked to write an evaluation, your instructor probably has particular conventions in mind. Regardless of formatting and arrangement issues, you can assume that the preceding two questions will be necessary. Additionally, you can use the sections in this chapter to create a more sophisticated argument with a revelatory and focused main claim.

Evaluation of "The Education of Ms. Groves"

JOHN ADAMS

John Adams teaches college writing. He wrote the following argument after seeing a *Dateline NBC* episode that aired in 2006. As many good arguers do, Adams saw past the apparent message of the television program. While *Dateline* intended to offer an informative report on education in America, Adams realized the subtle and deeply flawed assumptions at work. He saw how those assumptions quietly support an inaccurate and injurious mode of thinking. Like many academic arguments, Adams's argument tries to dig up and reveal the dangerous assumptions that people would otherwise gladly accept.

Dateline NBC is one of those TV shows that blurs the line between news and entertainment. The show's website says the show "bring[s] viewers compelling investigative reports and personal stories." "The Education of Ms. Groves," which recently aired on *Dateline NBC*, illustrates the dangers of mixing news and entertainment, investigative reporting and storytelling. The show engages its audience through classic storytelling techniques, beginning with the likeable and attractive Ms. Groves. She is an optimistic first-year teacher, quickly faced with many challenges. Every engaging story has a crisis to be resolved, and it remains suspensefully unclear up until the end whether or not Ms. Groves will resolve hers.

There are five parts to a plot line (exposition, rising action, climax, falling action, and resolution), and *Dateline NBC* employs them dutifully. While their storytelling technique keeps the viewer tuned in, their oversimplification of the complexities of education do a disservice to teachers and students and communities at large. "The Education of Ms. Groves" ends up being like a sitcom or a cheesy TV drama, not an insightful look at a troubled American education system. In the first half of the program, Ms. Groves has lots of problems; then in the last half, the crisis is simply resolved, as if teaching and learning is just that easy. While NBC claims to be "chronicling a new teacher's first year," it edits and oversimplifies in a way that reinforces harmful misconceptions about teaching and learning.

Of course the crisis is that Ms. Groves is having a hard time getting through to her students. They are unruly and, what's worse (according to the show), doing poorly on tests. How was the crisis resolved? Ms. Groves (who was underprepared as a teacher) learns a few tricks. She counts 3, 2, 1 and her previously unruly students become silent. She posts grades publicly and everyone, it seems, gets focused and motivated. (We see students eagerly rushing up to see their scores, then working harder than they were before.) The show suggests that had Ms. Groves simply done these things at first, she wouldn't have had any problems. *Her* foolish mistake was not to know these *simple* tricks of the trade. The show suggests that anyone can and should learn these things in college before entering the classroom as a teacher. (Ms. Groves was not an education major in college, but chose to join Teach for America, an organization that recruits outstanding college graduates to teach in low-income communities. Ms. Groves's father wanted her to go to law school.)

Certainly, tricks (techniques or strategies) help immensely in any profession, but the show oversimplified the messy issue of education—of teaching and of learning. And the degree to which it oversimplified something so complex, ongoing, and lifelong is what's stunning. The show told Americans frustrated with their education system that education is easy: Teachers simply need to be dedicated, love their students, and learn a couple nifty tricks. From the show, Americans are to conclude that students fail for one reason: because of bad teachers (because the teacher failed the student, the parent, and the country).

According to the show, a good teacher simply overcomes the rest of American culture. Of course

Joe Corrigan/Stringer/Getty Images Entertainment/Getty Images

a father must get out of prison (all's well when he does) and a homeless family needs a house (once in it, problem solved). But in "The Education of Ms. Groves," other complex factors such as media, consumerism, or diet simply don't exist. The show makes two big mistakes: (1) It oversimplifies what it does talk about, and (2) it doesn't mention some other very messy contributing factors.

Of course, a one-hour TV show can't cover everything. Producers must select and edit to put forth a certain argument, but the *Dateline NBC* argument is logically flawed. It relies, for example, on a strawperson fallacy—by flattening out and oversimplifying the qualities of the people and their situation: The show sets up at the beginning that Ms. Groves has had only five weeks of teacher training. So her first term is unsuccessful, why? Because of her lack of knowledge about teaching. But she perseveres; she doesn't quit. She gets the magic tips from the principal, and then she succeeds. Eureka, within the first year! Anyone thinking on this simplistic level would quickly conclude: Why not train the teacher a little better up front (tell her the tricks, stupid)? Or, one might conclude: Things worked out in the end, so there's no real harm. It's like a *Three's Company* episode. If Jack had simply taken out the garbage like Crissy told him to, there

wouldn't have been any misunderstanding, and all the wacky shenanigans would not have ensued.

Dateline NBC would have served viewers better by doing some in-depth analysis of this complex issue. Instead, they misrepresented and oversimplified, as they do with other issues (presidential elections, the environment, war). One consequence, whether positive or negative, of the show's "logic" may be that it motivates some people to try teaching. Golly, it looks so easy: All a teacher needs to do is get the tricks of the trade from the principal first, then he or she can avoid all the problems that Ms. Groves encountered. Of course, anyone who thinks this way isn't really thinking much. Many people will realize that the show ignored complexities (the way a politician does when he says the economy's good because more Americans own homes than ever before).

Many people will realize that *Dateline NBC* turned a complex issue into a TV drama like *Desperate Housewives* or *Grey's Anatomy*. It had an attractive leading character, some good drama (even a fight!), and an emotional (uplifting) ending. Unfortunately, though it will entertain, this show will disappoint a curious mind because it reduces a serious issue to a Hallmark card. A lot of dedicated, loving, trick-savvy teachers are probably laughing (though with frustration) at the TV-style docu-drama of American education. While it showed the father in prison, the homeless family, and so on, according to *Dateline NBC*, it can all be overcome (all of American culture can be overcome) if our teachers just know to count backwards. *Supernanny* and *Wife Swap* deal with complexity more than this.

Many of the cultural problems educators are up against are created, reinforced, and spread by American media. American children grow up immersed in a loud, often stupid, world of media and consumption (the two are really the same). Today's children and many adults are not comfortable with quiet. They're bombarded with noise; there is always something to watch, listen to, and do.

They're not permitted (or subjected to) a moment of peace and quiet so that they can learn to explore their own thoughts. Then we expect them to have completely different minds once they enter a classroom. "The Education of Ms. Groves" suggests that Ms. Groves overcomes all this somewhat magically, by counting backwards, 3, 2, 1, problem solved. (There's no place like home. There's no place like home. There's no place like home.)

NBC (and its brother, sister, and parent companies) creates a lot of that noise; thus, it has helped to create elementary schools full of restless consumers. "The Education of Ms. Groves" suggests that none of that matters. Instead, the problem is prison, homelessness, undertrained teachers. In the show, the media never looks at the media. It is apparently unable to see its own role in the culture that it reports on.

Ms. Groves had only five weeks of teacher training. And her first term as a teacher didn't go well. We know this, according to the show, because of students' test scores. This is another unfortunate oversimplification and misrepresentation. *Dateline NBC* simply bought into the idea that tests and scores measure learning, that they *make* learning, that they *are* learning. And it passed this assumption on to its viewers, unquestioned. After four months of experience and a little talking to the principal (him giving her the magic pill), all is well. This leads viewers to believe that the failures of the American education system (and there are many and they are complex) are because of one simple thing: bad teachers. The show claims that good teachers can overcome everything, if they care and love and know a few simple tricks. Apparently, according to the show, most American teachers don't do this. As *Dateline NBC* tells it, all it takes is a semester of teaching and some talks with a principal to correct a wrong answer.

Analyzing Argument

1. What is Adams's main claim about "The Education of Ms. Groves"?

2. According to this argument, what should an investigative news program do for viewers? Why does this particular *Dateline* episode fall short?

3. Chart out Adams's main line of reasoning. What are the stated and unstated premises that a reader must follow before accepting the argument's main claim?

4. Where does Adams qualify or concede points? How are those qualifiers or concessions important to the overall argument? How do they relate to Adams's voice?

5. Adams alludes to several television dramas and sitcoms. How do they make a point about an investigative report on *Dateline?*

6. Explain how Adams uses an understanding of logical fallacies. Why are logical fallacies important to this argument?

Adventure Is Calling

MICHAEL C. HILLIARD

Essays about video games, like essays about any topic, run the risk of being mundane. For example, they often make the same old points about video games leading (or not leading) to violent behavior. In "Adventure Is Calling," Michael C. Hilliard goes beyond the typical argument. He shares an insight about the nature of video games and how they compare to classic literary adventure stories.

I have always loved adventure stories. As I was growing up homeschooled, my mother imparted a love of reading early on in my life, first reading to me and my sisters, then encouraging us to read on our own as we grew older. The library was a favorite destination and we would often vacation there for hours at a time, getting to know Mrs. Bert, the children's librarian, discovering new books, and taking far too many back home with us. Getting our own personal library cards was a significant milestone in our lives and we were quite proud of the privilege—better still, now we could take out even more books.

Adventure and fantasy stories were my favorites. I couldn't tell how many times I've pored over tales of *Narnia, Middle Earth* and *Wonderland,* making dear friends of elves, dwarves, dragons, Hobbits who lived in holes, and a little girl who fell down another sort of hole entirely; not to mention all of the wonderful wizards, fauns and other manner of talking beasts along the way.

Introduces the topic of books, and then adventure and fantasy stories.

But it wasn't all fun and games or pleasant walks in the woods. Quite the contrary, the stories were filled with peril: Savage beasts, fearsome swordfights, and terrifying villains always seemed to lurk in the path of my beloved heroes, and their noble quests often seemed doomed to fail. And yet, no matter how dire the situation, no matter how impossible the odds or frightening the villain, the heroes would press on, even when they had the chance to run away. Choosing what was right instead of what was easy, they persevered and won the day.

Narrows the focus to peril and the importance of pressing on, choosing what was right instead of what was easy.

Adventure stories have always played a major role in the growth and development of a society. Instinctively, it seems, people crave stories of heroes and villains, strange lands and daring quests. Although we could venture an in-depth psychological analysis to attempt to identify just what it is that people love about adventure stories, I think the answer is simple: we need inspiration. As the heroes in our stories make brave choices and remain steadfast, we identify with them, making them role models for our own lives. In a world that often seems lost and broken—where monsters take the form of terrorist bombings and school shootings, when the

Connects adventure stories to the growth and development of society.

princess in need of rescue is a family member struggling with addiction, or a friend dealing with emotional abuse—we need stories of hope and determination, stories that inspire us to face the adversity head on, even when hope seems lost.

At the Gamescom trade fair in Cologne, Germany, two women dressed as video game characters.

JOERG CARSTENSEN/epa/Corbis

Evidence that video games are replacing books as a primary method for delivering adventure stories.

Until recently, books were the primary method for delivering adventure stories to the masses, but such is becoming a thing of the past; now, movies and video games are the media of choice. Video games in particular seem to be taking over the adventure market in recent years. Rarely do kids clutch a book to their chest; instead, they carry miniaturized video game systems ablaze with explosions of light and sound. And not just kids, either. As a matter of fact, the Entertainment Software Association reports that the average gamer is 35 years old, and there are more women over the age of 18 playing video or computer games than boys aged 17 or younger (NPD Group). A few short years ago, hardly anyone living in the sunlight knew what *WoW* referred to, but now it's safe to say that at least one person you know is playing *World of Warcraft* on a regular basis—heck, even Mr. T. of '80s *A-Team* fame is now appearing in TV commercials for the game. Skepticism has existed in equal measure—you hear complaints that video games are rotting the minds children, that people should read more, or that video game violence might be linked with cases of real-world violence— but in popular practice these arguments don't seem to have much effect, judging by the meteoric rise the video game industry has experienced over the past decade (NPD Group).

Question of value about video games versus books when it comes to delivering adventure stories to the masses.

As video games become one of the dominant forces for providing society with tales of adventure, it should give us pause to wonder if they are up to the task. All too often the fantasy worlds in which we attempt to immerse ourselves through graphic game play prove too shallow to offer any in-depth character or story development, which is essential for good adventure stories. Certainly, books are just as capable of failing in this regard. Poor writing can infect any mode of communication. However, a video game is all too often handicapped by conventions that detract from the storytelling. Instead of encouraging players to grapple with difficult circumstances in their lives, video games all too often distract us with illusions of adventure, action, amusement and escapism.

Genuine storytelling depends on some key elements. For one, any good adventure story will have a compelling crisis. In *Alice in Wonderland,* it started as little more than a dreary day; but, as the story progressed and down the rabbit hole we traveled, solving riddles, drinking potions, and avoiding the wrath of a head-hunting queen all became a part of Alice's crisis before the day was out. In perhaps one of the greatest fantasy adventure stories ever written, J.R.R. Tolkien's *Lord of the Rings,* a motley crew of characters must cross an entire continent, battling legions of powerful and deadly foes on a quest to destroy a powerful magical object upon which the fate of the world precariously hangs. Adventures thrive on dangerous quests with impossible odds. It is the very act of overcoming adversity that changes someone from ordinary to extraordinary, from "zero to hero" as the bard might say.

> Specific examples of books and crisis (*Alice in Wonderland; Lord of the Rings*).

Video games often present the player with a crisis, typically developed through a series of cut-scenes interspersed at regular intervals throughout the game. But how often do these brief scenes of exposition transcend the 30-second cut-scene to provide real depth of meaning for the much more dominant action sequences where players spend the vast majority of their time? In writing a good adventure story, an author is able to concern herself entirely with the workings of the story, the development of the characters and the crises they face. In writing a good video game, the studio's primary goal is to create a game that is enjoyable to play, because otherwise no one would buy it.

> Video games don't provide the depth of meaning books do when it comes to crisis.

Don't get me wrong. Book-publishers want to sell books just as much as game developers want to sell games, but one is successful through talented writing and a good story, while the other succeeds primarily if it is fun to play. In a normal adventure story, action scenes (battles and the like) are tools for the development of the story. In a video game, however, the story generally serves as the requisite base for developing the action scenes: fighting the *Balrog* isn't necessary so that the Fellowship will be forced to deal with the loss of the wise and knowing Gandalf when he falls into the abyss after fighting the demon; instead, it's just another boss fight at the end of a level.

> Further explanation of how video games treat crisis differently than books.

To work within the framework of game conventions based on character progression, plot development is boiled down to a series of required objectives or tasks the player must complete, but in this they become tasks of compulsion rather than tasks of purpose: the hero saves the princess because he must to get to the next level, not because of any sense of honor, love, or moral duty. For the player, actions performed become a matter of skill at operating a game controller rather than a question of perseverance in the face of fear or impossible odds. The traditional roles are reversed. In place of action and adventure as catalysts for character development, character development becomes a compulsory base for the—much more important—action sequences. Focus shifts from inspiration, imagination and learning to simple amusement.

I'm not arguing that video games never present interesting moral dilemmas or opportunities for learning. In his book *The Ethics of Computer Games,* Miguel Sicart attempts a thorough exploration of the many facets of ethics pertaining to society's interaction with video games. His case study of the 2007 release *Bioshock* tells of both the successes and failures present in video games as they attempt to provide a meaningful moral experience for players. In his review, Sicart praises the unique narrative development of *Bioshock,* where a final revelation in the plot forces players to reflect critically on the morality of their previous actions in the game. Indeed, video games rarely encourage moral reflections from players, and *Bioshock*'s unique plot twist represents a refreshing shift in game design. However, Sicart also criticizes several other aspects of *Bioshock*'s game play, particularly the very elements for which it was purported to present players with meaningful ethical dilemmas. In the supposed ethical exigencies, players of *Bioshock* are routinely presented with the choice of either killing or "saving" computer-controlled characters. The situation might be considered morally challenging, Sicart argues, except that the choice is deprived of meaningful consequences because game play and progression is not significantly altered based on either decision (151–63). *Bioshock* and many games like it fail to be compelling morally because developers don't want to create a game in which the consequences of a player's actions could prevent or inhibit their progression through the game. After all, who would want to play a game that would send you to jail and keep you from playing until you've served your time? In the end, although Sicart finds that many games do present interesting aspects of ethical design, he believes the industry on the whole cares very little, if at all, about creating ethical games (229).

I like video games. Starting back when all we had was a monochromatic green-screen computer, playing knock-off versions of *Space Invaders* or *Pong* on giant five-and-a-quarter inch floppy disks, to more recent times with games like *Star Wars: Knights of the Old Republic* on a PC, or *Fable* on the *Xbox,* I've happily whiled away many hours beating up bad guys and vying for high scores. After a long day at school or at work, I've often relaxed into a game's easy pleasure. I'm certainly not one to make the

---

Marginal notes:

In video games, unlike books, the "focus shifts from inspiration, imagination, and learning to simple amusement." Concession that video games do sometimes present interesting moral dilemmas and opportunities for learning.

An authority, Miguel Sicart, is used to help the reader understand and accept the main claim, that though video games amuse, they often fail to inspire.

Acknowledges the positive value, yet limitation, of video games.

argument that video game entertainment is all wrong. But, as a dominant force in providing tales of adventure to our society, video games too often amuse rather than inspire.

Works Cited

Entertainment Software Association. "Industry Facts." *The Entertainment Software Association.* N.p., 2010. Web. 24 Mar. 2010.

The NPD Group, Inc. "2009 U.S. Video Game Industry and PC Game Software Retail Sales Reach $20.2 Billion." *The NPD Group, Inc.* N.p., 14 Jan. 2010. Web. 10 Mar. 2010.

Sicart, Miguel. *The Ethics of Computer Games.* Cambridge: MIT, 2009. Print.

Analyzing Argument

1. What difference between adventure stories and video games does Hilliard draw the reader's attention to?

2. How does Hilliard use opposition to develop his argument?

3. What main criterion does Hilliard use to evaluate video games?

4. Identify a place where Hilliard carefully guides the reader from one idea to another. Explain his strategy.

5. What value is at the root of Hilliard's argument?

Higher Education through Discombobulation

BETSY CHITWOOD

In "'Have It Your Way': Consumerism and Education," Simon Benlow explains the important difference between a customer and a student. For example, he writes, "When I think back to the best teachers and professors in my education, I recall those who demanded everything contrary to the consumerist mentality. They insisted on active students; they made us read staggering amounts of material and then actively put that material to use; they prompted us into confusion and disorientation; they made us uncomfortable, and then, sometimes, offered paths to clarity." After reading Benlow's argument in her second-semester college writing course, Betsy Chitwood wrote the following essay in which she supports Benlow's point by arguing for the value of confusion in the learning process.

I have fond memories of my mother saying, "I'm all discombobulated!" It's really just an interesting way of saying you're confused or disoriented. Of course she said it to make me laugh and so I didn't see confusion as a negative aspect of life. But neither did I realize that confusion is an important element to learning. Confusion and disorientation are important in the learning process because these emotions force us to go beyond what we know in search of answers. Also called cognitive disequilibrium, confusion and disorientation create a motivating challenge to students to explore and take risks as they step out—or are pushed out—of their comfort zone.

My own experience is offered in support of this learning process. Stepping out from my familiar surroundings and entering the military brought about a disorientation that remains unmatched to this date. Military training included: becoming a member of a new culture, long hours of study, physical training, adhering to a regimented lifestyle, no personal time and all this (and more) on very little

or no sleep. This learning process, albeit an extreme example, motivated me to take risks and seek ways to succeed in my chosen career. The impact of the disorientation was in direct proportion to the personal growth brought about by my "education" and it definitely shaped who I am today.

Evidence from academic research supports this theory. In a study by Craig and Graesser at the University of Memphis, college students participated in an introduction to computer literacy by using AutoTutor, an intelligence tutoring system (ITS). The study, which tracked the effect of confusion and other emotions on student's responses, showed that a higher percentage (68%) of learning gains were achieved when the students were met with confusion (4). Researchers Dalton and Crosby, in their study of cognitive or psychological disequilibrium, note its usefulness in gaining higher understanding and personal growth. And developmental psychologist Erik Erikson used the concept of "crisis" to describe the experience of reaching the point where you wrestle with confusion to reach the higher ground of understanding (2). Students who are reluctant to take on the challenge will find their learning experience stifled and their education slow, but those who meet the challenge will realize a higher level of knowledge and self awareness. American psychologist Lawrence Kohlberg refers to disequilibrium as a means to improve understanding concerning moral and ethical situations stating, "Without such conflict and struggle moral reasoning can become stuck at conventional and conformist levels of thinking" (2). Psychologist and educator Nevitt Sanford suggests experiences of psychological discord produce internal conflict. This conflict pushes students to go beyond their inner limits and enter into new understanding, joining their previous knowledge with a new level of knowing.

Some may disagree with the use of confusion as a tool in the learning process, stating that students may remain at a standstill if the confusion or

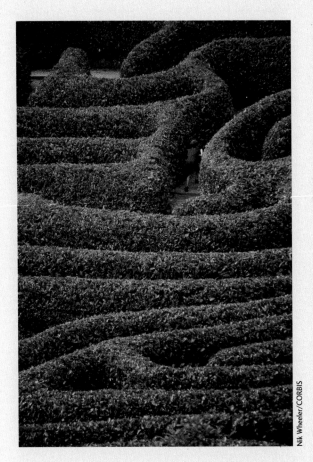

Nik Wheeler/CORBIS

challenge is too great. Since we are not all alike, not all techniques will have the same effect. Although students may be motivated by a challenge, some may need support in order to step into learning. Finding balance between challenge and support is the key. From parent to professor, a teacher needs an awareness of a student's ability to meet challenges *and* their need for support. Chickering suggests that an optimum learning climate uses a balance of challenge and support appropriate for each student's educational level (qtd. in Dalton and Crosby 1).

We must all face confusion at times. Anytime we encounter something we don't understand, and knowledge is required that is not stored in our memory banks, we will be confused. Confusion won't last long if we realize that it is a means to an end. We need to think it through, find answers—or whatever is required—and gain understanding to go on. Each time we find success, we can draw on this experience to take on the next challenge. If we are not willing to use confusion to our advantage as an educational tool, we may feel frustrated and not know where to turn. If this continues we may become discouraged in our education, lose motivation, and give up or struggle along while we seek ways to alleviate these feelings.

In his essay "'Have It Your Way': Consumerism Invades Education," Simon Benlow states, "the best teachers . . . prompted us into confusion and disorientation . . . and then, sometimes, offered paths to clarity." Paths to clarity must be found as we seek to restore an inner harmony. Students who search out their own paths will find these paths lead not only to higher understanding, but more importantly, they are building character, confidence and producing the content of who they are becoming.

Confusion and disorientation, appearing to some as negative, unwelcome intruders, are actually the seeds of personal growth and higher understanding. If we see these emotions as seeds of opportunity, and not something to be avoided or anesthetized, we will find that we have the fortitude to face them head on. If we take what knowledge we have and add what we can acquire, we will reach higher awareness on an educational and personal level.

Works Cited

Benlow, Simon. "'Have It Your Way': Consumerism Invades Education." Mauk/Metz. *The Composition of Everyday Life: A Guide to Writing,* 3rd ed. Wadsworth–Cengage Learning, 2010. 140–42.

Brennen, Annick M. "Articles & Resources on Educational Administration & Supervision." *Enhancing Students' Motivation.* 21 November 2009.

Craig, S. D. and A. C. Graesser. "Why Am I Confused: An Exploratory Look into the Role of Affect in Learning." October 2004. www.autotutor.org. 21 November 2009.

Dalton, Jon and Pamela Crosby. "Challenging College Students to Learn in Campus Cultures of Comfort, Convenience and Complacency." February 2008. *Journal of College & Character.* 21 November 2009.

Analyzing Argument

1. What is the essay's main claim?

2. What argument is the essay a response to?

3. What support strategies help the reader accept Chitwood's claims?

4. What additional support strategy might Chitwood use and why?

5. How does Chitwood's voice help the reader understand and accept her position? Use excerpts from the essay to support your claim.

6. How could Chitwood make her argument more insightful by introducing more opposition?

What is the value of a Happy Meal?

1. Make a list of details from the McDonald's photograph (Lego, Happy Meal, American flag, and so on). How does each detail appeal to the customer? How does the detail appeal to adults? How does it appeal to children?

2. Beyond this photograph, how does McDonald's appeal to logic, emotions, values, need?

3. Make a list of the positive and negative consequences of eating at McDonald's and other fast-food restaurants. What is the positive value of a Happy Meal, of McDonald's, of fast food in general? What is the negative value?

Exploring for Topics

While some things are obviously harmful and others are obviously good, this chapter focuses on topics about which people may disagree. As the chapter readings illustrate, good argument involves more than announcing opinions. It seeks to reveal a new way of thinking so that readers are jolted (or lulled) into re-seeing the topic. Using the following sections, explore a topic that might otherwise go unnoticed, or draw out unseen layers of a familiar topic. Then develop an insightful argument about that topic's value. Go beyond finding fault or giving unqualified praise and discover how a topic impacts the world around it: how does it affect a community, the environment, an organization, a business, animals, children, family members? Ask yourself: *How is this thing valuable or perilous?*

- On your college campus, examine a placement policy, absenteeism, student medical benefits, grading standards, the physical campus itself, administrator salaries, student dress, faculty dress, buildings.
- At an organization or corporation, evaluate a marketing campaign, staffing policies, slogans, individual products or product lines, individual services, sales strategies, mergers.
- In popular culture, defend a public figure or policy against popular sentiment.
- In the media, examine people or things that *seem* harmless but that actually influence the world negatively. Alternatively, examine people or things that *seem* harmful but actually have a positive role.
- At a sporting event or concert, consider a team's or a player's performance, audience behavior, facilities, staff.
- Closely examine an element of popular or consumer culture: a consumer trend, a musical genre, a news channel, a specific program, a newspaper article, a slogan, credit cards, a new look.
- Look into politics. Examine a particular policy, a campaign ad, a particular speech, anti-terrorism policies, an education reform bill, a health care approach, military strategy, a proposed solution.

What good is this?

Activity
In groups, generate several responses for the following statements.

1. _____ seems harmless, but actually, he/she/it _____.

2. _____ seems negative, but actually, he/she/it _____.

Try to generate topics that other groups may not consider—policies, attitudes, products, or services that normally get overlooked, but that need a close examination.

Arguments that point out the obvious or express often-stated opinions are not valued in academic writing, or in most other writing. Academic audiences value arguments that *reveal* something new—in this case, the deeply harmful or beneficial qualities of a subject. Such arguments evolve over time, beginning with an initial but thorough analysis. Use the following invention questions to launch your thinking:

▶ Who or what does the topic harm?

▶ Who or what does it benefit or help?

▶ Does the topic promote a particular kind of behavior, thought process, or attitude?

▶ What is its purpose or intent? (Is that purpose a good one? Why or why not?)

▶ Despite its intent, what are its hidden effects? (How does it impose on others, impede future action, oversimplify thinking, slow action, create frenzy, undermine principles, support core principles, enrich lives, free people, facilitate action?)

The most powerful insights lie beyond initial responses as you stretch the limits of what you normally think. Notice how John Adams develops his ideas about a TV program:

▶ Despite its intent, what are its hidden effects?

The show told the story of a first-year teacher having problems in the classroom: her students are unruly and they're not doing well on tests. After it shows the problems she's having, the show moves into the solution phase. It's somewhat suspenseful, just like the typical entertainment program on TV. You wonder if Ms. Groves is going to give up or persevere, if she's going to get through to her students or not. And just like the typical entertainment programs, there's a happy ending. But, what's the hidden effect of this? The program treats a complex issue with a basic plot—exposition, rising action, climax, falling action, resolution. This could be informative and instructive. But is it? Does the American TV viewer learn something important and valuable about education? Or does the viewer get an oversimplistic misunderstanding? Certainly, young teachers probably struggle, learn, improve, and become more effective. But the way *Dateline* presents the situation is too simple. It gives the viewer a harmful impression about education. It makes it seem simple and easy, and it suggests to Americans who are concerned about problems with public education that complex issues can be solved by learning a few basic tricks.

Adams uses this invention writing to move beyond his initial, gut reaction. His first few sentences are a summary that helps him eventually think more analytically and begin to work toward discovering an evaluative insight.

> ### Invention Workshop
>
> With one or two other writers, answer the preceding invention questions for your topic. Go beyond the initial answers for each. For instance, if someone suggests that an organization is harmful because it is dishonest, probe further, not only revealing the specifics of the dishonesty but also tracing the aftereffects of dishonesty. Use the discussion as a tool for *finding out,* for exploring layers beyond your group's initial preconceptions. During the discussion, record the evolution of ideas by taking notes.

Research

Although they may already have a sense of their position on a topic, before taking a firm stance, arguers use primary and secondary research to explore other positions. Surveys, a type of primary research, collect three layers of information: people's knowledge about, experience with, and opinions on the subject. Even if a survey has a small number of respondents, it can yield valuable insights. For instance, an arguer focusing on online courses could develop a short survey and use questions like the following:

- Have you ever taken a course online? How many?
- What influenced your decision to choose an online course?
- If given the choice between taking a course in person or online, which would you choose?
- What are the main reasons you would take an online course?
- What are the main reasons you would avoid taking an online course?

Depending on the answers, the researcher might get a deeper understanding of the topic. Respondents might explain that they took an online course because they thought it would be easier and less time consuming, yet it turned out to be the opposite, and this information might give a writer a sense of direction or purpose.

Arguers use electronic databases to find published discussions, a type of secondary research, about a subject. Keyword searches that allow you to enter various nouns connected by Boolean operators such as *and* provide good starting places. The trick is to explore various combinations of words. Too few words can yield too many sources to search through, and the wrong words can yield little or nothing. A careful search will yield a manageable and readable list of sources.

Activities

1. You can survey members of your class or a range of people outside of class. Ask respondents if they know about your topic, then delve into their opinions with specific questions. Be careful to gather information without leading the respondents to your position, and record their responses so you can return to them later. (See more about conducting surveys on pages 372–373.)

2. In groups, suggest various words and word combinations for searching each person's topic. For example, if researching the value of computers in education, one keyword search might be "computers *and* education." Then group members might suggest "online courses," "children *and* computers," "learning *and* technology," and so on.

An argument that does not deal with the world of thought surrounding the topic is merely an island of opinion.

Inventing a Claim

Since arguments exist within a context of public opinion, good arguers must know what others have said about a topic. Then they can engage other positions and put forth a persuasive argument.

Answers to the following invention questions will shed light on the way people think about the topic and help determine an argumentative strategy.

What Do Others Claim?

▶ What do others think about it, and why do they hold their opinions?

▶ If you have a particular source, what does the author of the source value? What does he or she assume (but not necessarily state) about the topic?

▶ Beyond explicit statements, how might people express their opinions about the subject (by passive acceptance, by votes, by direct marketing, by active public support, by purchasing a specific product or service)?

▶ What situations, media, traditions, policies, behaviors, or attitudes have kept people from evaluating the topic?

What Do I Claim?

▶ How do my views on the topic relate to others' views?

▶ What values and assumptions do I share with others?

▶ How do my values and assumptions differ from others'?

It is easy to characterize a topic as bad, evil, great, or interesting, but a main claim should do more. It will *reveal* something unique and particular about the subject. For instance, the first of the following statements is flat, uninteresting, and pretty obvious, but the second reveals a particular negative aspect:

Dateline NBC is wrong about education in America.

Dateline NBC oversimplifies the many complicated problems plaguing the American education system and leads us to the dangerous conclusion that bad teachers are simply to blame for the system's failures.

In the first statement, *wrong* can mean many things. It is a vague adjective that could be applied to nearly any subject. (Lying is wrong. You dialed the wrong number.) Adjectives like *bad, unfair, evil, odd, great,* and *wrong* do little more than share a general feeling about a topic. They do not focus an argument on a particular aspect or point, so they limit the intensity of a claim. In the preceding examples the first statement also contains a linking verb: *is*. Verbs such as *is, am, are, was, were* simply link the parts of the sentence that come before and after them: *Dateline NBC* = wrong about education in America. Linking verbs limit what a sentence can do. They can even encourage writers to use broad adjectives such as *bad, unfair, evil*. But when a writer uses an active verb, such as *oversimplifies* or *leads*, the sentence gains potential and the writer is able to see further possibilities for the argument. The words a writer uses actually impact the writer's own thinking, and bland words create bland thinking.

Good arguers watch out for words and phrases that work against the goal of developing a narrow and intense point. The following words and phrases can dull your thought:

Linking Verbs:	is, are, was, were, be, have been, etc.
Vague Adjectives:	bad, unfair, mean, broken, ridiculous, stupid, wrong, awful, interesting, etc.

To generate more intensive focus, writers changed the following flat statements into revelatory alternatives by changing linking verbs and vague adjectives.

Typical Flat Statements

- The parking situation on campus is unfair to students.
- High school education focuses too much on standardized tests.
- College classes outside student majors are unnecessary.
- Energy drinks are bad for today's kids.

Revelatory Alternatives

- The campus parking lots breed panic and competitive hostility in students—even before they get to class.
- Our culture's over-reliance on cars, rather than mass transportation, causes individual students undue anxiety.

- The campus parking lots demonstrate an uncomfortable truth: America's car culture has grown beyond convenience.
- Standardized tests have transformed students into budgetary items.
- The language surrounding standardized tests has made students see themselves as cash cows for their schools.
- The rhetoric justifying standardized tests has ruined the meaning and purpose of public education.
- Required college composition courses have made writing into a laborious performance rather than an intellectual tool.
- Red Bull and its weird chemical cousins provide more twitch to an already twitchy generation.

More Sample Claims

Politics

- Despite the open hostility against political campaign ads, they do force candidates to consider their constituents beyond the usual financial supporters.
- The lack of a viable third party in American politics diminishes real debate about the environment.

Education

- Despite teachers' grumpiness about text messaging, it does not diminish the English language.
- When students are comfortable, college has failed.
- Struggling to word the main idea of an argument in one clear and concise claim statement helps a writer to explore the complexities of an idea and develop critical thinking skills.

Popular Culture

- Applebee's and Chili's are ruining suburbia's taste for fresh food.
- The icons and eye candy encircling the television screen on major networks distracts viewers from any one particular news story.
- While steering consumers away from harmful junk foods, the low-carb diet craze has also diminished our collective joy in comfort food.
- The sex appeal sold on *American Idol* overshadows the nuances of live vocal performance.
- Microbrews have saved beer throughout the country by ending the reign of awful corporate beer and its dim-witted culture.

Professional Life

- Massage therapy, once thought a bourgeois luxury, rescues everyday people from heavy dosages of synthetic and quietly harmful prescription drugs.
- Contrary to popular opinion, an organization with many supporters and few members works more effectively than one with many members.

Activities

1. In small groups, add one claim to each category: Politics, Education, Popular Culture, Professional Life.

2. As you consider your evaluation, look back over your notes, especially at your responses to the invention questions so far, and try to make a specific and revealing point that goes beyond a bald statement. (You may find that changing linking verbs to active verbs helps in this process.)

3. In groups, narrow and intensify the following broad main claims:
- Too much money in politics is bad.
- The current college football playoff system leaves something to be desired.
- Restaurant chains are rotten places to eat.
- The college's new registration policies are unfair.

Share your revised claims with the class, and then discuss how your group proceeded through the task. What phrases or words did you target as you approached the statements?

Inventing Support

It is easy to pass off responsibility in an argument by saying that people should decide for themselves if something is good or bad. But the responsibility of an arguer is to convince people to see a topic a particular way—in this case, to see that something has a particular value. The goal is not to convince others to like or dislike something, but to convince them that something is just or unjust, ethical or unethical, manageable or unmanageable, practical or unpractical, prophetic or short-sighted, and so forth.

Criteria Nothing can be evaluated without criteria, or standards of judgment. Without a set of principles beyond our own opinions, an evaluation becomes a mere projection of personal likes and dislikes. The criteria for evaluating a restaurant might include the food quality, cost, service, atmosphere. The criteria for evaluating a movie might include the plot, acting, cinematography, special effects. An important aspect of any evaluation is deciding on appropriate criteria. For example, an evaluation of a romantic comedy might not speak to special effects, which might be an important criterion for evaluating an action-adventure movie.

John Adams gives a specific criterion in his evaluation of a *Dateline NBC* show: *News programs and investigative reports should not oversimplify complex social issues.* Although not stated directly, it is a key part of the argument:

> Many people will realize that *Dateline NBC* turned a complex issue
> into a TV drama like *Desperate Housewives* or *Grey's Anatomy.* It had
> an attractive leading character, some good drama (even a fight!), and an
> emotional (uplifting) ending. Unfortunately, though it will entertain, this
> show will disappoint a curious mind because it reduces a serious issue to
> a Hallmark card. A lot of dedicated, loving, trick-savvy teachers are prob-
> ably laughing (though with frustration) at the TV-style docu-drama of
> American education. While it showed the father in prison, the homeless
> family, and so on, according to *Dateline NBC,* it can all be overcome (all
> of American culture can be overcome) if our teachers just know to count
> backwards. *Supernanny* and *Wife Swap* deal with complexity more than
> this.

Analogical Reasoning Showing similarities to other subjects can add a powerful layer to an argument. An analogy can be explicit, drawing out many similar qualities between one thing and another and taking several paragraphs or pages to develop. Or a writer can make brief and more indirect comparisons to reinforce a key point. In "Adventure Is Calling," Michael Hilliard compares and contrasts adventure stories and video games. For example, after a paragraph explaining how overcoming adversity is key to an adventure story, Hilliard explains how overcoming adversity is also key to video games, but that video games lack the same depth of meaning:

> Video games often present the player with a crisis, typically developed through a series of cut-scenes interspersed at regular intervals throughout the game. But how often do these brief scenes of exposition transcend the 30-second cut-scene to provide real depth of meaning for the much more dominant action sequences where players spend the vast majority of their time? In writing a good adventure story, an author is able to concern herself entirely with the workings of the story, the development of the characters and the crises they face. In writing a good video game, the studio's primary goal is to create a game that is enjoyable to play, because otherwise no one would buy it.

Testimony Even in the most formal argumentative essays, writers may rely on personal experiences to support claims. While Betsy Chitwood provides support from researched, secondary sources, she also develops her argument with testimony. This testimony is an effective support strategy because Chitwood also uses researched sources, and her personal experience fits into an overall line of reasoning:

> My own experience is offered in support of this learning process. Stepping out from my familiar surroundings and entering the military brought about a disorientation that remains unmatched to this date. Military training included: becoming a member of a new culture, long hours of study, physical training, adhering to a regimented lifestyle, no personal time and all this (and more) on very little or no sleep. This learning process, albeit an extreme example, motivated me to take risks and seek ways to succeed in my chosen career. The impact of the disorientation was in direct proportion to the personal growth brought about by my "education" and it definitely shaped who I am today.

Hilliard also uses personal experience, but in a different way. The bulk of Hilliard's argument avoids personal testimony and the first-person pronoun "I," But Hilliard uses testimony in his first two paragraphs to move into his argument, and in the last paragraph to move out of it.

Literary Works One way writers help readers understand and accept claims is by alluding to literary works. In "Adventure Is Calling," to help the reader understand a key difference between video games and stories, Hilliard refers to *Alice in Wonderland* and *Lord of the Rings*. Notice how he introduces the literary works, summarizes the relevant information, and connects it to the claim the reader should accept:

> Genuine storytelling depends on some key elements. For one, any good adventure story will have a compelling crisis. In *Alice in Wonderland,* it started as little more than a dreary day; but, as the story progressed and down the rabbit hole we traveled, solving riddles, drinking potions, and avoiding the wrath of a head-hunting queen all became a part of Alice's crisis before the day was out. In perhaps one of the greatest fantasy adventure stories ever written, J.R.R. Tolkien's *Lord of the Rings,* a motley crew of characters must cross an entire continent, battling legions of powerful and deadly foes on a quest to destroy a powerful magical object upon which the fate of the world precariously hangs. Adventures thrive on dangerous quests with impossible odds. It is the very act of overcoming adversity that changes someone from ordinary to extraordinary, from "zero to hero" as the bard might say.

Appeals to Logic Lines of reasoning create logical connections that lead to a conclusion. Appeals to logic call on the reader to do more than accept a fact or statistic; they ask a reader, directly or indirectly, to think through various layers and follow a line of reasoning consisting of several related claims. Some of these claims get more support than others. An important part of making an argument is deciding how much support to provide for each claim. Readers will understand and accept some claims with little or no support, while other claims require much support.

For example, Hilliard's line of reasoning is built from a series of claims that walk the reader deeper into the issue, beginning with personal experience and observation (*Adventure stories were my favorite. The stories were often filled with peril.*) and leading up to more analytical and insightful territory (*Adventure stories have always played a major role in the growth and development of a society. We need stories of hope and determination, stories that inspire us to face the adversity in our lives head on, even when hope seems lost.*). These earlier claims and their support lead the reader to narrower and more insightful claims later in the argument:

- Instead of encouraging players to grapple with difficult circumstances in their lives, video games all too often distract us with illusions of adventure, emphasizing action, amusement and escapism over growing and learning from compelling stories and genuine role models.

- Unlike an adventure story, video games don't present a crisis with depth of meaning.

Claims in "Adventure Is Calling" Line of Reasoning:

- Adventure stories have always played a major role in the growth and development of a society.
- We need stories of hope and determination, stories that inspire us to face the adversity in our lives head on with courage, even when hope seems lost.
- Until recently, books were the primary method for delivering adventure stories to the masses, but such is becoming a thing of the past; now, movies and video games are the media of choice.
- Instead of encouraging players to grapple with difficult circumstances in their lives, video games all too often distract us with illusions of adventure, action, amusement and escapism.
- Unlike an adventure story, video games don't present a crisis with depth of meaning.
- As a dominant force in providing tales of adventure to our society, video games too often amuse rather than inspire.

Appeals to Value When writers appeal to values, they show how something or someone is either in tune or out of tune with key values such as equality, fairness, honor, and so on. For example, in "Evaluation of 'The Education of Ms. Groves,'" Adams shows that *Dateline* oversimplifies a complex issue. He argues that a news program should value critical thinking, not just entertainment.

> Certainly, tricks (techniques or strategies) help immensely in any profession, but the show oversimplified the messy issue of education—of teaching and of learning. And the degree to which it oversimplified something so complex, ongoing, and lifelong is what's stunning. The show told Americans frustrated with their education system that education is easy: Teachers simply need to be dedicated, love their students, and learn a couple nifty tricks. From the show, Americans are to conclude that students fail for one reason: because of bad teachers (because the teacher failed the student, the parent, and the country).

Throughout his argument, Adams reminds the reader of this appeal. For example,

- But in "The Education of Ms. Groves," other complex factors such as media, consumerism, or diet simply don't exist. The show makes two big mistakes: (1) It oversimplifies what it does talk about, and (2) it doesn't mention some other very messy contributing factors. [paragraph 5]
- *Dateline NBC* would have served viewers better by doing some in-depth analysis of this complex issue. Instead, they misrepresented and oversimplified, as they do with other issues (presidential elections, the environment, war). [paragraph 7]

In his essay, Hilliard appeals to values of hope, determination, and inspiration. For example,

As the heroes in our stories make brave choices and remain steadfast, we identify with them, making them role models for our own lives. In a world that often seems lost and broken—where monsters take the form of terrorist bombings and school shootings, when the princess in need of rescue is a family member struggling with addiction, or a friend dealing with emotional abuse—we need stories of hope and determination, stories that inspire us to face the adversity in our lives head on with courage, even when hope seems lost.

Use the following invention questions to develop both evidence and appeals for your argument:

▶ What criteria should I use to evaluate the topic?

▶ How can I compare or contrast my topic to something else? To what situation, person, or thing does my topic relate? What qualities do they share? How can I use those shared qualities to support my point?

▶ Have I experienced something that might reveal an important aspect of this topic? How could it fit into the argument?

▶ What claims will create a line of reasoning that leads the audience to my conclusion?

▶ What values does the subject compromise or challenge?

Arrangement

How Should I Begin? Writers often begin with a short introduction that leads up to the main claim. (See Chitwood's essay in this chapter.)

   This strategy helps take the reader from the outside world into the world of the essay; it walks the reader up to the main idea that the rest of the essay will support. But arguers don't always state the main claim in the first paragraph. For example, Adams and Hilliard spend several paragraphs establishing important background and building a line of reasoning that leads to a statement of the main claim later in the argument.

How Do I Lead the Reader from One Idea to the Next? Good arguments flow smoothly from one idea to the next. One claim in a line of reasoning follows logically from a previous claim, and arguers connect claims and support. Notice how Hilliard walks the reader from one idea in the line of reasoning (Adventure stories were often filled with peril.) to the next (Choosing what was right instead of what was easy, they persevered and won the day.):

> But it wasn't all fun and games or pleasant walks in the woods. Quite the contrary, the stories were often filled with peril. Savage beasts, fearsome swordfights, and terrifying villains always seemed to lurk in the path of my beloved heroes, and their noble quests often seemed doomed to fail. And yet, no matter how dire the situation, no matter how impossible the odds or frightening the villain, the heroes would press on, even when they had the chance to run away. Choosing what was right instead of what was easy, they persevered and won the day.

Once Hilliard has taken the reader to a new point, he is ready to make the next point: *Adventure stories have always played a major role in the growth and development of a society. . . .* While the content of Hilliard's paragraph carries the reader from one idea to the next, arguers also use transitional sentences, phrases, (such as *however, but, and*) so that readers don't get lost. In the preceding example, Hilliard uses *But, Quite the contrary,* and *And yet* to lead the reader from idea to idea.

Audience and Voice

Concessions and Qualifiers When arguers use concessions and qualifiers to acknowledge the validity of opposition, their arguments become more sophisticated and more appealing to a broader audience. *Concessions* are statements that acknowledge the value of an opposing claim, and *qualifiers* acknowledge limits on the writer's own claims.

When the argumentative stance is intense because the arguer is making heated points, concessions and qualifiers are especially valuable. Adams concedes two points in his essay. In the first concession, he admits that a single news program has certain limitations that can't be overcome:

> Of course a one-hour TV show can't cover everything. Producers must select and edit to put forth a certain argument, but the Dateline NBC argument is logically flawed.

In another paragraph, while he seems to oppose the notion of teacher tricks, he acknowledges they have some value:

> Certainly, tricks (techniques or strategies) help immensely in any profession, but the show oversimplified the messy issue of education—of teaching and of learning. And the degree to which it oversimplified something so complex, ongoing, and lifelong is what's stunning.

These concessions enhance Adams's voice by acknowledging other views. Without concessions and qualifiers, Adams would appear unaware of complexity, and the strength of his argument would suffer.

Asides (Parenthetical Comments) The aside or parenthetical comment allows writers a virtual space to stretch out and give the reader slightly more. Although the parenthetical comment is used for a broad range of purposes, three uses are dominant: (1) to give more detailed information; (2) to add an informal and often more opinionated assertion; (3) to emphasize or extend a point. In the following passage, John Adams uses asides (ideas placed within parentheses) for all three reasons. For example, in the first paragraph below, the aside "(presidential elections, the environment, war)" gives more detailed information about the "other issues":

> *Dateline NBC* would have served viewers better by doing some in-depth analysis of this complex issue. Instead, they misrepresented and oversimplified, as they do with other issues (presidential elections, the

environment, war). One consequence, whether positive or negative, of the show's "logic" may be that it motivates some people to try teaching. Golly, it looks so easy: All a teacher needs to do is get the tricks of the trade from the principal first, then he or she can avoid all the problems that Ms. Groves encountered. Of course, anyone who thinks this way isn't really thinking much.

Many people will realize that the show ignored complexities (the way a politician does when he says the economy's good because more Americans own homes than ever before). Many people will realize that *Dateline NBC* turned a complex issue into a TV drama like *Desperate Housewives* or *Grey's Anatomy*. It had an attractive leading character, some good drama (even a fight!), and an emotional (uplifting) ending. Unfortunately, though it will entertain, this show will disappoint a curious mind because it reduces a serious issue to a Hallmark card. A lot of dedicated, loving, trick-savvy teachers are probably laughing (though with frustration) at the TV-style docu-drama of American education. While it showed the father in prison, the homeless family, and so on, according to *Dateline NBC*, it can all be overcome (all of American culture can be overcome) if our teachers just know to count backwards. *Supernanny* and *Wife Swap* deal with complexity more than this.

Many of the cultural problems educators are up against are created, reinforced, and spread by American media. American children grow up immersed in a loud, often stupid, world of media and consumption (the two are really the same).

Activity

Several asides appear in the paragraphs above:

- (the way a politician does when he says the economy's good because more Americans own homes than ever before)
- (even a fight!)
- (uplifting)
- (though with frustration)
- (all of American culture can be overcome)
- (the two are really the same)

For each aside, does it 1) give more detailed information, 2) add an informal and more opinionated assertion, 3) emphasize or extend a point?

Revision

To revise, begin with the larger questions. You can find these global concerns by reviewing the chapter introduction, which emphasizes important general points when it comes to arguing about value. For example,

- What important idea—about something that is harmful or helpful, dangerous or valuable, and so on—does the essay communicate to the reader?
- How does the argument go beyond your gut reaction? How does it carefully weigh an issue or situation, analyze its layers, and claim something revelatory?
- What hidden value does it bring to light?
- Why is it important to help others accept the main claim and act accordingly?

Peer Review

Exchange drafts with at least one other writer. (If time allows, exchange with two or three writers to gather a range of perspectives or comments.) Use the following questions to generate specific constructive comments about others' drafts:

1. How does the argument answer this basic question: *What is the value of the topic?*

2. What is the argument's main claim? If it depends on linking verbs and general adjectives—"College athletics are unfair," "Liberals don't have a clue," "Required courses are unnecessary"—how can it be more focused on a particular aspect or point?

3. What is the most supportive passage? Describe why it works well in the argument. What passage might the arguer delete and why?

4. How is this argument *revelatory*? (What genuinely new perspective does it offer? How does it help us to re-see the topic?)

5. How could the writer use more allusions, examples, scenarios, or testimony to illustrate specific points?

6. How does the argument respond to opposition? What counter-arguments does the writer make? What points might the writer concede or qualify?

7. What phrases or passages could be more focused, more specific? Comment on any phrases, sentences, or passages that speak broadly

about the topic and lack a specific explanation or detailed support strategy.

8. Check for paragraph coherence: What paragraphs shift focus or take on too many separate points without a clear line of reasoning?

9. Are sources integrated smoothly, not forced into passages? Explain any gaps between the writer's line of reasoning and the ideas from an outside source. (See pages 395–410.)

10. If you used outside sources, consider the following questions:

- Have you used research as means of discovery? (pages 360–383)

- Have you evaluated sources for ideology, reliability, relevance, timeliness, and diversity? (pages 384–394)

- Are the ideas from outside sources integrated smoothly into your ideas? (pages 395–410)

- Are the sources documented appropriately (with in-text and end citation)? (pages 411–438)

Arguing Crisis

What Are We Going To Do?

R hetoricians in ancient Greece and Rome taught students about argument by using examples of crises. They would place students in hypothetical situations: *The barbarians are coming over the hill and attacking the city; what should we do?* Their students would create arguments that addressed the complexities of the situation. Such lessons were important because they illustrated the vital role of argument in everyday life. Public crises almost always give way to arguments, and the most persuasive arguments have dictated the direction of local, national, and international policies in all civilizations.

Saul David Alinsky, a Chicago community organizer, said, "When written in Chinese, the word 'crisis' is composed of two characters—one represents danger, and the other represents opportunity." From a rhetorical perspective, crises are opportunities to think differently, to act differently, to develop new ideas. In fact, in a crisis situation, thinking in the same old ways can lead nowhere. (The status quo can be downright dangerous!) Good arguers know how to bring their audiences out of intellectual, social, political, economic, and spiritual crises.

Crises loom in nearly every situation, whether social, institutional, professional, or political. Something unsavory that no one predicted is bound to happen. And once something does go awry, the arguments begin: Should we sell the company, downsize, or retool the inventory? Should we call a plumber or fix it ourselves? Should we run for the hills or stay here and fight? Should we start driving cars with better gas mileage or revamp the public transportation system in this country? Should we make friends with these pale-skinned settlers, drive them back to their boats, or ignore them and hope they go away?

Any one crisis prompts a huge variety of possible responses. But those often get whittled down to two options, and advocates of either side A or B argue over the worth of one response while tearing apart the other. This focus on only two options, however, blurs other possibilities. During the Cold War, for example, many people in the Soviet Union and the United States imagined that one side would attack the other: "It's either them or us." But a third course of events took place: the Soviet economy slowly caved in, and the standoff between the two nations faded into history.

Insightful thinkers try to see through the crossfire, beyond the two common possibilities. Imagine the following: A group of managers at a small company are faced with a dilemma. The materials they use for shipping and packaging have not arrived, and they need to ship their product to a customer who needs it on time. One manager suggests calling the customer and breaking the news but also giving a discount on the product. Another manager argues that they should ship the product without the proper packaging so the order arrives on time. While the managers debate the value of those two options, someone raises a third option: They could buy a limited amount of material from a nearby pack-aging service so a portion of the shipment could be sent and then wait to ship the remainder. The third, slightly more involved, option would probably best address the crisis. Like this situation, most crises can be handled in a variety of ways, but the realm of possibility may lie hidden behind a wall of common practices, traditional perspectives, or a per-ceived either/or choice.

A crisis is a crucial or decisive situation in which things are about to change with potentially severe or intense consequences. Experts in all fields and academic disciplines must deal with crises:

- Engineers scramble to develop new plans for a bridge that must account for new information about the shifting sediment on the river's flood plain.
- A nursing staff must respond to increased patient care demands and a projected decline in hiring.
- A council for regional artists must address an anticipated cut in funding for the National Endowment for the Arts.
- Because a local school tax levy failed, teachers must figure out how they will staff an important after-school program for junior high students.

Regardless of the particular situation, those who react to crises and pro-pose the best possible solutions (the most manageable, ethical, practi-cal, economic, far-reaching, etc.) are often the most valuable individuals in a given situation. They can see hidden implications, blurred boundar-ies, and potential consequences.

Arguments about crisis involve two layers: (1) the crisis, and (2) possible solutions. The essays in this chapter spend more time developing the first layer—attempting to persuade readers that a particular crisis exists. Tracy Webster, Amber Edmondson, and Laurie Schutza focus on crises related to homes, consumer behavior, and hoarding. Their essays focus primarily on the crises and not so much on solutions. Because readers may not see the urgency of each situation, these writers devote most of their arguments to the crisis layer. Curtis White takes a slightly different approach by focusing on the complex cause of the crisis. He claims that the environmental crisis continues because mainstream society is too weak to acknowledge it and because environmental activism is incapable of addressing its real origins. Curtis argues that solutions become possible only if we understand the complexity of the crisis. As these arguments illustrate, the emphasis on crisis or solution depends on the topic, the opposing voices, and even previous solutions.

Proposals

A proposal is an argument that calls for a particular course of action. Proposals are one type of argument that emerges from a critical social situation—a situation that warrants collective or public action. They take many forms. Business proposals, course proposals, and congressional or legislative proposals are more formal types, which require specific formatting conventions. But proposals also come in more generic and informal arguments. In fact, the proposal essay is a common form, and it usually contains the following elements:

- **Description of the situation that warrants action (the crisis):** evidence for or appeals about the crisis situation.

- **Counterarguments:** why people should accept the situation as warranting action, despite other portrayals of the situation.

- **Description of the proposed solution:** how it would address the situation, how life would look once it is implemented.

- **Support (evidence and appeals) for the solution:** why it should be implemented or at least attempted.

- **Counterarguments against other solutions:** how other solutions (beyond the writer's) might fall short.

- **Concession about other solutions:** how other solutions (beyond the writer's) might be of value.

The proposal argument has no universal formula. Its elements change depending on the situation. For instance, if a writer is addressing a relatively common crisis, something that many other people have acknowledged as important, then he will spend less time describing that crisis but more time dealing with other solutions. If a writer is taking on a relatively new crisis, something readers have not generally acknowledged, then she would spend more time on the description and little or no time discussing other solutions. But despite the potential difference, one quality remains consistent: The proposal writer foregrounds or prioritizes the action to be taken. While some arguments prioritize the crisis itself (getting readers to believe that a particular crisis exists), proposals spend more energy on asserting and defending the steps to address the crisis or a plan of action.

The invention work throughout this chapter will generate important rhetorical strategies for a proposal argument. Specifically, the following questions should be considered for a successful argument:

- **The crisis:** What is the critical situation? Do readers need to be introduced to it and convinced that action should be taken? Why might people dismiss the situation? What reasons would they give for dismissing it? Can you address those reasons?

- **The solution:** What particular strategy can you assert? How will your solution address specific elements or causes of the crisis? How is your solution particularly practical, logical, manageable, ethical, humane, or economical?

- **Other solutions:** What else has been tried or proposed? Why might your solution be more practical, manageable, logical, ethical, cost-effective, or necessary?

The proposal writer foregrounds or prioritizes the action to be taken.

The Idols of Environmentalism

CURTIS WHITE

In this essay, White makes a powerful move: he explains how the environmental crisis continues despite, and even because of, environmentalists' arguments. While many essays about the environment blame particular people or policies for ongoing destruction, White walks readers toward increasingly subtle layers of cause and effect. For him, the crisis lingers in the very language most people use to discuss the crisis. In this sense, White argues about the nature of the argument. The article was first published in *Orion Magazine* in 2007.

Environmental destruction proceeds apace in spite of all the warnings, the good science, the 501(c)3 organizations with their memberships in the millions, the poll results, and the martyrs perched high in the branches of sequoias or shot dead in the Amazon. This is so not because of a power, a strength out there that we must resist. It is because we are weak and fearful. Only a weak and fearful society could invest so much desperate energy in protecting activities that are the equivalent of suicide.

For instance, trading carbon emission credits and creating markets in greenhouse gases as a means of controlling global warming is not a way of saying we're so confident in the strength of the free market system that we can even trust it to fix the problems it creates. No, it's a way of saying that we are so frightened by the prospect of stepping outside of the market system on which we depend for our national wealth, our jobs, and our sense of normalcy that we will let the logic of that system try to correct its own excesses even when we know we're just kidding ourselves. This delusional strategy is embedded in the Kyoto agreement, which is little more than a complex scheme to create a giant international market in pollution. Even Kyoto, of which we speak longingly—"Oh, if only we would join

it!"—is not an answer to our problem but a capitulation to it, so concerned is it to protect what it calls "economic growth and development." Kyoto is just a form of whistling past the graveyard. And it is not just international corporations who do this whistling; we all have our own little stake in the world capitalism has made and so we all do the whistling.

The problem for even the best-intentioned environmental activism is that it imagines that it can confront a problem external to itself. Confront the bulldozers. Confront the chainsaws. Confront Monsanto. Fight the power. What the environmental movement is not very good at is acknowledging that something in the very fabric of our daily life is deeply anti-nature as well as anti-human. It inhabits not just bad-guy CEOs at Monsanto and Weyerhaeuser but nearly every working American, environmentalists included.

It is true that there are CEO-types, few in number, who are indifferent to everything except money, who are cruel and greedy, and so the North Atlantic gets stripped of cod and any number of other species taken incidentally in what is the factory trawler's wet version of a scorched-earth policy. Or some junk bond maven buys up a section of old-growth redwoods and "harvests" it without hesitation when his fund is in sudden need of "liquidity." Nevertheless, all that we perceive to be the destructiveness of corporate culture in relation to nature is not the consequence of its power, or its capacity for dominating nature ("taming," as it was once put, as if what we were dealing with was the lion act at the circus). Believing in powerful corporate evildoers as the primary source of our problems forces us to think in cartoons.

Besides, corporations are really powerless to be anything other than what they are. I suspect that, far from being perverse merchants of greed hell-bent on destruction, these corporate entities are as bewildered as we are. Capitalism—especially in its corporate incarnation—has a logos, a way of reasoning. Capitalism is in the position of the notorious scorpion who persuades the fox to ferry him across a river, arguing that he won't sting the fox because it wouldn't be in his interest to do so, since he'd drown along with the fox. But when in spite of this logic he stings the fox anyway, all he can offer in explanation is "I did it because it is in my nature." In the same way, it's not as if businessmen perversely seek to destroy their own world. They have vacation homes in the Rockies or New England and enjoy walks in the forest, too. They simply have other priorities which are to them a duty.

The idea that we have powerful corporate villains to thank for the sorry state of the natural world is what Francis Bacon called an "idol of the tribe." According to Bacon, an idol is a truth based on insufficient evidence but maintained by constant affirmation within the tribe of believers. In spite of this insufficiency, idols do not fall easily or often. Tribes are capable of exerting will based on principles, but they are capable only with the greatest difficulty of willing the destruction of their own principles. It's as if they feel that it is better to stagger from frustration to frustration than to return honestly to the question, does what we believe actually make sense? The idea of fallen idols always suggests tragic disillusionment, but this is in fact a good thing. If they don't fall, there is no hope for discovering the real problems and the best and truest response to them. All environmentalists understand that the global crisis we are experiencing requires urgent action, but not everyone understands that if our activism is driven by idols we can exhaust ourselves with effort while having very little effect on the crisis. Most frighteningly, it is even possible that our efforts can sustain the crisis. The question the environmental tribe must ask is, do our mistaken assumptions actually cause us to conspire against our own interests?

The belief that corporate power is the unique source of our problems is not the only idol we are subject to. There is an idol even in the language we use to account for our problems. Our primary dependence on the scientific language of "environment," "ecology," "diversity," "habitat," and "ecosystem" is a way of acknowledging the superiority of the very kind of rationality that serves not only the Sierra Club but corporate capitalism as well. For instance:

- "You can pump this many tons of greenhouse gases into the atmosphere without disturbing the major climatic systems."
- "This much contiguous habitat is necessary to sustain a population allowing for a survivable gene pool for this species."
- "We'll keep a list, a running tally of endangered species (as we'll call these animals), and we'll monitor their numbers, and when that number hits a specified threshold we'll say they are 'healthy,' or we'll say they are 'extinct.' All this is to be done by bureaucratic fiat."

I am not speaking here of all the notorious problems associated with proving scientifically the significance of environmental destruction. My concern is with the wisdom of using as our primary weapon the rhetoric and logic of the very entities we suspect of causing our problems in the first place. Perhaps we support legalistic responses to problems, with all their technoscientific descriptors, out of a sense that this is the best we can do for the moment. But the danger is always that eventually we come to believe this language and its mindset ourselves. This mindset is generally called "quantitative reasoning," and it is second nature to Anglo-Americans. Corporate execs are perfectly comfortable with it, and corporate philanthropists give their dough to environmental organizations that speak it. Unfortunately, it also has the consequence of turning environmentalists into quislings, collaborators, and virtuous practitioners of a cost-benefit logic figured in songbirds.

It is because we have accepted this rationalist logos as the only legitimate means of debate that we are willing to think that what we need is a balance between the requirements of human economies and the "needs" of the natural world. It's as if we were negotiating a trade agreement with the animals and trees unlucky enough to have to share space with us. What do you need? we ask them. What are your minimum requirements? We need to know the minimum because we're not likely to leave you more than that. We're going to consume any "excess." And then it occurs to us to add, unless of course you taste good. There is always room for an animal that tastes good.

We use our most basic vocabulary, words like "ecosystem," with a complete innocence, as if we couldn't imagine that there might be something perilous in it. What if such language were actually the announcement of the defeat of what we claim to want? That's the worm at the heart of the rose of the "ecologist." It is something that environmentalism has never come to terms with because the very advocates for environmental health are most comfortable with the logic of science, never mind what else that logic may be doing for the military and industry. Would people and foundations be as willing to send contributions to The Nature Conservancy or the Sierra Club if the leading logic of the organization were not "ecosystems" but "respect for life" or "reverence for creation"? Such notions are, for many of us, compromised by associations with the Catholic Church and evangelicalism, and they don't loosen the purse strings of philanthropy. "Let's keep a nice, clean scientific edge between us and religion," we protest. In the end, environmental science criticizes not only corporate destructiveness but (as it has always done) more spiritual notions of nature as well.

Environmentalism seems to conclude that the best thing it can do for nature is make a case for it, as if it were always making a summative argument before a jury with the backing of the best science. Good children of the Enlightenment, we keep expecting Reason to prevail (and in a perverse and destructive way, it does prevail). It is the language of "system" (nature as a kind of complicated machine) that allows most of us to feel comfortable with working for or giving money to environmental organizations. We even seem to think that the natural system should work in consort with our economic system. Why, we argue, that rainforest might contain the cure for cancer. By which we also mean that it could provide profitable products for the pharmaceutical industry and local economies. (God help the doomed indigenous culture once the West decides that it has an economy that needs assistance.) Al Gore's *An Inconvenient Truth* may have distressing things to say about global warming, but subconsciously it is an extended apology for scientific rationality, the free market, and our utterly corrupted democracy. Gore doesn't have to defend these things directly; he merely has to pretend that nothing else exists. Even the awe of Immanuel Kant's famous "starry skies above" is lost to modern environmentalism, so obsessed is it with what data, graphs, and a good PowerPoint presentation can show.

In short, there would be nothing inappropriate or undesirable were we to understand our relation to nature in spiritual terms or poetic terms or, with Emerson and Thoreau, in good old American transcendental terms, but there is no broadly shared language in which to do this. So we are forced to resort to what is in fact a lower common denominator: the languages of science and bureaucracy. These languages have broad legitimacy in our culture, a legitimacy they possess largely because of the thoroughness with which they discredited Christian religious discourse in the eighteenth and nineteenth centuries. But many babies went out with the bath water of Christian dogma and superstition. One of those was morality. Even now, science can't say why we ought not to harm the environment except to say that we shouldn't be self-destructive. Another of these lost spiritual children was our very relation as human beings to the mystery of Being as such. As the philosopher G. W.

Leibniz famously wondered, "Why is there some-thing rather than nothing?" For St. Thomas Aqui-nas, this was the fundamental religious question. In the place of a relation to the world that was founded on this mystery, we have a relation that is objec-tive and data driven. We no longer have a forest; we have "board feet." We no longer have a landscape, a world that is our own; we have "valuable natural resources." Even avowed Christians have been slow to recall this spiritualized relationship to the world. For example, only recently have American evangel-icals begun thinking of the environment in terms of what they call "creation care." We don't have to be born again to agree with evangelicals that one of the most powerful arguments missing from the environmentalist's case is reverence for what sim-ply is. One of the heroes of Goethe's *Faust* was a character called Care (Sorge), who showed to Faust the unscrupulousness of his actions and led him to salvation. Environmentalism has made a Faustian pact with quantitative reasoning; science has given it power but it cannot provide deliverance. If envi-ronmentalism truly wishes, as it claims, to want to "save" something—the planet, a species, itself—it needs to rediscover a common language of Care.

Brooks Kraft/Corbis

The lessons of our idols come to this: you cannot defeat something that you imagine to be an external threat to you when it is in fact inter-nal to you, when its life is your life. And even if it were external to you, you cannot defeat an enemy by thinking in the terms it chooses, and by doing only those things that not only don't harm it but with which it is perfectly comfortable. The truth is, our idols are actually a great convenience to us. It is convenient that we can imagine a power beyond us because that means we don't have to spend much time examining our own lives. And it is very conve-nient that we can hand the hard work of resistance over to scientists, our designated national problem solvers.

We cannot march forth, confront, and defini-tively defeat the Monsantos of the world, especially

not with science (which, it should go without saying, Monsanto has plenty of). We can, however, look at ourselves and see all of the ways that we conspire against what we imagine to be our own most urgent interests. Perhaps the most powerful way in which we conspire against ourselves is the simple fact that we have jobs. We are willingly part of a world designed for the convenience of what Shakespeare called "the visible God": money. When I say we have jobs, I mean that we find in them our home, our sense of being grounded in the world, grounded in a vast social and economic order. It is a spectacu-larly complex, even breathtaking, order, and it has two enormous and related problems. First, it seems to be largely responsible for the destruction of the natural world. Second, it has the strong tendency to reduce the human beings inhabiting it to two func-tions, working and consuming. It tends to hollow us out. It creates a hole in our sense of ourselves and of this country, and it leaves us with few alter-natives but to try to fill that hole with money and the things money buys. We are not free to dismiss money because we fear that we'd disappear, we'd be nothing at all without it. Money is, in the words of Buddhist writer David Loy, "the flight from empti-ness that makes life empty."

Needless to say, many people with environmental sympathies will easily agree with what I've just said and imagine that in fact they do what they can to resist work and consumption, to resist the world as arranged for the convenience of money. But here again I suspect we are kidding ourselves. Rather than taking the risk of challenging the roles money and work play in all of our lives by actually taking the responsibility for reordering our lives, the most prominent strategy of environmentalists seems to be to "give back" to nature through the bequests, the annuities, the Working Assets credit cards and long distance telephone schemes, and the socially responsible mutual funds advertised in Sierra and proliferating across the environmental movement. Such giving may make us feel better, but it will never be enough. Face it, we all have a bit of the robber baron turned philanthropist in us. We're willing to be generous in order to "save the world" but not before we've insured our own survival in the reigning system. It's not even clear that this philanthropy is a pure expression of generosity since the bequest and annuity programs are carefully measured to provide attractive tax benefits and appealing rates of return.

Even when we are trying to aid the environment, we are not willing as individuals to leave the system that we know in our heart of hearts is the cause of our problems. We are even further from

knowing how to take the collective risk of leaving this system entirely and ordering our societies differently. We are not ready. Not yet, at least.

Analyzing Argument

1. Summarize White's argument in one or two sentences. Try not to lose the complexity of his main claim.

2. White makes many claims in the essay, but what are his most important claims? In other words, what are the main premises (steps in his line of reasoning)? What logical steps must you, as a reader, make to accept his point about the crisis?

3. How does White use appeals to value? Point to one passage that relies on an appeal to value and explain its role in the overall argument.

4. How does counterargument work in White's essay? Focus on one passage and explain how it takes on (pushes against, refutes, or overturns) an opposing position.

5. Do you detect a solution in White's argument? If so, what kind of solution does he suggest?

6. Describe White's voice in this argument. Point to a particular passage that illustrates your understanding of his voice.

Big House in the Wilderness: Moratoriums on Building and Individual Irresponsibility

TRACY WEBSTER

Tracy Webster developed this argument after reading Anna Quindlen's 2003 *Newsweek* article, "A Shock to the System," which proposes a moratorium on building permits. Webster seems to understand what he's up against: an ideology of self-righteousness and privilege. He knows that most readers feel entitled to do, buy, and build whatever they please. It's the American way. Therefore, he takes on that ideology directly and figures it into his argument for a radical solution. Webster's response also illustrates one way an outside source can be used in an argument: as a springboard into one's own set of assertions.

It's hunting season. I hear guns. Where I live, you can't drive home at night without stopping for a deer in the road, an elk, or even a moose. A bear ran alongside my car one night, and in the same place a few months later, one chased a jogger. What a great place this must be to hunt. In October, when it snows in the mountains, wild animals come down into the valley, and hunters shoot them. Even buffalo are in danger. They call it "harvesting" buffalo, and when the great bovines wander down into the lower elevations and cross a certain line (thus, "leaving the park"), hunters are there, to harvest them. The ranchers like this because they are afraid that the buffalo will infect their cattle with brucellosis, a bovine disease that the buffalo carry. No record of buffalo infecting cattle exists.

This is not an anti-hunting essay, though. Where I live, people build houses where buffalo live. They like it here. So they see a nice spot, a 20-acre parcel; deer graze on it and perhaps an eagle nests high in a tree. And the people build a 3,000- or 4,000- or

David Prince/Corbis

5,000-square-foot home, right there where the wild animals used to live. The people are proud of their homes. They show them off to their friends. Their homes make them feel good about themselves. If you live in such a home, you are no doubt successful. No doubt. But the deer eat their saplings and the mud swallows make nests in their eaves. And it's off: the battle between the homeowner and the nuisance, wildlife. So, the homebuilders are as big a threat to the wildlife as are the hunters. A bigger threat, really.

In "A Shock to the System," *Newsweek* essayist Anna Quindlen says that "no one seems to have considered the obvious alternative: instead of issuing hunting permits, call a moratorium on building permits. Permanently." (She's referring to hunting permits in New Jersey, for bear.) To some, Quindlen's argument may seem extreme, unnecessary, and perhaps un-American, taking away honest, hardworking Americans' rights to "life, liberty, and the pursuit of happiness." If they have, or can borrow, the money to buy property and build a home, don't they as Americans have the right (the freedom) to build as large a home as they individually choose to build anywhere they can buy to build it? It is, after all, their money, their home, their inalienable right, isn't it?

A moratorium on building, at this time, anywhere, seems unlikely. With the current American mindset, it is more likely that a building permit will be granted for yet another big home building supply store, one of those massive cathedrals to home building which helps make it cheaper and easier to conquer and destroy nature through construction. But are moratoriums on building permits, as Quindlen suggests, really necessary?

One question is: Can't individual Americans simply build differently? (Are moratoriums necessary?) Of course, to pursue this question (this line of thinking), the reader must accept the premise that Americans are overbuilding, and that by overbuilding, Americans are foolishly and unnecessarily overdestroying nature, the environment, wildlife. They have to accept the premise that current building practices are somehow harmful. Some Americans, to be certain, don't accept this premise. Here's why they should:

As Americans, we must walk a narrow path. The cities are dirty and crowded and dangerous. The countryside, the mountains, the wilderness are clean and peaceful. Who can blame someone for fleeing the city—or, even more, for fleeing the suburbs? What an awful place suburbia can be. It's thick with traffic and littered with strip malls. If it's all you know, it's not that bad; but to the more rural-minded, it can be quite offensive. And as millions of suburbanites and city dwellers discover the pain and misery and hell of their lives, they dream of getting out. And some do.

But Americans, perhaps more than any other people who have ever lived, are terrible at walking narrow paths. They cannot just move to the wilderness and live. They must pound the wilderness to death. They must beat it to hell. They must drive gas-guzzling, polluting, school-bus-sized SUVs a hundred miles to work and back. They must build huge homes, large enough to be small hotels.

Anna Quindlen says that according to the National Association of Home Builders, "the average American home has doubled in size in the past century." Some see this, no doubt, as a great achievement—a sign of their own and their country's success and prosperity. But family size hasn't doubled; it has decreased. Americans have come to simply want, expect, and possess *more stuff*. And along with this, they cannot merely displace a few animals and live in relative peace with the rest. Instead, they see it as their right to destroy the homes—and what have been the homes for centuries—of more wildlife than a thousand humans have any acceptable reason to destroy, simply because they'd like to have a large and impressive home in a pretty place. Sadly, this is why Quindlen's proposed moratorium is necessary, and why it is the only solution.

Americans, left alone, will not build smaller or smarter or more compassionately. Instead, a few concerned activists, those who truly see the issue, must build a coalition to force others, through government action (a moratorium on building permits) to live more responsibly.

I began this essay by thinking out loud how it seems odd that men come here to hunt deer that you have to try not to hit with your car. The deer aren't hard to find, and when they see you they just stand there, motionless, staring. Of course, you can't shoot the ones standing on the road. You have to drive out a ways, then walk a bit farther, and then shoot one. Back there, in the woods, the deer might have a better chance, by blending in with the trees and hearing or smelling or seeing you before you see them.

But this is not an anti-hunting essay or an anti-house-in-the-wilderness essay. It is an anti-big-house-in-the-wilderness essay. The big house in the wilderness is more dangerous than any hunter is. It's the big house, the too-big house, that is unjustifiable. Quindlen compares the way that Americans act with their animal counterparts today to the way our ancestors once acted toward Native American people: We are willing to "tolerate" them as long as "they don't demand to share." She says, "If they don't cooperate, we slaughter them." We "harvest" them, she means. She is right to make connections between the past and the present, and between building permits and hunting permits: *Homebuilders are slaughtering buffalo.*

Moratoriums on building permits would not be necessary if individual homebuilders acted more responsibly, but how in our present culture could Americans ever bring themselves to act more responsibly? Some do, of course. But most can't. They simply see it as their right to do whatever they feel like doing. They see anything else as an infringement on their freedom, a personal insult, and a public injustice. Quindlen's suggestion requires collective, or government, action—a more extreme measure that must be taken to prevent individual freedom-loving Americans from eating the whole pie, instead of having just one piece. As more and more Americans, attracted to a beautiful life among wildlife, build homes in deserts and forests and fields, their own sensitivity and integrity is at stake. We would all benefit if individual homebuilders had in the past considered, *or would in the future consider,* a few hard questions before changing the landscape so drastically:

- How large a home should I build? How destructive to the plants and animals should it be? How important or necessary is it that I build such a large home where animals once lived, and won't be able to live anymore?
- What, honestly, is my relationship to nature? Am I mostly appreciating it, or am I mostly torturing it?
- How might I build differently out of respect for what I claim to value and love—wildlife?

What would happen if Americans could somehow overcome their own selfish and hypocritical desires to overbuild and overdestroy, and instead make *every* effort, not just *some* effort, to peacefully and respectfully coexist with nonhuman life? Doing this would require a new sort of vision—seeing all the wildlife that they presently overlook. It would also require a new look at rhetoric, replacing words like "harvest" with "slaughter" and "environment" with "home." What would happen if all new homebuilders saw themselves more as visitors, guests, and newcomers? And better yet, as intruders, conquerors, and imperialists?

If Quindlen's proposal seems extreme, it is because in American society where narrow paths have become unimaginable to many, individual freedom allows for, and encourages, individual *irre*sponsibility. As long as Americans are free to build obscenely large houses, to destroy acres of wildlife habitat, to pollute the air and rivers, many Americans are going to do exactly that. Why? Because they see it as their right, because they are free, because they are Americans. Quindlen is right: Moratoriums on building permits are the obvious alternative.

Analyzing Argument

1. Why does Webster connect hunting and home building? How is that connection important to his line of reasoning?

2. In paragraph 4, Webster says, "With the current American mindset, it is more likely that a building permit will be granted for yet another big home building supply store. . . ." To what mindset does Webster refer?

3. Describe Webster's use of counterargument, concession, and qualifier. How do they function in his argument? Which does he rely on most?

4. As a secondary source, Quindlen's argument is vital to Webster. In your own words, how would you describe the relationship between Quindlen's and Webster's arguments?

5. Webster says, *"Homebuilders are slaughtering buffalo"* (paragraph 11). What is the effect of this phrase on readers? What is the effect of the italics?

The Pack Rat Among Us

LAURIE SCHUTZA

Laurie Schutza developed the following argument over several weeks in her English composition course. As with many good academic arguments, Schutza's began with a personal problem—one that worked quietly in her own life. She even wondered if it was appropriate for the public context of academic argument. But as she invented layers of her initial thoughts and researched others' struggles with hoarding, she realized the significance of the topic. Her argument, then, attempts to drag this quiet crisis into the light of day.

I look up at the house on the hill. Situated in a relatively affluent neighborhood, overlooking the ocean, it looks like a normal, well-maintained home from street level, but as I walk up the driveway and it comes into full view, the reality of the situation hits me like a stack of old newspapers. There is no doubt this is the home of compulsive hoarders. It is also the home of people I love.

The contents of the garage, filled with unpacked moving boxes of twenty years, unfinished projects, and every tool known to mankind are spilling onto the driveway. There is an old Chevy van with peeling paint that has been sitting up for years. Several working refrigerators and freezers filled with food that will spoil before eaten line the narrow pathway to the front door. Along this obstacle course, I must watch my step, for there are many tripping hazards. A tangle of old hoses and extension cords roam and twist like snakes along the trail. Mountains of long-forgotten objects peek from under tattered tarps overgrown with ivy. I walk past old tires, car parts, construction materials, broken-down appliances, and old machinery in need of repair. Standing water, fallen leaves, moss, and lichen form the frosting on top of the layers of debris. The front porch is lined with boxes and bags of unknown contents.

As I enter the front door, I am greeted with disorganized heaps and stacks of papers, plastic bags, more cardboard boxes, and various junk drawers. Finding a place to sit becomes a scavenger hunt. If I investigate further, I can see the sofas, chairs, tables, antiques, and decorations that furnished what was once a tasteful living room, now made unlivable by the clutter. The dining room is covered with piles of paper. Family meals at the table are nonexistent. Junk mail, newspapers, magazines, videotapes, vitamin supplements, dishes, and stockpiles of food and paper products fill the kitchen counter space. Even the stove is unusable unless one moves the piles. Empty milk jugs, cans, containers, and general trash line the kitchen floor.

The rest of the house is no better. I squeeze myself through cramped paths where cobwebs drape from the ceiling and a thick veil of dust covers everything. The closets are full to capacity and are spilling into every bedroom. Clothes, books, knick-knacks, brand-new electronic equipment never even taken out of their boxes, and more magazines and paper fill every nook and cranny. Items such as food, batteries, flashlights, tools, work gloves, and office supplies are stashed and stockpiled "just in case." Family treasures, mementos, and heirlooms languish under the junk like relics waiting to be discovered. It's impossible to find anything when needed, time is wasted, and important things get lost. There is no space to work, play, sit, eat, or even sleep. No longer can any of the rooms be used for their intended purpose. As I maneuver my way through the house, I feel like the walls are swallowing me: "I'm suffocating," I think to myself. How has this happened? How has the house on the hill become such an insurmountable nightmare?

To many observers this is certainly an extreme situation, but the inhabitants of this house did not start out this way. It was a slow process of accumulation over years. These family members are not idle or lazy, but hard-working, well-educated individuals. To the outside world, they seem perfectly normal and no one would ever suspect. But they are experts at hiding their secret life, never inviting guests in and only meeting friends in places other than their chaotic home. Hoarders are generally misunderstood by the public and are jokingly referred to as "pack rats." Most of us would be appalled and say, "Why don't they just clean up the junk?" But hoarders have extreme difficulty giving up their possessions and become emotionally attached to everything they own. They don't like living this way and would like to change, but the task seems too overwhelming, the clutter so pervasive that they can't figure out where to begin. Living in fear, embarrassment, and shame, they have built a fortress of stuff that isolates them from the outside world. Feeling out of control, they can eventually give up.

Why do hoarders attach themselves to things? Is it because of fear and what are they afraid of? Have they been adding things to their existence to fill an emptiness or void? Are they hiding within the walls, battling the inevitable realities of life such as new relationships, careers, and even death? The fortress of stuff may be a defense against fear. Like a security blanket giving them a layer of comfort that insulates them from the outside world, their possessions may help them to feel safe and secure. Maybe by attaching themselves to things, they are fulfilling a need for security.

Many people are happy to be considered pack rats, collecting items and storing them until needed. Our homes may even have one of those junk rooms, hidden behind closed doors that we would rather forget about. But when this mentality is taken to an extreme, and every room is crammed with large disorderly quantities of things, the home can become dangerous and unlivable. This condition is known as compulsive hoarding. It is a debilitating mental illness related to obsessive-compulsive disorder (OCD). And more common than one might think: "2.5 percent of Americans suffer from OCD, which translates into approximately seven million people or roughly one out of every forty adults . . . between one-quarter to one-third of those with

OCD also have hoarding symptoms" (Neziroglu, Bubick, and Yaryura-Tobias 2). Researchers say this estimate may be low because of the secretive nature of the hoarder. According to The Children of Hoarders, a support group devoted to helping those with this disorder, "more than 1.4 million homes in the United States alone are . . . hoard homes" (Children of Hoarders). There are even studies showing that hoarding can be genetic. One such study "found that 84% of compulsive hoarders reported a family history of hoarding behaviors in at least one first-degree relative" (qtd. in Saxena and Maidment 1144). There are numerous motivations behind hoarding, and even though the volume of items differentiates us from the hoarders, we may recognize some of these tendencies in ourselves.

What is the fundamental reason behind hoarding and collecting stuff? Humans developed approximately 100,000 years ago as hunter/gatherers. To survive brutal winters, drought, and famine, our ancestors were genetically programmed to eat and store calories when food was abundant. Likewise, they learned it was to their advantage to save and store anything that was important for survival. But what else motivated them to save? According to the authors of the book *Overcoming Compulsive Hoarding*, "fear is the basic reason behind the drive to save. . . . If you think about the bare essentials for human survival, food and shelter are crucial. . . . [Hoarders] may have learned to temporarily avoid feeling fear by feeling secure and safe with [their] possessions" (Neziroglu, Bubick, and Yaryura-Tobias 31).

To acquire more and save is fundamentally human. No wonder the tendency to stockpile and hoard is affecting our daily lives. As Mary Duenwald writes in her article for *Discovery*, "That compulsion, scientists now theorize, is a natural and adaptive instinct gone amok" (30). Whereas at one time, only royalty and the wealthy could afford material extravagances, the Industrial Revolution and mass production created a middle class that could finally enjoy affordable goods. Now that food and material things are plentiful, we have developed problems of overindulgence.

But what motivates hoarders to amass huge quantities of stuff? The reasons vary, but the fear of being without is the common thread that runs through the compulsion. They are afraid to discard anything that might be useful some day, so they decide to keep everything. The "just in case" scenario comes into play (Neziroglu, Bubrick, and Yaryura-Tobias 133). Hoarders live in fear of being unprotected if anything goes wrong. They acquire junk as insurance against any conceivable future need. They feel their very survival depends on it. (And many elderly hoarders are products of the Great Depression where they were taught to save everything or the Cold War where they were taught to stockpile and always be prepared.)

Every item seems unique and therefore irreplaceable. Hoarders tend to keep what many may consider useless items such as empty food containers or cardboard boxes. They may even place the same importance on items like empty milk jugs, light bulbs, or a gold necklace. One may find all three of these items in one of the many piles of a hoarder. They have difficulty categorizing so everything ends up in disorganized heaps. Printed information such as newspapers and magazines are not thrown out until they are read and understood (Neziroglu, Bubrick, and Yaryura-Tobias 35). They actually fear losing information that may change their lives for the better. The amount of paper coming into all our homes is staggering. Tons of junk mail, magazines, and newspapers worm their way in, and if one doesn't stay on top of the paper flow, it can stack up fast. Reading it all can become a monumental task. Unread reading material is one of the most common items kept by hoarders. They think, one of these days they will read it all. But that day never comes.

Hoarding can actually replace spending time with loved ones. Hoarded objects fill the emptiness and loneliness. Empty nesters replace their grown children, retired people replace a lost career, and a widow replaces a deceased spouse.

Inability to prioritize and indecisiveness is perhaps the most pervasive problem facing the hoarder. Having to decide what to get rid of, they begin to feel anxious and uncomfortable (Neziroglu, Bubrick, and Yaryura-Tobias 36). They overthink every item, so they end up keeping it all. A phenomenon called "churning" may occur (qtd. in Neziroglu, Bubrick, and Yaryura-Tobias 38) when one tries to clean one pile and it is intermixed with another. Things get lost, creating more disorder, and piles never leave the house.

Hoarders tend to have many interests and can be quite creative, seeing the potential in everything. They want to do it all themselves at their own pace, considering it an extravagance or a sign of weakness to enlist the help of others. In reality they think no one else can do the job to their standards. Having big, ambitious ideas, they may decide to start several projects all at once, but they bounce back and forth between the tasks and cannot seem to follow through. There is an inclination to avoid the task because everything they do becomes tedious and overwhelming. This difficulty to prioritize can lead to procrastination. Hoarders have this utopian vision that one day there will be enough time to finish all they plan to do, including cleaning up the mess. The problem is there's never enough time and in actuality, they would need several lifetimes to accomplish all they set out to do. This way of thinking may even be their defense against the inevitabilities of life and death; their way of displaying their invincibility. As long as these ongoing works in progress are alive and well, they are too. Unfortunately, time marches on all too quickly, and all the items bought and saved, with the best of intentions, are just added to the other piles of grand dreams.

These are some of the more common traits of the hoarder. They may sound extreme, but how far removed are we, the consumers, from this tendency to collect and save? Are we just a few steps away from extreme hoarding? Do we *really need* everything we buy and save? Although the hoarder's behavior is taken to a pathological extreme, we all seem to share the same basic tendency to avoid fear by acquiring and collecting possessions that create that feeling, or at least impression, of safety and security. And maybe the pathology is somewhat collective. America has become a nation of mass consumers. We are encouraged to be good shoppers and it's our obligation as citizens to buy, because it fuels greater productivity, creating more jobs that lead to more wealth for consumers to buy more stuff. It's the American way. Life might be just a little more perfect if we just had that new television, computer, or car. We are constant upgraders and are driven to buy the newest, up-to-date gadget proclaiming, "Just get rid of the old model," creating our so-called "throwaway" society. The problem is, hoarders don't throw anything away and consider themselves resourceful recyclers. In the past thirty years, we've gone from records, reel-to-reel, eight-track, cassettes, compact discs, and now MP-3 players all in a blink of an eye. Every year the technology gets smaller, sleeker, and faster. Consumers want "it" and have to have "it" now (whatever "it" may be). The whole system is geared to help us acquire all that we desire, but the hawkers of products haven't addressed how to rid ourselves of these things when they become undesirable.

Advertising is built around and for consumption. We are constantly being force-fed stuff—and the need for more stuff. We can't escape the barrage. According to University of Victoria Professor Daniel Laskarin:

> We live in a culture of consumption. . . . Many of us sacrifice more than half of our lives doing things we don't enjoy to buy things we don't need. We have plenty, yet feel dissatisfied. . . . The only way out is to stop and ask what we really want instead of letting the media and big business tell us (qtd. in Gibson 61).

Television commercials try to convince us that our dreams will come true if we buy their products. Celebrities promote spending money to achieve a certain look. Newspapers are full of shopping "bargains" we can't resist. They lure us in with early-bird specials and enticing coupons. Holiday advertising encourages us to buy gifts to show our love for one another. But stores can actually create a sense of urgency unleashing shopping frenzies turning violent and ugly, where people fight over merchandise and possibly get trampled in the process. The ads can convince us to buy things we didn't even know we needed.

There are more and more ways to acquire things. Department, specialty, and discount stores are old reliables. The arrival of online shopping and television shopping channels has made purchasing even more accessible. Items can be ordered without having to leave home or interact with people, creating more separation from the outside world. And now popular warehouse stores such as Sam's Club and Costco encourage us to stockpile. Garage sales, resale shops, flea markets, and antique malls are favorite places to find bargains. Television shows like *Antiques Roadshow* give us false hope that our treasures will become valuable someday. This encourages us to save items that maybe we shouldn't. Some of these treasures may end up on eBay and the cycle goes on. Compulsive shopping is now a common form of shopping. It sends millions of "average" consumers spiraling into debt. Meanwhile, the average home becomes a warehouse for all the stuff. Junk drawers spill over to kitchen counters and tables. Closets, attics, and basements overflow into bedrooms. Crammed garages lead to storage rentals. Our possessions elbow us into bigger homes so we can fill more rooms with even more stuff. According to Anna Quindlen, "the average American home has doubled in size in the past century" (qtd. in Webster 302). Tracy Webster continues, "Some see this, no doubt, as a great achievement—a sign of their own and their country's success and prosperity. But family size hasn't doubled; it has decreased. Americans have come to simply want,

Kathy Bishop/morguefile.com

from letting anything new into our lives. We may miss out on blossoming relationships, fascinating careers, or exciting trips if we continue to dwell in the past. The key is "to stop saving memories and start making them" (Children of Hoarders).

If possessions get too out of hand, they can create dangerous health risks, including tripping and fire hazards and allergies due to molds and dusts. Many hoarders are elderly with health problems such as osteoporosis or blindness. Just one fall can send them to the hospital, never to return home. There are even instances where people have been buried alive by their own junk. The most legendary is the case of two hoarding brothers, Homer and Langley Collyer. They were discovered dead in their New York City mansion in 1947 buried under tons of debris collected over a forty-year period (Duenwald 30).

Clutter can put a strain on relationships. Our neighbors don't appreciate junked-up houses in their communities. Homes that are overflowing, spilling into driveways and yards are unsightly and may cause property values to lower in the neighborhood. There are cases where the stuff gets so out of hand that either neighborhood associations or the public health department must step in. Friends stop coming over or calling. Wives have given husbands ultimatums: "Clean it up or I'm leaving you." It's difficult for family members to visit when the stuff becomes the main focus. It's a huge distraction, making it impossible to relax and converse. Tension builds up, tempers flare, and feelings get hurt. It can literally tear families apart. This burden, this legacy of stuff, will eventually be handed down to the next generation to deal with.

I would like to save the people that live in the house on the hill, but it is an imposing job. I have attempted to tackle a closet or a room, but to my dismay, any empty space that I create is immediately filled. Sometimes it seems hopeless. Their things seem to come first, because they are so emotionally tied to them. The stuff keeps them occupied, but they miss out on new opportunities. These new situations can be scary, but they use their possessions

expect, and possess more stuff" (302). As comedian George Carlin once quipped, "Your house is just a pile of stuff with a cover on it . . . a place to keep your stuff while you go out and get more stuff."

Our homes can become museums of our own personal artifacts. Souvenirs from every trip we took over the years, programs from every event we've attended, and boxes stuffed with childhood memories. Sometimes these things can keep us living in the past. Memories are attached to objects and in turn we attach ourselves to those objects. We may feel if the item is discarded, we are somehow throwing a part of ourselves away with it. Some things are important to keep such as photos, letters, and mementos of very special occasions. But when we keep too many of these things, it can become a compulsion and we can't let go. If we keep a whole lifetime's worth of possessions, they can prevent us as an excuse to further separate themselves from society. They feel safe and secure in their own little world they have created: *this fortress of isolation*. If I could break through those walls, I would, but it's an arduous task to try to change people so set in their ways. As much as I want to alter their behavior, hoarders can't bear to part with their stuff.

I look at myself and wonder: Do I have these tendencies? Am I destined to become a pack rat? I look in my closets crowded with clothes and shoes, much I don't wear. Stacks of mail that I keep saying I'm going to sort and read are piled up around my house. My grown kid's artwork, clothing, and toys fill the attic, but I can't part with so much of it for sentimental reasons. Who among us can say we have none of the characteristics of the hoarder? Haven't we all taken pleasure from buying and owning things? The motivation to collect and store is powerful. Our ancestors used this survival technique to their advantage, but today, "living in a land of wants, not needs, creates its own dilemmas" (Vanderbilt). Do we buy it or not . . . do we keep it or throw it out? That's the big question. There are so many choices; maybe too many. Most of us can make these decisions efficiently, but the hoarder agonizes over each and every item and ends up keeping it all. But aren't we all attached to our possessions to a certain extent? We like our things until they threaten to control us. That need to feel safe and secure to avoid feeling fear is what links all of us to the hoarder. Even the most organized and efficient among us must admit to feeling a bit overwhelmed by the volume of stuff and junk we possess, accumulate, and think we need. In our quest to acquire and attach ourselves to things, are we just a few steps away from the inhabitants of the house on the hill? Perhaps a little "pack rat" resides in all of us.

Works Cited

Children of Hoarders. *Can't Let Anyone in Your House*? N.p.: Children of Hoarders, 2006. *Children of Hoarders.* Web. 15 Nov. 2006.

Duenwald, Mary. "The Psychology of . . . Hoarding." *Discovery.* Oct. 2004: 30–31. Print.

Gibson, Katherine. *Unclutter Your Life: Transforming Your Physical, Mental, and Emotional Space.* Hillsboro: Beyond Words, 2004. Print.

Neziroglu, Fugen, Jerome Bubrick, and Jose A. Yaryura-Tobias. *Overcoming Compulsive Hoarding: Why You Save and How You Can Stop.* Oakland: New Harbinger, 2004. Print.

Saxena, Sanjaya, and Karron M. Maidment. "Treatment of Compulsive Hoarding." *Journal of Clinical Psychology* 60 (2004): 1143–54. *Academic Search Elite.* Web. 20 Nov. 2006.

Vanderbilt, Tom. "Self-Storage Nation." *Slate.* Washington Post, 18 July 2005. Web. 20 Nov. 2006.

Webster, Tracy. "Big House in the Wilderness: Moratoriums on Building and Individual Responsibility." *Inventing Arguments.* Ed. John Mauk and John Metz. 2nd ed. Boston: Wadsworth-Cengage, 2009. 301–03. Print.

Analyzing Argument

1. What is the most important appeal in this argument? What passage best illustrates that appeal?

2. Schutza does not develop an explicit solution to hoarding. Although she implies a set of personal goals or hopes, she does not explain them and call for a particular policy or action. Why might this particular topic, at this particular point in time, lack a direct and collective solution?

3. In several passages, Schutza blurs the line between hoarders and the average consumer. How does this affect the argument? As you read, how did it affect you?

4. Examine Schutza's use of secondary sources. Choose a particular quotation and explain how the quoted source functions in the argument—for example, as part of an appeal, concession, counterargument, or evidence.

5. What values or assumptions does Schutza share with the other writers in this chapter (White, Webster, and Edmondson)?

Citizens and Consumers

AMBER EDMONDSON

Amber Edmondson argues about a crisis in community. It is not merely the crisis of big box stores in small towns, but the loss of culture in those towns. While her argument uses secondary research, her starting place and most of her examples come from the real geography of Edmondson's life. She wrote this essay for the final research project in her first-year college writing course and used the invention tools in this chapter.

Scottville, my hometown, consisted of two blocks of commercial Main Street—and it really was called "Main Street"—surrounded by sightless miles of plowed fields. The downtown was small, housing a handful of the necessities: a hardware store, a grocery store, a tractor supplier, whose titles were each preceded by a family name. Schoenberger's Market, Frosty's Flicks, Cox's Sales and Service. But Scottville always seemed to be more than a tumbleweed-infested one-horse farm town. Instead, the downtown was blocked off every autumn and hosted the Harvest Festival that crowned the Asparagus Queen. Through all seasons, the Scottville Clown Band serenaded the town, led then by the mayor and sheriff. Every winter, an arts and craft show was held at the middle school. Even as the big box stores moved into neighboring Ludington, family-run businesses dominated Scottville.

Growing up in a small farming community can have a profound effect. While my family did not farm, reverence for the land was instilled at an early age. When we bought our groceries, we knew that all the produce had been sown and harvested nearby. The citizens were very resourceful and self-reliant. No Walmarts or Meijers came to town, nor did the people ever see the need for any. This resourcefulness was particularly evident to my family, whose breadwinner was a hairdresser trying to make money in a town that cut its own hair. We eventually packed up and moved north to Cadillac where people, I would discover, were much more dependent.

Cadillac's boundaries stretched farther than Scottville's and were teeming with streets and buildings and cars, yet seemed much emptier. The town showed irreparable scars from the hard fist of corporate power, having seemingly allowed the big box stores in during economic hard times. They promised jobs and price-lowering competition and quickly put the downtown shops out of business. No longer was it sensible for consumers to venture downtown for trips to the grocery, a shoe store, and the pharmacy when they could simply get it all in one place. The slogan for their newest welcomed big box is "A million reasons, a single store." One by one, letters fell from the downtown marquees and windows became

Introduction paints a picture of Scottville, which faces a crisis.

Description of the people of Scottville.

Describes the harmful effects of box stores.

cloudy and dark on the main street. But the growing north end glowed and pulsed with neon excess. It became apparent that this excess, this growing corporate presence, was making itself the economic and cultural center of town, while Cadillac neglected to preserve its culture, its own unique intellectual and artistic tastes.

Appeal to value: culture should be preserved.

While it may seem that the Walmarts and Meijers of the world bring variety to their host towns, thereby adding to the local culture, these giants truly have the opposite effect. Instead of joining the existing culture, big box stores work independently to duplicate their product line and game plan. They decide what books, music, and films get stocked as well as what fashions are peddled. Walmart HQ doesn't know or care about the Scottville Clown Band or Elk Rapids poet Terry Wooten. Instead, Britney Spears and *Chicken Soup for the (fill in the blank) Soul* are imported into towns across the nation. These decisions are made in remote board-rooms "where the values and needs of the local community carry little or no weight," according to Stacy Mitchell of the New Rules Project in Minneapolis (qtd. in "New" 25). This homogenization of regional cultures makes it easier for citizens to let go of their downtowns—nay, for citizens to even be unaware of the existence of downtown at all—at the beck and call of a mega-chain store.

Responds to claim that box stores are good for the community.

Local culture, however, is not the only aspect of a community that these corporations affect. Economically, allowing chain stores into a town would seem like a sound game plan. They offer jobs, cheaper products, and perhaps the security that comes along with national brand recognition. However, the money grossed at these stores does not stay in the community, save the meager employee paychecks. Often, these stores offer no benefits to employees and "[give] very little back to the community," according to We're Against the WAL campaign organizer Albert Norman (18).

Transition from culture to economics.

And it is shortsighted to say that the products are cheaper even if the price tag displays a smaller number. If the health of downtown is taken into account, the price is rather quite high. Local businesses cannot compete with the low prices available to larger corporations and many are forced to close their doors for good, putting an end to a possible family legacy. Instead of becoming the sun they promised to be at the center of a community, these chain stores turn into black holes, slurping a town's money "somewhere else."

Counterargument anticipates the argument that products are cheaper.

According to economic development consultant Donovan D. Rypkema in "The Importance of Downtown in the 21st Century," not only are these chains harming our downtowns economically and artistically, they are also threatening the social communities in which they feed. Rypkema describes downtown as the gathering place of citizens and as the center of local

Refers to an authority for support.

culture. Once people are relegated to the outskirts of town to work in large chain stores and factories, social bonds begin to deteriorate. When people work at corporate department stores, they are often paid just enough to get by, making it difficult to achieve personal happiness. Psychologist Abraham Maslow's hierarchy of needs places physiological, then psychological, security at the very base of his pyramid (Gwynne). Before moving up to the next level, love and belongingness, one must first be able to eat, have shelter, and be mentally and emotionally sound. When people are just scraping by, they don't have time to worry about being part of a community. This, however, is in keeping with the entrepreneurial every-man-for-himself spirit of the capitalist system.

This economic system is a fairly young experiment that seems to contradict our natural tendencies toward community. When citizens in a community become simply consumers in an economy, they forget how to operate as a cooperative and the benefits of doing so. When local restaurants bow out to more expensive, more upscale operations like Ruby Tuesday, "regulars" disappear and servers lose that bond with their customers and their connection to the community. When local farmers are forced out of work by corporate farms and chain stores that stock food from unknown origins, communities lose a source of local food and quickly forget that food comes from anywhere but the supermarket.

Personal testimony used for support.

A gentleman I was speaking to recently explained that less than twenty years ago, he could walk down the road to buy his eggs, milk, and meat for a wholesale price from a local farmer. His farming neighbor made a living off these transactions and the money stayed in the community, while the gentleman retained the peace of mind that comes along with knowing where your food is coming from and knowing where your money is going. After a while, with corporate farms shipping food into the new corporate supermarkets, the farmer could no longer make ends meet and was forced to sell his farm and work in a factory. Both the gentleman and the farmer now get their food at a higher cost from Meijer and eat strawberries that have traveled countless miles, while the farmer, left with no skills applicable to the influx of corporate jobs, has lost forty years of his life and his occupation.

Values social, not just economic, growth.

This assault on independence and self-reliance is perhaps the most destructive threat to our communities by these corporations. When the leaders of a town become focused on economic growth while ignoring social growth, businesses most often win out in the end, and they have very different goals and needs than the average citizen. It may seem, then, that little difference exists between small local businesses and the department store giants. However, while local businesses can still affect town leaders' decisions, the added profits that are gained as a result stay within the community. When Walmart influences town decisions in its favor, the money it makes is shipped out to Walmart headquarters states away. Also, notes Mitchell, "large corporations are required by law to maximize returns to shareholders, [while] locally owned businesses can be guided by other values besides the bottom line" (qtd. in "New" 25). When control over the economic forces of small towns is taken away from citizens—business owners included—people can easily forget what it means to help out locally if there is no such thing as "local."

There can exist a middle ground, however, between "local" and "corporate." After fleeing Cadillac to pursue a college degree in Traverse City, I expected little more than another version of Cadillac, merely with a mall and more square miles of neon. I did find those elements, but I also found a surprisingly well-developed downtown. It stretched for several blocks, spilling onto perpendicular streets off the main drag, and incorporated shops frivolous and necessary, cultural and touristy. It appears that while Traverse City allowed in the big boys, it also nurtured the business district that formed the town and, while citizens may not go downtown for all of their basic shopping needs, Front Street remains a cultural center of the town. The Cherry Festival, Friday Night Live, and the Open Space are all guests of and products of the downtown, offering artistic and intellectual gatherings throughout the year.

Along with the seasonal events held downtown, Front Street also offers many unique shops owned and operated by local citizens. It may be more convenient and perhaps cheaper to shop at a big box store for these specialty wares, but a consumer might only be skimming the top of a particular hobby or interest such as beading. While most anything that could be bought downtown can also be bought in bland, generic form at Walmart or Meijer, the downtown specialty shops offer higher quality goods, often made right in town or perhaps only as far away as Leelanau County.

As well as helping the community as a whole, the downtown shops offer benefits to individual community members. Instead of going to work at Walmart, people can be employed at these locally owned stores and have much more access to the intricacies of operating a business. Employees also get to learn more about the specialties of these stores, be it beading, crystal meditation, brewing specialty espresso drinks, or making fudge. As a Walmart employee, one merely learns to run a cash register, to put boxes on a shelf, and to get paid very little. So, while these megastores may hire several hundred people in the community, these people—largely adults—are merely focused on getting by and not on bettering themselves.

What is more disturbing than even the personal deterioration of individuals occurring today is the possibility of their communities becoming a Cadillac tomorrow. In his "Apology to Future Generations," Simon Benlow

Suggests solution to crisis.

Is Edmondson's description of working at locally owned stores or at Walmart effective?

suggests that people no longer see themselves as part of society as a whole but instead are focused on their own selfish desires and instant gratification. While it may seem better for people to choose today to discard their membership to a community and allow themselves to operate solely as a consumer, that course leaves the children of tomorrow without the option of simply being a citizen. When local businesses cannot succeed and citizens cannot offer their own unique skills to a community, children have only the choices of submitting to lifelong employment at Walmart or having to leave their community in search of another where their skills have a chance of contributing. While Benlow talks about consumerist tendencies in general, much of his essay can be applied to what people have done to their communities: "As [consumerism] came through every town, no one could resist it. It banged and clamored and woke everyone from dreamy isolation, and so even the most ascetic types played along in some small way" (416). Benlow makes it clear that while consumerism and the corporations that encourage such behaviors deteriorate communities, citizens are the ones with the power to decide how far the destruction will go.

Citizens must resist being reduced to merely consumers if they are to preserve their communities. In Albert Camus's "The Myth of Sisyphus," the protagonist learns after being tethered to an eternity of futile labor that people may not have control over their situation, but they do have control over their behavior within that situation. It seems to be taking a while for most of America to realize not only how much power they have but also that something is wrong. Instead of turning away in droves once Walmart was discovered to have been employing illegal immigrants, consumers caused the megastore's stock to rise three-quarters of a percent that day ("Moyers"). When people should have been appalled at the store's behavior, they were reminded of "always low prices, always Walmart" and started Christmas shopping a bit early.

But citizens are starting to stand up to the corporations that threaten their areas, seemingly as a direct result of the strength of their communities. While the one political action undertaken by Cadillac citizens was a poorly planned and executed protest against a tire-burning plant, Traverse City is a hotbed of grassroots action, most likely due to the focus on community development, which allows for personal development. Recently, a group advocating local currency has formed, the local food cooperative is flourishing, various peace groups meet frequently and march periodically, and the local bookstore hosts local musicians as well as philosophy and Green Party meetings. The local Sweetwater Alliance has taken extensive action with some success against a water-bottling factory that had moved into the local area to filter not just money from the region, but to remove the community's resources as well. This seeking out of like-minded others

Uses Benlow to explain how consumerism is harmful.

Provides examples of what can be done.

is the level after security in Maslow's hierarchy of needs and can be found in its truest sense in our local communities.

This belonging is perhaps the most important element offered by our communities, and it may be the element most likely to save them. In Traverse City, this seeking out of the like-minded led to the formation of the Traverse Area Community Currency Initiative (TACCI), whose goal is to create a local currency for the area. Modeling their system after that which is succeeding in Toronto and Madison, TACCI is one of many groups working toward similar causes. These groups will someday achieve great change for their areas, but they would not have formed without an already strong community. Cadillac may be many years away from forming its own version of TACCI, and Scottville may never need that, but it all comes back to community.

Scottville is strong because of its community and its reverence of its culture. Cadillac, on the other hand, has a very weak culture but could make the shift to improving it. Before any of this can happen, however, the citizens must acknowledge this importance of community through a concerted educational effort by those in charge. Citizens must also reject the big box stores that threaten their economies and must weigh the importance of convenience versus community. This addiction to convenience needs to be stopped before our communities can again be strong. We need to emphasize our own local cultures and again become citizens instead of consumers.

Works Cited

Benlow, Simon. "An Apology to Future Generations." *The Composition of Everyday Life: A Guide to Writing.* Ed. John Mauk and John Metz. 3rd ed. Boston: Wadsworth-Cengage, 2010. 413–17. Print.

Camus, Albert. "The Myth of Sisyphus." *The Mercury Reader.* Ed. Maurice Scharton. Boston: Pearson Custom, 2001. Print.

Gwynne, Robert. *Maslow's Hierarchy of Needs.* U of Tennessee, Knoxville, 1997. Web. 30 Nov. 2003. [http://web.utk.edu/gwynne/maslow.htm].

"Moyers and Brancaccio Track the News." *NOW with Bill Moyers.* PBS. WCMU, Mount Pleasant, 7 Nov. 2003. Television.

"New Rules for the New Localism: Favoring Communities, Deterring Corporate Chains (an Interview with Stacy Mitchell)." *Multinational Monitor* Oct.– Nov. 2002: 25–29. *Academic Search Elite.* Web. 1 Dec. 2010.

Norman, Albert. "Eight Ways to Stop the Store: Up against Wal-Mart." *Nation* 28 Mar. 1994: 418. *Academic Search Elite.* Web. 1 Dec. 2010.

Rypkema, Donovan D. "The Importance of Downtown in the 21st Century."
Journal of the American Planning Association 69.1 (2003): 9–15. *Academic
Search Elite.* Web. 1 Dec. 2010.

Analyzing Argument

1. Explain how Edmondson responds to opposing positions or perspectives. Describe specific passages in which she counters or concedes.

2. According to Edmondson, why are "big box stores" so popular? What does their popularity tell us about American values?

3. Choose four statements from Edmondson's essay that you consider premises in her line of reasoning. Explain how each statement functions as a premise in her argument.

4. How does Edmondson use Scottville and Cadillac to develop her argument?

5. What values underlie Edmondson's statement: "It became apparent that this excess, this growing corporate presence was making itself the economic and cultural center of town, while Cadillac neglected to preserve its culture, its own unique intellectual and artistic tastes" (paragraph 3)? Choose another key sentence from Edmondson's argument, and explain the underlying values.

6. Edmondson uses sources throughout her argument. Which ones are most effective? Why?

John Mauk

Is bottled water a crisis?

1. What arguments have you heard for and against bottled water?

2. How does bottled water pose a threat to the public? How does this image make a case for or against bottled water?

Exploring for Topics

A crisis is more than a rupture in the flow of normal events. It is a crucial or decisive situation. In a crisis, severe or intense consequences are at stake; things are teetering on a line between beneficial and disastrous outcomes. A crisis also can occur when something goes totally awry, when an expected outcome or routine is nowhere in sight, when systems and organizations break down just when they are needed most. As you scan your environment for possible topics, look for critical situations, those on the brink of drastic change. The following strategies can help you focus on a specific crisis.

- In a local, college, or national newspaper, look for crises in any of the following: school budgets, city government, labor, transportation, health care, environment, entertainment, energy, or day care.
- In your town or neighborhood, look for crises with security, equality, zoning, sprawl, policing, agriculture, traffic, or safety.
- Check out school-sponsored documents (posters, fliers, signs, letters, websites, and so on). Does your school claim that any crises exist? If so, how are those crises characterized? Would you characterize them differently?
- Tune in to a political talk show. Listen for social and political crises such as military conflict, terrorism, trade disputes, state budgets, the Medicare budget, or corporate fraud.
- Use the following prompt to explore for crises that usually go unnoticed: While people go on with their everyday lives, they do not recognize _____ and its looming threat.
- Investigate your academic major. Speak with a professor or read a journal in your field and search for crises involving labor, research strategies, funding, the environment, big business, assessment, control, salaries, reporting, and so on. What crisis affects the most people? What crisis affects you?
- With a group of peers, examine the world around you and ask questions about social problems. Be adventurous: *What will we do with all the used tires? How can so many people vote against their own best interests? Doesn't anyone care that prime-time television shows are ruining people's ability to think clearly? What social crises do graffiti artists point out?*
- Focus on a crisis described in one of the chapter readings, but try to see the crisis from a different perspective and characterize it in your own words.

To view this video, visit the English CourseMate at CengageBrain.com.

Top to bottom: Randall Hop/stockxchng.com; AP Photo/Petar Petrov; Madhouse: Minnesota Historical Society/CORBIS; From CourseMate video (BBC: Bee Disappearance)

The first move of any good writer is some basic detective work—to look closely and see what others might overlook. Use the following invention questions to help probe the particulars of the situation. Make certain to focus on particulars. Be careful not to simply answer the questions; rather, use the questions to *explore* the real complexities of the issue:

▶ What makes the situation a crisis? (How is it a critical turning point?)

▶ What is being threatened—what cherished thing, value, principle, resource?

▶ What is the threat? A way of thinking? A behavior? Something else?

▶ Who or what caused the crisis? How did the situation evolve into a crisis?

▶ When might it climax (or go to the point of no return)?

▶ What can be done to resolve the crisis?

Invention Workshop

With one or two other writers, answer the preceding invention questions for your topic. Let the ideas evolve. For instance, if someone explains the cause of a crisis, ask whether it may have begun before that, in some less obvious way. Use the discussion as a tool not simply for *talking about* the topic, but for *finding out* more—for exploring layers beyond your group's initial preconceptions. As the discussion evolves, record the ideas by taking ample notes.

Hint: Keep asking questions about the situation to discover the most basic cause of the crisis. For instance, you might ask: *What basic human need is not being addressed? What oversight put things in motion? What misunderstanding or natural occurrence cultivated the crisis?* Try to discover what the people involved do not see because they are too close to the events or blinded by their own biases or perceptions.

Inventing a Claim

In addition to a close examination of the topic itself, it is important to know what opinions are circulating—how people characterize the crisis, or if they even acknowledge it at all. Writers sometimes discover voices that oppose their initial thoughts on a topic. Such discoveries can be of great value. They can help a writer to build a bridge, to shape an argument so that doubtful or even hostile readers will consider a claim, a possibility beyond their own perspectives.

As in Tracy Webster's case, writers may find sources that completely coincide with their own point of view or extend that point of view. But finding these connections is not easy. Writers must be able to see past the surface of articles—past titles, main claims, or even the primary focus. Often, the deepest and most helpful connections lie in the underbrush. For example, Tracy Webster's argument focuses on big houses in the wilderness. His main source, Anna Quindlen's article, is titled "A Shock to the System." The "shock" refers to a regional power outage in the Northeast. A novice researcher may have overlooked Quindlen's article, dismissing it because the title has nothing to do with Webster's main focus. But Webster sees past the surface difference (between his topic and Quindlen's article) and finds a shared set of values and beliefs.

Webster's topic: Big houses in the wilderness.

Quindlen's title: "A Shock to the System."

Webster's focus: Big houses that destroy natural habitat.

Quindlen's focus: Power outage and bear hunting in the Northeast.

Webster's assumption: Humans should live in harmony with their surroundings.

Quindlen's assumption: Humans should live in harmony with their surroundings.

Had Webster skipped over Quindlen's article, he would have missed a supporting voice. Even though their essays emerge from different situations, Webster and Quindlen share important values and assumptions. As you scan databases or the Internet for sources, keep Webster's discovery in mind: Often, the most helpful source looks very different once you get past the title and initial claims.

Using your library's periodical databases or the Internet, find published discussions about the crisis you have chosen. If the crisis is fairly recent (in the past few months), you will probably have success finding related newspaper articles rather than journal articles. If the crisis is very local, like the strike at a local factory, you may find articles in local newspapers. You could also extend the search to find how people tend to argue about your topic. (For more on finding and integrating outside written sources, see pages 395–410.)

Although you may not find people arguing about your particular crisis, you can use other arguments to understand related values and claims. After collecting outside opinions on the situation (through surveys, secondary research, or both), use the following questions to explore the various possible positions related to the crisis:

What Do Others Claim?

▶ How do other people or sources characterize the crisis?

▶ What possible actions or solutions are put forth?

▶ What do other arguments seem to value (money, progress, children, equality)?

▶ If solutions have been suggested, how thorough are they? (What details do they omit? What significant factors do they ignore?)

What Do I Claim?

▶ How do I see the crisis differently from others?

▶ What values and assumptions do I share with others?

▶ Based on my values and assumptions, I believe the crisis can be addressed by _____.

Of course, there are limitless ways to approach a crisis and make an argumentative claim. But it may help to understand some of the common approaches. Consider the following formula. Even though you may not maintain the exact structure, try one of the formulas to help you get traction:

A. Because _____ is _____, there is no stopping it.

B. Because _____, we should _____.

C. To address the current _____, we should

_____.

D. The _____ crisis continues primarily because _____ do not recognize _____.

More Sample Main Claims

Politics

- Because the United States has strategic and economic interests in Afghanistan, there is no stopping the ongoing war.
- Because corporate lobbyists now control politics in Washington, DC, states must begin taking back governmental control.
- To end the constant "pork" projects in federal government, public citizens must call for strict term limits for members of Congress.

Popular Culture

- The corporate news networks have created a citizenry that is dangerously close to losing control of, or happily letting go of, its democracy.
- Hard-hitting, shrewd comedy is necessary in a free society, and it is nearly gone from mainstream American entertainment.
- Because of the toxic chemicals released during the manufacturing and discarding of plastic bottles, bottled water should be taxed to reduce its popularity.

Education

- Because the minds of our generation are consumed and distracted by sports, the only alternative is to remove athletics completely from public high schools.
- Because corporate testing services now dictate curriculum while sucking huge amounts of money from public education, teachers and parents must unite and halt the entire system.
- College curricula continue to shape students into consumers and button pushers, which means that yet another generation will go into the workforce and the voting booths without critical literacy.

Town and Community

- The disappearance of senior citizens from the center of civic life has created a psychological void.
- Because township officials have allowed low-end national food and hotel chains to colonize the beaches, we are in danger of losing the most unique qualities of our area.

Activity

Which is the most insightful claim in the preceding list? Why?

Inventing Support

Lines of Reasoning A crisis may seem like chaos, so a good argument provides a logical path away from the crisis. When writers develop a set of connected premises, they establish that path. Sometimes, writers even draw attention to each premise. Notice how Tracy Webster directly discusses an important premise:

> One question is: Can't individual Americans simply build differently? (Are moratoriums necessary?) Of course, to pursue this question (this line of thinking), the reader must accept the premise that Americans are overbuilding, and that by overbuilding, Americans are foolishly and unnecessarily overdestroying nature, the environment, wildlife. They have to accept the premise that current building practices are somehow harmful. Some Americans, to be certain, don't accept this premise. Here's why they should:

Webster then goes on to develop his line of reasoning and support the premise that Americans are overbuilding and destroying nature.

An argument about a crisis may have several layers of cause and effect. And writers often need to argue that particular behaviors, ideas, or practices created the crisis. In his argument about the environment, Curtis White walks readers through complex layers. For him, the crisis is not simply about pollution, degradation of resources, or even evil corporate executives. The crisis is hidden in the actual language about the environment. White's courageous argument takes readers, one step at a time, into deeper and deeper layers:

> Perhaps we support legalistic responses to problems, with all their technoscientific descriptors, out of a sense that this is the best we can do for the moment. But the danger is always that eventually we come to believe this language and its mindset ourselves. This mindset is generally called "quantitative reasoning," and it is second nature to Anglo-Americans. Corporate execs are perfectly comfortable with it, and corporate philanthropists give their dough to environmental organizations that speak it. Unfortunately, it also has the consequence of turning environmentalists into quislings, collaborators, and virtuous practitioners of a cost-benefit logic figured in songbirds.

Appeals to Value Many arguments about crisis call readers to act—or at least to imagine the best action possible. And an appeal to value is a powerful tool for motivating action. Notice Webster's argument, which subtly calls on the audience's sense of responsibility:

> But Americans, perhaps more than any other people who have ever lived, are terrible at walking narrow paths. They cannot just move to the wilderness and live. They must pound the wilderness to death. They must beat it to hell. They must drive gas-guzzling, polluting, school-bus-sized SUVs a hundred miles to work and back. They must build huge homes, large enough to be small hotels.

Later in the argument, Webster goes even further with the appeal, and makes it more explicit:

> Moratoriums on building permits would not be necessary if individual homebuilders acted more responsibly, but how in our present culture could Americans ever bring themselves to act more responsibly? Some do, of course. But most can't. They simply see it as their right to do whatever they feel like doing. They see anything else as an infringement on their freedom, a personal insult and a public injustice. Quindlen's suggestion requires collective, or government, action—a more extreme measure that must be taken to prevent individual freedom-loving Americans from eating the whole pie, instead of having just one piece.

Authorities Consider the various possible ways that outside sources can help develop your ideas:

- To help explain the nature of the crisis
- To help explain a solution
- To integrate an opposing perspective on the crisis or a solution
- To explain a related value or way of thinking

Remember that helpful authorities are sometimes voices from the past. Philosophers, writers, scholars, scientists, and thinkers from history can give much to a current argument. In his essay, Curtis White borrows statements from philosophers of the past to explain a way of thinking. While the philosophers were not speaking about White's topic (the environmental crisis), their perspectives support one of White's key premises:

> Even now, science can't say why we ought not to harm the environment except to say that we shouldn't be self-destructive. Another of these lost spiritual children was our very relation as human beings to the mystery of Being as such. As the philosopher G. W. Leibniz famously wondered, "Why is there something rather than nothing?" For St. Thomas Aquinas, this was the fundamental religious question. In the place of a relation to

the world that was founded on this mystery, we have a relation that is objective and data driven. We no longer have a forest; we have "board feet." We no longer have a landscape, a world that is our own; we have "valuable natural resources."

As this example shows, authorities need not match your position exactly. They often help give dimension to an argument by reinforcing a broader concept, a way of conceiving an issue, even a way of seeing the world.

Testimony When a writer shares something personal, the argument itself becomes more human and more immediate. Testimony brings a topic into the real (even intimate) dialogue between writer and audience.

> I look up at the house on the hill. Situated in a relatively affluent neighborhood, overlooking the ocean, it looks like a normal, well-maintained home from street level, but as I walk up the driveway and it comes into full view, the reality of the situation hits me like a stack of old newspapers. There is no doubt this is the home of compulsive hoarders. It is also the home of people I love.

Schutza's experience does more than suggest, "This happened to me." Rather, it humanizes a potentially distant topic, hoarding, and brings it closer. But her argument does not rely exclusively on the personal. Her own experience is rounded out with a variety of other support strategies.

Literary Works Fiction, poetry, and drama often speak to the human foibles that create and sustain crises. In fact, some see this as literature's power: it shows us the effects of our weird moral, social, and psychological hiccups. In his argument about the environment, White alludes to the fictional character Faust, who makes a deal with the devil. In White's argument, the devil is quantitative reasoning:

> We don't have to be born again to agree with evangelicals that one of the most powerful arguments missing from the environmentalist's case is reverence for what simply is. One of the heroes of Goethe's *Faust* was a character called Care (Sorge), who showed to Faust the unscrupulousness of his actions and led him to salvation. Environmentalism has made a Faustian pact with quantitative reasoning; science has given it power but it cannot provide deliverance. If environmentalism truly wishes, as it claims, to want to "save" something—the planet, a species, itself—it needs to rediscover a common language of Care.

As White's move illustrates, integrating a literary work requires some imaginative analysis. We have to think beyond the specific crisis and inspect the deeper sources of tension—people's greed, ignorance, fear, detachment, and so on. Then, we can try to recall works that explore those tensions. To develop support for your argument, use the following questions to explore possibilities:

▶ What logical appeals are necessary for my argument? (What line of reasoning do I want my audience to follow?)

▶ What authorities can I use? What philosophers, novelists, poets, or thinkers from the past uphold a way of thinking that might help make my case about the current crisis?

▶ What personal situations can I use? (What situations from my life reveal something important about the nature of the crisis or the solution?)

▶ What appeals to value can I make? (What values are tucked inside my argument? Can I call on the audience's sense of duty, justice, family, personal responsibility, or something else?)

Arrangement

Where Should I Distinguish between the Crisis and the Solution? Each argument is different from the next. While some arguments about crisis focus significant attention on solutions, others attempt only to draw out the nature of the crisis and characterize it as worthy of attention. Still others may explain the nature of the crisis and then counterargue the worth of others' proposed solutions. While the arguments in this chapter vary significantly in their emphases, they all share some common ingredients:

- Description of the crisis
- Description of life without the crisis
- Evidence or appeals about the crisis
- Counterarguments
- Description of the solution
- Support (evidence and appeals) for the solution
- Counterarguments of other solutions
- Concession about other solutions

Notice the arrangement of Webster's essay:

Paragraphs 1–2	Description of the crisis (or the starting place)
Paragraph 2	Qualifier (describing the specific nature of the crisis)
Paragraphs 3–4	Authority (Quindlen) and a proposed solution
Paragraphs 5–9	Counterargument (and appeal to logic in support of the solution)
Paragraphs 10–11	Qualifier (reinforcing the specific nature of the crisis)
Paragraphs 12–14	Appeal to logic in support of the solution

What's important is that the basic ingredients of an argument can be arranged in an unlimited number of ways, depending on the nature of the crisis and the stance of the writer.

How Should I Begin? In any argument, introductions vary depending on the nature of the topic, the nature of the writer's voice, and the nature of the audience. An informal strategy might involve a personal narrative (such as Schutza uses). A more formal approach may give a less personal report on the crisis. In his essay, White begins broadly. But he does not say what his readers already know (that environmental destruction is bad, that it is increasing, that it hurts us all). Instead, he begins his analysis of cause:

Environmental destruction proceeds apace in spite of all the warnings,
the good science, the 501(c)3 organizations with their memberships
in the millions, the poll results, and the martyrs perched high in the
branches of sequoias or shot dead in the Amazon. This is so not because
of a power, a strength out there that we must resist. It is because we are
weak and fearful. Only a weak and fearful society could invest so much
desperate energy in protecting activities that are the equivalent of suicide.

Despite different approaches, one quality is consistent in good argumentative essays: they avoid squeezing in too much information in the
introduction, such as a description of the crisis and an articulation of
the solution. Instead, they attempt, simply, to introduce a crisis.

How Should I Include Counterarguments, Concessions, or Qualifiers?

Doing counterargument involves challenging other
positions—and showing why any opposing claims are not as reasonable as one's own. Other opinions must be addressed, even confronted
directly. Confronting other opinions, or counterarguing, helps create
sophisticated and more persuasive arguments. In an argument about
crisis, opposition to your main idea might arise at two primary places: at
your characterization of the crisis, and at your solution. In other words,
people might disagree with the way you portray a critical situation, and
they might also disagree with the effectiveness of your solution (if you
propose one). It might help to consider all the possible opposing views
and then respond directly to each—or to the most important.

Your portrayal of the situation	*Possible opposing views:* "It's not as bad as you suggest." "It's much worse than you suggest." "Your description is short-sighted." "Your understanding of the cause/effect is wrong."
Your proposed solution	*Possible opposing views:* "It won't work." "It's too dangerous, unethical, unmanageable, costly, unpop-ular, etc."

Of course, opposition can come in many other places in an argument.
(Generally, people can disagree with any claim made.) However, be especially cognizant of these two important layers.

Audience and Voice

Arguers use various strategies to get an audience involved in a crisis. Some create a voice of urgency; others project calmness. And even though writers do not benefit from using the sound of their voices (with changes in pitch and volume), they can use a variety of tools for attracting readers.

Informality An informal voice can be an asset—even in formal academic argument. Strategies for developing an informal voice include strategically placed slang or idiosyncratic phrasing. Webster creates informality by linking words together in an unorthodox manner:

> But this is not an anti-hunting essay or an anti-house-in-the-wilderness essay. It is an anti-big-house-in-the-wilderness essay. The big house in the wilderness is more dangerous than any hunter is. It's the big house, the too-big house, that is unjustifiable.

Informality is also created with certain pronouns, specifically, by drawing attention to "you" and "I." For instance, Laurie Schutza begins with personal testimony and returns to it at key points in the essay. And her conclusion reinforces her personal connection, in part by cataloguing her own collection of saved items:

> I look at myself and wonder: Do I have these tendencies? Am I destined to become a pack rat? I look in my closets crowded with clothes and shoes, much I don't wear. Stacks of mail that I keep saying I'm going to sort and read are piled up around my house. My grown kid's artwork, clothing, and toys fill the attic, but I can't part with so much of it for sentimental reasons. Who among us can say we have none of the characteristics of the hoarder?

Formality Formality in writing is the degree to which the features correspond to standard conventions or expectations. In formal academic settings, readers expect to encounter writing that does not veer too far off course and does not draw attention to itself or to the writer's emotions. Notice, for example, Amber Edmondson's final paragraph. Although it makes a strong appeal, it also refrains from sounding too plaintive or accusatory:

> Scottville is strong because of its community and its reverence of its culture. Cadillac, on the other hand, has a very weak culture but could make the shift to improving it. Before any of this can happen, however,

the citizens must acknowledge this importance of community through a concerted educational effort by those in charge. Citizens must also reject the big box stores that threaten their economies and must weigh the importance of convenience versus community. This addiction to convenience needs to be stopped before our communities can again be strong. We need to emphasize our own local cultures and again become citizens instead of consumers.

Edmondson could have easily drawn attention to her own anger or frustration. Instead, this passage reinforces key points of her argument without turning overly emotional.

Accusation A strong stance on a topic often comes along with a stern voice, and sometimes the arguer wants to create a voice that targets another position. Notice Webster's accusation of particular homebuilders:

If Quindlen's proposal seems extreme, it is because in American society where narrow paths have become unimaginable to many, individual freedom allows for, and encourages, individual irresponsibility. As long as Americans are free to build obscenely large houses, to destroy acres of wildlife habitat, to pollute the air and rivers, many Americans are going to do exactly that. Why? Because they see it as their right, because they are free, because they are Americans. Quindlen is right: Moratoriums on building permits are the obvious alternative.

In these passages, the voice of accusation is concise. It depends upon short and clean phrasing that draws attention away from the writer and toward the culprits. For your own argument, consider the following:

▶ Is the argument too informal or formal? How can I create a formal, but engaging, academic voice?

▶ How can allusions help to create the most appropriate voice?

▶ Is there someone to blame for the crisis? If so, can I accuse him or her without sounding too harsh?

Revision

Revision—or re-seeing—involves evaluating one's own work: identifying its strengths and weaknesses and making effective changes. Rethink your essay by reconsidering the chapter introduction:

- "Insightful thinkers often see through the crossfire, beyond the two common possibilities." How does the essay get readers beyond common possibilities?
- "Regardless of the particular situation, those who react to crises and propose the best possible solutions (the most manageable, ethical, practical, economic, far-reaching, etc.) are often the most valuable individuals in a given situation." How does your argument propose the best way out?
- "The emphasis on crisis or solution depends on the topic, the opposing voices, and even previous solutions." If you do not propose a direct solution, why? Does the argument do something equally important?

Peer Review

In peer review, writers have an opportunity to understand how their ideas influence others—not simply if their ideas are wrong or right, if the spelling is good and the grammar correct. The process can actually make an argument come to life. If the reviewers read closely and offer focused comments, they can help to add new dimensions to the argument. Notice that the following questions do not focus on editing (or correctness and grammar rules). Rather, they focus on the argumentative moves in the essay—on intensifying the claims and support strategies where possible.

Exchange drafts with at least one other writer. (If time allows, exchange with two or three writers to gather a range of perspectives or comments.) Use the following questions to generate specific constructive comments about others' drafts:

Main Claim

1. Does the argument focus your attention on a specific crisis? Are you convinced that it is a crisis worthy of public attention? If not, what could the writer do to convince you?

2. How does the essay go beyond discussing obvious possibilities? Could the writer go further in suggesting a way out of the crisis?

Support

3. What support strategy is most effective? What support strategy could be deleted without weakening the argument?

4. Identify appeals to logic in the essay. Explain how the writer could further develop a specific logical appeal so that you better understand the nature of the crisis or the validity of the proposed solution.

5. Identify an appeal to value, and explain how it figures into the argument. How, for example, does the essay call on the reader's sense of fairness, justice, honor, or duty? Explain how the writer could further develop the appeal. How might the writer draw more attention to the shared value?

6. Consider outside sources. How do they help support the writer's claims? Do outside sources take over any portions of the argument? Do they overwhelm the writer's voice?

Counterarguments/Concessions/Qualifiers

7. Consider counterarguments. How might a reader remain unconvinced because the essay did not anticipate and respond to some other valid viewpoint? What additional counterarguments would be helpful?

8. Should the writer concede or qualify any points to help strengthen the argument?

Arrangement

9. How might the argument be more engaging if ideas were arranged differently? For example, should the crisis be described sooner, or more quickly? Should long sections of narrative (or storytelling) be helped along with connections to the essay's main idea?

Audience and Voice

10. What makes the writer sound fair and informed? What focuses too much on personal feelings, attacks, and accusations?

WILLIAM H. WEST'S
BIG MINSTREL JUBILEE

CARROLL JOHNSON

TOM LEWIS

ED. HOWARD

GEO. B. MACK

FOUR OF OUR NATION'S FUN MAKERS

Arguing the Past

What Happened?

People are prone to repetition. Companies continue policies (which may or may not work well); countries keep laws on the books (which may or may not coincide with core national principles); and, of course, individuals knowingly continue bad habits (which may hurt them or others around them). In short, we are willing to base the present on the past—unless an argument about the past changes our perspective. Imagine, for instance, a large company that keeps a particular sales policy in place for years because it assumes the policy has been successful. Then a manager argues in a detailed report that the policy has not been successful and actually has added to unnecessary costs throughout the years. If this new argument is persuasive enough, it may cause the company to restructure its sales policy entirely.

Such arguments regularly occur in professional life. In fact, many organizations hire people whose sole job is to study and make arguments about past actions and policies. Colleges hire institutional researchers to examine the success of past hiring practices; businesses of all types hire accountants to examine their economic histories and make recommendations based on those histories; institutions hire quality control officers to not only examine present operations but also scrutinize past operations; and huge organizations (from NASA to the Environmental Protection Agency) hire specialists in many different fields to examine their corporate history and make suggestions about present and future action.

Arguments about the past occur in almost all aspects of life. People argue about the justice or injustice of past action, debating, for instance, if the purchase of Manhattan from the Native Americans was fair or, more recently, if the North American Free Trade Agreement (NAFTA) has benefited or hurt U.S. workers. Politicians argue over the country's past condition: Was it a good year for manufacturing, or was it bad? Was it a successful or unsuccessful economic policy? Was it a justified or unjustified military action? Depending on the answers (the arguments) to such questions, people make decisions about the future (whom to vote for, which policy to support, and so on).

All of this assumes that the past is important—it is not dead. And anyone bound for serious study of the present and future must first understand the link to the past. History itself is a collective debate about what happened, who was involved, and who was responsible. As you examine the readings in this chapter, notice how the arguments, regardless of their specific position or focus, make an important link between the past and the present. They each argue for a different way of seeing the past.

Activities

1. Think of a moment from history when new evidence prompted people to rethink a past event or historical figure. What specific evidence prompted the rethinking? Specifically how did people's thinking change? What conflicting views still exist?

2. Humans are part of history; each person has a past that is connected to other people's pasts. What histories are you a part of? Search through a school yearbook, family photos, a stack of old family letters, a town history. Look for a connection to the past that you haven't thought about before. For example, how might something about your school, classmates, grandparents, or town history have influenced your current interests, values, struggles, or psychoses?

3. People in all walks of life and in all academic disciplines return to the past to discover if present versions of the past accurately portray reality. For example:

- Psychologists argue over the influence Freud had on clinical practices.
- Art historians debate the role of political influence on particular artists or even entire movements.
- Nursing professionals argue about the wisdom of past hiring practices, which have led to present staffing shortages.
- Geographers argue about the role the Appalachian Mountains played in the development of the American frontier.

Add two examples to this list—one related to a particular career or field of study.

Shakespeare and Narcotics

DAVID PINCHING

When the Shakespeare Birthplace Trust in Stratford-upon-Avon permitted researchers to perform chemical tests on twenty-four pipe fragments from Shakespeare's house and nearby sites, two of the pipes showed traces of cocaine and hallucinogenic drugs. The findings were reported in the *South African Journal of Science* in 2001. "Shakespeare and Narcotics" was published on www.Bibliomania.com in response to reaction to the findings.

The recent discovery of a drug-tainted clay pipe in Stratford-upon-Avon, home of Shakespeare, has caused some fervent discussion on the topic of the Bard's possible cocaine usage. In early March of this year, some South African researchers explained that their chemical analysis of seventeenth-century pipes had revealed traces of cocaine, compounds created by the burning of cannabis, and hallucinogenic substances. Apparently, then, Shakespeare and his contemporaries had access to a number of narcotics. Naturally, tabloids and websites alike responded by claiming that Shakespeare was inspired by drugs. A few choice headlines include everything from "Drugs Clue to Shakespeare's Genius" and "Did Shakespeare Seek Inspiration in Cocaine?" to the less subtle "Shakespeare's 'Cannabis Sonnet'" and "Shakespeare May Have Been Stoned on Pot." Every academic who could be bothered to dip into the mire of such shock journalism shrieked back that there was no proof that Shakespeare took the substances and that, crucially, he was a genius regardless of his lifestyle. In the lather of spurious information from the drug lobby, entirely innocuous phrases such as "noted weed" and "compounds strange" were cited as proof that the writer of *Much Ado About Nothing* and *Romeo and Juliet* was drugged up to the ruff. Actually, in the relevant context, "noted weed" means "famous type of clothing" and a "compound strange" is nothing more exciting than an unusual word construction.

Steven Vidler/Eurasia Press/Corbis

Oddly, in all the desperate kafuffle to find some loose reference to narcotics that could appear in a twenty-line tabloid article, journalists failed to note more suspect goings-on in the plays themselves. Was it not Macbeth who saw a dagger floating in the air in front of him, Hamlet who ran about murderously after being visited by his father's ghost, and Othello who babbled incoherently about "goats and monkeys"? Almost the entire cast of *A Midsummer Night's Dream* are given drugs and sleeping potions at some point and one is entirely convinced that he is a wall (actually, he is one of the few not drugged, but the point holds). The fact that the journalists and academics alike seemed to avoid studiously was that there was nothing remotely illegal about the drugs found in the pipes in Shakespeare's day. As most people are aware, Queen Victoria herself took cannabis for the relief of period pains and every poet worth his or her salt in the nineteenth century ingested enough laudanum and opium to make the Beatles blush. The fact that we seem to want Shakespeare to have taken drugs for sensational value says more about our age of celebrity than it does about the great playwright. Those who like to degrade the great and promote the sensational would like to imagine Shakespeare, spliff in mouth like the ridiculous and once ubiquitous "psychedelic" poster of the *Mona Lisa*. It is a lot easier to debunk some-thing than to create something worthwhile oneself.

The mindset behind such an outlook is the really depressing thing. People like to imagine Shake-speare freebasing and rolling up joints because they see him as an establishment figure. As such, portraying him as a junkie causes amusement and indignation because of our modern attitude to sub-stances that allows certain kinds of intoxication but not others. Shakespeare would not have understood our simultaneous and hypocritical prudishness and excess. He was, in his time, a radical, a novelty, and far more dangerous to the establishment with his damning indictments of royalty in *King Lear, Rich-ard III,* and *King John,* among others, than any of our media starlets. The idea that you can be anti-establishment by becoming incapable of thinking properly is pretty out of date anyway. And, as the worst excesses of post-Sixties fiction, music, and art have proved, "mind-altering" does not necessarily mean "art-improving." Ann Donnelly, the curator of the Shakespeare Birthplace Trust, was unimpressed with the evidence from the pipes and claimed that people are always trying to "come up with reasons for saying Shakespeare was not a genius." This may be something of a spoilsport attitude, but it is a fair one. Everyone in England is forced to read Shake-speare at school, and plenty of other countries have a similar policy regardless of the fact that Shake-speare is hardly the easiest entry point into the Eng-lish language. However, one suspects that if cream buns and Britney Spears were forced on pupils as Shakespeare is, they too would become distrusted at an early age. As such, Ms. Donnelly is right in say-ing that people often look for a way to knock Shake-speare off his high horse. There was the school of thought that said that Shakespeare was not even the author of the plays published under his name but that, in fact, an aristocrat wrote them. Others have claimed that Ben Johnson and other worthies of the age were responsible. Generally, it seems that peo-ple have a problem accepting that one man wrote so much, let alone so much great literature. What we are effectively saying in insisting that Shakespeare probably smoked drugs is that given the task of try-ing to write all the plays Shakespeare did we would probably turn to narcotics. The fact is that reading the Bard's works or going to see a good production of one of his plays is infinitely more rewarding than taking drugs. Thankfully, Shakespeare's plays are also cheaper and more freely available. Read them all on Bibliomania.

Analyzing Argument

1. What basic principle, issue, or value is at the root of the argument?

2. What is the main claim?

3. What values are at play in the following statements?

It is a lot easier to debunk something than to create something worthwhile oneself. (paragraph 2)

People like to imagine Shakespeare freebasing and rolling up joints because they see him as an establishment figure. (paragraph 3)

The fact is that reading the Bard's works or going to see a good production of one of his plays is infinitely more rewarding than taking drugs. (para-graph 3)

4. What other values (in addition to the ones from question 3 above) are important to Pinching's argument?

5. How does Pinching connect the past to a larger point about contemporary Western culture?

6. How does Pinching help readers to rethink the past?

A Nation Made of Poetry

JOANNIE FISCHER

When the U.S. National Archives and Records Administration compiled a list of 100 milestone documents in U.S. history from 1776 to 1965, Joannie Fischer, a contributing editor for *U.S. News and World Report*, responded by exploring the role of unofficial documents (speeches, songs, novels, and so on) in American history. The official documents are available at www.ourdocuments.gov.

The official documents now on display in Washington, D.C., offer one version of America's story. It's an authorized biography of sorts, screened and sanctioned. But the beauty of words in a democracy is that anyone can offer them up, and they live or die not by a ruler's dictate, but by their ability to permeate hearts and minds, to ignite passions, and to provoke action. Throughout our history, we have learned that words with enough resonance—whether from a slave, a student, or a songwriter—can change history as dramatically as any decree.

In fact, for every official document marking our nation's progress, there are countless others that have steered events, whether by inciting, critiquing, warning, encouraging, cajoling, enraging, or inspiring. Sometimes the words in these unofficial manifestos are so powerful that they still echo through time, blending with other potent phrases from other outspoken souls to form a grand montage of ideas and urgings, odes and rants, tall tales and truthful testimonies. This "unauthorized" biography of our nation is scrawled in letters and diaries, in pamphlets and propaganda, in poems and rock concerts, in novels and essays. From the whole, vast array, we each pick and choose those lines that move us most, and piece together our own story of what it really means to be an American.

To be sure, without some of these scripts, key moments in U.S. history might never even have taken place. Without Thomas Paine's elegant and angry prose, for example, we might not even exist as an independent country today. In 1775, Colonial leaders were torn by warring views about how to deal with mother England. Then, in January 1776, Paine's pamphlet *Common Sense* was published in Philadelphia, opening with the legendary phrase, "These are the times that try men's souls." It argued forcefully for the necessity of revolution and sold 150,000 copies overnight. It's widely credited with overcoming dissenters' qualms and unifying opinion enough to make the Declaration of Independence possible. "Without the pen of Paine," said John Adams, "the sword of Washington would have been wielded in vain."

So, too, was the Civil War sparked not by the flare of a cannon but by a flair for language. Although slavery had been controversial for 100 years, and tensions between the North and South ran strong and deep, it took novelist Harriet Beecher Stowe's *Uncle Tom's Cabin* to convey in intimate detail the horrors of slavery and galvanize the abolitionist movement. In 1851 and 1852, roughly 10 years before the siege of Fort Sumter, some 300,000 people had devoured her tome, published in weekly installments in a magazine and ending with this exhortation: "On the shores of our free states are emerging the poor, shattered, broken remnants of families. . . . They come to seek a refuge among you." Stowe so famously fueled fevers that Abraham Lincoln, upon meeting her in 1862, is said to have declared, "So you are the little woman who wrote the book that started this great war!"

And, ironically, if not for a letter signed by the great pacifist Albert Einstein, we might never have dropped atomic bombs on Hiroshima and Nagasaki, plunging the world into the nuclear age. In 1939, when physicists found a way to split uranium atoms and release immense amounts of energy, the American press was abuzz with the expert opinion that such energy would never be harnessed into a bomb—a claim that the U.S. government bought into. But Einstein, a refugee from Nazi Germany, became convinced by colleagues not only that a bomb was scientifically feasible but that if the United States didn't build one first, the Nazis would, thereby gaining an unbeatable advantage over the rest of the world. On Aug. 2, 1939, he signed a letter to President Roosevelt advising him the atomic bomb was not only possible but imminent. The letter also warned that Germany had commandeered Czechoslovak uranium mines and halted further sales of the ore. To ward off disaster, he urged the president to sponsor a fast-moving U.S. atomic project. Einstein's letter launched the Manhattan Project and the nuclear arms race, which led six years later to the devastation of Hiroshima and Nagasaki. Toward the end of his life, Einstein said that sending the letter was "the greatest mistake" he ever made.

At times in our history, laws on the books had declared an issue resolved, a case closed, but informal voices sprang up and forced us as a people to reconsider. In 1963, for example, decades after a constitutional amendment gave women the vote and supposed equality, Betty Friedan wrote in her book *The Feminist Mystique* about "the problem that has no name." As she described it, "Each suburban wife struggled with it alone. As she made the beds, shopped for groceries, matched slipcover material . . . chauffeured Cub Scouts and Brownies, lay beside her husband at night—she was afraid to ask even of herself the silent question—'Is this all?'" With these words, Friedan awakened women of the "silent generation" and spawned a movement for women's rights that continues even today.

And in the same year, a century after the Emancipation Proclamation and years after the official end of racial segregation, Martin Luther King Jr. reminded the country: "We must face the tragic fact that the Negro is still not free." His words were epic: "When the architects of our republic wrote the magnificent words of the Constitution and the Declaration of Independence, they were signing a promissory note," King said. "It is obvious today that America has defaulted . . . insofar as her citizens of color are concerned." The force

and eloquence of his words emboldened crusaders, and within two years both the Civil Rights Act and the Voting Rights Act were enacted. To this day, his words challenge each American to answer whether our black citizens can truly say, "Free at last! Free at last! Thank God Almighty, we are free at last!"

No matter what the time or place, our unofficial scribes have helped us to define our national character. Acting as mentors, they have fostered traits such as our famous individualism. Ralph Waldo Emerson did this when he wrote in *Self-Reliance:* "Whoso would be a man must be a nonconformist." And Henry David Thoreau echoed that sentiment in a personal diary that's been as influential in American culture as many archived documents: "I went to the woods because I wished to live deliberately . . . and not, when I came to die, discover that I had not lived." These philosophers and essayists have held up models for us to emulate, with stories of strong heroes like Paul Bunyan and courageous pioneers like Davy Crockett. And they have encouraged our world-renowned work ethic, as in Walt Whitman's celebration of carpenters and mechanics and shoemakers in *I Hear America Singing,* or more recently Woody Guthrie's and Bob Dylan's and Bruce Springsteen's paeans to American folklife and the nobility of labor.

Yet we often stumble into virtually irreconcilable tensions in trying to derive solidarity and community from millions of ambitious individualists. Indeed, our wordsmiths have often warned us when we have tipped too far off balance. Robert Frost was cautioning the nation when he wrote, "Something there is that doesn't love a wall . . . before I built a wall I'd ask to know what I was walling in or walling out." (Yet so wed are we to the values of freedom and solitude that we tend to skip over Frost's intended irony and quote his final phrase as words to live by: "Good fences make good neighbors.")

It took an outsider, the French social critic Alexis de Tocqueville, to alert early Americans to the "restlessness in the midst of their prosperity." Indeed, he chastised Americans for their "taste for physical gratifications," for "brooding over advantages they do not possess," and for the "vague dread that constantly torments them lest they should not have chosen the shortest path" to success. Writing in 1835, he concluded: "It is impossible to spend more effort in the pursuit of happiness."

In the almost two centuries since *Democracy in America* appeared, countless homegrown sages have tried to warn us of the deceptive lure of the pot at the end of the rainbow. There was the folktale of John Henry, who out of pride worked himself to death in order to beat a steam engine blasting holes through a mountain. There was F. Scott Fitzgerald's tragic Gatsby, doomed by his materialistic appetites, and at the opposite pole, John Steinbeck's hardworking but lost families in *The Grapes of Wrath,* cast into wretchedness by forces beyond their control. The folk duo Simon and Garfunkel sang cautionary rhymes about a fraudulent "big, bright green pleasure machine" and about the superficially successful Richard Cory—first the subject of an 1897 Edwin Arlington Robinson poem—who despite all his worldly riches and power was so miserable as to put a bullet through his own head.

Some influential writers have gone so far as to reject our capitalist ways altogether. In his 1906 polemic *The Jungle,* socialist Upton Sinclair argued: "There is one kind of prison where the man is behind bars, and everything that he desires is outside; and there is another kind where the things are behind the bars, and the man is outside." Half a century after Sinclair was writing, a new generation of young socialists would spark the wave of 1960s protests. "The American political system is not the democratic model of which its glorifiers speak," declared the Port Huron Statement, the manifesto of Students for a Democratic Society. "In actuality it frustrates democracy by confusing the individual citizen, paralyzing policy discussion, and consolidating the irresponsible power of military and business interests." One 1960s peace activists' motto—"make love, not war"—still reverberates today, and more recent counterparts of the antiwar activists have added "no blood for oil" to the unofficial national lexicon.

To its credit, America has always shown a great measure of tolerance for such self-criticism. Indeed, even when we have disagreed most vehemently, Americans have tended to agree on basic principles like the right to disagree. Again, Emerson's words have guided us: "Nothing is at last sacred but the integrity of your own mind." Others have created icons of integrity, such as Harper Lee's character Atticus Finch, a southern lawyer who in *To Kill a Mockingbird* defends a black man whom everyone else would scapegoat. Such high principle may be best portrayed by the ultimate American hero, the scrappy Huck Finn, who after much soul-searching decides that the right course of action is to defy all authority and help the runaway slave, Jim, to escape to freedom.

Freedom: the term Americans say best defines our nation. It's the juncture at which all of our most defining documents—both official and unofficial—always intersect. Our government proclaims freedom as a God-given right, and our songs chime "let freedom ring." Our activists protest freedoms still denied, and our sages remind us time and again that freedom is only truly worthwhile when we use it to "do the right thing." Perhaps that is why, indelibly engraved into our collective conscience, are not only the words "land of the free" but also "home of the brave."

Analyzing Argument

1. What basic principle, issue, or value is at the root of Fischer's argument?

2. What is Fischer's main claim?

3. How does Fischer's argument rely on shared values? Point to specific passages to support your answer.

4. How does Fischer engage opposition? Where does she counter, concede, or qualify her own claims? Explain how that move (or moves) functions in her argument.

5. How could Fischer's claim be more focused and revelatory?

Red (White and Blue) Scare

STEPHEN PELL

Stephen Pell developed this argument in his second-semester college English course, using ideas about spin and propaganda from essays in the previous edition of *Inventing Arguments*. Pell's argument not only sheds light on the past, but it also reveals a connection between past and current events.

After World War II, after the Nazis had been pushed back into Germany, after Hiroshima and Nagasaki, a new power threatened our way of life: its name, communism. Josef Stalin reigned supreme over the Soviet Union. He had killed and imprisoned numerous citizens of his own country during now infamous purges, and ruled his country with an unflinching iron fist, oppressing his citizens with sheer brutality and show of force. The Russian poet Anna Akhmatova, whose poetry inspired many of her countrymen during these dark times, describes, in haunting verse, the horror that was impressed upon the population by Stalin's atrocities. Akhmatova herself had been an unintentional victim of the Stalinist purges; her husband and son were both imprisoned. The poem, often considered her most famous piece, is entitled "Requiem." In one passage, she remembers those who stood beside her outside the prison walls, waiting in futility, "The fading smiles upon submissive lips, / The trembling fear inside a hollow laugh. / That's why I pray not for myself / But all of you who stood there with me / Through fiercest cold and scorching July heat / Under a towering, completely blind red wall" (Akhmatova).

This terrifying account is the communism Americans knew and feared. Fear of "Reds" was palpable throughout the country. As Michael Barson and Steven Heller point out, the angst towards communism boils to the surface in Steinbeck's classic, *The Grapes of Wrath:* "A red is any son of a bitch that wants thirty cents when we're paying twenty-five" (qtd. in Barson and Heller 8).

The "Red" threat wasn't completely illegitimate. The purges that took place under Stalin certainly warranted a fair amount of opposition, and the Cuban missile crisis was nothing to sneeze at. To be fair to the American public living through these dark times, communism, as they knew it, was a serious concern to the way in which they lived. The problem, however, was that communism itself became synonymous with Stalin. This correlation had already embedded itself deep within the public psyche, making it easy for the government to capitalize on the public's premonitions. Continued use of the public's own fear of communism allowed the government to justify aggression against communist states such as Cuba, Guatemala, and Korea.

The Guatemalan conflict was relatively short compared to other anti-communist military actions of the time period, such as Korea and Vietnam, but it was well publicized. In June 1954, *Time* took a close look at the Guatemalan civil war. As expected of an article featured in a popular American magazine during the Cold War, sensationalism of glorious triumph over the "Reds" nearly oozes from the pages ("Battle"). The author of the article has the uncanny ability to present a gray situation, like a civil war, in such a fashion that the gray areas seem to fade away, leaving a defined line between black and white. The communist president of Guatemala, the enemy, is portrayed as a backstabbing, bloodthirsty madman. Throughout the article, the ideal of communism is presented as though it is a lesser form of government, as "rudimentary." This and other articles in popular magazines became some of the strongest forms of propaganda available to the masses.

The U.S. government was not only waging the war abroad, but back home as well. Paired with the national media, the government controlled its own people, not with guns, but with words. Americans were being attacked on all fronts with anticommunist propaganda: everything from movies to posters to public service announcements, speeches, articles in magazines, books, and even real-life world events. These world events often centered around military or paramilitary action towards a select group of communists or a country, usually ending with the communist forces being crushed to illustrate the superiority of capitalism.

Naturally, the dirty details of these paramilitary operations were never divulged to the American public until many years after the fact, making these operations a form of intense propaganda, in many ways more effective than conventional forms of propaganda. A government could *claim* that a rival nation's economy was failing. They could *say* that a nation's leader was an evil madman who violently oppressed his people. Posters could be pasted on the sides of buildings; radio waves could be broadcast to the masses; schools could be required to educate on the dangers of a communist government; but nothing convinces the population of a truth better than creating the truth firsthand.

Anti-communist advocates argue that the communist system of government was overtly oppressive and vastly inferior to capitalism. They may cite the economic instability in countries such as the Soviet Union and Cuba. However, it was not revealed until later that one of the biggest contributors to the instabilities of these countries was none other than our own CIA. These events of sabotage were planned as full-scale paramilitary operations, the most notable being "Operation Mongoose," which was primarily designed to cripple Cuba's economy and incite an uprising from within the country. Author James W. Symington writes in his article for the *National Review*:

> In sum, if the intent of the past two generations of U.S. policy towards Cuba has been to render its economy comatose—energy consumption cut in half, vehicular travel horse- and mule-drawn or fixed in time to the 1950s, agricultural production inadequate, diet restricted, plumbing and street lamps non-operational, professional classes earning less than busboys in the gleaming Veradero tourist hotels, and too many of her fairest daughters walkers of the night streets—I would have to pronounce the policy an unqualified success. (37)

Symington's article is calling for the stoppage of America's trade embargo of Cuba, an embargo started during the Kennedy administration, that is only hurting an already economically battered country.

How did they do it? How could a nation's government convince an entire population to think the same way about an issue without tanks rumbling through the streets or by leveling the business end of a rifle at the collective mass? Propaganda.

America had had a history of utilizing propaganda to either stir up the masses or subdue them. "Loose talk" was a common issue addressed in American propaganda during World War II and the years following. One poster in particular illustrates how much America emphasized the value of keeping quiet. The poster bears the image of a GI helmet draped over a white cross with the words: "A careless word . . . another cross." Still another poster bears the image of a housewife and the ridiculous claim that her "loose talk" cost lives. What information could she possibly know?

This theme trickled beyond issues of national security and into everyday life. Americans were warned of "petty squabbles" among coworkers. A piece of propaganda during the early '40s features a bird's head and these words: "IF you MUST TALK about your boss or the person working alongside *(squawk squawk)* wait till the war is over. Office and factory politics and jealousies are destroyers of production. Chew a piece of gum instead" ("Petty Squabbles").

Propaganda during the Cold War took on many forms. It was a poster plastered to the side of a building, reminding the American public of the dangers the communists posed. It came in the form of blockbuster Hollywood hits like *I Married a Communist, The Red Menace,* and of course, every James Bond film up until the collapse of the Soviet Union. Articles detailed nightmare scenarios, such as communist guerillas taking over Detroit. *Look* magazine became the premiere periodical for sensationalized articles intent on stirring up the American public's anti-communist imagination. *Look* even featured a helpful template to be used to identify American communists with greater ease.

Americans faced propaganda from all angles during the Cold War. Not even the children were safe from the onslaught of anti-communism. Comic books of the time featured subtle and not-so-subtle undertones of capitalism, in the form of their favorite superhero vanquishing an ominous villain, clearly representing the Soviet Union. Bubble gum contained "Children's Crusade Against Communism" cards in every pack. Instead of the pictures of their favorite ballplayers, children were greeted with the wrinkled face of Josef Stalin or an artist's interpretation of what New York City *would* look like in the aftermath of a nuclear attack.

These appeals to everyday Americans' logic were by no means lofty. The propaganda was directed squarely at the middle class, which was not likely to dissect the hidden arguments lacing each and every propaganda poster. This attack on a specific class is a proven and effective method in the art of propaganda. Hitler states that "[for the intellectual class], propaganda is not suited. . . . All propaganda must be presented in a popular form and must fix its intellectual level so as not to be above the heads of the least intellectual of those to whom it is directed" (qtd. in Mauk and Metz 129). Propaganda posters were often bright and colorful, with few words. The posters presented their ideas and hidden ideas quickly and easily. However, when text was necessary to convey the complete argument against communism, it was often in the form of an article in a popular magazine, circulated throughout the middle classes. There was no escaping it. The "Red Scare" seeped its way into every form of

media available to the masses. Everyday life became saturated with the appeals against communism.

The threat of communism was taken very seriously during the Cold War era. The Soviet threat became an excuse to take drastic measures against countries that posed no real danger to our way of life. Such was the case in Guatemala, when our nation's government justified to the American public that serious action against Guatemala was imperative, simply by scaring them with the "monster" that was communism. Noam Chomsky, a well-known and often controversial voice when it comes to America's foreign relations, writes in his book *Hegemony or Survival,* "The Soviet threat was routinely invoked, abetted by Guatemala's appeal to the Soviet bloc for arms after the U.S. had threatened attack and cut off other sources of supply. The result was a half-century of horror, even worse than the U.S.-backed tyranny that came before."

Hegemony. A thousand times more effective than the physical display of power, hegemony is power internalized within the very psyche of a group of people, altering how they think, directing who they associate themselves with, and making its presence known whenever a tough decision should arise. The government's control over information was the equivalent of covering up all but a small portion of a painting. The public wasn't getting the whole picture. Thus, the government had great leverage in establishing what the public *should* think about communism. Presenting only one side of communism, the dark side, the American government was able to simultaneously encourage hostility towards the Soviets while winning the trust of the American public.

Americans were living in a bubble. Petrified of the outside world of "Reds" and rebels and dictators, Americans clung ever tighter to Uncle Sam, if only to protect themselves from impending doom. Thomas Hobbes' 17th-century book, *Leviathan,* describes the motives behind the formation of the first commonwealths:

[The commonwealth] is the foresight of their own preservation, and of a more contented life thereby; that is to say, of getting themselves out from that miserable condition of war which is necessarily consequent, as hath been shown, to the natural passions of men when there is no visible power to keep them in awe, and tie them by fear of punishment to the performance of their covenants, and observation of those laws of nature.

The first governments were founded on the idea that an individual could not withstand the tumult of the outside world alone. The only safety came in groups. A commonwealth of individuals banded together to establish a larger body, a stronger body, one that could keep them safe from surrounding barbarism. In the case of the United States during the Cold War, the barbarism was replaced by communism, and Americans, driven by fear, voluntarily sacrificed their freedoms for security, positioning themselves further under the wing of the Republic, allowing the roots of hegemony to penetrate free thought.

The notion of a people sacrificing individuality and imagination for alleged security and blissful ignorance vaguely resembles the predictions found in Aldous Huxley's dystopic future in *Brave New World*. Characters are described as "bottled" from the outside world, and from themselves. The term "bottled" is used as a euphemism for *intoxicated* on the drug of choice, *soma*. In the novel, soma, along with years of subliminal conditioning, allows the government to maintain order among a society ranging in the billions. However, while the soma brings peace, it strips its users of freedom, rational thought, and individuality altogether. Users (everyone) stumble about in a dazed state, delightfully unaware of their surroundings. This is how propaganda leaves the average citizen. It is the opiate of the masses, the intellectual assault that makes hegemony within our society a very real, past and present danger.

Hegemony is so powerful because it targets the mind. A physical show of force, such as armed guards stationed on every corner or the threat of imprisonment for any suspicious activity against the government, is an effective method of controlling a population, but it has its downside. A select few will always fight against such obvious power, and though their bodies are being oppressed, their minds are free to think, free to reason, and free to conceive plots of a revolution. Hegemony attacks the mind, smothering the fires of change before they have a chance to ignite. Its effectiveness lies in its subtlety. A hegemonic authority can implement fear and sensationalism to convince the public that a certain choice is more acceptable or inherently right. Adolf Hitler himself addressed this potency: "Here the art of propaganda consists in putting a matter so clearly and forcibly before the minds of the people as to create a general conviction regarding the reality of a certain fact, the necessity of certain things and the just character of something that is essential" (qtd. in Mauk and Metz 129).

Communist Controlled Countries - 1980

Ambrose Video

Hegemony is still present today. Communism is certainly still unwelcome in this country, but now there is a new threat to our culture: terrorism. In the months following the attacks of September 11th, an all-out war on terror was declared while we continued to ponder the motives behind the attacks. During these initial months, any questioning of the government's actions in dealing with this new threat was enough to get oneself alienated from society. It was a vulnerable point in our nation's history. Trust in the government was high, as well as fear of the outside world. The masses could be easily swayed with a dramatic speech or sensationalized news piece. A unified mindset could be sensed throughout the majority of the population. The mere hint of hostile countries possessing weapons of mass destruction was enough to send people into a panic. We were afraid of another September 11th, as illustrated by the hasty creation and ratification of the Patriot Act, an act that trades freedom for security. Most Americans were unfazed. They had come to believe that it was the right thing to do. The painful memories of 9/11 swarmed in the back of their minds, memories that could be harnessed.

Hegemony and democracy cannot coexist. Anti-communist propaganda during the Cold War presented a one-sided view of communism, instilling fear in the population and restricting rational thought. This blatant bid for total thought control reveals the hidden motives of those in power, those who wish to control rather than to sustain freedom, those who wish to present a black-and-white description of what is right and what is wrong. Though such a tightly controlled view of the world promises unity, it comes at the price of truth and intellectual liberty.

Works Cited

Akhmatova, Anna. "Requiem." *Poemhunter.* Poemhunter, n.d. Web. 30 Apr. 2006.

Barson, Michael, and Steven Heller. *Red Scared! The Commie Menace in Propaganda and Popular Culture.* San Francisco: Chronicle, 2001. Print.

"Battle of the Backyard." *Time.* Time, 28 June 1954. Web. 28 Apr. 2006.

Chomsky, Noam. "Cuba in the Cross-Hairs: A Near Half-Century of Terror." *Hegemony or Survival.* New York: Metropolitan, 2003. *chomsky.info.* Web. 1 May 2006.

Hitler, Adolf. "Mein Kampf." *Inventing Arguments.* Ed. John Mauk and John Metz. Boston: Wadsworth-Thomson, 2006. 128–30. Print.

Hobbes, Thomas. "Of the Causes, Generation, and Definition of a Commonwealth." *The Leviathan.* London, 1651. Oregon State University. Web. 30 Apr. 2006.

Huxley, Aldous. *Brave New World.* 1932. New York: Perennial Classics, 1998. Print.

"Petty Squabbles." *CafePress.com.* CafePress.com, n.d. Web. 28 Apr. 2006.

Symington, James W. "Into Cuba." *National Review* 10 Nov. 2003: 36–38. *Academic Search Elite.* Web. 1 May 2006.

Analyzing Argument

1. According to Pell, what happened?

2. How does the argument connect the Red scare of the past to the reader's life today? How important is the connection?

3. What types of support are used, and how? Consider evidence, examples, and appeals.

> **Evidence:** authorities, testimony, facts, statistics
> **Examples:** allusion, anecdote, illustration, scenario
> **Appeals:** to logic, emotion, character, value, need

4. Academic audiences look at the inner workings of an argument. To examine Pell's argument more carefully, ask:

- What does the argument assume the reader values?
- What assumption (from the previous question) might a reader object to? Make an argument in support of the assumption. That is, argue for why the reader should accept the assumption.
- What assumptions might Pell have argued for, and why? Were all his assumptions safe ones to make?

Somewhere in the Past: Clarksville's School and Community Life

CAMERON JOHNSON

Using the invention prompts in this chapter, Cameron Johnson explored the complexities of a common topic: school funding. While Johnson concedes that class size has remained consistent and school buildings have been well-maintained, he unearths a less obvious and extremely important consequence of budget cuts, and he cautions the citizens of Clarksville (and other communities) that such cuts extend beyond school and into the very life of the community.

School funding has been steadily decreasing in the Clarksville Area School district for the past decade. While the district has managed to keep the schools running, providing lunches, busing, and textbooks, cuts in funding have hurt Clarksville Schools and Clarksville, the community, in subtle and important ways. When school funding does not keep up with the growing needs of students, the whole community pays the price.

Some influential community leaders have argued for years that schools, like all companies, organizations, and households, should "tighten their belts" in times of economic woe. And, for years, that is what our schools (and most others around the country) have been doing. So while those community leaders can applaud the school board, superintendent, teachers, and students for getting by on less, citizens of Clarksville should be cautious about their optimism. While class size has remained consistent and school buildings are well maintained, lack of funding has hit the schools and our community in other places.

Appeal to value. (The passage engages the values of those who prefer spending less on schools.)

Deceptively important academic programs and extracurricular activities have been cut. A 1990 *Oracle,* the school's yearbook, includes photographs of several groups and clubs that no longer exist: perhaps most notably, the Junior High Drama Club and the Senior High Thespians, but also the Jazz Ensemble, Sundancers, Future Business Leaders, and more. None of these losses alone is devastating, yet many Clarksville citizens have fond memories of high school musicals, such as *Guys and Dolls* and *Bye-Bye Birdie,* musicals replaced now by an evening watching TV or a movie at the local cinema. High school musicals, and other extracurricular events, help to connect school, student, and community, not just the night of the event, but for years to come.

"Deceptively" = there is more going on with these programs than meets the eye.

This is the main idea of the argument.

Another example helps illustrate the vital connection between school and community. Many Clarksville citizens grew up in, and have fond memories of, the school's summer recreation program that was cut back steadily each year and finally abandoned in 1996. While this program can

Cameron Johnson, "Somewhere in the Past: Clarksville's Schools and Community Life." Reprinted by permission of the author.

Addresses potential opposing position—that only essential programs should be funded.

The series of points is an appeal to logic. Here we see the line of reasoning at the heart of the argument.

This is a more generalized expression of the claim.

The secondary sources show that Clarksville's funding issues are common throughout the country. (The information about other schools reinforces the point about Clarksville.)

Before we move into Putnam's points, the writer sets up the points and creates appropriate context for the quotations.

Although the quotation is lengthy, all the information is relevant to the argument. It reinforces Johnson's key point: that public interaction is shrinking in communities like Clarksville.

be seen as nonessential, it was hardly fluff in the budget. The summer recreation program was an important link between school and community. It not only gave kids something to do, but it helped forge a stronger bond between school and student, and this bond created other bonds: between school and community and between community and student. Because of less funding, schools end up offering less support (for academics) and less attraction (for extracurricular activities). In the long run, schools with less funding become less important to students and less important within the community as a whole. The summer recreation program is just one example of this subtle, or silent, breakdown.

All across America, local school systems have been facing consistent budget cuts, and as in Clarksville, the cuts impact the delicate layer of social life around the schools: summer school, sports, music, and art programs have consistently been lopped off the agendas. Some districts, such as one in Orange County, Florida, are considering moving back starting times to 10:30 or 11:00 a.m. (Stover). It is easy to see that budget cuts have made schools shrink inward—balling themselves into smaller space and smaller bits of time. And even when communities pass local levies, they are often not enough to turn the tide. Increased taxes have not always kept up with the rate of inflation. According to the organization Funding for Washington Schools, for example, the purchasing power for education in the state of Washington has actually decreased 33% since 1992 because of inflation. And when that loss is projected over the coming decades, it is easy to imagine the economic effect: a consistent reduction of programs and a consistent reduction in the role that schools once played in their communities.

In previous generations in America, the people of small towns convened—perhaps at the church, a town hall, a school, or all of these. Some institution served as an assembly place. But now, American communities are less communal than they have ever been. According to sociologist Robert D. Putnam, "There is striking evidence . . . that the vibrancy of American civil society has notably declined over the past several decades" (65). Putnam's important essay, "Bowling Alone: America's Declining Social Capital," details a range of individual and collective behavior that illustrates diminishing civic engagement in American towns:

A series of identical questions posed by the Roper Organization to national samples ten times each year over the last two decades reveals that since 1973 the number of Americans who report that "in the past year" they have "attended a public meeting on town or school affairs" has fallen by more than a third (from 22 percent in

1973 to 13 percent in 1993). By almost every measure, Americans' direct engagement in politics and government has fallen steadily and sharply over the last generation, despite the fact that average levels of education—the best individual-level predictor of political participation—have risen sharply throughout this period. Every year over the last decade or two, millions more have withdrawn from the affairs of their communities. (68)

In other words, people may be getting more schooling (graduating from high school, going to college), but they are doing so in a more private manner. Their educational experiences are more divorced from their community experiences—and so the whole purpose of education seems more wrapped in individual private success. Even parental involvement has waned:

> The parent-teacher association (PTA) has been an especially important form of civic engagement in twentieth-century America because parental involvement in the educational process represents a particularly productive form of social capital. It is, therefore, dismaying to discover that participation in parent-teacher organizations has dropped drastically over the last generation, from more than 12 million in 1964 to barely 5 million in 1982 before recovering to approximately 7 million now. (Putnam 69)

This is not to say that parents are generally less engaged in their children's schooling. They may, in fact, be more engaged than before. But if they are, it is a private engagement, one not dramatized in public life.

Putnam's study corresponds to my own experiences. In the 1970s and 1980s, when I was coming through the public schools, they were more central to town life than they are now. I remember huge turnouts for a wide range of school-sponsored events (even beyond the Friday night football games): ice-cream socials, plays, orchestra concerts, spelling bees, even marching band *practice.* But something has changed fundamentally.

Somewhere in the past is the community of Clarksville. Certainly, it is still a town. But it is slightly less alive than it was. It may have a strip mall and two more fast-food establishments than it did ten years ago, but it is less involved in its own affairs. The public schools were a key part of a past vitality. But as funding has been cut, extracurricular programs, the ones that created an intensive social life around the schools, have also been cut. We have let something important, something about our community, fade into history.

*Side notes:*

Johnson follows up the quotation and makes it feel even more relevant to the argument.

Here's another follow-up. Johnson qualifies the point of the quotation.

A transition from the outside source to Johnson's personal testimony.

Johnson returns to the specific focus on Clarksville. He is careful to qualify the claims.

Works Cited

Putnam, Robert D. "Bowling Alone: America's Declining Social Capital." *Journal of Democracy* 6.1 (1995): 65–78. Print.

Shutz, Byron and Barb Billinghurst. "School Funding Facts." *Funding Washington Schools.* Funding Washington Schools Advocates, n.d. Web. 24 Oct. 2010.

Stover, Del. "Stretching the Incredible Shrinking School Budget." *Education Digest* Sept. 2003: 59. Print.

Analyzing Argument

1. What basic principle, issue, or value is at the root of Johnson's argument?

2. Does the argument convince the reader of its main point? In other words, is anything left hanging that might call the argument into question?

3. What logical appeal is important to the argument, and how?

4. Fill in the following:
   Main Claim:
   Unstated Assumption(s):
   Support:

5. In groups, identify several unstated assumptions that are crucial to Johnson's argument. How might Johnson have argued for the validity of the unstated assumption?

6. What attempt does the argument make to connect with the audience? Does the argument concede, qualify, or counterargue? Does the language or voice engage people with a different position or perspective?

Apache children on arrival at the Carlisle Indian School in Pennsylvania.

Apache children four months after arrival at the Carlisle Indian School in Pennsylvania.

Carr Fork Canyon, Utah (circa 1939–1945)

We should never have made cars so affordable to the masses.

WHAT HAPPENED?

Real family entertainment died with *The Waltons* and *Little House on the Prairie.*

To view this video, visit the English CourseMate at CengageBrain.com.

op to bottom: Madhouse; Library of Congress; ─adhouse; © Photodisc; From CourseMate ─deo (BBC: Civil Rights March)

Exploring for Topics

Arguments often emerge from conflicting perspectives about the past. A topic might involve a highly debatable issue such as the circumstantial evidence used to convict or set free someone accused of a crime. But a topic need not concern an event already surrounded by debate. Some of the most engaging arguments involve topics that at first seem beyond argument. As you examine the world around you, pay attention to how the past has been described and look for any discrepancy between your perspective and others'. Or look for tension among different accounts of the past. If you discover tension in the way someone has been characterized, something has been defined, or something has been sequenced, you may have a topic that will develop into an argument. Use the following prompts to find topics and begin developing your own argument:

- Consider past national or world events: a military action, governmental election, political scandal, economic crisis, marketing campaign, political protest.
- Read about an era or time: prewar Europe, the Jazz Age, the golden age of Greece, the Reagan years, the Clinton years, the Cold War, the Beat Generation.
- Recall a past local event: an election, high school sporting event, political scandal, industrial accident, schoolyard mishap, business deal, violent crime, festival, parade.
- Read an old magazine or newspaper and look for behaviors, trends, or fashions from the past: architectural trends, gender roles in the workforce or at home, educational practices, work schedules, standards of beauty, hairstyles.
- Visit a place that characterizes the past: a museum, national monument, historical landmark, amusement park, corporate headquarters.
- Explore your academic major: browse through a related textbook or journal, or ask someone involved in the field (a professor or even a student who has taken several classes) about the history and development of the discipline. The following questions may be helpful: What particular past events are still being debated in the discipline? Is there debate about the cause of any trends, situations, or events in the discipline? Is research in the field or discipline on the right track? Why or why not?
- Consider the opening image for this chapter: What does it suggest about America's past? What does it say about fun, entertainment, American spirit, or race relations?

- Consider the readings and images from this chapter: Which makes you want to speak out? What point is not resolved in your mind? From your perspective, which raises an especially important topic?
- What song or songs argue about the past? What version of the past does the song argue for? Do most people accept that version of the past?

To fully explore the past, arguers go beneath the obvious information and examine details, acting like detectives collecting clues. From these clues, they build and argue for a valid account of events. Use the following invention questions to explore your topic. While it may be tempting to answer quickly and move on, the insights you are seeking lie beyond the first, quick response:

▶ Who was involved? Explain their influence.

▶ What factors (natural, political, etc.) were involved, and what was their influence?

▶ How were institutions or policies involved?

▶ What were the consequences of the event or behavior in question?

▶ How were people's lives directly or indirectly affected?

▶ Might other effects become clear at some point in the future?

▶ What are the hidden effects (the layers no one can actually see)?

Now, notice how Cameron Johnson takes one of the questions and explores:

▶ How were people's lives directly or indirectly affected?

When school funding does not keep up with the growing needs of students and teachers, the whole community pays the price—not financially, but in other ways. When schools can't afford to pay for after-school programs, clubs, and teacher assistants (the kind of things that are the first to go when funding gets low), the schools become less of a center for student life. The schools shrink inward and involve fewer people. The schools offer less support (for academics) and less attraction (for extracurricular activities). In the long run, schools with less funding become less important to students—and within the community as a whole. And when that happens, ironically, the communities go downhill (slowly but surely). And when communities go downhill, property values go downhill (slowly but surely). This is what has happened in Clarksville. School funding has slowly been decreasing over the years. As a result, the public schools have shrunk away from the community.

Johnson's invention writing explores the direct, and also the indirect and subtle, effects of the situation. Now he might look for additional effects by asking, *So what if the public schools shrink away from the community? Who or what might be affected? What problem(s), if any, might arise?*

Invention Workshop

For your topic, with one or two other writers answer the invention question, "How were people's lives directly or indirectly affected?" Then identify an indirect or subtle effect that more people should be aware of.

Exploring for Principles and Precedent Good arguers go beyond a topic's specific details to discover relevant principles (standard rules that govern behavior) and precedents (cases that came before). Johnson's topic, Clarksville public school funding, relates to general principles about school funding and the general relationship between communities and schools. During invention, he writes:

> In the long run, schools with less funding become less important to students—and within the community as a whole. And when that happens, ironically, the communities go downhill (slowly but surely). And when communities go downhill, property values go downhill (slowly but surely).

Here we see Johnson making a general claim about the school/community relationship, pointing to a principle beyond Clarksville, and applying it to the specific topic:

> This is what has happened in Clarksville. School funding has slowly been decreasing over the past fourteen years. As a result, the public schools have shrunk away from the community.

Johnson could go even further and investigate the relationship between public institutions and communities:

> Communities are better off when they nurture their public institutions. From libraries to city park services, public institutions make a community better. When those institutions are developed with care and proper funding (with sustained attention), they give back to the community in many unseen ways—in essence, they offer a huge financial, cultural, and civic return.

Johnson's exploration transcends the particulars of Clarksville. This exploration pays off because the broader principles can be applied to the specific case. Johnson could also explore precedent (similar cases that have occurred) by asking, *How has public school funding worked in America? How have most public schools fared under decreasing tax dollars?* In general, these questions ask: *What has happened before?* As you consider your own topic, ask yourself the following:

▶ What bigger principles, issues, or values are involved?

▶ What other situations are like this? What has happened in these other situations?

Collecting Opinions Answers to survey questions can help writers understand conventional views and imagine some unconventional or peculiar ones. But informal surveys rarely yield highly credible support. The responses do not amount to a collective truth about the topic; instead, they reveal patterns of perception in particular communities. Claims from surveys should be used accordingly—not as ultimate grounds for claims, but as tools of exploration.

Conducting Secondary Research Writers use secondary sources (articles, books, websites, and so on) to find out what has already been said and to develop a sense of their own position. If little has been said directly about a topic and published arguments are hard to find, this does not mean all hope is lost. On the contrary, it means you have some open argumentative terrain.

Because every topic is related to broader principles and precedents, research can take many different paths. For instance, Johnson's focus on Clarksville relates to the broader relationship between communities and public institutions. So a range of relevant information could emerge from a database search of the following keyword combinations: *school funding and property value; public institutions and funding; public institutions and funding and communities.* These searches could lead to sources that address broader issues such as the general decline in civic engagement or the national trends in school funding, and these sources would shed light on the particular situation in Clarksville. Research includes different layers—both particular details and broader principles. While researchers sometimes pursue a particular fact or statistic to support their position, they also look for theories and arguments that help them see the topic in a new way. This is the heart of inventive research.

Activities

1. As a class, discuss what types of sources may best develop arguments about the past—or which ones might help you to see the past in a new way. Consider the following source types:

Primary Sources	Secondary Sources	
Interviews	Books (nonfiction)	Government documents
Surveys	Newspapers	Pamphlets
Literary works	Magazines	Speeches
Novels	Journals	Performances
Short stories	Online periodicals	Films, television, music
Poetry	Websites	Posters
Religious texts	E-mails	

2. Survey at least five students from your class and at least five people not in your class. First ask if they know of the event or situation you have chosen. Then ask them to give their accounts. Do not lead them to an answer, but ask for their opinions of what happened and how they characterize the events. Listen for descriptive words such as *terrible, excellent, proud, guilty, surprising, irresponsible, brave, correct*. Record the responses and look for how others perceive the topic, what patterns exist, and any unconventional ways of thinking.

Inventing a Claim

To make a persuasive argument about the past, arguers must first become aware of other versions or accounts. Only then can they plan an effective argumentative strategy. Use the following questions to examine possible arguments about your topic.

What Do Others Claim?

▶ What is the mainstream or official account? (What do most people say happened?)

▶ How is the event or situation characterized or defined? (What key descriptive words or adjectives do people use?)

▶ What are the marginalized accounts (those that are rarely mentioned)?

What Do I Claim?

▶ Do you agree or disagree with any accounts you have heard or read?

▶ How is your own perspective different from or similar to others'?

For any one situation or event, an unlimited number of points can be argued. For example, you may argue that something caused an event, that a past behavior was warranted or unwarranted, that a past situation is deeply misunderstood, or that someone was guilty or innocent. The following are standard types of arguments about the past, focused in different ways:

Cause/Effect Arguments Cause/effect arguments assert a claim for or against a particular cause:

- The freedom of the Jazz Age was, in part, a response to the tightly controlled behavior of the preceding decades.
- The rawness of the grunge sound was a backlash against the slick fashions of mainstream 1980s music.
- The train collision last month occurred because Westway Railroad refused to address major mechanical deterioration.

Definition Arguments Definition arguments assert a particular characterization about a topic:

- The Jazz Age was more about sexuality than jazz.
- Grunge was not necessarily the music of a generation.
- Last month's railway collision was a classic example of corporate irresponsibility.

Evaluation Arguments These arguments assert some claim of value (that some event or situation was good/bad, wrong/right, misguided/appropriate, and so on):

- Jazz was America's most important cultural discovery.
- The grunge sound of the early 1990s saved the music industry from heading in an insipid direction.
- Westway Railroad Company was guilty of gross negligence in last month's train collision.

Now that you have a topic in mind, choose an argumentative path. Ask yourself:

▶ What exactly can be argued about the topic?

▶ What path do I want to take?

▶ Is the tension based on the cause or sequence of events, the characterization of people or things, or the evaluation of something or someone?

Write out the claim you are making about the past, and view this claim as a work in progress. Notice Johnson's working claim, which changed as the argument evolved:

> The people of Clarksville may not realize it, but the town's vitality has been left in the past—along with well-funded schools.

A Caution about Clichés Clichés, worn-out expressions that people use in everyday conversation, should be avoided in formal arguments. Johnson's working claim would be made less clear with a cliché: *The people of Clarksville may not yet realize it, but they have sealed the deal on their own community, which will spiral downward along with its underfunded schools.* Clichés don't offer particular information. For example, "seal the deal" could mean nearly anything. It is better to avoid such vague phrases and articulate more specific ideas.

Narrowing Claims Claims should focus on a precise and intense idea—one worthy of exploration. They should make readers aware of a single point. Generally, the more precise the point, the more intense the argument. Notice the difference between the following statements:

- Music of the 1960s was better than the music of today.
- The culture of hope in the 1960s gave the popular youth music more significance than the popular music of today has.
- The civic unrest of the late 1960s made rock-and-roll music seem more artistic than it actually was.

The first statement has a broad subject, and the verb *was* does not focus the reader on a particular quality or issue. The statement does not reveal an insight, but flatly states a broad opinion ("better" in what way?). The second and third statements go further and invite readers to see a particular aspect about popular music in the 1960s. As you develop your claim, consider the subject and verb: Are they specific enough? If the subject of the sentence is not specific, how can you better focus your thoughts? Does the verb direct attention to a particular quality or action?

More Sample Claims

A focused, revelatory claim will create a more intense argument for any topic. The following claims point readers (and their writers) in very particular argumentative directions:

Politics

- As the Clinton era illustrated, federal fiscal discipline, once a trademark of the Republican Party, has been taken over by the Democrats.
- Contrary to modern romantic notions, Native Americans were often territorial and fought to defend or occupy new land before European settlers brought their notion of war to this continent.

Community Issues

- Had the township elected not to allow big box stores to take over the outskirts of the city in the early 1990s, the downtown, and perhaps the outlying region, would still be thriving today.
- Like many small towns in America, Coventry emerged only because of the farming that surrounds it.

Popular Culture

- Commercials are not getting less sophisticated. Since the beginning of television, they have been insufferably dim-witted, aimed at the lowest possible level of consciousness and self-awareness.
- The hope of the hippy era faded into history because, like any mass movement in America, its collective energy focused on fashion and image, not real political change.

Environment

- When it comes to the health of the environment, the "scientific community" has always been dismissed by the masses, and—as history shows—the masses have consistently been wrong.
- The attempts to clean up the Great Lakes in the 1970s and 1980s were met with derision and contempt, showing that mainstream political ideology has valued the right to poisonous living conditions for decades.

Inventing Support

Building an argument is not simply a matter of saying what you think. It is a process of supporting a debatable claim or set of claims. Writers develop arguments with various support strategies.

Testimony Testimony is an individual's personal portrayal or understanding of events. In an argument about the past, testimony can be especially persuasive. Firsthand testimony can be used to capture the details or emotion of a past situation, or to show a particular account:

> In the 1980s, the standardized test craze was just beginning to enter public schools. Certainly, students had been taking standardized tests, such as the California Achievement Test, for years, but in the '80s, the once-a-year testing sessions started to climb. In fact, my memories of the sixth grade are filled with hours of the fill-in-the-bubble, number-2-pencil-only tests, the names of which I do not recall. Nor do I recall receiving anything back about my scores.

Arguers can also use the testimony of others:

> Some historians with an ax to grind are quick to dismiss Woodstock as a mere incident—as something that had little meaning outside of the drug culture of the era. However, the drug culture was only a single layer of Woodstock, and many participants still explain that they were very much aware of the significance of the event. According to Bill Crandle, the meaning was palpable in the air: "We all knew that it was something special, and that history would remember us. People even talked about it, saying things like 'people won't ever forget it.'"

Examples Examples are specific cases or illustrations of phenomena. They help to make an abstract point clearer or more concrete. Examples also can help narrow down generalizations or broad claims. In her article "A Nation Made of Poetry," Joannie Fischer argues that America's past is built on great poetic texts, and most of her article offers examples through history:

> To be sure, without some of these scripts, key moments in U.S. history might never even have taken place. Without Thomas Paine's elegant and angry prose, for example, we might not even exist as an independent country today. In 1775, Colonial leaders were torn by warring views about how to deal with mother England. Then, in January 1776, Paine's pamphlet *Common Sense* was published in Philadelphia, opening with the legendary phrase, "These are the times that try men's souls."

Authorities Authorities are sources or people who can substantiate points based on their research or professional qualifications. Authorities are important to use when offering specialized information (anything that might require focused research or experimentation). Notice how Johnson uses an organization as a source:

> It is easy to see that budget cuts have made schools shrink inward— balling themselves into smaller space and smaller bits of time. And even when communities pass local levies, they are often not enough to turn the tide. Increased taxes have not always kept up with the rate of inflation. According to the organization Funding Washington Schools, for example, the purchasing power for education in the state of Washington has actually decreased 33% since 1992 because of inflation.

Johnson uses the source to show historical precedent and explain a dimension of public school funding. The sentence immediately following brings the reader back to his main point:

> And when that loss is projected over the coming decades, it is easy to imagine the economic effect: a consistent reduction of programs and a consistent reduction in the role that schools once played in their communities.

Analogies Analogies compare a less familiar thing to a familiar thing to make the less familiar more understandable. To draw an analogy is to draw out the similarities between two different phenomena. This is often done in arguments about the past. If someone wants to prove something about past event A, he or she may show how it is like event B:

> In some ways, the search for the source of the river Nile was like the search for the fountain of youth: European explorers plunging into foreign (and conquerable) lands to gain notoriety, to gain immortality.

Analogies are often used to discuss past political affairs:

> Only twice in American history have we had father/son presidents: the Adams and the Bush families. In some ways, the families are much alike. Both had immense power in the country, which enabled the sons to be channeled into the positions. The difference, however, lies in the nature and use of that power.

Literary Works Literary works such as novels, poetry, drama, and short stories can be used in various ways to support a writer's claims. In "Red (White and Blue) Scare," Pell uses Aldous Huxley's novel *Brave New World* to help the reader understand his claim that "people [sacrifice] individuality and imagination for alleged security and blissful ignorance."

Pell states his claim, introduces Huxley's novel, makes specific references to the novel, and connects those references to the larger points of his argument about propaganda and hegemony:

The notion of a people sacrificing individuality and imagination for alleged security and blissful ignorance vaguely resembles the predictions found in Aldous Huxley's dystopic future in *Brave New World*. Characters are described as "bottled" from the outside world, and from themselves.

> The term "bottled" is used as a euphemism for *intoxicated* on the drug of choice, *soma*. In the novel, soma, along with years of subliminal conditioning, allows the government to maintain order among a society ranging in the billions. However, while the soma brings peace, it strips its users of freedom, rational thought, and individuality altogether. Users (everyone) stumble about in a dazed state, delightfully unaware of their surroundings. This is how propaganda leaves the average citizen. It is the opiate of the masses, the intellectual assault that makes hegemony within our society a very real, past and present danger.

Appeals to Logic This type of appeal calls on the audience to follow a line of reasoning. In an argument about the past, the logical appeal often is based on cause and effect: the arguer would like the audience to see a reasonable relationship between an action and a reaction. For example, notice Johnson's final paragraph:

> Somewhere in the past is the community of Clarksville. Certainly, it is still a town. But it is slightly less alive than it was. It may have a strip mall and two more fast-food establishments than it did ten years ago, but it is less involved in its own affairs. The public schools were a key part of a past vitality. But as funding has been cut, extracurricular programs, the ones that created an intensive social life around the schools, have also been cut. We have let something important, something about our community, fade into history.

Johnson's argument provides a direct connection between the cause (funding cuts in the school district) and the effect (loss of community). The passage invites readers to understand that one impacted the other.

Appeals to Value Appeals to value make a connection between the topic and a value such as fairness, equality, duty, or responsibility. Notice how Johnson engages the values of those who prefer spending less on schools:

> Some influential community leaders have argued for years that schools, like all companies, organizations, and households, should "tighten their

belts" in times of economic woe. And, for years, that is what our schools (and most others around the country) have been doing. So while those community leaders can applaud the school board, superintendent, teachers, and students for getting by on less, citizens of Clarksville should be cautious about their optimism. While class size has remained consistent and school buildings are well maintained, lack of funding has hit the schools and our community in other places.

Deceptively important academic programs and extracurricular activities have been cut.

Johnson acknowledges the value of being frugal and makes frugality shared common ground. With the shared value established, he turns to a new idea: "Deceptively important academic programs and extracurricular activities have been cut."

For your own topic, use the following invention questions to develop support:

▶ What specific situations show my point about the past?

▶ What people or events from history, popular culture, or literature show my point?

▶ What line of reasoning should the reader follow to understand my point? (How can I best walk the reader through that line of reasoning?)

▶ What emotions can I evoke in the reader? How will those help the reader understand my position?

▶ What values underlie my position? How can I invite the reader to share those values?

▶ What literary works help to illustrate my point about the past?

Invention Workshop

With one or two other writers, answer the preceding invention questions for your topic. See how many types of support you can find for each topic.

Types of Support

Evidence: authorities, testimony, facts, statistics

Examples: allusion, anecdote, illustration, scenario

Appeals: to logic, emotion, character, value, need

Arrangement

Arranging an argument means arranging how the reader will experience the issue. In this case, the arrangement will determine how the reader returns to the past, experiences particular claims and details, and then returns to the present. The writer is a guide to the past, taking the reader on a persuasive tour, and the arrangement of a text is the path the reader takes.

How Should I Begin? Arguments about the past can begin with a current event that prompted the argument. For example, in "A Nation Made of Poetry," Joannie Fischer begins her argument by referring to official documents now on display.

> The official documents now on display in Washington, D.C., offer one version of America's story. It's an authorized biography of sorts, screened and sanctioned. But the beauty of words in a democracy is that anyone can offer them up, and they live or die not by a ruler's dictate, but by their ability to permeate hearts and minds, to ignite passions, and to provoke action. Throughout our history, we have learned that words with enough resonance—whether from a slave, a student, or a songwriter—can change history as dramatically as any decree.

In "Shakespeare and Narcotics," David Pinching uses the same strategy, starting with a current event:

> The recent discovery of a drug-tainted clay pipe in Stratford-upon-Avon, home of Shakespeare, has caused some fervent discussion on the topic of the Bard's possible cocaine usage.

In "Somewhere in the Past: Clarksville's Schools and Community Life," Johnson begins by illustrating what happened in the past:

> School funding has been steadily decreasing in the Clarksville Area School district for the past decade. While the district has managed to keep the schools running, providing lunches, bussing, and textbooks, cuts in funding have hurt Clarksville Schools and Clarksville, the community, in subtle and important ways. When school funding does not keep up with the growing needs of students, the whole community pays the price.

Johnson's first sentence illustrates the past (what has been happening); the second sentence asserts a problem (cuts in funding have hurt the school *and* the community); the third sentence transcends the particulars of Clarksville and points to a principle (the importance of schools to the community). The rest of the essay develops Johnson's claim "When school funding does not keep up with the growing needs of students, the whole community pays the price."

Where Should I Detail the Past? Joannie Fischer details the past throughout most of her essay, always connecting past details with their significance to the present:

> To be sure, without some of these scripts, the key moments in history might never even have taken place. Without Thomas Paine's elegant and angry prose, for example, we might not even exist as an independent country today. In 1775, Colonial leaders were torn by warring views about how to deal with mother England. Then, in January 1776, Paine's pamphlet *Common Sense* was published in Philadelphia, opening with the legendary phrase, "These are the times that try men's souls." It argued forcefully for the necessity of revolution and sold 150,000 copies overnight. It's widely credited with overcoming dissenters' qualms and unifying opinion enough to make the Declaration of Independence possible. "Without the pen of Paine," said John Adams, "the sword of Washington would have been wielded in vain."

Like Fischer, the other writers in this chapter detail the past throughout their essays. Pell focuses on the past for eighteen paragraphs, then changes focus to the present:

> Hegemony is still present today. Communism is certainly still unwelcome in this country, but now there is a new threat to our culture: terrorism. . . .

How Can I Briefly Explain Accounts of the Past? While accounts of the past are sometimes explained at length (a chapter or even an entire book can explain an account of the past), accounts are often explained briefly and then responded to. Notice how Johnson creates an account of the past in his first two sentences, and then develops how and why that account has changed:

> In previous generations in America, the people of small towns convened—perhaps at the church, a town hall, a school, or all of these. Some institutions served as an assembly place. But now, American communities are less communal than they have ever been. According to sociologist Robert D. Putnam, "There is striking evidence . . . that the vibrancy of American civil society has notably declined over the past several decades" (65). Putnam's important essay, "Bowling Alone: America's Declining Social Capital," details a range of individual and collective behavior that illustrates diminishing civic engagement in American towns. . . .

Invention Workshop

With one or two others, discuss how you might explain accounts of the past in your essay.

1. How many accounts of the past will you explain and why?

2. How much detail is necessary to bring the reader's thinking in line with your own?

3. What details would take away from the argument's intensity?

4. Will you explain an account at length, or can you sum it up in a sentence or two?

5. Will you explain an account by correcting some other account, as Pinching does?

Activity

For practice in describing the past, and to help figure out how you might describe the past for your argument essay, describe your version of the past in two pithy sentences, then describe it in a paragraph or more.

Audience and Voice

Bridging Values Writers use their understanding of the audience to find common ground and bridge values. Building a bridge to the values of one's opponents is an especially powerful argument strategy. As Fischer argues the importance of unofficial documents in American history, she connects individual voices and documents to American values such as *individualism* and *hard work:*

> No matter what the time or place, our unofficial scribes have helped us to define our national character. Acting as mentors, they have fostered traits such as our famous individualism. Ralph Waldo Emerson did this when he wrote in *Self-Reliance:* "Whoso would be a man must be a nonconformist." And Henry David Thoreau echoed that sentiment in a personal diary that's been as influential in American culture as many archived documents: "I went to the woods because I wished to live deliberately . . . and not, when I came to die, discover that I had not lived." These philosophers and essayists have held up models for us to emulate, with stories of strong heroes like Paul Bunyan and courageous pioneers like Davy Crocket. And they have encouraged our world-renowned work ethic, as in Walt Whitman's celebration of carpenters and mechanics and shoemakers in *I Hear America Singing,* or more recently Woody Guthrie's and Bob Dylan's and Bruce Springsteen's paeans to American folklife and the nobility of labor.

While Fischer connects Emerson, Thoreau, Bunyan, Crocket, Whitman, Guthrie, Dylan, and Springsteen to individualism and hard work, she connects other voices to *self-criticism,* another important American value:

> In the almost two centuries since *Democracy in America* appeared, countless homegrown sages have tried to warn us of the deceptive lure of the pot at the end of the rainbow. There was the folktale of John Henry, who out of pride worked himself to death in order to beat a steam engine blasting holes through a mountain. There was F. Scott Fitzgerald's tragic Gatsby, doomed by his materialistic appetites, and at the opposite pole, John Steinbeck's hardworking but lost families in *The Grapes of Wrath,* cast into wretchedness by forces beyond their control. The folk duo Simon and Garfunkel sang cautionary rhymes about a fraudulent "big, bright green pleasure machine" and about the superficially successful Richard Cory—first the subject of an 1897 Edwin Arlington Robinson

poem—who despite all his worldly riches and power was so miserable as to put a bullet through his own head.

Fischer's many examples help the reader accept her account of the past in which unofficial documents resonate and steer history.

For your own topic, use the following invention questions to build bridges to opposing viewpoints:

▶ When you picture yourself arguing this topic, who is on the receiving end?

▶ What values do you share with that audience?

▶ What values might you not share? (Do you, for instance, value individual rights more than your audience does or vice versa?)

▶ What connections can you make between your values and the values of those who might disagree with you?

Counterarguments, Concessions, and Qualifiers Another way writers connect with their audience is through counterarguments, concessions, and qualifiers. Notice how Cameron Johnson explains and then refutes an opposing position:

> Some influential community leaders have argued for years that schools, like all companies, organizations, and households, should "tighten their belts" in times of economic woe. And, for years, that is what our schools (and most others around the country) have been doing. So while those community leaders can applaud the school board, superintendent, teachers, and students for getting by on less, citizens of Clarksville should be cautious about their optimism. While class size has remained consistent and school buildings are well maintained, lack of funding has hit the schools and our community in other places.

Not all opposing positions can be explained away. Some have value, and good arguments acknowledge that value by conceding opposing points or by qualifying their own points. Notice how Johnson acknowledges an opposing view and then responds:

> Another example helps illustrate the vital connection between school and community. Many Clarksville citizens grew up in, and have fond memories of, the school's summer recreation program that was cut back steadily each year and finally abandoned in 1996. While this program can be seen as nonessential, it was hardly fluff in the budget. The summer recreation program was an important link between school and community. It

not only gave kids something to do, but it helped forge a stronger bond between school and student, and this bond created other bonds: between school and community and between community and student.

Johnson concedes that the summer recreation program can be seen as nonessential. Then he counters that position by arguing the summer program had value as an important link between school and community ("it was hardly fluff").

Authority One strategy for building authority is to project a voice that is more discerning than popular opinion. Notice how David Pinching corrects an opposing, popular view and creates a sense of authority:

> In the lather of spurious information from the drug lobby, entirely innocuous phrases such as "noted weed" and "compounds strange" were cited as proof that the writer of *Much Ado About Nothing* and *Romeo and Juliet* was drugged up to the ruff. Actually, in the relevant context, "noted weed" means "famous type of clothing" and a "compound strange" is nothing more exciting than an unusual word construction.

Whenever writers can legitimately correct opposing views, or even point out a fact that others ignore, they indirectly build authority, which then gives credence to their other claims.

Activity

Ask two peers to read your essay, then discuss the following audience and voice issues: How does the argument build a bridge to shared values? How does it connect with readers through counterarguments, concessions, and qualifiers? How does the writer establish authority? How might the argument do these things more effectively?

Revision

During revision, writers see their argument with more clarity and get their most powerful ideas. Good revision requires two things: the willingness to step back from one's work and see it from a new perspective, and the willingness to make significant changes. As you respond to the following revision questions, refer to the relevant sections of this chapter. Rereading the discussions and responding again to the invention questions will help you explore ideas further and develop new, more persuasive support.

Claim

1. What is the main claim about the past? Could any clichés be replaced with specific language? How could the main claim be more precise and intense?

Support

2. What basic principle or value is at the root of the argument? How could it be brought more to the foreground?

3. How does the argument convince the reader? Is anything left hanging that might call the argument into question?

4. Is the past event or situation explained sufficiently? Where and how would more detail help persuade readers to accept the main claim?

5. Is the past event or situation explained in too much detail? Which details could be deleted without weakening the argument?

6. Does the argument depend too much on one kind of support? If so, which support is overused, and what other strategies might be employed instead?

7. How does the argument respond to opposing positions? What counterarguments, concessions, and qualifiers could strengthen the argument?

Arrangement

8. How does arrangement keep the argument interesting? How might ideas be rearranged, or even deleted, to give the argument more momentum?

Audience and Voice

9. How does the language or writer's voice invite people with a different perspective into the argument?

10. Is the argument lively and intense enough? How could it be more so?

Sources

11. If you used outside sources, consider the following:

- Have you used research as a means of discovery? (pages 360–383)
- Have you evaluated sources for ideology, reliability, relevance, credibility, timeliness, diversity? (pages 384–394)
- Are the ideas from the outside sources integrated smoothly into your ideas? (pages 395–410)
- Are the sources documented appropriately with in-text and end citations? (pages 411–438)

Peer Review

In a group of four, take turns workshopping one essay at a time:

1. One writer reads his or her essay to the group.

2. Other group members write down their initial ideas about the essay.

3. The writer reads his or her essay again, and group members write down more specific comments. (To generate specific comments, use the preceding Revision Questions.)

4. Each group member shares his or her comments with the writer, as the writer takes notes.

Group members will be tempted to discuss ideas, but this method of peer review discourages discussion. Instead, it is designed to provide four writers with feedback from three readers in a short period of time.

Arguing the Future
What Is Going to Happen?

No one can be certain of the future. However, popular culture offers a constant stream of prophetic visions. Films *(Planet of the Apes, The Matrix* trilogy, *The Day After Tomorrow)*, novels *(Brave New World)*, and short stories ("There Will Come Soft Rains") have attempted to warn us of an impending, perilous future. Meanwhile, swarms of advertisements try to convince us that the future will be full of more and better conveniences, products, and services. From the most sophisticated literary work to the most simplistic ads, many texts in our daily lives make bold assertions about the future. They shape how we imagine ourselves, our civilization, our species, and our planet in coming years.

But the future is not written only by fiction writers, Hollywood directors, and marketers. Every day, we make personal decisions based on our assumptions about the future. We sign apartment leases and assume that our financial situations will remain stable; we buy a week's worth of food and assume that the electricity will continue powering our refrigerators; we store our personal money in banks and assume that the institutions will remain solvent. And we often have to argue about the way we see the future. Business leaders, for example, must make their peers believe in or doubt the staying power of current trends. Imagine a sales executive for a major automaker arguing that the company should maintain its SUV output because, she argues, the price of oil will eventually stabilize and then decrease as tensions in the Middle East are resolved. Another executive argues that gas prices are certain to increase as Iran gains power in the region. Depending on the most acceptable view of the future, the automaker will make a decision on SUV production.

Arguments about the future are always based on the past and present. Therefore, convincing arguments about the future are connected to what people already know about patterns of behavior:

- Having traced the past migratory patterns of butterflies, a scientist argues that certain species will continue to move northward.
- Based on past findings about children's television viewing habits and the link to attention deficit disorder, a psychological study predicts that American children will become increasingly less able to focus in formal academic settings.
- Pointing to the population shifts of the twentieth century, a sociologist argues that the twenty-first century will challenge major metropolitan areas to invent new modes of transportation.
- Basing its conclusions on trends from the past 100 years, a committee of climatologists argues that average global temperatures will continue to increase in the next century.

But an argument about the future can diverge from the past: someone might argue that the future will look radically different from the past and present. That person must argue especially well to make the future seem plausible. Imagine a writer who focuses on the future of higher education. Although the latter half of the twentieth century saw increasing access to higher education, he argues that college will become *less* accessible to the middle and working classes. Because this claim counters the past trend, the writer must provide reasoning for this shift, arguing, for instance, that several factors (global markets, political access, changing political ideology) will establish new conditions. (See Charles Nelson's essay, "Investing in Futures," in this chapter.)

The future is open to interpretation. When we argue about the future, we must take into account not only what has happened and what is likely to happen, but also what could possibly happen. We must imagine a realm of scenarios—and then convince others that one particular path, out of unlimited possibilities, is the most likely. As you examine the following readings, notice how the authors present a possible (or even likely) future based on the trends of the present. And when you explore topics for your own argument, consider present trends and make it your job to convince readers that a particular trend is likely to impact the future.

Live Forever

RAYMOND KURZWEIL

Not long ago, most people could not imagine personal computers, satellites, or cell phones. In this essay, Ray Kurzweil suggests a version of the future unimaginable to most people today—a version in which humans merge with the technology they have created and then live forever. Kurzweil is an inventor, author, and editor of KurzweilAI.net, a website that "features the big thoughts of today's big thinkers examining the confluence of accelerating revolutions that are shaping our future world." "Live Forever" was first published in *Psychology Today* magazine in 2000.

Thought to Implant 4: OnNet, please.

Hundreds of shimmering thumbnail images mist into view, spread fairly evenly across the entire field of pseudovision.

Thought: Zoom upper left, higher, into Winston's image.

Transmit: It's Nellie. Let's connect and chat over croissants. Rue des Enfants, Paris in the spring, our favorite table, yes?

Four-second pause.

Background thought: Damn it. What's taking him so long?

Receive: I'm here, ma chère, I'm here! Let's do it!

The thumbnail field mists away, and a cafe scene swirls into place. Scent of honeysuckle. Paté. Wine. Light breeze. Nellie is seated at a quaint table with a plain white tablecloth. An image of Winston looking 20 and buff mists in across from her. Message thumbnails occasionally blink against the sky.

Winston: It's so good to see you again, ma chère! It's been months! And what a gorgeous choice of bodies! The eyes are a dead giveaway, though. You always pick those raspberry eyes. Très bold, Nellita. So what's the occasion? Part of me is in the middle of a business meeting in Chicago, so I can't dally.

Nellie: Why do you always put on that muscleman body, Winston? You know how much I like your real one.

Winston morphs into a man in his early 50s, still overly muscular.

Winston: (laughing) My real body? How droll! No one but my neurotechnician has seen it for years! Believe me, that's not what you want. I can do much better! He fans rapidly through a thousand images, and Nellie grimaces.

Nellie: Damn it! You're just one of Winston's MI's! Where is the real Winston? I know I used the right connection!

Winston: Nellie, I'm sorry to have to tell you this. There was a transporter accident a few weeks ago in Evanston, and . . . well, I'm lucky they got to me in time for the full upload. I'm all of Winston that's left. The body's gone.

When Nellie contacts her friend Winston through the Internet connection in her brain, he is already, biologically speaking, dead. It is his electronic mind double, a virtual reality twin, that greets Nellie in their virtual Parisian cafe. What's surprising here is not so much the notion that human minds may someday live on inside computers after their bodies have expired. It's the fact that this vignette is closer at hand than most people realize. Within 30 years, the minds in those computers may just be our own.

The history of technology has shown over and over that as one mode of technology exhausts its potential, a new, more sophisticated paradigm emerges to keep us moving at an exponential pace. Between 1910 and 1950, computer technology doubled in power every three years; between 1950 and 1966, it doubled every two years; and it has recently been doubling every year.

By the year 2020, your $1,000 personal computer will have the processing power of the human brain—20 million billion calculations per second

(100 billion neurons times 1,000 connections per neuron times 200 calculations per second per connection). By 2030, it will take a village of human brains to match a $1,000 computer. By 2050, $1,000 worth of computing will equal the processing power of all human brains on Earth.

Of course, achieving the processing power of the human brain is necessary but not sufficient for creating human-level intelligence in a machine. But by 2030, we'll have the means to scan the human brain and re-create its design electronically.

Most people don't realize the revolutionary impact of that. The development of computers that match and vastly exceed the capabilities of the human brain will be no less important than the evolution of human intelligence itself some thousands of generations ago. Current predictions overlook the imminence of a world in which machines become more like humans—programmed with replicated brain synapses that re-create the ability to respond appropriately to human emotion, and humans become more like machines—our biological bodies and brains enhanced with billions of "nanobots," swarms of microscopic robots transporting us in and out of virtual reality. We have already started down this road: Human and machine have already begun to meld.

It starts with uploading, or scanning the brain into a computer. One scenario is invasive: One very thin slice at a time, scientists input a brain of choice—having been frozen just slightly before it was going to die—at an extremely high speed. This way, they can easily see every neuron, every connection, and every neurotransmitter concentration represented in each synapse-thin layer.

Seven years ago, a condemned killer allowed his brain and body to be scanned in this way, and you can access all 10 billion bytes of him on the Internet. You can see for yourself every bone, muscle, and section of gray matter in his body. But the scan is not yet at a high enough resolution to re-create the interneuronal connections, synapses, and neurotransmitter

concentrations that are the key to capturing the individuality within a human brain.

Our scanning machines today can clearly capture neural features as long as the scanner is very close to the source. Within 30 years, however, we will be able to send billions of nanobots—blood cell–size scanning machines—through every capillary of the brain to create a complete noninvasive scan of every neural feature. A shot full of nanobots will someday allow the most subtle details of our knowledge, skills, and personalities to be copied into a file and stored in a computer.

We can touch and feel this technology today. We just can't make the nanobots small enough, not yet anyway. But miniaturization is another one of those accelerating technology trends. We're currently shrinking the size of technology by a factor of 5.6 per linear dimension per decade, so it is conservative to say that this scenario will be feasible in a few decades. The nanobots will capture the locations, interconnections, and contents of all the nerve cell bodies, axons, dendrites, presynaptic vesicles, neurotransmitter concentrations, and other relevant neural components. Using high-speed wireless communication, the nanobots will then communicate with each other and with other computers that are compiling the brain-scan database.

If this seems daunting, another scanning project, that of the human genome, was also considered ambitious when it was first introduced 12 years ago. At the time, skeptics said the task would take thousands of years, given current scanning capabilities. But the project is finishing on time nevertheless because the speed with which we can sequence DNA has grown exponentially.

Brain scanning is a prerequisite to Winston and Nellie's virtual life—and apparent immortality.

In 2029, we will swallow or inject billions of nanobots into our veins to enter a three-dimensional cyberspace—a virtual reality environment. Already, neural implants are used to counteract tremors from Parkinson's disease as well as multiple sclerosis. I have a deaf friend who can now hear what I'm saying because of his cochlear implant. Under development is a retinal implant that will perform a similar function for blind people, basically replacing certain visual processing circuits of the brain. Recently, scientists from Emory University placed a chip in the brain of a paralyzed stroke victim, who can now begin to communicate and control his environment directly from his brain.

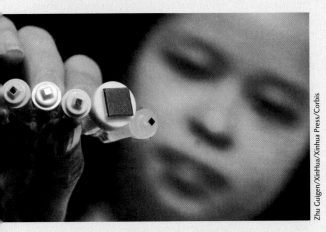

Drug delivery tools made with nano-technology.

But while a surgically introduced neural implant can be placed in only one or at most a few locations, nanobots can take up billions or trillions of positions throughout the brain. We already have electronic devices called neuron transistors that, noninvasively, allow communication between electronics and biological neurons. Using this technology, developed at Germany's Max Planck Institute of Biochemistry, scientists were recently able to control from their computer the movements of a living leech.

By taking up positions next to specific neurons, the nanobots will be able to detect and control their activity. For virtual reality applications, the nanobots will take up positions next to every nerve fiber coming from all five of our senses. When we want to enter a specific virtual environment, the nanobots will suppress the signals coming from our real senses and replace them with new, virtual ones. We can then cause our virtual body to move, speak, and otherwise interact in the virtual environment. The nanobots would prevent our real bodies from moving; instead, we would have a virtual body in a virtual environment, which need not be the same as our real body.

Like the experiences Winston and Nellie enjoyed, this technology will enable us to have virtual interactions with other people—or simulated people—without requiring any equipment not already in our heads. And virtual reality will not be as crude as what you experience in today's arcade games. It will be as detailed and subtle as real life. So instead of just phoning a friend, you can meet in a virtual Italian bistro or stroll down a virtual tropical beach, and it will all seem real. People will be able to share any type of experience—business, social, romantic, or sexual—regardless of physical proximity.

The trip to virtual reality will be readily reversible since, with your thoughts alone, you will be able to shut the nanobots off, or even direct them to leave your body. Nanobots are programmable, in that they can provide virtual reality one minute and a variety of brain extensions the next. They can change their configuration, and even alter their software.

While the combination of human-level intelligence in a machine and a computer's inherent superiority in the speed, accuracy, and sharing ability of its memory will be formidable—this is not an alien invasion. It is emerging from within our human-machine civilization.

But will virtual life and its promise of immortality obviate the fear of death? Once we upload our knowledge, memories, and insights into a computer, will we have acquired eternal life? First we must determine what human life is. What is consciousness anyway? If my thoughts, knowledge, experience, skills, and memories achieve eternal life without me, what does that mean for me?

Consciousness—a seemingly basic tenet of "living"—is perplexing and reflects issues that have been debated since the Platonic dialogues. We assume, for instance, that other humans are conscious, but when we consider the possibility that nonhuman animals may be conscious, our understanding of consciousness is called into question.

The issue of consciousness will become even more contentious in the 21st century because non-biological entities—read: machines—will be able to convince most of us that they are conscious. They will master all the subtle cues that we now use to determine that humans are conscious. And they will get mad if we refute their claims.

Consider this: If we scan me, for example, and record the exact state, level, and position of my every neurotransmitter, synapse, neural connection, and other relevant details, and then reinstantiate this massive database into a neural computer, then who is the real me? If you ask the machine, it will vehemently claim to be the original Ray. Since it will have all of my memories, it will say, "I grew up in Queens, New York, went to college at MIT, stayed in the Boston area, sold a few artificial intelligence companies, walked into a scanner there, and woke up in the machine here. Hey, this technology really works."

But there are strong arguments that this is really a different person. For one thing, old biological Ray (that's me) still exists. I'll still be here in my carbon, cell-based brain. Alas, I (the old biological Ray) will have to sit back and watch the new Ray succeed in endeavors that I could only dream of. But New Ray will have some strong claims as well. He will say that while he is not absolutely identical to Old Ray, neither is the current version of Old Ray, since the particles making up my biological brain and body are constantly changing. It is the patterns of matter and energy that are semipermanent (that is, changing only gradually), while the actual material content changes constantly and very quickly.

Viewed in this way, my identity is rather like the pattern that water makes when rushing around a rock in a stream. The pattern remains relatively unchanged for hours, even years, while the actual material constituting the pattern—the water—is replaced in milliseconds.

This idea is consistent with the philosophical notion that we should not associate our fundamental identity with a set of particles, but rather with the pattern of matter and energy that we represent. In other words, if we change our definition of consciousness to value patterns over particles, then New Ray may have an equal claim to be the continuation of Old Ray.

One could scan my brain and reinstantiate the new Ray while I was sleeping, and I would not necessarily even know about it. If you then came to me, and said, "Good news, Ray, we've successfully reinstantiated your mind file so we won't be needing your old body and brain anymore," I may quickly realize the philosophical flaw in the argument that New Ray is a continuation of my consciousness. I may wish New Ray well, and realize that he shares my pattern, but I would nonetheless conclude that he is not me, because I'm still here.

Wherever you wind up on this debate, it is worth noting that data do not necessarily last forever. The longevity of information depends on its relevance, utility, and accessibility. If you've ever tried to retrieve information from an obsolete form of data storage in an old obscure format (e.g., a reel of magnetic tape from a 1970s minicomputer), you understand the challenge of keeping software viable. But if we are diligent in maintaining our mind file, keeping current backups and porting to the latest formats and mediums, then at least a crucial aspect of who we are will attain a longevity independent of our bodies.

What does this super technological intelligence mean for the future? There will certainly be grave dangers associated with 21st-century technologies. Consider unrestrained nanobot replication. The technology requires billions or trillions of nanobots in order to be useful, and the most cost-effective way to reach such levels is through self-replication, essentially the same approach used in the biological world, by bacteria, for example. So in the same way that biological self-replication gone awry (i.e., cancer) results in biological destruction, a defect in the mechanism curtailing nanobot self-replication would endanger all physical entities, biological or otherwise.

Other salient questions are: Who is controlling the nanobots? Who else might the nanobots be talking to?

Organizations, including governments, extremist groups, or even a clever individual, could put trillions of undetectable nanobots in the water or food supply of an entire population. These "spy" nanobots could then monitor, influence, and even control our thoughts and actions. In addition, authorized nanobots could be influenced by software viruses and other hacking techniques. Just as technology poses dangers today, there will be a panoply of risks in the decades ahead.

On a personal level, I am an optimist, and I expect that the creative and constructive applications of this technology will persevere, as I believe they do today. But there will be a valuable and increasingly vocal role for a concerned movement of Luddites—those anti-technologists inspired by early 19th-century weavers who in protest destroyed machinery that was threatening their livelihood.

Still, I regard the freeing of the human mind from its severe physical limitations as a necessary next step in evolution. Evolution, in my view, is the purpose of life, meaning that the purpose of life—and of our lives—is to evolve.

What does it mean to evolve? Evolution moves toward greater complexity, elegance, intelligence, beauty, creativity, and love. And God has been called all these things, only without any limitation, infinite. While evolution never reaches an infinite level, it advances exponentially, certainly moving in that direction. Technological evolution, therefore, moves us inexorably closer to becoming like God. And the freeing of our thinking from the severe limitations of our biological form may be regarded as an essential spiritual quest.

By the close of the next century, nonbiological intelligence will be ubiquitous. There will be few humans without some form of artificial intelligence, which is growing at a double exponential rate, whereas biological intelligence is basically at a standstill. Nonbiological thinking will be trillions of trillions of times more powerful than that of its biological progenitors, although it will be still of human origin.

Ultimately, however, the Earth's technology-creating species will merge with its own computational technology. After all, what is the difference between a human brain enhanced a trillion-fold by nanobot-based implants, and a computer whose design is based on high-resolution scans of the human brain, and then extended a trillion-fold?

This may be the ominous, existential question that our own children, certainly our grandchildren, will face. But at this point, there's no turning back. And there's no slowing down.

Analyzing Argument

1. What assumptions are important to Kurzweil's argument? That is, what must the reader assume in order to accept his version of the future?

2. How does Kurzweil attempt to bring the reader from the present to the future? Describe how specific passages serve in his line of reasoning.

3. What is Kurzweil's main claim?

4. Explain how the opening scenario figures into Kurzweil's argument.

5. How does Kurzweil engage the opposition? How does he address potential doubters?

6. Why might the reader have trouble accepting this view of the future? What changes might help the reader accept the view?

The End of the Handshake

JOEL COLLINS

Good writers examine the habits and reflexes of everyday life. They imagine quiet trends and subtle changes. In the following essay, Joel Collins considers a widely used social convention—and he points to the signs of its demise. Collins wrote the essay for his second-semester English composition course.

The handshake is everywhere. Hands connect after football games, when a guest comes out on a talk show, and when the president meets with diplomats. The gesture occurs on a private scale when a teenage boy meets his girlfriend's father, when a woman greets a potential boss at a job interview, or when a principal congratulates a student for good marks. Over many years, the handshake has become a symbol of courtesy and the go-to move for anyone trying to make a good impression. It is as common as any other greeting, but despite its popularity, the handshake is about to be no more. As people become more germophobic and technologically advanced, the handshake will disappear from our customs.

The origins of the handshake are still uncertain, but there is no denying that the gesture has been around for a long time. Some speculate that handshakes actually originated with chimpanzees as a way for them to calm each other (Bering). Others say that humans started the handshake as a "demonstration of helplessness" upon meeting a superior (Bering). Despite its beginnings, it stuck, and it has become a staple of any meeting between two individuals. However, over the years, the handshake has undergone plenty of change. People have tried for years to come up with unique ways to greet one another. Simple waves, hugs, head nods, and the relatively new fist bump have all arisen as popular greetings in America. As a society, we have always wanted the newest and the best, whether in transportation, media, medicine, or anything else.

If there is something new we can have or do, we do our best to get it. Our value in all things new will not skip over ways of greeting one another. Granted, we also place great importance on tradition and familiarity, but those values can blend with our drive to change. The tradition of people greeting one another will remain, but the handshake, in its traditional form, will fade. Be it the fist bump or some new greeting that has not yet come about, something less involved, less intimate will make it irrelevant.

In addition to the importance we put on finding newer and better things, modernized countries value reaching out, bridging distances. With the invention of ships and airplanes and the internet, we have connected all corners of the world. A person in New York can do business with a Japanese firm which had gotten some of its materials from France. People of different cultures are increasingly interacting with one another. With those interactions comes a blending of cultures. The American may want to greet her Japanese partner with a handshake while the Japanese woman will be more likely to bow. If the French man comes to the meeting, he will be used to greeting people with a kiss on the cheek. As globalization continues to unite different regions of the world, cultures will continue to meet and, in some instances, clash. For example, Michelle Obama recently went to Indonesia, and on her trip she shook hands with an Indonesian official. It turns out that in their society, men are not supposed to have physical contact with women that are not a member of their family, so that man came under intense criticism ("Minister Admits"). Although American culture has a vast impact on the rest of the world, we are not influential enough to change long-established religious customs wherever we want to. The Muslim faith is deeply rooted in the Middle East and Southeast Asia, places where we have great economic interest, and we won't be able to change their customs. Muslim culture has been able resist American influence thus far, as shown by artifacts such as hijabs, which women must wear to cover their hair (Amirahmadi).

And it's not simply a matter of custom. With every handshake comes an opportunity for bacteria to move from one host to another. Each person carries nearly 5,000 different species of bacteria and countless amounts of each species just on the palms of their hands, and they are all looking to spread to new areas ("The Irresistible Rise"). With new diseases that threaten to reach pandemic levels seemingly every year, people are starting to take strides to clean up and get healthier. We have been scared by swine flu, bird flu, SARS, the West Nile Virus, MRSA, mad cow disease, and an array of other diseases, many of which are not even able to spread from person to person. These diseases did provide a real threat, but their seriousness was exaggerated by mass hysteria and media hype. The news claimed that it might not be safe to go to work, the airport, or the shopping center because disease was sure to strike. Americans increased their fixation on hygiene.

In recent years, a whole new industry has popped up with hand sanitizers being available everywhere. There are cleaners at grocery stores to swab down shopping carts, hand sanitizer pumps at the entrances to restaurants, and even mini tubes of hand cleaner that millions of people carry around in their purses or pockets. Clean hands have come to the forefront of American values. Given this new health kick, it makes perfect sense that handshake will be on its way out in coming years. People do not want extended contact with others, especially with strangers. (Who knows where those hands have been, if that person has been sick, and how many harmful bacteria that person is carrying on the palms?)

Some may argue that the handshake will stick around because of our need for physical contact—the basic emotional need to engage in with others. Certainly, people need the touch of others for emotional comfort and strength; however, that does not include handshakes. Hugging or holding hands with a loved one is vital to human life, but shaking the hand of a stranger or even a friendly acquaintance does not fill the same need. There is very little true emotion behind most handshakes; they are a social convention, not a sign of deep care or intimacy. The drive to avoid contaminants will trump the convention.

Since we no longer live in a time when it is common for people to carry firearms when they travel, the handshake is no longer necessary as a safety precaution. It lingers still because it is now considered a polite greeting, something that people do to gain respect, trust, and compassion from others. However, we live in a world fixed upon what is quick, easy, and necessary. Fast food, texting, and YouTube have replaced sit down dinners, long conversations, and to some extent, movie going. We like to get straight to the point now and cut through the fluff, so what is keeping handshakes alive now? They waste time before the meaty part of a meeting. Since we care less and less about niceties and because efficiency weighs heavier than courtesy, the handshake is on the verge of nonexistence.

In the future, technology will continue to make communication between people even easier. With Skype and other instant video tools, people currently meet across long distances. Technology is even in the works to have 3-D replicas of people beamed to wherever they are needed. Japan, if awarded the right to host the 2022 World Cup, has promised 3-D hologram broadcasts of every game that can be displayed on soccer fields in stadiums throughout the world as if the games were actually taking place in those stadiums (Neild). In time, that same technology will be able to put business people in any meeting room desired without leaving the comfort of their own offices. In this hologram and digitized world, the handshake will become irrelevant.

Almost all aspects of the world we live in are changing, including the ways humans greet each other. As the world advances and becomes more focused on health, convenience, and technology, the handshake will lose its place as a customary greeting and will no longer be used at all.

Works Cited

Amirahmadi, Hooshang. "Islam in the Contemporary West." *American Iranian Council—A Platform for Dialogue.* American Iranian Council, 12 Dec. 2006. Web. 2 Dec. 2010. http://american-iranian.org/publications/articles/2006/12/islam_in_the_contemporary_west.html.

Bering, Jesse. "Bering in Mind: Limp Wrists and Tight Fists: What Your Handshake Says about You." *Scientific American.* Scientific American, 18 Feb. 2010. Web. 2 Dec. 2010. http://www.scientificamerican.com/blog/post.cfm?id=limp-wrists-and-tight-fists-what-yo-2010-02-18.

"Minister Admits Reluctant Michelle Obama Handshake." *Yahoo! News.* Associated Press, 9 Nov. 2010. Web. 2 Dec. 2010. http://news.yahoo.com/s/ap/20101109/ap_on_re_as/as_indonesia_michelle_s_handshake.

Neild, Barry. "Can Japan Deliver a Holographic World Cup?" *CNN Tech.* CNN, 30 Nov. 2010. Web. 2 Dec. 2010.

"The irresistible rise of the hand bacteria." *New Scientist* 199.2681 (2008): 17. *Academic SearchElite.* Web. 2 Dec. 2010.

Analyzing Argument

1. Collins points to specific signs (specific indicators) of the handshake's demise. Which seem the most telling? Which situations or trends seem most indicative of the future he envisions?

2. How does Collins use his understanding of basic human needs or reflexes in his argument?

3. An argument about the future relies on a line of reasoning that begins in the past or present. Explain how Collins walks the reader forward through time. How does he, for instance, bring the reader from a current trend to a future condition?

4. How does Collins engage opposing positions or doubt about his vision of the future?

Investing in Futures: The Cost of College

CHARLES NELSON

In this essay, Charles Nelson responds to a college writing assignment to explore the future viability of college. Specifically, he focuses on increasing college tuition costs and their effect on lower-paying vocations. He shows how a present trend will project into the future and how that trend will directly impact career choice. Notice that his line of reasoning relies on some simple calculations.

It is widely known that college has been a good investment for students. It has traditionally offered many advantages, the most obvious being that some degrees pay off financially. For example, according to the National Association of Colleges and Employers' 2002 Salary Survey, starting salaries for some majors exceed $50,000—chemical engineering: $51,254; electrical/electronics and computer engineering: $50,387; computer science: $50,352; mechanical engineering, management information systems/business data processing, accounting, civil engineering, and economics/finance all start above $40,000 (Geary). Students in these majors lay down twenty or forty or eighty thousand dollars, then after several years of schooling land a fine-paying job. The school loan can be paid off in a reasonable time while the graduate earns, and spends, and enjoys a rewarding career.

Explains the financial payoff of a college education.

Degrees pay off in other ways too: College exposes students to new issues and subject areas; it helps students to consider the value of things that might otherwise seem pointless; college graduates may lead more rewarding lives, being more mentally engaged by their surroundings. According to *Preparing Your Child for College* a United States Department of Education resource book for parents, reasons to attend college include greater knowledge, more money, greater potential, and more job opportunities. The Department of Education report explains that "a college education will increase your child's ability to understand developments in science and in society, to think abstractly and critically, to express thoughts clearly in speech and in writing, and to make wise decisions. These skills are useful both on and off the job." The Department of Education report continues: "a college education can help increase your child's understanding of the community, the Nation, and the world—as he or she explores interests, discovers new areas of knowledge, considers lifelong goals, and becomes a responsible citizen."

Explains the nonfinancial rewards of a college education.

But if college costs continue to rise at recent rates, in a few years graduates will have spent two or three hundred thousand dollars for a

Reprinted by permission of Charles Nelson.

Introduces a possible future—one
that is based on the present.

The math works to reinforce
the line of reasoning—and the
projection about the future.

Quotes an authority.

The next step in the line of
reasoning: if college costs
do increase as above, formal
education will become obsolete.

Offers a slight concession—that
the future is impossible to predict
exactly.

college education. Sound crazy? According to data collected in the College Board's Annual Survey of Colleges, 2003–2004, college tuition increased 14.1 percent over the past year at four-year public institutions, 6 percent at private ones, and 13.8 percent at two-year public institutions, and at four-year public institutions, tuition, fees, room, and board averaged $10,636; at private ones, $26,854 *(Tuition Levels Rise)*. If college expenses increase 15 percent a year again and again, an annual tuition of $10,000 becomes $11,500 the next year, $13,225 the year after that, and $15,209 the year after that. The student whose first year costs $10,000 pays a total of $49,934 for all four years. If a bachelor's degree ends up taking that student five, not four, years, make that $67,424.

The math becomes daunting. Simply adding 15 percent each year to a student's tuition and fees raises the future cost of college to a spectacular amount. $15,209 plus 15% equals $17,490. $17,490 plus 15% equals $20,114. $20,114 plus 15% equals $23,131. $23,131 plus 15% equals $26,601. In just eight years, one year of college has increased $16,601—from $10,000 (which doesn't sound like much) to $26,601. The student who begins college at $26,601 a year will end up paying $26,601 + $30,591 + $35,180 + $40,457, equaling $132,829. If it takes that student a fifth year to get a degree, add $46,526 for the extra year, and the cost will be $179,355.

But doesn't college tuition increase at roughly the rate of inflation? Doesn't it all even out? No. College tuition since the 1980s has increased at twice the rate of inflation, with no sign of slowing down. As Scott Ross, the executive director of the Florida Student Association, puts it, the tuition button is stuck in the "up-fast" position (qtd. in Clayton). And while some jobs—chemical engineering, electrical/electronics and computer engineering, and so on—keep pace with college tuition, others can't. So, which majors are we willing to delete?

Unless they can earn back significantly more than they invest, students will be faced with some serious questions: Is learning to think better worth the cost? Can't I expose myself to new issues and subject areas *without college?* What is the value of a $200,000 college degree? Many potential graduates are bound to decide that college, unfortunately, just isn't worth it.

Perhaps educators, politicians, and banks will find ways to keep college costs down, especially for those students who major in the financially less lucrative fields. For example, because a history degree pays less in the marketplace than an engineering degree, a history major might pay less. Of course there's no way to accurately predict a student's future earnings based on his or her major (or based on anything else). A philosophy major could somehow earn millions, while an engineering major may be unable to hold down a steady job. Still, the general concept applies: Students are paying the same tuition for different degrees, and some of those degrees will eventually be boxed out of college because students graduating with the degree won't be able to pay back the loans. Unless something gives, when the cost of a college degree hits two or three hundred thousand dollars, colleges may be void of students studying art, poetry, or (in some states) education. If college tuition continues to increase at its present rate (and there's nothing to suggest it will not), higher education might price itself out of teaching literature, humanities, anthropology, sociology, philosophy . . . all the disciplines that explore what it means to be human. From there, it doesn't take a science fiction writer to imagine the ill effects on our little civilization.

Appeal to value: exploring "what it means to be human" is a worthy practice.

Leaves the reader considering serious consequences.

Works Cited

Clayton, Mark. "Backlash Brews over Rising Cost of College." *Christian Science Monitor.* Christian Science Monitor, 17 June 2003. Web. 26 Aug. 2004.

Geary, Leslie Haggin. "Highest Paying College Degrees." *CNN/Money.* Cable News Network, 5 Apr. 2002. Web. 26 Aug. 2004.

Tuition Levels Rise but Many Students Pay Significantly Less than Published Rates. N.p.: College Board, 21 Oct. 2003. *College Board.* Web. 4 Sept. 2004.

United States. Dept. of Educ. Office of the Under Secretary. Planning and Evaluation Service. *Preparing Your Child for College: A Resource Book for Parents.* 2000. *United States Department of Education.* Web. 27 Aug. 2004.

Analyzing Argument

1. According to Nelson, what is going to happen?

2. What are the most effective support strategies in the essay? Consider specific appeals, examples, and evidence.

3. How does Nelson engage opposition or doubt? How does he counter or concede to outside perspectives?

4. How do Nelson's calculations (in paragraphs 3 and 4) help to develop his line of reasoning?

5. Explain the rhetorical effect of Nelson's last statement—about "the ill effects on our little civilization."

Around the Table in Traverse City

JOEL PAPCUN

Making broad claims about the future can be perilous. A claim about the future of all food, for example, would be almost impossible to support. Because communities, states, entire regions evolve (or devolve) in different ways, more focused claims are safer bets. It's more reasonable to imagine the future of one area than the future of all places. Joel Papcun, a culinary arts instructor at Northwestern Michigan College, makes a focused claim about the future of food in his specific region. He supports his vision of the future with specific local trends.

As folks drive through the Grand Traverse region, it is impossible not to recognize the familiar signs of corporate, upscale-casual, family-friendly restaurants that line the busiest corners. The marketing gurus of these corporate giants have long known the formula for successfully luring the tourist and, to some extent, the local patron into their well-placed eateries. Red Lobster, Applebee's, Outback Steakhouse and Hooters to mention a few, the names read like a "who's who" list of fun, entertaining venues that offer everything from soup to nuts. Everything except nutritionally sound food, that is.

Inside these colorful, media-energized dining rooms, patrons' senses are aroused by chemically enhanced aromas emanating from the modern kitchen that lay hidden behind traditional swinging doors. Almost all these restaurants provide local appeal by including locally themed menus highlighted with regionally noteworthy products (which are not necessarily obtained from regional farms). For the educated local diner, the enchantment often wears off after a visit or two, as the flavors seem to blend into a salty, sugary, fatty combination of highly processed foodstuffs.

Almost any region in the country can be found to support a similar cultural attitude. The big brand name restaurants provide a familiar facade to the droves of tourists looking to sate the need of food during their journey. The Grand Traverse region, although still affected by the corporate eating culture of the nation, is different. While we are home to a range of big brand restaurants, a strong cultural drive for "all-things local" resides and thrives here. Local farmers' markets abound during the growing and harvest seasons. Indoor markets pop-up as the winter season bears down on the region. The Grand Traverse area is also home to several newer companies that work to provide a connection between local farmers and the region's stores, restaurants and food processors. The finer restaurants seek out local products before looking to the commercial variety that is easily had through mega-suppliers. Local companies such as "American Spoon" and "Food For Thought" minimally process and can regional food products for year-round consumption.

We have a diverse population, if not by ethnicity, by age group and income. Having been named the third best city of the nation in which to retire ("25 Best"), Traverse City continues to lure baby boomers looking to relocate or build a second home in the area. These boomers, many of whom makeup the demographic of well-educated, healthy, culturally aware folks, take the meaning of fitness to heart. Seeking quality of life that is inclusive of the area's offerings, food, nutrition, and dining play a considerable part in their quest for vitality. Twenty- and thirty-somethings, of which there is a growing number, make up the demographic that is ever-increasingly aware of environmental concerns and their effects on everyday life.

Although the State of Michigan as a whole is experiencing financial troubles and a population exodus as never seen before, the Grand Traverse region continues to grow both in population and industry base. The area's open spaces, wildlife, and opportunity for healthy activity continue to create a quality of life environment that is sought after. Tourists in search of an "active" vacation may seek out one of the area's many wineries, equestrian ranches, or community supported agriculture (CSA) farms. Increasingly popular, agritourism accounts for a growing segment of the area's revenue. In ten short years, the number of CSA farms has more than quadrupled, growing from nearly 400 to more than 1,800 nationally (Gogoi 3). Farmland preservation, benefiting directly from the agricultural interest created by this segment of the tourism industry, resonates with the stewardship-minded. Consequently, the client base for quality food will expand to the far reaches of the region as the area continues to cultivate agritourism and the dollars that come along with it.

Desiring to produce the best quality food possible, several area chefs have led the way to a "locavore" mentality that is spreading through the region. Seeking all things locally produced, raised and grown, these chefs are creating a "foodie Mecca." Local wineries, breweries and distilleries all add to the expanding food culture of the region. Recently asked to cook at the prestigious Beard House in New York City, local chef Myles Anton of Trattoria Stella is a dominant force in the Grand Traverse "locavore" movement. His reliance on regional products to reproduce the ethnically themed menu at Stella's is proof that the area supports a variety of crops and products worthy of national attention.

In addition to the local restaurant and hospitality offerings, the region is home to a state-of-the-art culinary school that draws would-be chefs from around the multi-state region. Placing an emphasis on local, seasonal, and sustainable foods, the Great Lakes Culinary Institute is a valuable and lasting force on the food culture of the area. Many culinary students explore the region's offerings; often deciding to stay in the area after their training has been completed, thus extending the local, sustainable mindset of the area. The local community college is also the Midwest home of the annual Bioneers Conference. This national conference focuses on sustaining the earth's resources through natural

bioengineering, organic farming, and sustainable growing and living practices. A co-sponsor of the Bioneers Conference, the Oryana Natural Foods Cooperative located in Traverse City is a conduit for the sustainable food and living culture found here. This locally owned co-op has undergone considerable growth in the last decade.

Local projects continue to play a part in the natural food culture as well. "Taste the Local Difference" and the "Fresh Food Initiative" are two such projects. Bolstering "real food" awareness and providing education to those who are not versed in scratch cooking, or who are part of the non-cooking portion of society, these organizations provide the basic lessons that may transcend the marketing onslaught of the commercial food conglomerates and bring the cooking of whole foods back into the limelight.

Eating local, sustainable foods can, at times, be more expensive than the mass-produced varieties found in large discount grocery stores. While this factor may deter some lower-income families from the nutritional benefits of a potato less traveled, it will not thwart folks determined to find healthy alternatives through a "local" diet. Assistant professor of Health and Wellness at the University of North Carolina at Ashville, Amy Lanou claims, "[local] meat producers . . . can't keep up with demand even though their product costs $1 more per pound than meat in the supermarket" (qtd. in Taylor).

The drive for local food is aided, at least in part, by the desire to maintain the look and feel of the area. Here in Northern Michigan, farmland and open space are important to the overall feel of the region. The sustainability of the soil and ground water is also important to the local communities. Michigan is surrounded by the world's largest fresh water supply. Seemingly pristine, the Great Lakes are still recovering from over a century of ecological abuse that a fledgling, industrialized nation threw at them. Preservation of the Great Lakes is part of being better stewards of the natural resources to which we have been entrusted. To that end, Traverse

City is home to the Water Studies Institute. Situated at the south end of West Grand Traverse Bay, the institute is the first to offer an Associate in Science and Arts Degree for Freshwater Studies in the United States. Continued regional efforts to maintain quality fresh water resources will benefit the area and the nation for years to come.

Another spoke in the wheel of the "real food" bandwagon is the recent enactment of a law allowing the raising of chickens for food or eggs within the Traverse City limits. The ability, or more importantly, the *right* to provide a nutritionally sound, sustainably raised, and economical alternative to mass-produced foodstuffs was confirmed in a majority vote of the local city commission. Due in part to the community voice being heard, this change reinforces the local mentality of self-reliance often found in thriving areas around the country.

The local projects and environmental interest currently seen will continue to prod the communities of the greater Grand Traverse region toward sustainable, natural foods that are grown without the carbon footprint of the resource-gulping factory farms used to produce the worlds Frankenfood supply. The desire to enjoy food, as it was intended, flavorful and full of rich nutrients, will continue to influence the local restaurant menu. In fact, if trends are an indicator, the majority of restaurants will succumb to the demands of an educated, foodies-dominated patronage and provide mostly local, mostly natural and sustainable menu items.

A generation from now, there will surely be those who disregard the social call for personal responsibility, for healthy choices and natural diets full of real, whole, foods. The non-foodie or uninformed consumer, a diminishing demographic of society in the Grand Traverse region, will still make poor choices in food selection, whether in a grocery store or a restaurant. Continued growth of the locavore movement will likely limit the opportunity for such poor choices. Local, sustainable, and natural foods have so much to offer, the extraordinary will become the norm in the next few decades.

Works Cited

Connell, David J. "On the Challenge of Creating Sustainable Food Systems." *Environments Journal* 36.1 (2008): 75–77. *Academic OneFile*. Web. 15 Dec. 2009.

Gogoi, Pallavi. "The Rise of the 'Locavore.'" *BusinessWeek*. Bloomburg, 20 May 2008. Web. 15 Dec. 2009.

Taylor, David A. "Does One Size Fit All? Small Farms and U.S. Meat Regulations." *Environmental Health Perspectives* 116.12 (2008): A528+. *Academic OneFile*. Web. 15 Dec. 2009.

"25 Best Places to Retire." *CNNMoney.com*. Cable News Network. A Time Warner Co, 24 Sept. 2009. Web. 28 Nov. 2009. http://money.cnn.com/galleries/2009/moneymag/0909/gallery.bpretire_top25.moneymag/index.html.

Analyzing Argument

1. Papcun points to several demographic trends that will lead to increased locavore culture. In your own words, explain how those demographic trends allow for Papcun's vision of the future.

2. All arguments about the future rely on some assumptions about continued collective behavior. Explain how Papcun's argument relies on specific assumptions. Are his assumptions acceptable? Why or why not?

3. How does Papcun engage opposition? Where does he counter, concede, or qualify?

4. What is the most effective supporting passage? What kind of support is Papcun using? A type of appeal? Evidence? Example? Perhaps a combination?

5. Arguments for this chapter assert and defend claims of fact. For the most part, they veer away from value judgments. However, some hint of value does inevitably slip into the arguments. Where do you find value operating in Papcun's argument? Does it help or hurt his case?

A smart car parked beside a Hummer.

1. What does the juxtaposition of the Humvee and the smart car suggest about the past, present, and future?

2. The future does not simply arrive. Technologies, customs, conventions, and habits have to be changed. How does the smart car represent the tension that is always at work in projections about the future?

Exploring for Topics

Robert G. Ingersoll, American politician, abolitionist, and lecturer, said, "The present is the necessary product of all the past, the necessary cause of all the future." Ingersoll prompts us to see a deep connection among the past, present, and future. Whenever people argue about the future, they must keep the past and present in mind—because the future does not emerge from thin air but from real material conditions and real human attitudes. Writers who take on the future must also take on the biases, prejudices, fears, values, beliefs, and assumptions of their present readers.

This chapter is about inventing a particular view of the future. Your readers must believe that a present situation is leading toward a particular future. They must be able to see how the present will evolve, devolve, or in some sense, stay the same. Ultimately, the argument you generate will invite readers to participate in an imagined world—one that does not yet exist.

It would be impossible (or at least unhelpful) to make an argument about "the future" in its entirety. To generate a reasonable argument, we must focus on a particular topic that is set in the future. As in all argumentative situations, the more focused and narrow the topic, the more intensive and engaging the writing process. Use the following prompts to explore for possible topics and begin developing your own argument:

- What particular change in the future will impact your life or your readers' lives?
- What changes do you see as inevitable? Will gay marriage be legal across the United States? Will all employers provide health care for significant others, regardless of gender or marital status? Will only the wealthiest citizens be serious candidates for president? Will women hold fifty percent of Congressional and Senate seats?
- Imagine possibilities and fill in the blanks in the following statement: Most people assume that _____ will continue as is; however, _____.

- Watch a futuristic or science fiction movie, such as *Fahrenheit 451*, *Gattaca*, *Idiocracy*, or *The Matrix*. According to the movie, what will the future hold for _____? (Consider particular topics such as the state of technology, the role of law enforcement, the relationships between men and women, the character of government, the relationship between nations.)
- Consider your academic major. How long will it survive as an academic focus? How will economic, demographic, or environmental trends impact it? How will technology impact its future?

- What topic interests you? Imagine how it will look in the future. Consider specifics: a musical genre, college athletics, a political party, the gender ratio in a particular career, megastores, a health care policy, cell phones, online gaming, traditional marriage, profanity, body piercing, religious divisions, comedy films, romance novels, CO_2 emissions, college grades, and so on.
- Closely examine a reading from this chapter. How might the future be different from what is portrayed in the reading? What else can you imagine about the future of that particular topic?
- With a group of peers, think of several futuristic or science fiction movies. Choose one movie that everyone has seen. List the topics that the movie suggests through characters, action, plot, and setting. Then discuss what argument the movie makes.

Activity

1. With a group of peers, continue adding ideas to your lists of topics. Continue until each group member has accumulated several possible topics of interest.

2. As a group, discuss one of the topic ideas from above. Imagine how it might be different in the future. Consider social customs, emotional responses, and even legal issues. How might they all impact the topic?

To understand how something might fare in the future, we must first understand how it functions in the present and what factors (internal and external) are likely to influence it. We must also qualify the vague phrase *the future*. It might mean tomorrow or thousands of years from now. The meaning depends upon the topic and the nature of the argument. For some topics, such as the preservation of species or space travel, *the future* means hundreds, even thousands, of years. For other topics, such as access to higher education, *the future* might mean five, ten, or twenty years.

Decide how far into the future you want to look, and then apply the following invention questions to your topic:

▶ What factors presently influence the topic?

▶ How has it evolved or developed?

▶ What influential factors are likely to change in the future? What effect will those changes have?

▶ What political, social, cultural, environmental, and global factors will influence the future of this topic?

▶ How will the near future differ from the distant future?

Inventing a Claim

As with all arguments, writers arguing about the future must explore the common (and uncommon) opinions surrounding the topic. For this chapter, exploring opinions may be a tricky process. Rather than finding direct assertions about the future, you may find only hopes mixed with present attitudes and behaviors. You may have to infer what people think or fill in the gaps between people's hopes and beliefs.

You can monitor opinion on your topic by browsing the Internet. Search for your topic and seek out personal, professional, nonprofit, governmental, and educational sites. Scan through the sites and read for opinions or characterizations of the topic. You might also take a more focused and intensive research approach, and examine periodical databases.

Charles Nelson discovered specifics by reading published research on funding in higher education. He sought out trends in funding, average college costs, and average increases. He also tried to find the average student loan debt in the country and researched the economic factors that play into college tuition. He used several periodical database searches with the following keywords:

college and tuition and state and funding

college or university and tuition and state and funding

higher and education and funding and state

student and loans and cost and trends

student and college and loans and debt

student and loan and average and debt

Not all of these searches were fruitful; some simply gave too many results. But others helped Nelson find trends in loans, debt, and college tuition.

Despite your particular research requirements, it is crucial to understand how others imagine the future. As you read through potential sources, use the following questions to distinguish between your vision and others' stated or unstated notions:

What Do Others Claim?

▶ What do people normally think of when they imagine the future of your particular topic? What do they think is going to happen?

▶ What is the time frame that other people work with? That is, *when* do they think something is going to happen? (Next week? Next month? In the next century?)

▶ Why do they believe in that particular version? To accept their version of the future, what do they have to assume, value, or believe?

▶ What do experts in the field believe will happen in the near future? The distant future?

What Do I Claim?

▶ How is my vision of the future different from the common vision or from expert projections?

▶ What assumptions (about the topic, about social change, about people, about institutions) underlie my vision of the future?

▶ What do others not see or consider when they imagine the future of this topic?

Anyone can look forward and imagine the future. But a good argument about the future focuses on some specific condition or situation. We should be cautious of generalized statements that make safe and uncontestable claims. For instance, imagine if Nelson argued the following: *College tuition will be too high for most people in the future.* The claim is safe; it is hardly arguable and contains vague generalities such as "too high" and "most people." Nelson is better off thinking of specific effects of high college costs. Notice how his main idea evolved into increasingly sharper statements:

- College tuition will be too high for most people in the future.
- College tuition will eventually go beyond what the middle class can afford.
- The cost of college education will eventually transcend its earning value.
- In the coming decades, perhaps within the next generation, the cost of college education will transcend its earning value.

Nelson's claim goes beyond broad descriptors (such as "too high") and, instead, offers a particular future condition.

To sharpen your focus, consider the following questions:

▶ What are the possible specific outcomes for this topic?

▶ What is the single most important or significant outcome?

▶ What is not apparent now that will become apparent in the future?

More Sample Claims

Technology

- As the world becomes increasingly technologically complex, more government regulation will be necessary for the protection of all citizens, even those who oppose increased regulation.
- As TV programs like *CSI* suggest, crime fighting in the near future will be characterized not by bullets and badges but by science and forensic technology.

Education

- Because memorization of content lies at the center of American education, standardized testing will likely become the primary mode of teaching and learning.
- If the United States remains a viable democratic nation in this century, its citizens will look back on this era and scoff at the college degree mills now infecting higher education.

Popular Culture

- Based on current trends, the future half-hour sitcom will soon be half commercial and half sitcom. In other words, the *com* will stand for *commercial*.
- In the near future, the American consumer will shift away from the programmed reflex of buying "name brands" and seek out local food that is safer, healthier, and less expensive in the long run.
- There's no stopping it: the antibacterial craze will undoubtedly create a future of rampant and incurable sickness.

Politics

- In the next election cycle, the Tea Party will overtake the Republican Party as the reigning conservative force across the country.
- Before the next national election, the Tea Party will further alienate itself from mainstream views on taxes and gun laws.

- After the Baby Boomers finally relinquish political control, it will take the next generation only a few political cycles to rid the country of the irrational fear of marijuana and legalize its purchase.
- In thirty years, mainstream America will look back with horror and disgust at the homophobic propaganda of today's politicians, just as we now look at the chest-beating and banner-waving racism in 1950s and '60s political campaigns.

Invention Workshop

Your main claim for this argument should answer this question: *Given past or present trends, what is likely to happen in the future?* Notice how Nelson answers it:

> In the coming decades, perhaps within the next generation, the cost of college education will transcend its earning value.

1. Write out your main claim about the future, and share it with several other writers. As a group, examine each claim and make sure that each addresses the key question: *Given past or present trends, what is likely to happen in the future?*

2. Next, try to sharpen the focus of each claim. As a group, suggest how broad words and phrases could be more specific.

Inventing Support

Supporting an argument about the future (something that has not yet happened) can be tricky. It involves establishing logical connections between what has happened, what tends to happen, and what you think will happen. In other words, it depends on logical appeals. But you are not limited to logical appeals. Explore all the following possible strategies.

Allusions Because you cannot point directly at the future to support your points, you will have to depend on past and present trends or events. For example, in "Live Forever," Raymond Kurzweil alludes to the human genome project to support his version of the future. After describing a future in which billions of nanobots enter the bloodstream and scan the brain so that it can be re-created, Kurzweil says,

> If this seems daunting, another scanning project, that of the human genome, was also considered ambitious when it was first introduced twelve years ago. At the time, skeptics said the task would take thousands of years, given current scanning capabilities. But the project is finishing on time nevertheless because the speed with which we can sequence DNA has grown exponentially.

Readers who doubt Kurzweil's claims (about scanning machines the size of blood cells) must think again because of his allusion to the success of the human genome project.

Literary Works Remember that novels, poems, plays, and songs can help give form to your vision of the future. Because literary works deal with some fundamental questions, tensions, and assumptions about our world, they can help to establish what may or may not change in the future. The literary work need not be set in the future. In fact, it may even take place long ago. In his argument, Ray Kurzweil deals with some fundamental assumptions about human identity—assumptions that have been debated for millennia. In alluding to ancient Greek thought, Kurzweil shows the significance of the issue:

> Consciousness—a seemingly basic tenet of "living"—is perplexing and reflects issues that have been debated since the Platonic dialogues. We assume, for instance, that other humans are conscious, but when we consider the possibility that nonhuman animals may be conscious, our understanding of consciousness is called into question.

Facts Although facts about the past and present can be disputed, they are necessary for an argument about the future. *What will be* emerges out of *what is*, so a good argument carefully describes the relevant aspects of the present. Notice how Kurzweil always grounds his projections in the certainty of the present. Consistently, he makes clear that we are "already" on the way to his vision:

> In 2029, we will swallow or inject billions of nanobots into our veins to enter a three-dimensional cyberspace—a virtual environment. Already, neural implants are used to counteract tremors from Parkinson's disease as well as multiple sclerosis. I have a deaf friend who can now hear what I'm saying because of his cochlear implant. Under development is a retinal implant that will perform a similar function for blind people, basically replacing certain visual processing circuts of the brain. Recently, scientists from Emory University placed a chip in the brain of a paralyzed stroke victim, who can now begin to communicate and control his environment directly from his brain.

The established fact that neural implants are already used to treat disease helps the reader accept Kurzweil's vision that we will someday swallow or inject billions of nanobots. The paragraph communicates facts that create a logical line of reasoning:

Present Facts

–Neural implants are already used to counteract tremors.

–A deaf friend has a cochlear implant, and a similar retinal implant is under development.

–A chip has recently been placed in a stroke victim's brain.

Future Condition

–We will someday swallow or inject nanobots.

The facts that Kurzweil provides do not prove him right. Instead, they make his case stronger and more believable. They make it easier for the reader to accept.

Statistics/Authorities Statistics can be compelling because they help paint a picture of reality. But they should always be used as part of a larger argumentative strategy. In Charles Nelson's argument, numbers from the past and present help him to build a case about the future:

> If college expenses increase 15 percent a year again and again, an annual
> tuition of $10,000 becomes $11,500 the next year, $13,225 the year after
> that, and $15,209 the year after that. The student whose first year costs
> $10,000 pays a total of $49,934 for all four years. If a bachelor's degree
> ends up taking that student five, not four, years, make that $67,424.

But the numbers themselves do not mean anything unless we accept his
other points and assumptions about the nature of college, the nature of
mainstream culture, the continuation of middle-class life. These statistics
are a compelling part of Nelson's argument, but they make sense only
because of his broader line of reasoning.

In his essay, Joel Papcun integrates some important statistics to help
establish a current trend. The passage is only one, but an important,
step in his overall line of reasoning:

> Increasingly popular, agritourism accounts for a growing segment of the
> area's revenue. In ten short years, the number of CSA farms has more
> than quadrupled, growing from nearly 400 to more than 1,800 nationally
> (Gogoi 3). Farmland preservation, benefiting directly from the agricul-
> tural interest created by this segment of the tourism industry, resonates
> with the stewardship-minded. Consequently, the client base for quality
> food will expand to the far reaches of the region as the area continues to
> cultivate agritourism and the dollars that come along with it.

Appeals to Logic Like all arguments, those about the future are supported by various forms of evidence. Perhaps most significant here is the
logical appeal, or a line of reasoning that moves readers from the past
and present to the future. For example:

Premise: Because A has happened,

Premise: Because conditions are favorable for A to happen again,

Conclusion: A will probably happen again.

Premise: Because B has been increasing/decreasing,

Premise: Because conditions allow for B to continue increasing/
decreasing,

Conclusion: B will continue to increase/decrease.

In "Investing in Futures: The Cost of College," Charles Nelson's argument
depends upon a line of reasoning. First, he establishes the trend:

> According to data collected in the College Board's Annual Survey of
> Colleges, 2003–2004, college tuition increased 14.1 percent over the past
> year at four-year public institutions, 6 percent at private ones, and 13.8

percent at two-year public institutions, and at four-year public institutions, tuition, fees, room, and board averaged $10,636; at private ones,
$26,854 (*Tuition Levels Rise*).

Then, in the same paragraph, Nelson explains how the trend may
continue.

Although Nelson takes several paragraphs to develop the point, we
can abbreviate his line of reasoning to the following:

Premise: College tuition has increased 15 percent each year.

Premise: This trend is likely to continue.

Conclusion: College tuition will continue to increase 15 percent each
year.

Each step in this line of reasoning requires some support, and each step
comes with its own set of concerns and opposing points. Notice how
Nelson deals with the second premise:

> But doesn't college tuition increase at roughly the rate of inflation?
> Doesn't it all even out? No. College tuition since the 1980s has increased
> at twice the rate of inflation, with no sign of slowing down. As Scott Ross,
> the executive director of the Florida Student Association, puts it, the
> tuition button is stuck in the "up-fast" position (Clayton).

Once he has established the nature of the trend and its future direction,
he argues its likely effect on college programs. Over several paragraphs,
Nelson develops another line of reasoning based on the first:

Premise: College will continue to increase 15 percent each year.

Premise: Most post-college careers will not pay enough to cover the
cost of a college degree.

Conclusion: The degrees associated with those careers will become
too costly for students to consider.

Or, as he explains in his concluding paragraph:

> Unless something gives, when the cost of a college degree hits two or
> three hundred thousand dollars, colleges may be void of students study-
> ing art, poetry, or (in some states) education. If college tuition continues
> to increase at its present rate (and there's nothing to suggest it will not),
> higher education might price itself out of teaching literature, humanities,
> anthropology, sociology, philosophy . . . all the disciplines that explore
> what it means to be human.

Like any writer, Nelson must convince his readers that each premise is acceptable and that each one leads to his conclusion. He cannot simply state each premise: He must use a variety of support strategies to make each premise acceptable. Nelson's argument illustrates the way in which appeals involve, and sometimes depend on, other forms of support. (For more on appeals to logic see Chapter 3.)

As you consider your own argument, use the following questions to develop appeals and evidence:

▶ What line of reasoning do I want my readers to accept? (What premises about the past, present, and future must readers accept?)

▶ What novels, films, television shows, or poems have suggested a future that relates to my argument?

▶ What other behaviors, policies, situations, animals, institutions, laws, and so forth relate, in some surprising way, to my topic?

▶ How do authorities or statistics support or oppose my argument?

▶ What historical trends, human behaviors, or natural/physical laws suggest that my vision of the future is reasonable or possible?

Activity

Construct two premises that lead to each conclusion:

1. Standardized testing services will eventually control curriculum in public schools.

2. Standardized testing services will eventually be driven out of public schools.

3. The record industry will succeed in closing down online music services.

4. Most new music will be consumed through online services.

Arrangement

How Do I Establish a Present Trend? Before zooming into the future, some of the writers in this chapter work to establish a present trend. For example, Charles Nelson begins with a widely accepted notion—that college has traditionally been a good investment. He spends two paragraphs describing the relationship between college cost and its rewards. Then he takes the reader to a future in which a college education costs a staggering amount:

> But if college costs continue to rise at recent rates, in a few years graduates will have spent two or three hundred thousand dollars for a college education. Sound crazy?

In "The End of the Handshake," Joel Collins consistently describes the relevant trend before he makes a claim about the future. Whether he is detailing a trend in technology, business affairs, or hygiene, he first focuses on the present:

> In recent years, a whole new industry has popped up with hand sanitizers being available everywhere. There are cleaners at grocery stores to swab down shopping carts, hand sanitizer pumps at the entrances to restaurants, and even mini tubes of hand cleaner that millions of people carry around in their purses or pockets. Clean hands have come to the forefront of American values. Given this new health kick, it makes perfect sense that handshake will be on its way out in coming years.

In his essay, Joel Papcun devotes several paragraphs to present trends— initiatives, events, and growing organizations that signal a particular kind of future. He uses paragraphs to focus on a community initiative, event, or a growing organization. And, as in the following passage, he makes sure to show how the trend is rooted in the culture—that it's not going away any time soon:

> In addition to the local restaurant and hospitality offerings, the region is home to a state-of-the-art culinary school that draws would-be chefs from around the multi-state region. Placing an emphasis on local, seasonal, and sustainable foods, the Great Lakes Culinary Institute is a valuable and lasting force on the food culture of the area. Many culinary students explore the region's offerings; often deciding to stay in the area after their training has been completed, thus extending the local, sustainable mindset of the area.

How Should I Connect the Past/Present and Future? An argument builds a version of the future from the pieces and parts of the past and/or the present. Notice how Raymond Kurzweil makes claims about the future, and then supports them by referencing the past:

> But while a surgically introduced neural implant can be placed in only one or at most a few locations, nanobots can take up billions or trillions of positions throughout the brain. We already have electronic devices called neuron transistors that, noninvasively, allow communication between electronics and biological neurons. Using this technology, developed at Germany's Max Planck Institute of Biochemistry, scientists were recently able to control from their computer the movements of a living leech.

Charles Nelson uses the particulars of the present to project a version of the future:

> The math becomes daunting. Simply adding 15 percent each year to a student's tuition and fees raises the future cost of college to a spectacular amount. $15,209 plus 15% equals $17,490. $17,490 plus 15% equals $20,114. $20,114 plus 15% equals $23,131. $23,131 plus 15% equals $26,601. In just eight years, one year of college has increased $16,601—from $10,000 (which doesn't sound like much) to $26,601. The student who begins college at $26,601 a year will end up paying $26,601 + $30,591 + $35,180 + $40,457, equaling $132,829. If it takes that student a fifth year to get a degree, add $46,526 for the extra year, and the cost will be $179,355.

Activity

Write two introductions for your argument. One should take the reader from a common meeting space to a new version of the future. The other should immediately take the reader to the new version of the future—without establishing common ground.

Audience and Voice

Whenever writers assert anything about the future, they tap into a long tradition: from astrologers, palm readers, and fortune cookies to prophets, visionaries, and shamans. From the mundane to the exotic, from the informal to the ritualistic, people who ask others to envision a future are working in a rich tradition and a potentially powerful situation. An argument about the future thus can be an opportunity to explore voice. The situation might call for a somber and grave voice warning of coming peril; it might call for a voice projecting wonder or curiosity; it might even call for an informal, comedic voice.

Question/Answer Why ask questions while making an argument? How do questions affect the writer's voice? And can one ask too many questions? Writers ask questions for different reasons. For example, rhetorical questions are more like statements: they assert something and are not meant to be answered. *How many times do I have to tell you to shut the door?* really means *I've told you to shut the door several times. I'm getting tired of telling you. PLEASE, shut the door next time.* At the end of a paragraph discussing the popularity of hand sanitizers, Collins uses a common question to voice the kind of concern people often have about germs:

> People do not want extended contact with others, especially with strangers. (Who knows where those hands have been, if that person has been sick, and how many harmful bacteria that person is carrying on the palms?)

In addition to rhetorical questions, writers sometimes ask questions they don't have answers to. While an arguer should make and support claims, this doesn't mean every question can be answered—that every suggestion can be tightly packaged and necessarily concluded. Sometimes it is fair (and even necessary) to leave the reader with unanswered questions. Notice how Raymond Kurzweil asks and answers a question in first paragraph below, and then asks two additional questions in the second paragraph below. Kurzweil does not answer the last two questions because he doesn't know the answers; one might argue that those questions are unanswerable but important to consider:

> What does this super technological intelligence mean for the future? There will certainly be grave dangers associated with 21st-century technologies. Consider unrestrained nanobot replication. The technology

requires billions or trillions of nanobots in order to be useful, and the most cost-effective way to reach such levels is through self-replication, essentially the same approach used in the biological world, by bacteria, for example. So in the same way that biological self-replication gone awry (i.e., cancer) results in biological destruction, a defect in the mechanism curtailing nanobot self-replication would endanger all physical entities, biological or otherwise.

Other salient questions are: Who is controlling the nanobots? Who else might the nanobots be talking to?

Writers often ask questions and then answer them, as Nelson does:

But doesn't college tuition increase at roughly the rate of inflation? Doesn't it all even out? No. College tuition since the 1980s has increased at twice the rate of inflation, with no sign of slowing down.

Nelson could have forgone the question/answer approach, conveying the same idea with only the assertion: *College tuition since the 1980s has increased at twice the rate of inflation.* While the questions do not provide the reader with more information, they do affect Nelson's voice and audience. The questions slow the pace of his argument, and they act as a common ground where writer and reader can meet up before moving on to an important point.

However, writers must be careful not to ask too many questions. Some essays can be effectively arranged based on a question/answer approach, and a paragraph full of questions can be effective in some cases. But too many questions can create a frustratingly slow read. In some cases, the reader may even feel talked down to.

Credibility While writers may generate intrigue and curiosity, they must also appear credible. The voice coming at the reader needs to sound insightful but not divorced from a reality that the writer and reader both share. Of course, credibility comes from a reasonable argument, one with adequate support and logical claims. But voice is also vital. In fact, no amount of support can help a voice that sounds noncredible.

A credible-sounding voice in an argument about the future invites the reader into a logical perspective and helps establish a reasonable and believable vision. In the following passage, Charles Nelson suggests a negative effect of increasing college costs:

Unless something gives, when the cost of a college degree hits two or three hundred thousand dollars, colleges may be void of students studying art, poetry, or (in some states) education. If college tuition continues to increase at its present rate (and there's nothing to suggest it will not), higher education might price itself out of teaching literature, humanities, anthropology, sociology, philosophy . . . all the disciplines that explore what it means to be human. From there, it doesn't take a science fiction writer to imagine the ill effects on our little civilization. (331)

Nelson is careful not to project outlandish consequences. Rather, he leaves the reader to imagine. He might have gone further:

> If college tuition continues to increase at its present rate (and there's nothing to suggest it will not), higher education might price itself out of teaching literature, humanities, anthropology, sociology, philosophy . . . all the disciplines that explore what it means to be human. From there, our civilization is likely to forget the more reflective pursuits. We will be in danger of losing our already tenuous understanding of human complexity. We will have more difficulty understanding each others' hearts and minds. We may even become less inclined to ask the big questions than we are now.

These musings are interesting, but perilous. Not only are they logically unsound (bordering on slippery slope and non sequitur), but they also create a voice that seems detached and overly insistent. While writers should appear intense and focused, they should also appear clearheaded. Nelson's strategy, in the original passage, adeptly gets readers to more grounded and insightful points.

"No amount of support can help a voice that sounds noncredible."

Revision

Intensity is the result of intensive invention. Assuming you have explored your ideas thoroughly, now you can revise to make your argument more forceful and engaging.

1. In the introduction, delete any sentences that do not provide new and important information.

2. Sharpen the opening sentence by eliminating unnecessary words or expressions.

3. Now go through the other sentences in the essay, doing the same as above. What can be deleted? Consider entire paragraphs, sentences, phrases, and words. Avoid cutting out ideas and specific examples; rather, focus on shaving off vague statements, clichés, expletives (*there are, it is*), wordy phrases, and unnecessary attention to yourself as a writer (*I think that . . . , It is my belief that . . .*).

Peer Review

Exchange drafts with at least one other writer. (If time allows, exchange with two or three writers to gather a range of perspectives or comments.) Use the following questions to generate specific constructive comments about others' drafts:

1. Does the argument answer this question: Given past or present trends, what is likely to happen in the future?

2. What are the most effective support strategies in the essay? What additional support strategies could help to persuade the reader? (What allusions, examples, or scenarios might help create the connection between a present trend and a future reality?)

3. What assumptions might the audience reject? How can questionable assumptions be supported?

4. How does a connection between the past/present and the future help the reader to accept the argument? What other connections between past/present and the future might help a reader to accept the argument?

5. Why might the reader have trouble accepting this view of the future? What changes might help the reader accept the view?

6. When writers conjure visions of the future, they may fall into the slippery slope fallacy—arguing that all will be lost if we continue down

a particular path. If writers claim that a catastrophic end will come, for instance, they must provide logical steps to that end. (Readers cannot be expected to accept an extreme picture of the future without the logical steps to get there.) Has the writer provided those necessary logical steps? Has the writer avoided the slippery slope fallacy?

7. If the writer used outside sources, do they seem reliable, relevant, credible, timely, and diverse? Do you have any reason to question the sources? If so, how might the writer address your doubts?

8. Are the ideas from the outside sources integrated smoothly into the ideas?

9. Are the sources documented appropriately (with in-text and end citations)?

Revising in the Future

Perhaps the real value of revising your essay is applying what you have learned through revision to future writing projects. Consider the following questions about revision, and discuss your responses with others:

- What is the most notable improvement in your essay as a result of revision?
- What was most difficult about revising your essay, and how might you cope with this difficulty in the future?
- How, specifically, did revision help to intensify your argument?

Research can be seen as an
intensely interactive process
in which the researcher
is engaging with a huge
number of other lives.

Part Three
RESEARCH

The Research Guide

Overview of Research

The Research Path

When we take a trip, we may follow busy highways that a million others have taken. We may stop at the same places along the way and see the same sights as countless others. We may pay the same tolls, eat the same types of food, travel at the same pace, and make the same turns as those around us. And sometimes, we diverge from the main highways, take smaller roads, and drive through small towns. But even if we travel along with others, our journey will be unique. Ultimately, all travelers end up diverging from others—taking an exit where others stay on the highway, taking a left while others take a right, pulling into a side street while others stay on the main road.

Likewise, a researcher often begins with questions that have been asked countless times before. He or she goes to sources that many others have sought out, and may even take away the same key ideas from those sources. However, as a researcher moves from source to source and generates ideas from each, his or her path starts to become unique. The more the researcher actively reads and generates ideas, the more those ideas start to take on particular nuances. And as the path becomes unique, the insights it generates do as well.

Research is a path filled with twists, turns, and surprises. Like any journey, a particular research path can start in one place, move through several stages, and take the researcher to totally new ground. No matter where it leads, a research path should be seen as a continuous intellectual journey.

Inventive Research

If researching is like traveling, then inventive researchers are like adventurous travelers. They take back roads; they visit small towns. They may depend on interstates at times, but they also explore two-lane country roads and city neighborhoods. And in those small towns and city side streets, they are bound to see life beyond the repetitive march of fast-food joints and green highway signs.

Rather than reading only the most accessible source (say, the first listed on a database), inventive researchers also read others that may seem irrelevant at first. Rather than seeking only those sources in line with their initial thinking, inventive researchers explore articles that seem opposed to their original positions. They go after essays with strange titles; they crack open dusty books and review obscure websites. Inventive researchers take a particular posture as they encounter sources. They do more than simply read or listen. They also:

- **Look beneath the meaning of each keyword or phrase.** Inventive researchers see key terms and phrases as opportunities for more exploration. They assume that a word or phrase might generate new ideas. For instance, imagine that a writer is researching labor strikes. Rather than seeking out information only on *strikes,* she thinks about *labor.* She explores the word itself and discovers that philosophers and economists have defined the word according to different views of economy. Suddenly, her way of thinking about labor strikes connects with broader economic theories.
- **Go back in history to find the origin of words, attitudes, and beliefs related to the topic.** For example, imagine a writer is exploring sources for an essay on minstrel shows of the nineteenth century. While he initially believes that they were racist and demeaning to African Americans, he also wants to explore how audiences received them. He looks up "minstrel," which leads him to "blackface" performances. He discovers that the shows climaxed in popularity after the Civil War. He then continues by examining attitudes toward African Americans in the postwar years.
- **Look for principles and precedents.** Every topic connects to general principles (standard rules that tend to govern behavior) or precedents (previous cases). So, beyond their particular focus, inventive researchers imagine how their topics resonate with some broader set of rules or earlier cases.
- **Imagine analogies.** Making comparisons while reading and researching helps writers to see new layers of a topic. A well-crafted comparison may lay the foundation for an argument and create an

interesting direction for research. Imagine an argument about the U.S. military action in Afghanistan. A writer may see a connection between it and the Vietnam War. This comparison may become a springboard to further research. For instance, the writer might explore the difference between troop numbers in Afghanistan and Vietnam.

For more on hidden arguments and assumptions, see Chapter 5: Hidden Layers.

- **Read for underlying values.** All arguments reflect values or assumptions that lie beneath the surface. This layer of an argument can be as important as, if not more important than, the surface statements. The inventive researcher seeks out this layer and asks important questions for further research: What are the arguer's assumptions? How does the presentation of information impact the meaning? What is the reader prompted to value? What fundamental values (related to duty, country, progress, community, family) does the text project? What people or groups share these values? The answers to such questions might prompt the researcher to explore further, to look beyond the main topic and to investigate the value or belief systems beneath it.

Seeking Research

Not all research is exploratory. Researchers sometimes need to find particular information, such as data, a specific historical account, or examples to support a claim. They need to find a direct path to particular information, to go from point A to point B. They are tracking down something they assume has been formulated by someone else, and they want to find the best route to that information. They should first evaluate their needs by asking some basic questions:

- What type of information do I need? (Consider theories, historical dates, conclusions from laboratory experiments, demographic information, public opinion, historical precedent, famous quotations, biographical specifics, etc.)
- What discipline or field of study (history, philosophy, economics, etc.) has explored this issue?
- What type of publication is likely to offer such information (journals, magazines, theoretical books, etc.)?
- What is the best way to access that publication (periodical database, website, library shelves, etc.)?

Writers should proceed with caution when looking for particular information: The most prevalent mistake for beginning researchers is assuming that they should do seeking research when they actually need inventive research.

Conducting Primary Research

Academic writers do both *primary* and *secondary* research. In primary research, information is gathered firsthand by the researcher. A writer doing primary, or field, research makes observations or does experiments, interviews, and surveys. He or she participates in the original actions of gathering data or making conclusions. The writer/researcher is "in the field", collecting opinions, interpreting experiment results, and gaining insights from interviews. Such work allows the researcher to experience events and issues without the influence of someone else's interpretation.

Beyond these physical activities, in which the researcher actively collects or generates information, some texts are considered primary sources. Literary and religious texts are primary sources because the researcher is not *gathering* others' conclusions but is responsible for *making meaning* out of texts. In other words, when researchers use literature or religious texts, they must shape the text's possible meaning and make it relevant to a particular argument. (For more on literary and religious works, see Chapter 3, pages 41–43.)

Interviews

At a basic level, interviewing involves gathering information from a single person. But it can mean a great deal more. A good interview, like a good essay, goes beyond basic knowledge and provides insight. Good interviewers seek to engage interviewees in intensive conversations; they probe for knowledge and ideas, but they also allow interviewees to explore and develop ideas. The goal of an interview is not simply to record someone's opinion; rather, it is to prompt someone with particular experiences and insights to reveal something new and valuable.

Interview Questions Good interview questions create focus, yet allow interviewees to explore. Although they may seek out specific information, such as facts and dates, interview questions should go beyond collecting basic knowledge. In fact, asking interviewees basic information that can be retrieved through other sources undermines the interview process and wastes both parties' time. A more valuable strategy is to prompt interviewees to reflect on the meaning of issues or to make connections between ideas. Notice the difference between the following:

What's it like being a doctor?

How has working in the medical field influenced your personal life?

Primary Sources

Interviews
Surveys
Literary Works
Religious Texts
Autobiographies

Secondary Sources

Books (nonfiction)
Newspapers
Magazines
Journals
Government Documents
Reference Books
Websites
Blogs/Chats
Visual Media

The distinction between secondary and primary sources sometimes blurs. For instance, although news articles are usually considered secondary, a researcher arguing about news articles, as a topic, might treat them as primary sources, inspecting them as one might inspect a literary work. The categorizations *secondary* vs. *primary*, then, can depend on how the source is used.

The first question does not focus attention on any particular issue; the interviewee could talk about anything related to the medical profession. The second question, however, draws attention to a particular issue and asks the interviewee to consider a particular relationship. It is more specific than the first question and still calls for a certain degree of exploration.

Follow-up Questions Following up on answers is the interviewer's most powerful research tool. A survey asks a list of preformulated questions, but an interview can follow a line of thought that comes from someone's response. Imagine the following scenario, in which a researcher is interviewing a civil engineer:

INTERVIEWER: Is being a civil engineer interesting?

ENGINEER: Sure. I get to deal with all kinds of people and very real situations.

INTERVIEWER: Is being a civil engineer hard?

ENGINEER: Well, some of the work can be difficult. Trying to figure in all the variables in a given project can be a mathematical nightmare.

INTERVIEWER: What would you tell someone who wants to become a civil engineer?

Here, the interviewer comes up short in several ways. First, the questions are too general to yield focused and insightful answers. They prompt the engineer to respond in equally general terms. They are surface questions (the kind one might ask at a party) that invite short and uncomplicated answers. Second, the interviewer misses opportunities to follow up. After the engineer's responses, the interviewer could have asked about the "very real situations" or the "mathematical nightmare" but ignores both ideas and, instead, moves to the next question. This interview does not probe for insight or engage the thoughts of the interviewee. Notice the following example, which evolves within the space of only a few questions:

INTERVIEWER: How is a civil engineer important to society?

ENGINEER: Well, civil engineers conceptualize living space for the public. They envision what it might be like to live in a particular place, say, a downtown area, and then lay out plans to make a park, an intersection, even an entire downtown livable—and they do it all while considering how an area will grow and how people's needs may change.

INTERVIEWER:	So civil engineers have to be visionaries?
ENGINEER:	Yes! They are not simply figuring out formulas about buildings and zones and land; they are imagining what it might be like to live and work within a given area in the present and future.
INTERVIEWER:	And they do all this while accommodating the demands of city officials?

Here, the interviewer starts with a more insightful question. While the first interviewer depends on a vague concept ("interesting"), the second interviewer seeks out the meaning of a potential relationship (between civil engineers and society) and consequently receives an insightful response. Also, the interviewer in the second scenario springboards from the engineer's answers ("So, civil engineers have to be visionaries?"), thereby extending the initial thoughts.

Planning an Interview When setting up an interview, be sure to respect the position and accommodate the schedule of the interviewee. Researchers should never impose themselves on potential interviewees. Use the following tips and strategies:

- Always request an interview well in advance of your own deadlines so that you can accommodate the interviewee's schedule.
- When making a request, introduce yourself and the reason for the interview: Explain the nature of your research and how the interview will be integrated into it.
- Beforehand, negotiate a reasonable amount of time for the interview (such as thirty minutes) and stick to it so as not to impose on the interviewee's time.
- Plan out your method of recording responses—writing, audiotaping, or videotaping. Ask the interviewee if his or her answers can be recorded and if his or her name can be used in the final work.
- At the end of the interview, thank the interviewee for his or her time, and leave promptly.

Using Interviews An interview can be used to support claims made in argument, to help explain an idea, or even to help explain the history or significance of a topic. In the following example, the writer is trying to persuade readers that the water treatment system in her town is inadequate. The claim made by the interviewee supports the writer's idea:

Most often the water sewers can withstand the runoff from storms, but the past season has illustrated the inadequacy of the current sewer system. According to Harold Johnston, director of town utilities, the sewer system was overwhelmed twice in the past three and a half months, and the result was that untreated sewage flowed out into Silver Lake. When an overflow occurs and untreated water spills into the natural water system, the high amounts of bacteria affect the wildlife and jeopardize the health of swimmers and water enthusiasts. In essence, anyone or anything in the lake for days after an overflow is swimming in sewage.

Although the writer probably collected extensive information about the treatment system during her interview, she used only one particular point in this paragraph because it directly supports the main idea. (Other information might be used in later passages.)

The Letter Interview and the Research Process

GARYN G. ROBERTS

Garyn G. Roberts is an award-winning author. His most celebrated works include *Dick Tracy and American Culture: Morality and Mythology, Text and Context* (1994), which was nominated for the Mystery Writers of America Edgar Allan Poe Award, and *The Prentice Hall Anthology of Science Fiction and Fantasy* (2001), which he edited and which won the National Popular Culture Book Award. Roberts is authoring a bio-bibliographical history of Chester Gould and Dick Tracy. Much of his scholarly work through the years has depended upon primary research—specifically, the letter interview.

There exist a number of "truths" and generalizations about writing and the writing process. For example, in the strictest sense, all writing, at least on some level, is autobiography, metaphor, and fiction. But, this statement is not the focus here. In general, people are most successful as writers when they write about subjects in that they are not only interested, but also passionate. Though this may seem pedestrian and obvious on the face of it, we write best about subjects and topics that we already know to an extent and/or which we are willing to fanatically pursue. In addition, as clichéd as it may seem, the research process is a grand treasure hunt and the ensuing written product is a treasure realized at the end of the successful hunt. The research process often yields many "doubloons" and "pieces of eight." An essential tool or method used in much of my quest for treasure is oral history, and more specifically the personal interview, and by extension the letter and email interview. Letter and email interviews as research tools are the focus here.

In December 1965, as a first grader, I wrote President Lyndon Baines Johnson. President Johnson responded to my letter and sent photos of his family for my school. A couple of years later, I read my first series of *Dick Tracy* newspaper comic strips by Chester Gould (1900–1985) and I wrote Mr. Gould at the *Chicago Tribune.* We were friends and pen pals from that time into my graduate school years and until the time of his passing more than fifteen years later in 1985. I have interviewed many famous writers by mail and in person, and I did a great deal of marketing research for university business classes via interviews during my undergraduate education in the late 1970s and early 1980s.

It has been my privilege to have met famous people through the interview process (written and oral), and I am very fortunate to know and count some of the world's most famous authors as my friends. In a public presentation he did with me Spring 2003 celebrating the fiftieth anniversary of his novel *Fahrenheit 451,* Ray Bradbury stopped his part of the program to publicly thank me for my friendship and my years of work on his behalf.

Some of my favorite stories of interviews and oral histories, and subsequent research writing success, have come from my students, who have used letter and email interview techniques taught to me in the 1970s by Chester Gould.

Though maybe not thoroughly profound, the format for that letter interview (and now email interview) is based on sound reasoning and common sense, and invariably yields tremendous results. Mr. Gould laid it out for me this way, and I have used this method and taught my students the same for more than twenty-five years.

The philosophy of this type of interview is multifaceted, and designed to create a highly professional, trusting and friendly relationship between interviewer and interviewee. This letter and electronic format establishes the credibility of the writer/researcher, delineates the already existing knowledge and honorable intent of that person, and elicits detailed and important information from the uniquely informed interviewee.

This form of interview facilitates the interviewee's "buy-in" to the efforts of the researcher,

Garyn Roberts, "The Letter Interview and the Research Process." Reprinted with permission of Garyn Roberts, Ph.D.

and also opens the door for further communication between the writer and receiver of the interview. (It often leads to additional written communications, personal interviews, and enduring professional relationships and friendships.) And, this format politely creates a "contract" between the researcher and that person interviewed.

Amazingly simple in some ways, the letter interview begins with a neatly typed and specifically addressed envelope in which the letter will be sent. Next, and here is where the "contract" is established, a self-addressed stamped envelope is included for the return of written responses made to questions posed. The SASE makes the responder's efforts easier than they might be otherwise. In addition, few people want to ignore and waste the unused stamp on that return address.

In the case of the email interview, the principal is the same—without the stamp. Again, the writer of the interview seeks to establish a bond or even a "contract" of sorts with the interviewee. The sender of the email interview must, like the letter interview writer, remain vigilant when it comes to matters of formality, form, and grammar. It is important to get a sense of the interviewee's preferences. Some may prefer and might only respond to paper letters sent through the U.S. Postal Service; others may prefer and be tolerant of the electronic form. As with the letter interview, the goal of the electronic interview is to make the process as attractive and as comfortable for the interviewee as possible.

Use of appropriate letterhead is helpful, but not necessary, in the case of the letter interview. The letter or email itself begins with relevant inside addresses and date. After an appropriate salutary greeting such as "Dear Mrs. . . ." or "Dear Dr. . . . ," the first paragraph—concise but detailed and carefully worded—introduces the researcher/writer to the person addressed. Credibility and dedication to the topic at hand are critical, and are established here. As a student (high school, college, university or otherwise), you, the researcher, are already

stereotyped in a universally positive way. Identify yourself as a student working on a research paper for an English, Sociology, History or (fill in the blank) course. Presented correctly, students are revered in our culture, and people want to advance education of these fine people.

That first paragraph is also where the researcher acknowledges the expertise of the person who receives the letter interview. Always being genuine (not artificial and overly flattering), the researcher pays tribute to the person addressed, and briefly showcases what he/she already knows about that person and the subject at hand. Be polite and unassuming, and after identifying yourself, turn your focus to the person interviewed and topic at hand. This all contributes to matters of credibility, trust, and intent. And, it occurs in an introductory paragraph of five to seven well-conceived sentences.

Conclude that first paragraph by stating that you have some questions you would like to ask, and have included these questions in this very letter. In the last sentences of that paragraph, state, "I have included a few questions here, and would greatly appreciate your responses. If it most convenient for you, please answer these on this letter or in this email, right after each question, and mail these responses back to me in the SASE or at my email address." If you are sending an email, make sure that your interviewee can both open your message with the computer software they have available to them, and can easily respond to that message.

Wishing to avoid overtaxing your respondent, keep these questions to about five or six in number. With this relatively small number of questions, make each question count. Avoid the obvious and questions that can be answered by other general resources. This whole process is designed to celebrate the expertise of the person receiving the letter interview and to facilitate information.

The quality of answers you will receive is directly dependent on the quality of questions posed. Here, again, you are interested in politely, discretely, and without a great deal of fanfare, showcasing your knowledge of the subject already. The kinds of question you ask contribute directly to this goal.

Next, after that introductory paragraph, list those five or six questions. On a paper letter, leave ten to fifteen lines between questions so that your respondent can provide answers right after each question. (The interviewee does not have to go to any extra effort to answer your questions—you have made things as easy as possible for that person.)

The concluding paragraph does three things. First, it emphatically but evenly thanks the interviewee for his/her time. Second—optional but recommended—it asks if the interviewee would like a copy of your final research project. (A little extra work on your part, this gesture reassures that your intentions are genuine and your final writing is open to scrutiny. Trust is further strengthened.) Third, it asks one last question and makes one last statement: "May I approach you with follow-up questions as they arise? Thank you again."

This written interview is closed "Sincerely, . . ." and provides contact information—address, telephone, FAX, email, and related and potentially useful information.

Some final words of advice: Send this letter interview, or email interview, at least three to five weeks before the information is needed. Send these interviews to more than one expert. While the return rate on this particular letter interview process is quite high—in the case of the letter interview you sent that stamp and politely foisted off an obligation in your letter—you are not guaranteed a quality response. Your chances are good, and you have helped make these better with a professional and personal written interview, but you never know. Besides, more than one expert has never compromised a research project and related treasure hunt.

Through the years, I have received responses to such written interviews from people after their deaths (sent just before they died, or by their estates after they passed on). Such was the case with Dick Moores (1909–1986), Chester Gould's first assistant on *Dick Tracy* in the early 1930s and famous Walt Disney Studios artist. My dear friend Robert Bloch (1917–1994), famed author of short stories, novels—including *Psycho* (1959)—radio plays, screenplays, teleplays—including three episodes of the original *Star Trek* (1960s)—writers' writer, and mentor to contemporary authors—including Stephen King, dying of cancer, sent me material (including permissions and photos from Hollywood) for his biography he wanted only me to have. He wrote the introduction to that book, "knowing that he would not live to see it in print." Great fun, heavy responsibility, and a way to contribute meaningfully to the heritage and culture that is ours.

Sample Interview Letter

Dear *Formal Name of Interviewee:*

Mrs. Jean Gould O'Connell and I are working on two book-length projects on the life and career of her father, Chester Gould. In doing so, we are most interested in the insights and inputs of people who knew and were closest to Chester and Edna Gould. Could I trouble you to answer the following questions and relate any stories you think might be of importance, then send your responses back to me? Feel free to write your responses on this and other paper. Please be as detailed in your responses as you like. (What might seem unimportant may very well be important. So, please provide as much detail as you can.) Enclosed is a self-addressed stamped envelope for your convenience. All unique ideas and direct quotes will be appropriately credited and documented in our book projects. If you have any questions about this or any other matters, please let me know. Thank you in advance for your time and efforts.

1. How and when did you know Chester and Edna Gould?
2. Do you remember any specific events or people from Chester and Edna's lives that were reflected in Chester's famous comic strip *Dick Tracy?* What and who were these?
3. What memories do you have regarding Chester and Edna helping other people? Please explain.
4. Did Mr. Gould ever relate stories about . . .
   A. His youth in Oklahoma? What were these?
   B. His early years in the Chicago area (1921–1935)? What were these?
   C. His years at Bull Valley (near Woodstock, 1935–1985)? What were these?
5. Do have any stories you can relate regarding Chester's parents (Gilbert and Alice)? Or about his brother Ray and sister Helen? Please explain.
6. Do you remember any special stories about Edna (Mrs. Gould)? Please explain.
7. Is there anything you would like to add? What do think should be said in biographies of Chester Gould?

8. Can you provide me with any names and addresses of people you think I should contact regarding their knowledge of, professional relationships with, and friendship with Chester Gould and his family?

9. Are there any photographs you would like to share for this project? All appropriate credits would be provided for such pictures. (Original copies would be returned.)

This summer, during Dick Tracy Days in Woodstock, Illinois, I will be interviewing people in person regarding their memories of the Goulds and *Dick Tracy.* If you would be willing or would like to meet with me at that time to further discuss your memories and talk about these projects, please let me know. May I send you a second set of follow-up questions?

Thank you again for all your time and efforts. If it has not yet been stated directly here, it is important for you to know that we are interested in paying tribute to Chester and Edna Gould, *Dick Tracy,* and the many important friends and relatives that were part of their lives. We are very excited about these projects and you sharing your stories with us.

Sincerely,

Garyn G. Roberts

Surveys

While an interview is based on an individual's ideas and knowledge, a survey attempts to find public opinion on a topic. An interview is driven, in part, by the interviewee; his or her insights can influence the direction or emphasis of the interview. In surveys, by contrast, the researcher pre-arranges the direction and emphasis with carefully formulated questions.

Generating Questions In generating survey questions, a researcher should consider three points.

1. Survey questions seek to find out—not *influence*—people's thinking. For example, a question that draws attention to a president's "wealth and privilege" may lead respondents toward a specific response. Instead, the question should be phrased objectively, not leading the respondent in any particular direction.

Leading Question: Because of his enormous wealth and privileged upbringing, is the president out of touch with labor issues affecting average hardworking Americans?

Objective Question: Is the president in touch or out of touch with labor issues in the United States?

2. Just as they should not influence the respondents' thinking on an issue, good survey questions should focus on a specific topic.

Less Focused Question: Do you like our current president?

More Focused Question: Do you approve of the president's current policies on education funding?

3. Questions should use common, nonspecialized language (unless you are surveying only specialists in a particular field, such as doctors or engineers). Because survey respondents may come from different walks of life, survey questions should avoid technical jargon or specialized terminology.

Technical Question: Given recent research by CERRIE on genomic instability and mutations in mini-satellites, do you feel that radiation exposure guidelines should be revised?

Nontechnical Question: Given recent research about the long-term effects of low-level radiation, do you feel that radiation exposure guidelines should be revised?

Choosing Respondents Surveyors must consider the demographics (or characteristics of specific populations) of their potential respondents. A well-designed general survey should include a representative cross-section of the population. Consider the following:

- What is the age range in the respondent group?
- What is the racial makeup of the respondent group?
- What is the gender makeup of the respondent group?
- What is the occupational makeup of the respondent group?
- What is the geographical origin of the respondent group?

Recording Responses Responses can be recorded in various ways. Perhaps the easiest means is to elicit written responses by asking the respondents to write or check off their answers. But if that is not possible, the researcher must do the recording by writing or taping. (If you plan to tape answers, either on video or audio equipment, you should always obtain the respondents' permission in advance.)

Using Responses Survey responses are most often used to show public opinion about a topic. Although a survey may collect many different opinions (and opinions about a variety of issues), the results are often boiled down to a particular issue. In other words, the survey generates a particular insight that the researcher presents to the audience. For example, notice how the following paragraph presents a particular insight that was generated by a survey:

> Gone are the days when the average college student dedicates most of his or her time to study. Now, college students are increasingly apt to work. They hold part-time jobs, where they work a few hours per week, and full-time high-stress positions, where they work forty-plus hours per week. At Bay College, nearly 80% of surveyed students said they have some kind of outside employment. And 40% of those work more than thirty hours per week ("Campus Study" 4). Such figures correspond to a growing trend across the country.

Conducting Secondary Research

In contrast to primary research, secondary research is the examination of others' theories, conclusions, and ideas. Secondary sources (such as books, articles, and websites) help researchers to understand the history of a topic, to comprehend what has been said and what else can be said. Secondary sources also help writers get acquainted with others' values and assumptions and with the precedents of a particular field of study or discipline.

Regardless of the topic or discipline, every good researcher benefits from a wide understanding of and familiarity with that field's sources of information. Each type of source represents a possible research direction. And when researchers are familiar with many possible directions, they are bound to discover more than if they were stuck in a singular rut.

Books (Nonfiction)

Nonfiction books can be valuable secondary sources. Although their information may not be as up to date as some other types of sources, such as journals, they can be excellent resources for an in-depth understanding of your topic. There are six main categories of books that will help you in your research.

Theoretical Books, which are common in academia, explore ideas. The main goal of theoretical works, in any field, is to reinvent (or help to reinvent) how people think about an issue. Theoretical books are usually aimed at a specialized audience, people who already know something about the subject and who have some sense of other texts written on the matter. Notice the titles of some theoretical books on rhetoric and writing:

Rhetoric and Reality

Fragments of Rationality

The Methodical Memory

Textual Carnivals

Even though theoretical books can be tough going at first, they can help expand your topic. Because they work at the conceptual level and usually aim to redefine something in a field of study, they can generate new (often revelatory!) ways of thinking.

Historical Analyses focus on specific issues or particular historic periods. They involve significant research from authors and usually give surprising and detailed bits of information. Notice, for example, this passage from David Russell's *Writing in the Academic Disciplines, 1870–1990:*

> But the transition from oral to written requirements [at Harvard] was not easy to make, for the new university was no longer a single discourse community with a single curriculum. Even in the early 1870s, the struggle to find a place for writing in an increasingly elective and departmentalized curriculum was already in evidence. Shortly after Eliot became president, students were no longer required to read their compositions aloud. (52)

Historical analyses like Russell's make claims about the nature of events in the past, and they provide ample, detailed evidence that illustrates and supports those claims. (There are even history books about history. These highly theoretical texts, called *historiographies*, usually examine how history has been told.)

Edited (Thematic) Collections are groups of essays that focus on one topic. The essays may have been published elsewhere prior to their appearance in the collection. An editor or group of editors selects the essays, arranges them in the book, and usually provides some introduction to the whole collection that explains the nature of the topic. For example, *Women and Power in Native North America* was edited by Laura F. Klein and Lillian A. Ackerman. The editors provide a brief introduction (thirteen pages) that gives a broad overview. Each chapter is an essay from an individual author, and each focuses on slightly different aspects of the broader topic. Notice the titles of the first several chapters:

Women and Power in Native North America

1. "Introduction," Laura F. Klein and Lillian A. Ackerman

2. "Gender in Inuit Society," Lee Guemple

3. "Mother as Clanswoman: Rank and Gender in Tlingit Society," Laura F. Klein

4. "Asymmetric Equals: Women and Men Among the Chipewyan," Henry S. Sharp

Edited collections like this are valuable finds for researchers. They can be used in several ways:

1. The introductions or final chapters (which may also be written by the book's editors) often make general claims about the topic at hand. These sections might characterize the history or future direction of a

topic and thus help a researcher to get a handle on some of the more significant events, theories, or approaches to the topic.

2. Each chapter in an edited collection can be read as a separate article—its own statement about a given topic.

3. Several chapters in an edited collection can provide a range of perspectives (and sometimes contradictory opinions) about a topic. In this sense, collections can help a researcher see an ongoing debate and understand competing assumptions, values, and claims.

4. Edited collections usually provide thorough lists of sources, either at the end of each chapter or at the end of the book itself. These lists can be used as starting places for further research.

Textbooks aim to introduce readers (usually students in a specific course) to a discipline or field of study. They assume that readers need many terms defined, and they present information in digestible units or sections. A reader can examine a chunk of information from the middle of the text without having to read everything before it. Textbooks are also relatively user-friendly: information is presented in various ways, so readers can conceptualize, rather than just consume.

It is important to note that textbooks explain theories or principles but do not seek to *create* new theories. For instance, a psychology textbook is apt to discuss important figures such as Freud, Skinner, and Milgram, but it will not seek to transform how people think of those figures.

Biographies cover the life of an individual, as told by someone else. Most often, a biographer attempts to reveal hidden layers of someone's life and to show something intimate or especially significant about that person. David McCullough's biography of President John Adams, for instance, delves into the character traits of the president and shows how those traits corresponded to his life in office.

Autobiographies are personal narratives; they cover the life of the writer. For instance, in his 2004 release, *My Life,* former U.S. president Bill Clinton tells his own story.

Newspapers

Newspapers cover a broad range of topics. They are most valuable for highly publicized topics, such as political events, controversial public figures, national or local disasters, and significant cultural events. National newspapers, such as the *New York Times* or the *Washington Post,* also offer lengthy and in-depth analyses. In a sense, newspapers represent collective responses to the political and cultural events of the day.

Most academic and public libraries have newspaper databases and access to past editions. Practically all newspapers also have websites. And while city newspapers feature local issues, the following cover a range of national and global events: *Afro American Newspaper, American Banker, Atlanta Journal-Constitution, The Boston Globe, Chicago Tribune, The Christian Science Monitor, Denver Post, Detroit News, Houston Chronicle, Los Angeles Times, The New York Times, San Francisco Chronicle, Los Angeles Sentinel, St. Louis Post-Dispatch,* [New Orleans] *Times-Picayune, USA Today, The Wall Street Journal, The Washington Post.*

Magazines

Magazines are for general or casual readers, people who are not specialists in a given field. They range dramatically in style, subject matter, and editorial policy. There is a magazine for every conceivable layer of personal and public life: from gardening to bow hunting, from stamp collecting to hiking, from political intrigue to Hollywood gossip. Some magazines are more news oriented than others. *Newsweek* or *Time,* for instance, is more concerned with delivering world and national news than *People* or *Better Homes and Gardens.* But all magazines have the same goals: to make a profit and to stay in business.

Ultimately, magazines must appeal to two groups: their advertisers and their subscribers (in that order). Without advertising money, magazine budgets would run dry. Therefore, the stories and coverage in magazines rarely run contrary to the values of their advertisers. For instance, a general-interest magazine with major advertising from a car company is not apt to run a story that connects car exhaust to asthma. This is not to say that magazines are entirely controlled by their advertisers' values, but readers should know that choosing magazine content is a highly political process. Magazine editors must consider the financial impact of their decisions.

Activity

Look through a magazine. Based on its articles, advertisements, and images, explain its ideology, the hidden values that underlie the content and appeal to readers.

Magazines also cannot afford to alienate readers. Information is the product in a magazine, and if that product is distasteful in any way, readers simply may not buy it. Therefore, magazines tend not to sell information that might offend their readers, even if that information is credible and reliable. Magazine articles, then, are apt to engage the values their readers share. The information will likely resonate with a particular ideology. This is not to say that magazine articles are bound to lack reliability or credibility. But researchers should always be aware of the broader, business-related purpose of magazine articles and look for their underlying ideology and warranting assumptions.

Journals

In contrast to magazines, journals are written for a specialized audience in a particular field of study or discipline. They feature an array of articles by different authors, as magazines do, but differ in key aspects from magazines. Journals explore matters within a specialized field. They are often associated with academic disciplines:

Quarterly Journal of Speech

Management International Review

Mathematics of Computation

Journal of Materials Chemistry

College English

Nurse Researcher

Environmental History

Each discipline has many related journals, each with a specific focus. For instance, notice these chemistry-related journals found in one college library:

Chemical Business

Chemical Business Newsbase

Chemical Equipment

Chemical Market Reporter

Chemical Monitor

Chemical News and Intelligence

Chemical Specialties

Chemical Week

Chemical Week Asia

Chemical Week Internet Focus

Chemical and Industry

Chemistry Review

Another important difference between magazines and journals is in the nature of the articles. Magazines primarily set out to inform readers (give information), but journals set out to argue for new ways of thinking. Journal articles work to transform theories, practices, and policies within a field. Additionally, journals are generally nonprofit, often run by a nonprofit organization. Therefore, they lack advertisements or keep them isolated to the front and back pages. (The few advertisements, like all the content in journals, tend to be black and white—not replete with flashy colors and attention-grabbing devices.)

Journal articles are judged (or "refereed") by anonymous scholars before they are published. For instance, consider this typical scenario: An economist discovers a growing trend in personal debt among consumers. She writes a lengthy essay explaining the nature of the trend and what it may mean for the country and its future, according to a specific school of economic theory. Before the essay is accepted for publication in an economics journal, the editor sends it to several economics scholars throughout the country, perhaps even throughout the world. These scholars examine the research, judge the logic of the claims, recommend changes, and then recommend that the essay be published or rejected. Only after this intensive process (which may repeat several times) does an essay become a journal article. These rounds of judging help to ensure the information in the article is accurate.

Journal articles can be powerful research tools. They are generally available on research databases (such as InfoTrac® College Edition or Academic Search Elite), and they are highly focused, offering specific conclusions, theories, and information. Like theoretical books, journal articles can be filled with technical jargon and dense language. They are not for casual readers. But they often feature a short abstract or concluding section that summarizes the main points.

Journal articles are written when a scholar:

- Applies an ongoing theory to a particular situation.
- Discovers a likely cause or effect that has not previously been imagined.
- Redraws the boundaries of a given discipline or practice.
- Expands or rethinks a previously accepted theory.
- Discovers something previously overlooked in the history of the field.

Is It a Journal or a Magazine? At first glance, journals and magazines may look a lot alike. But closer inspection will reveal significant differences. Generally, journals are written for academic or highly specialized readers, and the articles put forward new theories or practices in a particular field of study (sociology, psychology, nursing, English, chemistry, history, etc.). Magazines are written for general readers, who may have a particular interest (cycling, running, gardening, etc.). If you are not certain what kind of periodical you have, use the following criteria:

Journals

- Seek to advance knowledge in a field of study.
- Deal with principles, theories, or core practices in an academic discipline.

- Are associated with a particular discipline or field of academic study.
- Have few advertisements, which usually appear only at the beginning and end (not between or among articles).
- Have few colors and flashy pictures (unless they are related to a study or article).

Magazines

- Report information and news or offer advice.
- Offer the latest technique in a hobby or sport.
- May appeal to readers with a particular interest.
- Have advertisements throughout the pages, even interrupting articles.
- Tend to use lots of color and pictures.

Activity

In groups, decide whether a journal or a magazine probably published the following articles. As a class, discuss the reasoning behind your decisions:

"Make Way for the Cherry Festival!"

"The End of Humanism: An Examination of Postmodern Thought"

"Angina and the Elderly"

"Are the National Parks in Trouble?"

"Climatic Change and Insect Migration"

Government Documents

Government documents include reports, transcripts, pamphlets, articles, speeches, books, maps, films, and more. While the U.S. government is the nation's largest publisher, state and city governments also publish documents. They can be of great value in one's research, and can be found online using keyword searches, going to the website of the relevant agency, or going directly to the Government Printing Office (GPO) website at www.access.gpo.gov.

Reference Books

Reference books, such as dictionaries, encyclopedias, and almanacs, can be helpful, but they should not be relied upon as the only sources for a college research paper. Using only reference books for research suggests that a researcher was unable or unwilling to find a range of sources, which in turn suggests a lack of depth in the exploration and discovery of ideas. Reference materials are usually found in a library's reference room (or in smaller libraries, a reference area) and cannot be checked out. They can be located, as with other library materials, by searching the library's catalog of holdings.

Websites

Websites are as diverse as the people who create them. (And everyone from a fourth-grader in rural Montana to a senior advisor to the president can create a website.) As most people know, the World Wide Web is a lively, confusing, and enormously diverse space. It contains nearly every type of information, theory, law, policy, reference, and idea imaginable.

For more specific advice on evaluating websites, see page pages 384–410.

The value of the web is fairly obvious to anyone who has spent a few minutes using any search engine: you quickly find vast amounts of information on anything from monkey droppings to Olympic history archives. The downside of the web is fairly obvious as well: the information may be questionable or only slightly relevant to your topic. Although it is easy to find general information on a topic, it is more difficult to find specific theories, conclusions, and data. Also, the web is populated with two significant annoyances: sales pitches and pornography. It is a playground for people selling junk and hawking porn. A serious researcher has to navigate his or her way through advertisements, posters, popups, and "opportunities" of all kinds. However, despite these difficulties, focused web searches can generate interesting results and can function as valuable inventive research.

Blogs/Chats

Blogs (web logs) and Internet chat rooms feature personal and largely informal postings. Although a writer should not rely on blogs and chat rooms for reliable information, these sources can be valuable stops along the research path, revealing new ways of thinking and new directions for further exploration. Ideas gleaned from these sources should be evaluated, integrated, and documented, just as ideas from websites and reference books should be. Because they are not edited by outside parties, these sources should be seen and used as personal statements rather than as proof for any claim.

Visual Media

Visual media include film, digital video, posters, photography, graphics, maps, and so on. Like articles or books, visual media can make arguments. For example, a poster, illustration, or map can assert an important political position or aesthetic judgment: Consider Edward Tufte's visual argument against a popular software program.

Edward R. Tufte

The Cognitive Style of PowerPoint

Military parade, Stalin Square, Budapest, April 4, 1956.
Copyright © 2003 by Edward R. Tufte   November 2004
Published by Graphics Press LLC   P. O. Box 430   Cheshire, Connecticut 06410   www.edwardtufte.com

Even if visual media do not argue directly, they function within an argument. A visual source of any kind is an artifact of a culture—a representation of certain values and collective assumptions. A film might reveal something about the attitudes of a particular time and place; a poster or advertisement may show what people value or how they think.

Searching the Library

Books, periodicals, newspapers, government documents, reference books, audiovisual materials, and websites can all be valuable sources of information. All of these sources can be found by searching a library's catalog of holdings and/or the Internet. Knowing how to navigate library catalogs and cyberspace is the first step in finding valuable sources. You might begin by getting familiar with your library's website. The website will explain all the library's resources, and it may provide links to other useful websites and databases.

When searching your library's catalog, you may be given the option of doing an author search, a title search, a subject search, or a keyword search. Do an author search if looking for works by a particular author; do a title search if you already know the title of the specific work. Subject searches are organized by headings (such as "agriculture," "government," "gender") and will usually produce many sources for a particular topic. Keyword searches can be used to focus the research process. For example, a slightly different keyword search produces widely varying numbers of entries:

Keyword Search	Entries Produced
weight	804
weight *and* body	146
weight *or* body	3,993
body weight	93
bodyweight	0

Searches can be made more efficient by using the following words (called *Boolean operators*):

- Using *and* between words narrows a search by finding documents containing multiple words—*weight and body.*
- Using *or* between words broadens a search by finding documents with either word in a multiword search—*weight or body.*
- Using *and not* between words finds documents excluding the word or phrase following "and not"—*weight and not body.*
- Using *near* between words finds documents containing both words or phrases that are near, but not necessarily next to, each other—*weight near body.*

Evaluating Sources

Good researchers always evaluate the nature of their sources. They look closely at the source, the argument it offers, and its hidden arguments. They do not ask if the source agrees with their own way of thinking. Evaluating a source has little or nothing to do with agreeing or disagreeing with it. (In other words, a source is not good because you agree with it or bad because you disagree.) Sources should be evaluated according to their adherence to specific criteria, such as those outlined in this section. Finally, as we will show, sources often do have biases—and some may be highly biased. However, bias in itself is not a flaw. Be cautious, though, about sources that attempt to conceal their bias.

Evaluating sources keeps researchers agile, able to do more than simply ingest facts and fit them into their arguments. The following criteria (relevance, reliability, credibility, timeliness, diversity, the nature of underlying values) can be used to evaluate any source.

Relevance

Relevance refers to the relationship between the source and the writer's topic and particular stance. A source that is relevant is appropriately related to the writer's argument. Perhaps the first inclination regarding relevance is to find those sources that directly support a main claim—sources that specifically speak about the writer's particular subject and espouse his or her particular stance on it. However, this is very limiting, especially since the research process might (and should!) develop or change how a writer thinks about a subject. Sources do much more than back up a writer's opinion. They can help to explain the subject's complexities, explain its history, explain the writer's position, support the writer's position, show claims that oppose the writer's, or show claims that are different from the writer's.

Because sources can be used in a variety of ways, a source that seems only remotely related to your project might be valuable in the long run. Consider the following example: A writer is researching voting practices in his community and wants to make a claim about low voter turnouts in recent elections. He finds a newspaper article about a local school scheduled for demolition that previously had been used as a voting location.

This article might seem irrelevant at first. After all, how does this particular school relate to voting trends in the community? But it actually may suggest a great deal about voting. One factor in voter turnout is proximity to voting locations. This article might show a trend of declining number of voting locations. The same writer might find a government web page about the history of voting in his state. At first, this source may not seem valuable because the writer is primarily concerned with recent voter activity. However, the history may provide some clues about the system itself, about the reasons for establishing Tuesdays as election days, or about the number of constituents in a given area, all of which are potentially valuable factors in understanding the complexities of recent voter turnout.

Use the following questions to weigh the relevance of sources you find:

- How does the source support or oppose my own opinions or hunches about the topic?
- How does the source help to explain something about the topic (its history, its evolution, its nature, etc.)?
- How does the source help to shape the values beneath my opinions?

Reliability

Reliability refers to the quality of information in the source. A reliable source documents the information it offers or proves that its claims can align with others' arguments. It documents claims involving statistics or data and offers paths to other research that supports the main argument. It makes a clear connection to a body of knowledge, to other scholars, thinkers, and researchers who have explored the issue at hand. The most obvious way to make this connection is with formal documentation (in-text citation and a bibliographical list). In effect, formal documentation says to readers, "Here is the path to other relevant research."

For journal articles, reliability may not be a problem because such sources endure a process of critical peer review. However, other publications do not have peer reviews. And magazines and newspapers do not have room to include formal documentation; their editorial policies exclude in-text documentation and Works Cited lists. But there are other ways for writers to signal reliability, such as an appositive phrase:

> Deirdre Mahoney, *a professor of writing at Northwestern Michigan College and a scholar of rhetoric,* argues that online courses are significantly more challenging for college students than traditional face-to-face courses.

Notice that the information after the name indicates the source's credentials. When a formal Works Cited list is not possible, writers use such phrases to document the reliability of their sources.

Consider the following questions for each source you find:

- Does the source offer formal documentation? Do other sources check out? Are they available?
- If there is no formal documentation, does the source acknowledge others with related credentials or qualifications?
- What about the source itself? Is it published by a reputable organization?

Credibility

In academic writing, previous publications and research credentials act as appeals to character. See page 52.

Credibility refers to the internal logic and validity of the information presented in the source. While a *reliable* source resonates with other research or corresponds to a body of knowledge, *credibility* is all about the source itself. A credible source does not attempt to hide its biases or its argument. It makes logical claims and helps the reader to follow its logic. If the source offers an argument, it makes its position clear and reveals its biases. (Of course, it is free of logical fallacies.) If the source attempts to inform rather than persuade, it does not spin information or conceal its biases.

Credibility may also involve the author of a source. Some authors have more credentials than others. However, a book or article by a well-known author should not automatically outweigh one by a less familiar writer. Many academic and professional writers are not big names in popular media but are well respected within small communities because they have spent years researching a particularly focused issue. For instance, Patricia Limerick, a highly respected history scholar, has written a great deal about the American West. Although her name is not recognizable to the general public, it is often noted in history scholarship. It is relatively easy to research authors' credentials.

Use the following questions to check the credibility of sources you find:

See Logical Fallacies in Chapter 3, pages 49–51. See Spin in Chapter 5, pages 91–93.

- Are the argument's claims well supported and well reasoned?
- Do you sense any logical fallacies?
- Does the source attempt to "spin" information or conceal its biases?
- Do you have reason to question the author's credibility? (If so, do a quick web or database search to see if he or she has written previously or is referenced in other publications.)

For more specific information on credibility and statistics, see Julie Burks's essay on pp. 398–400.

Timeliness

Timeliness refers to the appropriate relationship between the source's publication date and its content. A significant concern in academic research is the date of the sources. It is important that claims are supported with sources that are not obsolete or outdated. But this criterion depends upon the issue and the claim being made. Some claims require very current sources; for example, a writer making a claim about the state of cloning in the United States would be wise to consider sources published only within two to three years of her research. (Because the science of biotechnology evolves so rapidly and because each new advancement prompts significant public debate, claims that are ten years old probably would be antiquated.) However, that same writer might also want to discuss the role of science in human development, and discover a valuable text by a nineteenth-century philosopher who speaks about the role of machines in the evolution of the modern consciousness. In this case, the writer could use current texts to support claims about time-sensitive topics and refer to an older source to express an issue that stretches beyond a particular era.

The focus of certain topics can change because of events in popular culture, politics, and everyday life. Certainly the terrorist attacks of September 11, 2001, changed the way people think about a host of issues. *The 9/11 Commission Report*, released in July 2004, impacted policy decisions in government. Such events create a before-and-after gap, so certain information that would otherwise be considered relatively current might suddenly become outdated.

Although current information is important, the most valuable source is not necessarily the most recent. For some topics, writers may find value in older sources that have had significant impact on writers and researchers. For instance, a writer focusing on contemporary political protests would certainly discover recent sources about protests against the World Trade Organization. However, he might also find texts by Henry David Thoreau, Martin Luther King Jr., or Mahatma Gandhi to be of value. Although such sources are significantly older than a recent article on the Internet, they would provide depth to any discussion about political protests. Of course, a hundred-year-old text would be used differently than a contemporary text: The writer might use Thoreau to explain the importance of civic action as a general principle and turn to a recent source to articulate the present condition of political protest groups.

Use the following questions to help you weigh the timeliness of sources:

- Is the information time-sensitive? Is the topic apt to change dramatically from year to year?
- If the information is time-sensitive, is the source current?
- Has anything significant occurred in the field of study (or in everyday life) that may have changed or influenced the information in the source or the nature of the topic?
- If the source is not current, does it help to illustrate something that is timeless (some human, natural, or physical trait)?

Diversity

Here, diversity refers to the variety of sources a writer uses. Writers develop their views on a subject from different sources, much in the same way as people develop their views on religion or marriage or education from taking in and making sense of information from various sources. For example, our social values may have been influenced primarily by our parents; but other sources, such as childhood friends, books, movies, and music, also influenced us. Even views that oppose our own are important because they help us to define the borders of our beliefs. This process of making our own sense out of various pieces of information is called *synthesis*. It is what writers do when researching their topics. Writers need to consider and synthesize various sources about their topics; otherwise, their perspectives and, ultimately, their positions will be limited.

This does not mean that every research project must consult websites, journals, books, and newspapers. A perfectly sound project can emerge from a focus on the journals in a given field. It does mean, however, that writers should be cautious of depending on information from only one publication. If a writer made several claims about the state of American foreign policy, all based on *Newsweek* articles, some important perspectives would be missing. Or if a writer relied heavily on unaffiliated websites (those not associated with a professional organization or institution), the information could have significant gaps.

Underlying Values

Beneath the most objective looking source, there lies a layer of shared values and hidden assumptions. From heated argumentative essays to brief factual news articles, the claims emerge from and rely on some unstated ideas and shared beliefs about the world. This does not mean that a secret agenda, or subliminal message, lurks beneath our sources—or that the government is trying to brainwash us. It simply means that information grows out of what people value. A simple news article, for instance, might report on some "promising new technology" that will help American car companies to increase fuel efficiency. The article may not explain that fuel efficiency is inherently good, that saving money on gasoline is good, that diminishing our collective impact on the environment is good. Such value claims would go unstated and readers would likely accept them as part of the article itself. (For more on underlying values, see page 81 in Chapter 5.)

When we read sources, we should acknowledge the quiet and shared values that may come along beneath the obvious claims and information. Quite often, we will discover some obvious and widely accepted notions about the world—about good/bad, right/wrong. Sometimes, we might discover some complexity, a school of thought, a hope, a yearning, a fear, or a principle that is not so easily accepted.

Use the following questions to consider the underlying values beneath the surface of a source:

- What is the reader prompted or invited to value? (What ideas, people, attitudes, policies, or behaviors are held in high regard?)
- What broader set of beliefs or perspectives relates to those values?
- What assumptions can you detect in the argument?
- How are the main issues framed? That is, how does the writer characterize issues to be relevant in people's minds?
- What group, organization, or institution published the source? Might the values of that group influence the information offered?

The Patsy: A Story of a Number

JULIE BURKS

When evaluating a source, we should not be swayed too easily by numbers. Statistics can make a source seem instantly credible—more logical, less biased. But as Julie Burks, an accountant and auditor, explains, statistics themselves are fraught with potential shortcomings. Like any form of support, statistics can be tweaked and framed according to particular biases. This does not mean we should automatically toss out numerical support, but that we should not automatically accept it as beyond bias, beyond accident, beyond opinion.

Believers of statistics beware! Persuading an audience with a statistical analysis is an easy tactic. The reason: Numbers don't lie. However, the data behind the numbers, behind conclusions, behind completed reports, are like any part of human communication: full of potential flaws and misuse. In short, a responsible audience should practice some healthy skepticism when confronted with the mighty statistic.

Statistics are developed from testing samples of a population. The population is comprised of individuals. To most people, *individual* usually means human; but, to a statistician, individuals can also include animals and things. So when a study suggests that 8 out of 9 individuals prefer beef over tofu, it might be wise for the study's interpreter to know if the population being tested was a pack of Golden Retrievers or selection of human beings. Further, if the study focused on human responses, who were the humans? What demographic? Were they specifically selected McDonald's shareholders or randomly selected from cities in multiple states?

Even the timing of a survey can have dramatic effects. For instance, consider the outcome of a survey asking a sample population: Are American office workers subjected to weight-gain due to sedentary activities in the workplace? A survey such as this might bear differing conclusions if asked before or after lunch. Placing blame on externalities (such as the situational activities in the workplace) might come easy once the deep-fried Monte Cristo sandwich, followed by the hard-to-resist blueberry cheesecake, rests in the participant's belly after lunch hour. Conversely, if asked before lunch, the participant may conclude that one's diet and exercise routine has a greater impact on weight control than does the normal course of the work day.

Trusting the source of data often begins with the level of trust an audience has with the spokesperson. When Drew Barrymore lets a crowd in on a little secret about the "number one launch" mascara that doubles lash length, who wouldn't want to "join the six million and counting" (Cover Girl)? Cover Girl cosmetics selected Barrymore for her celebrity. Compound celebrity with statistics and cha-ching: Lash Blast mascara theoretically becomes an instant success. But what does the six million represent? Were these individuals independent consumers, Cover Girl employees, or artificial test eyelashes in the research and development laboratories? Is it the number one launch of all make-up companies world-wide? Or is the number one launch just for Cover Girl that year in America alone?

Another variable that can influence conclusions drawn from data is the scope of the data selected. Many savvy investors lost millions of dollars in the stock market in the late 2000's. After the peak of the housing bubble, investors started becoming wary and losing trust in financial markets. Scare tactics were flowing through various media channels disclosing short-term data (such as that shown on the following graph for the years 2006–2009) which was suggesting that the floor was going to fall out from under the feet of America. Everybody wanted out. The numbers become the scapegoat, the fall guy, the patsy, for irrational decisions and sporadic impulse. "People get scared in crowds; their confidence comes back one at a time," says Warren Buffet, one of the world's wealthiest investors and philanthropists.

The truth is revealed, however, when one observes the Dow Jones over a longer term (see the following graph). Even shortly after the bubble burst, this particular index is still better off than it was fifteen years prior. So what happened? Did investors neglect to look at the bigger picture? Were they relying on statistics from sources who had unidentified motives? Were the sources of this information jumping to conclusions before analyzing all the data? Regardless of the answers, such questions reveal possible biases or innocent inaccuracies.

Depending on who comprised the tested population, rhetoric within a survey can generate a preferred response for an intended audience. In fact, the entire study could be deliberately formulated to sway respondents. For example, if a group of American teens were asked whether or not they enjoy pâté, most participants would respond unfavorably. However, if the teens were asked if they enjoy meatloaf, the results would tilt in an entirely different direction.

Another concept in uncovering the misleading notions within data is manipulating statistical terminology. Much confusion arises (is created) from two statistical terms: *mean* and *median*. The terms both describe the center of a distribution but in different ways. The median is the number that sits perfectly in the middle of the distribution. The mean is the average of all values. For example, let's say we have the following values: 0, 2, 4, 7, 211. The median is 4 (sits perfectly in the middle) and the mean is 44.8 (the average: 0+2+4+7+211 divided by 5). These values also have what's called an *outlier*—an observation that is numerically distant from the rest of the data. In this case, the outlier is 211.

Let's say the example in the preceding paragraph was a test in which one table at Applebee's was selected. There were five individuals (humans

Top graph: Depicting a significant decline in the Dow Jones Industrial Average from the beginning of 2006 to mid-2009.
Bottom graph: Depicts the Dow Jones Industrial Average but extends the scope by 36 years (to 1970) to show larger trends.

in this instance) at the table, and these individuals were asked, "How many times do you use your cell phone in a day, whether calling or texting?" Wouldn't it be advantageous for a cell phone company to report that individuals with a median age of 67-years are texting on average 44.8 times per day? But let's look at our Applebee's table again. The ages of these fictitious individuals are 98-years, 68-years, 67-years, 14-years, and 6-years. The average age of this group is 16.4 years less than the median age. Including the outlier as a true representative of this population can lead to questionable results.

Age	# of Calls/Texts per Day
98	1
68	7
67	2
14	211
6	4

As with any argument, a responsibility rests on the interpreter/reader to question the underlying biases: Who is the source? Who is the intended audience? Who comprised the tested population? Is the test or study planned based upon desired results? Now, when persuasive, yet questionable, results emerge from a new study, one might inquire: "Where was the study conducted—a dog park?" The patsy, yet again: an innocent number.

Works Cited

Buffett, Warren. "Warren Buffet on the Economy, the Deficit, LeBron James and BP." *Huffington Post.* Huffington Post, 2010. Web. 24 July 2010. http://huffingtonpost.com

Cover Girl. *Covergirl Drew Barrymore's Lashblast Mascara Commercial. YouTube.* N.p., n.d. Web. 20 July 2010. http://www.youtube.com/watch?v=zILszWDXaYs

Moore, David S. *The Basic Practice of Statistics.* New York: W.H. Freeman and Company, 2004. Print.

Evaluating Electronic Sources

Writers should be especially careful about the information on websites because anyone with access to a computer can publish one and make any claim he or she wishes. Much information on the World Wide Web is thus potentially bogus. Bias must also be considered. The purpose of many sites is to sell something; therefore, the information may be slanted. Of course, bias is not inherently bad. It is only negative when it is concealed—or pitched as unbiased truth. How do you separate the bogus from the useful on the web? Try applying the following questions when considering websites:

- Who sponsors this site, and what credibility do they have for posting the information?
- Is the site attempting to sell something? If so, how might that impact the nature of the information?
- Does the site ask for personal information? (Does it state the purpose of this request?)
- Are statistics and data supported with appropriately documented sources?
- Is the information up to date? (Is the site updated consistently?)

➤ Evaluating Sources: In Brief

Evaluating sources depends on the application of key principles:

Relevance: the relationship between the source and the writer's topic and particular stance

Reliability: the quality of information in the source

Credibility: the internal logic and validity of the information presented in the source

Timeliness: the appropriate relationship between the source's publication date and its content

Diversity: the variety of sources a writer uses

Underlying Values: the collection of shared values and principles that rest beneath the claims

Activity

Wikipedia can be used for three types of research: preliminary survey of the topic, inventive research, and seeking research. To become more familiar with Wikipedia, use a topic you are currently researching or select one of these topics: No Child Left Behind Act, propaganda, Islam, credit cards, rhetoric, consumerism, marketing. Then answer the following questions:

- **Preliminary Research:** What important issues or aspects of the topic did you find out about through Wikipedia? Why should they be explored in your inventive research?

- **Inventive Research:** How did your thinking on a particular issue become more complicated because of the Wikipedia article? What source(s), besides Wikipedia, might you use to explore the issue further?

- **Seeking Research:** What facts from Wikipedia might be important to your argument, and what source(s) might you use to corroborate those facts?

Wikipedia In general, encyclopedias, including Wikipedia, are best used for initial research, to survey the broad territory of a topic before beginning inventive research. This preliminary research then leads to books, articles, and other sources that provide more detailed information that can be used for inventive and seeking research (see pp. 368–370). Wikipedia says,

> As with any source, especially one of unknown authorship, you should be wary and independently verify the accuracy of Wikipedia information if possible. For many purposes, but particularly in academia, Wikipedia may not be considered an acceptable source; indeed, some professors and teachers may throw Wikipedia-sourced material away out of hand. This is especially true when it is used uncorroborated. We advise special caution when using Wikipedia as a source for research projects.

(http://en.wikipedia.org/wiki/Citing_Wikipedia)

If used for inventive research, Wikipedia should not be used exclusively, since it is not exhaustive. Other key sources that are not mentioned in Wikipedia should be sought out as well. Nonetheless, by following links within articles and external links listed at the end of articles, writers can extend and transform their ideas. While it can also be used to find particular information such as a date (see "Seeking Research," pp. 369-370), Wikipedia is not just a place to locate facts but a place to explore possibilities.

Integrating Sources

Once writers have begun to work with other texts, or sources, they must integrate those texts into their own writing. Whether they are building bridges between positions, finding quiet connections, or counterarguing, they have to deal directly with others' words. They have to accurately portray what others have said and then work those ideas into coherent passages that explain their own position. (Some instructors consider this to be among the most difficult rhetorical work for writers!) Whether information is summarized, paraphrased, or directly quoted, it should be blended smoothly into the text so that the reader (1) understands its relationship to the writer's own ideas and (2) knows where the information came from. The challenge is to maintain coherence and flow while integrating others' voices and opinions.

Summary

As Chapter 4 explains, summary is expressing ideas from a source in your own words. Unlike a paraphrase (see pages 398–400), summary removes much of the detail from the original passage. The goal in summary is to abbreviate and reword the original text. In this sense, summary is a tool. It allows writers to place otherwise lengthy sources directly into their own arguments to support a claim of their own, to illustrate a point from an opposing position, or to help explain the topic itself. In other words, summary often serves a bigger purpose. It is also adaptable. A writer can shrink a mammoth Victorian novel into a few pages or a few sentences. Likewise, a ten-page article can be summarized in a page or a paragraph. It all depends on the writer's purpose. If a writer is using a source as one example among others, the summary of that source may be brief. But if the source is being used to illustrate a complex idea, the summary may be longer and more involved.

Summary walks a fine line between sufficient and excessive detail. The amount of detail always depends on the use of the source. Writers can ask the following questions when determining how best to summarize:

- What is the role of the source in my argument?
  - One example among many other examples?
  - An important tool for helping readers to think a particular way?
  - An illustration of a complex idea?
- How much detail would best illustrate my point?

Chapter 4, pages 101–106, explains steps for creating an accurate stand-alone summary. This section, however, shows how summary functions in a broader argument—how to summarize a source within an ongoing argumentative essay.

- How much detail would distract the reader away from my main point or derail the forward movement of my argument?

Notice how Joannie Fischer, in her essay "A Nation Made of Poetry," briefly summarizes lengthy literary works to illustrate her points:

> To its credit, America has always shown a great measure of tolerance for such self-criticism. Indeed, even when we have disagreed most vehemently, Americans have tended to agree on basic principles like the right to disagree. Again, Emerson's words have guided us: "Nothing is at last sacred but the integrity of your own mind." Others have created icons of integrity, such as Harper Lee's character Atticus Finch, a southern lawyer who in *To Kill a Mockingbird* defends a black man whom everyone else would scapegoat. Such high principle may be best portrayed by the ultimate American hero, the scrappy Huck Finn, who after much soul-searching decides that the right course of action is to defy all authority and help the runaway slave, Jim, to escape to freedom.

Two novels are boiled down to key statements that fit into Fischer's broader argument. The very short summaries leave out enormous amounts of plot and character detail. But this is appropriate for Fischer's purpose. Had she included further plot summary, her paragraphs would lose focus, and the reader would find it difficult to stay on the track of her main argument.

Example Summaries The length of a summary depends upon a writer's purpose. Most often, academic writers summarize in short passages—boiling down an entire article or book chapter into a paragraph or sentence. Because they want to maintain the forward momentum of their own arguments, they summarize sources quickly. But if a source is critical to the writer's argument, she may slow down and develop a longer summary, detailing key points from the source. The following summaries of Margaret Mead's essay "Warfare: An Invention—Not a Biological Necessity" (pages 136–140) illustrate three possible strategies:

- **Brief Summaries** give a concise rendering of the main idea:

    Margaret Mead argues that warfare is not a biological necessity or a sociological inevitability as some people believe. Instead, it is an invention, like writing or marriage.

- **Longer Summaries** give the main idea of the source and the most important reasoning:

    According to Margaret Mead, warfare, an organized conflict in which members of two groups fight and try to kill opposing members, is not a biological necessity or a sociological inevitability as some people believe. Instead, it is an invention, like writing or marriage. Some societies don't have warfare because they don't have the idea of it. And without the idea, they cannot have the thing.

Ultimately, people go to war not because of particular causes: disputes over land, struggle for power, or the attempt of a leader to gain prestige. They go to war because the idea of war exists in their culture.

Once an invention becomes known and accepted, people resist giving it up. But poor inventions do give way to better ones. First, people must recognize the defects of the old invention; then they must invent something better. Propaganda against warfare and documentation of its costs encourages people to see that warfare is a defective invention. And this allows people to believe that something better is possible.

• **Lengthy Summaries** give the main idea and supporting examples, reasoning, or evidence within the source:

In her essay, Margaret Mead explains that warfare, an organized conflict in which members of two groups fight and try to kill opposing members, is not a biological necessity or a sociological inevitability as some people believe. Instead, it is an invention, just as writing, marriage, cooking, trial by jury, using fire, or burial is an invention. People tend to think of these universal practices as necessary characteristics of humanity. But they are, in fact, inventions that can be replaced by better inventions that are more in accordance with the feelings and institutions of the times.

According to Mead, some societies don't have warfare, because they don't have the idea of it. Without the idea, they cannot have the thing. Eskimos, for example, have the personality and circumstances that could lead to war: They are simply not mild or meek people; they have fights, murder, and even cannibalism. Yet, they have no warfare. Ultimately, people go to war not because of particular causes: disputes over land, struggle for power, or the attempt of a leader to gain prestige. Instead, they go to war because war exists in their culture. Some might argue that warfare is absent among Eskimos because they have a low and undeveloped form of social organization. But the Pygmy peoples of the Andaman Islands in the Bay of Bengal and the Australian aborigines had a level of social organization similar to the Eskimos, and these two groups did have war simply because the idea of warfare was present.

Once an invention becomes known and accepted, people resist giving it up. But Mead argues that poor inventions do give way to better ones. First, people must recognize the defects of the old invention; then they must propose, or invent, something better. Public arguments against warfare and documentation of its costs encourage people to see that warfare is a defective invention. And this allows people to believe that something better is possible.

Activity

Identify which of the following summaries is best (1, 2, or 3), and explain the problems with the other choices.

Original

Organizing a text with sources may seem more difficult than organizing a text that is based exclusively on personal insights. However, the same principles apply: Paragraphs must be coherent, and transitions must be made between points. Whether information is paraphrased, summarized, or directly quoted, it should be blended smoothly into the text so that the reader (1) understands its relationship to the writer's own ideas and (2) knows where the information came from.

1. Organizing a text with sources is more difficult than organizing a text without sources, even though similar rules apply.

2. The same principles apply to organizing a text with or without sources: coherence and transitions are key. Source information should blend smoothly into the writer's ideas.

3. Although organizing a text with sources may seem more difficult than organizing one without sources, the same principles apply. Paragraphs must be coherent. Transitions must exist between points. Paraphrased, summarized, or directly quoted information must be blended smoothly into the writer's text so that the reader can understand its relationship to the writer's ideas and be able to see where the information originally came from.

Paraphrase

Paraphrase is a rewording of the original source using your own words and expressions. Unlike summary, paraphrase covers the detail and complexity of the original text. Following is a passage from Laura Tangley's article "Natural Passions":

There is "hard" scientific evidence for animal emotions as well. Neuroscientists who study the biology of emotions, a discipline still in its infancy, have discovered key similarities between the brains of humans and other animals. In all species studied so far, including our own, emotions seem to arise from long-evolved parts of the brain—particularly the amygdala, an almond-shaped structure in the brain's center. Working with rats, they have found that stimulating one part of the amygdala invariably induces a state of intense fear. Rats with damaged amygdalae exhibit neither normal behavioral responses to danger (such as freezing or running) nor the physiological changes associated with fear (such as higher heart rate and blood pressure).

A paraphrase of this passage might read:

Laura Tangley argues that laboratory experiments prove the existence of complex animal emotions. Some neuroscientists have recently begun studying the "biology of emotions" (120) and have found that human and animal brains are very much alike. According to the experiments, emotions come from parts of the brain that evolved long ago and that humans share with many other species. One such part is the amygdala, which rests in the center of the brain. Scientists found they could produce fear in the rats by stimulating parts of the amygdala. But rats with damage to that specific part of the brain lacked the normal range of responses to danger.

The paraphrase restates Tangley's ideas but does so in new language. In such a paraphrase, a writer might find a particular phrase important and quotable (such as "biology of emotions"), but the passage overall is rephrased and slightly summarized. A paraphrase is generally used because a writer wants to share the nuances of the original source but does not want the tone of the original to interfere with or take over his or her own text.

> **Paraphrasing is not merely changing a word or two, or shifting around sentence parts. Paraphrase demands a total rewording of the original source.**

Activity

Identify which of the following paraphrases is best (1, 2, or 3), and explain the problems with the other choices.

Original

Organizing a text with sources may seem more difficult than organizing a text that is based exclusively on personal insights. However, the same principles apply: Paragraphs must be coherent, and transitions must be made between points. Whether information is paraphrased, summarized, or directly quoted, it should be blended smoothly into the text so that the reader (1) understands its relationship to the writer's own ideas and (2) knows where the information came from.

1. Arranging an essay with outside sources is similar to organizing one without sources. For example, paragraphs should be coherent, and transitions should connect ideas. Information from sources (whether paraphrased, summarized, or quoted) must be integrated smoothly into the text so that readers understand how it fits in with the writer's ideas and know where the information came from.

2. Organizing a text with sources may seem harder than organizing one based only on personal insights. But the same guidelines apply: paragraphs have to be coherent, and transitions must exist between points. Whether information is paraphrased, summarized, or directly quoted, it should blend smoothly into the text so that the reader can understand its relationship to the writer's own ideas and know where it came from.

3. Organizing a text with sources is more difficult than organizing one without sources. The same rules apply, though. In both cases, paragraphs have to be coherent, transitions are essential, and information from sources must blend in with your own ideas.

Plagiarism

In short, plagiarism is the act of using other writers' words without attribution. It is stealing others' ideas in large chunks (entire essays or passages) or in small bits (a sentence or phrase). Whether in small or large chunks, stolen ideas are stolen ideas. To avoid plagiarism, writers must acknowledge their sources (also referred to as "citing" or "crediting" the source) whenever expressing someone else's idea or whenever providing information, such as a fact or statistic, that is not common knowledge. If writers use a source's exact words, they must put those words within quotation marks and credit the source (quotation marks alone are not crediting the source). If the information from the source is rephrased (paraphrased or summarized), it does not require quotation marks but does still require citation.

Most instructors recognize two different types of plagiarism:
(1) sloppy paraphrase and (2) intentional theft.

Plagiarism Type A: Sloppy Paraphrase Plagiarism can occur

because writers simply do not go far enough in their paraphrasing. That
is, they do not sufficiently reword the ideas from the original source.
Rather than reword the ideas of the source, they take a phrase here and
there, or mimic the sentence structure while changing only a few words.
For example, notice the similar phrases and word choice between Tangley's original and the passage after it. The writer does not rephrase Tangley's ideas but merely shifts words around and replaces others.

> **Original** There is "hard" scientific evidence for animal emotions as well.
> Neuroscientists who study the biology of emotions, a discipline still in its
> infancy, have discovered key similarities between the brains of humans
> and other animals. In all species studied so far, including our own, emo-
> tions seem to arise from long-evolved parts of the brain—particularly
> the amygdala, an almond-shaped structure in the brain's center. Working
> with rats, they have found that stimulating one part of the amygdala
> invariably induces a state of intense fear. Rats with damaged amygdalae
> exhibit neither normal behavioral responses to danger (such as freezing
> or running) nor the physiological changes associated with fear (such as
> higher heart rate and blood pressure).

> **Sloppy Paraphrase (Plagiarism Type A)** According to Laura Tangley,
> there is certain scientific evidence for animal emotions. Neuroscientists,
> who study the biology of emotions, have found important similarities
> between the brains of humans and other animals. In all species studied,
> including humans, emotions arise from long-evolved parts of the brain—
> particularly the amygdala, an almond-shaped piece at the center of the
> brain. Working with rats, these scientists discovered that stimulating one
> part of the amygdala induces intense fear. Rats with damaged amygdalae
> show neither normal behavioral responses to danger (freezing or run-
> ning) nor physiological changes associated with fear (higher heart rate
> and blood pressure).

Activity

What punishment is appropriate for intentional theft of others' ideas? As a
class, debate this question. As you develop reasoning, consider the following:
In a Rutgers survey, over one-quarter of college students admitted to plagiarizing an essay—and nearly 90 percent admitted to cheating on a test or quiz.

The writer of the second passage has only substituted some words and omitted others. This is not paraphrasing at all because the text retains the original flavor and expression of the author. Although the writer mentions Tangley's name, the passage masquerades as the writer's language. Quotation marks are not used, so it suggests that the writer has rephrased the ideas. While it may not seem like an egregious error, the writer has effectively stolen Tangley's language—and academic readers consider this plagiarism.

A paraphrase avoids using the same subjects and verbs as the original text. A good way to do this is to read the original passage carefully, set it aside, and restate the ideas in your own words. Remember that any one idea can be phrased in infinite ways.

Plagiarism Type B: Intentional Theft Writers sometimes plagiarize intentionally because they are desperate to complete an assignment or pass a class. They set out to steal or buy others' ideas. In this age of technology, students can easily download text from an online source or buy essays online. However, such essays are prepackaged, the topics are generalized, and the writing mediocre. Essentially, they are the opposite of what most college instructors want and are contrary to the invention strategies suggested throughout this book. As websites featuring prewritten essays increase, so does the ability of instructors to detect plagiarism.

Remember, the consequences for students caught plagiarizing are severe: Many colleges have campus-wide policies that punish intentional plagiarism with course failure, a permanent mark that denotes plagiarism, and expulsion. Such policies make a point: that academia values the honest work of the individual scholar and condemns any attempt to undermine that value system.

Quotation

Quotation, using the exact words of a source, allows writers to add an especially important phrase or passage to their own writing. Quotations can add flair and intensity to an argument. When an argument includes others' language, it suddenly becomes multi-voiced. You might imagine an academic essay like a dramatic reading, with the writer on a stage, speaking to the audience. Occasionally, the writer may step aside momentarily and bring on another speaker to express a particular point, thereby suggesting to readers, "This passage is so important that it should be given center stage." The key is to carefully select what ideas and manner of expression are worth quoting. Generally, writers do not allow quotations to take up more than fifteen percent of their texts, although certain situations may call for more.

When working with others' language, always quote sparingly—and focus on only the most striking parts. Follow these guidelines when using quotations:

- Choose only the most striking or revelatory passages.
- Cut out unnecessary or irrelevant information from the quote (using ellipses if necessary).
- Prune passages. Whenever possible, quote a sentence rather than a paragraph; quote a phrase rather than a full sentence.

Notice how a writer might pull only the most striking phrasing from a passage by Martin Luther King Jr.:

> In his "Letter from Birmingham Jail," Martin Luther King suggests that "human progress never rolls in on wheels of inevitability" (130).

Quotation Marks Only

When the quoted matter blends directly into your sentence without a speaking verb (*says, exclaims, proclaims, states,* etc.), no punctuation is required before the quotation. The sentence can be punctuated just as it would be if there were no quotation marks:

> We can then see what some more astute and careful readers of Housman's work have seen: namely, that "the undermining of romantic illusions yields first an appalling vision of death's reality which then creates a renewed appreciation of life in all its varied imperfections" (Lindsay 340).

> Quindlen compares the way that Americans act with their animal counterparts today to the way our ancestors once acted toward Native American people. We are willing to "tolerate" them as long as "they don't demand to share" (68).

Speaking Verb Followed or Preceded by a Comma

Speaking verbs (*say, says, said, exclaims, states,* etc.) indicate a shift from your voice to the voice of your source. In the second example below, *explains* tells the reader that the text is going to shift from the writer's voice to the voice of the source. A comma separates the quotation from the rest of the sentence:

> "Man is primarily an imagemaker," writes James Hillman, "and our psychic substance consists of images; our being is imaginal, an existence in imagination" (qtd. in *Re-Visioning Psychology* 23).

As Martin Luther King Jr. explains in his "Letter from a Birmingham Jail," "One day the South will know that when these disinherited children of God sat down at lunch counters, they were in reality standing up for what is best in the American dream" (43).

A speaking verb combined with a noun creates an attributive phrase that can be placed at the beginning, in the middle, or at the end of a sentence. Quoting involves carefully crafting sentences to create clear and natural-sounding connections between the writer's own ideas and the words of the source. Here are some standard strategies:

Quotation at the Beginning of a Sentence

"All voting is a sort of gaming, like checkers or backgammon, with a slight moral tinge to it," explains Henry David Thoreau (56).

Quotation in the Middle of a Sentence

As Thoreau points out, "all voting is a sort of gaming, like checkers or backgammon, with a slight moral tinge to it" (56), and it is this moral issue that is often overemphasized on ballots.

Quotation at the End of a Sentence

Henry David Thoreau claims that "all voting is a sort of gaming, like checkers or backgammon, with a slight moral tinge to it" (56).

Quotation Divided by Your Own Words

"All voting," explains Thoreau, "is a sort of gaming . . ." (56).

Sentence Followed by a Colon   The colon sets up or introduces the quotation. It tells a reader, "Here comes the quotation." The colon also allows the writer to explain the significance of the quotation beforehand:

Because Tenenbaum's quote is from an online article that does not include page numbers, no page number is given in parentheses.

One solution, according to Tenenbaum, is pretty simple: "Avoid making excess light, and use reflectors and shields to direct light toward the ground."

As George Williams notes, protection of white privilege is critical to patterns of discrimination: "Whenever a number of persons within a society have enjoyed for a considerable period of time certain opportunities for getting wealth, for exercising power and authority, and for successfully claiming prestige and social deference, there is strong tendency for these people to feel that these benefits are theirs by 'right'" (727).

Omitting Words Occasionally, writers want to quote a passage but leave out words or phrases. This is done by using ellipsis points (three consecutive periods). This construction tells the reader that words have been taken out of the original passage.

Original

When the leaders of a town become focused on economic growth while ignoring social growth, businesses most often win out in the end, and they have very different goals and needs than the average citizen.

Quotation

According to Amber Edmondson, "When the leaders of a town become focused on economic growth . . . businesses most often win out in the end, and they have very different goals and needs than the average citizen" (qtd. in *Inventing Arguments* 312).

The ellipsis indicates the missing phrase. The same strategy can be applied when cutting any amount of text from a quotation. For instance, notice how a whole sentence is removed from Laura Tangley's original passage. In this case, the ellipsis follows a period:

Original

Even scientists who are most opposed to the idea of animal passion acknowledge that many creatures experience "primary emotions"— feelings such as aggression and fear that are instinctive and require no conscious thought. Essential to escaping predators and other dangers, fear, in particular—along with predictable freeze, flight, or fight responses—seems to be hardwired. A laboratory rat that has never encountered a cat, for example, will still freeze if it is exposed to the smell of this predator.

Quotation

As Laura Tangley explains, "Even scientists who are most opposed to the idea of animal passion acknowledge that many creatures experience 'primary emotions'—feelings such as aggression and fear that are instinctive and require no conscious thought. . . . A laboratory rat that has never encountered a cat, for example, will still freeze if it is exposed to the smell of this predator" (118).

Adding Words It is occasionally helpful to add a note or comment within a quote. In this case, writers use square brackets to offset their own words. For example, a writer may insert a word in a quoted passage to clarify a vague pronoun or to give a brief explanation. In the following, the writer substitutes the actual noun for the pronoun "they." Without the noun, the reader may not understand the meaning of the quotation. As in this example, inserting bracketed comments within quotes can clear up any potentially vague information within a quote while maintaining the flow of the sentence:

Original

After months of exhausting research, they had finally come to understand the problem with their design.

Quotation

"After months of exhausting research, [the nuclear scientists] had finally come to understand the problem with their design" (Smith 82).

Noting an Error If a quotation is grammatically or syntactically flawed, a writer cannot change it. In such cases, the quotation must remain intact, and the writer must use square brackets and the three-letter word *sic* to acknowledge the error. A reader might otherwise assume that the error is on the part of the writer:

But the political party strategist saw things differently: "Even if we had waited on the Senate Arms Committee to release its findings, our move still would of [*sic*] been perceived as political" ("Politics of the Senate" 73).

Using Lengthy Quotes When writers quote more than four lines, they must use a block quote. As in this passage from an essay by Jay Harrington, writers often use a colon before block quotes:

As Pat Blashill notes in *Noise from the Underground:*

Alternative culture wasn't invented by Nirvana in 1992. They just brought an anthem of disaffection and anger to the top of the charts, to the malls, to the army bases, and into the living rooms of a nation that had spent most of the eighties trying to convince itself that it was a kind and gentle place. . . . America was all about shiny surfaces, and mainstream culture was about as deep as Bobby McFerrin's 1988 hit song, "Don't Worry, Be Happy." . . . Hollywood was again becoming a factory for empty escapism. The bestseller lists were rocked by *Slaves of New York, Less Than Zero,* and *Bright Lights, Big City,* three very hip novels about people with nice clothes, cocaine, and hardly anything to say. (16)

Using Double Quotes Occasionally, writers quote a passage that contains a quotation. In this case, single quotation marks are used inside the double quotation marks:

> As Maria Gallagher has argued, "It is time that we turn the corner on the road of national energy policies and begin to take 'alternative energy' seriously" (23).

Blending Information from a Source

Good writers use sources to forward their own arguments. They stay in control of their own writing. They frame the information from the source with their own language and provide commentary about that information. In the following, Tracy Webster refers to the source, gives a main idea from the source, and provides his own commentary on the idea:

> Anna Quindlen says that according to the National Association of Home Builders, "the average American home has doubled in size in the past century." Some see this, no doubt, as a great achievement—a sign of their own and their country's success and prosperity. But family size hasn't doubled; it has decreased. Americans have come to simply want, expect, and possess *more stuff.* And along with this, they cannot merely displace a few animals and live in relative peace with the rest. Instead, they see it as their right to destroy the homes—and what have been the homes for centuries—of more wildlife than a thousand humans have any acceptable reason to destroy, simply because they'd like to have a large and impressive home in a pretty place. Sadly, this is why Quindlen's proposed moratorium is necessary, and why it is the only solution.

In the following passage, Jennifer Worley sets up a main idea, gives background about a source, refers to the source, gives information from the source, and returns to her main idea:

> Idealization of women is nothing new. Nathaniel Hawthorne's 1846 short story "The Birthmark" illustrated the tragedy of seeking ideal beauty. In the story, a scientist attempts to remove a birthmark from his wife's face in order to perfect her appearance. Although he is successful at ridding the mark, the process kills her. In a recent essay, Chester McCovey discusses "The Birthmark" and its relevance to our own culture:
>
> > As for physical imperfection in the twenty-first century, it seems odd that on one level we promote respect for all sorts of human "imperfections," yet on the another level, we strive as we do to eliminate them

> whenever we can. It seems odd because so many times they are not imperfections at all.

> In other words, what we consider imperfections are also what make us unique, which we are told is important. Still, we make great effort to get rid of imperfections so we get closer to the ideal.

Webster and Worley both frame their sources' information and stay in control of the ideas.

Counterarguing Sources

Writers often directly refer to sources because the sources oppose their own claims. That is, they want to use the sources to show an opposing perspective. In these cases, the writers directly refer to the source (by paraphrasing, summarizing, or quoting), and then immediately respond. In the following paragraph, notice how Ben Stapleton briefly explains the opposing perspective (Breslau's characterization) and then responds to it for the remainder of the paragraph:

> In case it is not entirely clear, Breslau's characterization establishes a cause/effect that is out of sync with reality—but in line with Pickens's dream of controlling water for millions of people. Certainly drought causes water supplies to diminish, so does uncontrolled growth. But environmental restrictions *preserve* water. The only enemies of water preservation, in the true sense, are those super-capitalists who want to profit from moving it around. Breslau's spin on the facts turns the world upside down. In this quasi-reality, men like Pickens "provide" water and environmentalists keep it from people.

Counterarguing a source is often done in a *turnabout paragraph,* in which the writer gives the opposing side (by summarizing, paraphrasing, or quoting the source) and then responding, as Justin James does:

> The No Child Left Behind Act of 2001 was well intended, perhaps. Signed by President George W. Bush on January 8, 2002, the act "gives our schools and our country groundbreaking educational reform, based on the following ideals: stronger accountability for results, more freedom for states and communities, encouraging proven education methods, more choice for parents" (No Child Left Behind). The act has placed an emphasis on accountability, which is being determined by student test results. Test scores might rise. But does that really mean the schools are doing a better job or students are getting a better education? The current empha-

sis on testing can have harmful results. What's more, the method used to find out the scores teaches students a dangerous definition of *education.*

The writer's response might come in a new paragraph. In the following passage, notice Wendy Kaminer's counterarguing strategy. She devotes an entire paragraph to her source, Canli. She paraphrases, summarizes, and quotes the source. Then she breaks for a new paragraph (as if to prepare the reader for a change) and begins her response:

> Canli also reported that in brain scans taken while the subjects viewed pictures, "experience and memory is processed in the same location" in women, but not in men. This is how Canli explained the MRI evidence on CNN: "You are looking at a slice of brain tissue, and the red blobs on it indicate regions of activation that are associated with the emotional experience or with the emotional memory. When you look at the women, it's in the same place. . . . When you look at the men, the experience is on the left and the memory is on the right."
>
> I'm no expert on magnetic resonance imaging, but I've read that it's open to interpretation. And somehow I find these red blobs unconvincing as evidence that women are more emotionally retentive than men. You don't have to be a scientist to wonder whether a study suggesting that the emotional memories of 12 women were up to 15 percent more accurate than the emotional memories of 12 men is proof that men and women think differently; you merely need a knowledge of history.

Using Textual Cues

Whatever organizational strategy you use, make certain that you distinguish your ideas and claims from those of others. The reader must be able to tell whose ideas are being explained or asserted. Also, make certain you show the relationships between and among sources. In other words, make certain that you use appropriate *textual cues* (sentences, words, and phrases that explain the relationship between ideas, sources, or points in the paper) for the reader.

> Most music critics, *such as Smith, Castella, and Sanchez,* see the latest alternative genres as a collective response to the grunge scene of the early '90s.

The critics listed here have been discussed prior to this sentence, and the writer simply reminds the reader about these voices and how they relate to the present point being made. Simple phrases (like *such as*) cue the reader to make connections between passages in the text.

Jones's ideas are often seen as radical. Alberta Slavik, *for example,* casts Jones aside as a "hyper-liberal" journalist: "William Jones has gone too far, simply parading his politics at the cost of facts" (76).

The short phrase *for example* helps the reader keep track of the names. The phrase tells the reader, even before the quotation, that Slavik sees Jones's ideas as radical. Textual cues become increasingly important as writers add names and sources to their texts.

Using Paragraph Transitions

Integrating outside sources can make a text more sophisticated, but it can create confusion if the writer does not make clear connections between points. Because outside sources often increase the complexity of a text, paragraph transitions (sentences and phrases that join the content of paragraphs and show the logical connections) become vital to a coherent paper. Transition statements usually begin paragraphs and act as bridges from one paragraph to the next. The following sentences, which all begin paragraphs, act as bridges from previous points. Notice the key transitional words in each sentence: *however, despite, but, because of:*

- Not all farmers, however, agree with Johnson's strategy.
- Despite this overwhelming amount of evidence, some teachers refuse to acknowledge the way gender and race figure into the classroom.
- But all of the discussion on war distracts voters from significant domestic issues that will impact everyday life in the present and future.
- Because of Smith's recent book, many researchers have begun focusing their attention on the ways technology will change our ability to communicate.

Documenting Sources

Documenting sources is more than a formatting game. It is a process of sharing one's research path and leaving a trail for readers to follow. Good documentation shows how knowledge works—how ideas get borrowed, built upon, challenged, extended, and questioned. It also shows readers that a writer has conscientiously researched the subject.

In academia, writers must document all information that they gather from an identifiable source. In other words, if the information was found somewhere (anywhere), it must be cited. Academic writers also cite information that is not commonly known. *Common* may be a difficult concept to grasp. But think of common facts as those that could be heard from various sources at any given time. For instance, most people following mainstream news understand that BP owned the oil well that leaked into the Gulf of Mexico in 2010. The basic information is commonly known. But specific dates about the event or specific details about the leak (such as gallons of oil per day) are not commonly known. If such specific information were used in an academic essay, it would need to be cited. And even when academic writers know specialized or detailed information, they cite it. The citation has rhetorical force. It shows that the information can be examined on its own, beyond the framework of the project at hand. The citation also gives readers a place to find out more.

Activity

To Cite or Not to Cite: For each statement, decide if the information warrants a formal citation or if it can be considered common knowledge. Also, describe the reason for your answer:

1. The American Civil War divided the country into the Union states and the Confederacy.

2. It is well known that Michael Jackson's *Thriller* has been one of the most "culturally significant" records in history—selling more than 45 million copies throughout the world.

3. In the past ten years, Americans more than tripled their consumption of bottled water.

4. NASA is in charge of space shuttle missions.

5. In the coming week, NASA technicians will replace the shuttle's power drive unit (PDU), which will take up to three days.

6. The American Civil War claimed between 62,000 and 70,000 lives.

7. Michael Jackson, often referred to as the "king of pop," changed mainstream music with his ground-breaking record, *Thriller.*

8. The Onion began its hilarious parodies of American culture in 1988.

Because so many writers and thinkers participate in ongoing scholarly discussions, they need some agreed-upon conventions for sharing information. They need a standardized means of communicating where information has come from, where it is stored, and how it can be retrieved. Think of formal documentation, then, as a set of conventions—a style for sharing information. Like texting, like Morse code, like graffiti, like smoke signals, documentation styles are merely agreed-upon symbols for communicating across time and space.

The two most common documentation styles in academia are MLA (Modern Language Association) and APA (American Psychological Association). Regardless of the particular style of documentation, the basic concepts are the same. After learning the basic concepts, you can quickly learn the specific variations of a style when called upon to use it. Both styles depend on two basic components: (1) an in-text citation of a work and (2) a list of works at the end of the text (called Works Cited in MLA style and References in APA).

Think of formal documentation as symbols that communicate through time and space.

MLA Documentation Style

The Modern Language Association documentation style is used in English studies, humanities, and related fields. Each source requires two parts: an in-text citation and a Works Cited entry.

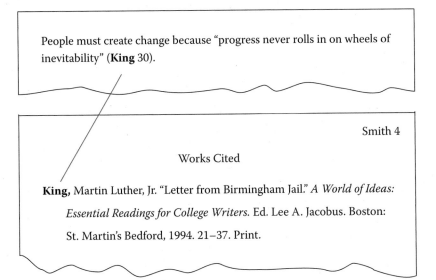

People must create change because "progress never rolls in on wheels of inevitability" (**King** 30).

King is used in parentheses because **King** is the last name of the source.

Smith 4

Works Cited

King, Martin Luther, Jr. "Letter from Birmingham Jail." *A World of Ideas: Essential Readings for College Writers.* Ed. Lee A. Jacobus. Boston: St. Martin's Bedford, 1994. 21–37. Print.

In-Text Citation An in-text citation involves referencing the original text in parentheses within the actual sentences of your text. Because the citation uses parentheses, it is sometimes called a *parenthetical citation*. An in-text citation must occur whenever a writer:

- Quotes directly from a source.
- Paraphrases ideas from a source.
- Summarizes ideas from a source.
- References statistics or data from a source.

The basic in-text citation includes the author's (or authors') last name (unless it is given within the sentence) followed by the page number of the source from which the cited material is taken (unless the source is electronic and lacks page numbers):

A revolution in medieval English poetry was "the gradual detaching of the lyric from music" (Lewis 3).

The end punctuation comes after the citation. Only a space separates the name and the page number.

If the author is referred to in the sentence, the author's name is omitted from the citation:

> Emphasizing her point, Miller demands that "it is now time for something drastic to change here on campus" (43).

If the source has no author, use the first word or phrase of the source's title and punctuate accordingly (quotation marks for articles and italics for books):

> The oil had spread over much of the shoreline and had "already begun its death grip on a vast array of wildlife" ("Black Death" 86).

If the source has two or three authors, use the last name of all authors:

> (Lunsford and Ede 158)

If the source has more than three authors, use the last name of the first author followed by "et al." (abbreviation for the Latin *et alii*, "and others"):

> (Margolis et al. 94)

If you have more than one work by the same author, insert a shortened title of the work after the author's name and before the page number:

> (Faigley, *Fragments of Rationality* 43)

If you are citing material that is quoted in the source, cite the source in which you found the quotation and add *qtd. in* before the author name or title:

> (qtd. in Smith 82)

If you want to acknowledge more than one source for the same information, use a semicolon between citations within one set of parentheses:

> (Lunsford and Ede 158; Smith 82)

If you have an electronic source with no page numbers, simply exclude the page number from the citation. Do not add page numbers, and do not use those that a computer printer assigns.

> According to Martha Smith, "untold numbers of children are negatively affected by the proficiency test craze."

Works Cited pages list the sources that are directly cited in the text. (Works Consulted pages, on the other hand, list all the sources that a writer has read and digested in the process of researching the project.) The first piece of information in each Works Cited entry should correspond to the in-text citation. In other words, the in-text citation and Works Cited entry should function together to form a trail for the reader to follow. For example, notice the relationship between the in-text citation for King and the entire bibliographic information in the Works Cited, as shown on page 421.

Entries in Works Cited pages must follow strict formatting guidelines, but the process is easy if you know the formulas involved. Although it may not appear so, documentation does follow a pattern. Despite the differences between sources, all entries give the same type of information in the same order:

1. Author name

2. Title of the work

3. Title of the bigger work (book, magazine, newspaper, etc.), if applicable

4. Place of publication or distribution (if unavailable, use *n.p.* for "no place of publication")

5. Publishing or broadcasting company or sponsoring organization (if unavailable, use *n.p.* for "no publisher")

6. Date of publication (if unavailable, use *n.d.* for "no date of publication")

7. Page numbers, if applicable (if unavailable, use *n. pag.* for "no page numbers")

8. For electronic sources: Tool of access (such as a particular database), if applicable

9. Publication medium (e.g., *Print, Web*)

10. For electronic sources: Date of access and URL (if needed to locate the source)

Formatting Authors and Titles

When it comes to author names and source titles, all entries (regardless of the source) adhere to the following:

- **Author Names:** are inverted unless the author is listed second or third:

  Smith, Lynda.

- **Multiple Authors:** For two or three authors, the second and third author names are not inverted and are listed directly after the first author. List the authors in the order they appear on the title page, not in alphabetical order. For more than three authors, you can avoid listing all the names and simply add *et al.* after the first name:

  Henderson, James, and Willa Henderson.
  Bryant, Nicole, William Leonard, and Cheryl Johnson.
  Johansen, Sturla, et al.

- **Titles:** Article titles are always in quotation marks, while the sources in which they appear—newspapers, magazines, and journals—are italicized. Titles always come directly after author names, unless no author appears on the source. In that case, the citation begins with the title. The beginning letters of all words are capitalized, except articles, prepositions, coordinating conjunctions, and *to* in infinitives.

Printed Books

All of the necessary information for books can usually be found on the title and copyright pages.

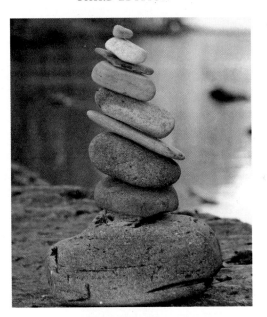

Inventing Arguments —— Title of the book

THIRD EDITION

John Mauk ——
Northwestern Michigan College
—— Author names
John Metz ——
Kent State University at Geauga

WADSWORTH —————— Publishing Company
CENGAGE Learning

Australia • Brazil • Japan • Korea • Mexico • Singapore • Spain • United Kingdom • United States

WADSWORTH
CENGAGE Learning™

Inventing Arguments:
Third Edition
John Mauk, John Metz

Senior Publisher: Lyn Uhl

Publisher: Monica Eckman

Acquisitions Editor: Margaret Leslie

Senior Development Editor: Leslie Taggart

Development Editor: Stephanie Pelkowski Carpenter

Assistant Editor: Amy Haines

Editorial Assistant: Danielle Warchol

Media Editor: Janine Tangney

Executive Marketing Manager: Stacey Purviance

Marketing Manager: Melissa Holt

Marketing Coordinator: Brittany Blais

Marketing Communications Manager: Courtney Morris

Content Project Manager: Corinna Dibble

Senior Art Director: Jill Ort

Manufacturing Planner: Betsy Donaghey

Rights Acquisition Specialist: Mandy Groszko

Production Service: Lachina Publishing Services

Text Designer: Greg Johnson

Cover Designer: Hanh Luu

Cover/title page Image: COPYRIGHT 2011 PHILWEBBPHOTOGRAPHY/Getty Images

Compositor: Lachina Publishing Services

For product information and technology assistance, contact us at **Cengage Learning Customer & Sales Support, 1-800-354-9706**

For permission to use material from this text or product, submit all requests online at **www.cengage.com/permissions**. Further permissions questions can be e-mailed to **permissionrequest@cengage.com**.

Library of Congress Control Number: 2011932605

Student Edition:
ISBN-13: 978-0-8400-2775-7
ISBN-10: 0-8400-2775-3

Wadsworth
20 Channel Center Street
Boston, MA 02210
USA —— City of publication

Cengage Learning is a leading provider of customized learning solutions with office locations around the globe, including Singapore, the United Kingdom, Australia, Mexico, Brazil and Japan. Locate your local office at **international.cengage.com/region**

Cengage Learning products are represented in Canada by Nelson Education, Ltd.

For your course and learning solutions, visit **www.cengage.com**.
Purchase any of our products at your local college store or at our preferred online store **www.cengagebrain.com**.
Instructors: Please visit **login.cengage.com** and log in to access instructor-specific resources.

Printed in Canada
1 2 3 4 5 6 7 15 14 13 12 11

Printed Books

General Format

Author's Name:
As in all sources
in MLA format,
single author
names are inverted.

The Title:
Book titles are italicized.

Ridl, Jack. *Losing Season.* Fort Lee: CavanKerry,

2009. Print.

City of Publication:
If multiple cities are listed
on the title page of the
book, give only the first.

Publishing Company:
Publishing companies
are always found on the
title page of the book.
List them in shortened
form, directly after the
city. A colon separates
the city of publication
and the company.

Date of Publication:
The date usually
appears on the
copyright page, which
is the back side of the
title page in a book.
(Always use the most
recent date listed.) Use
a comma between the
publishing company and
the date of publication.

Publication Medium:
For the print version of
a book, the publication
medium is Print. (See
pages 426–427 for
information on citing an
online book.)

Corporate Author

American Automobile Association. *Tour Book: New

Jersey and Pennsylvania.* Heathrow: AAA, 2001.

Print.

Use the name of the corporation as the author name.

Subsequent Editions

Wicks-Nelson, Rita, and Allen C. Israel. *Behavior

Disorders of Childhood.* 4th ed. Upper Saddle River:

Prentice, 2007. Print.

Find the edition information on the title page of the book, and place the information
in the entry directly after the title or the editor, if there is one. Use the abbreviations
2nd ed., 3rd ed., and so on, or *Rev. ed.* for "Revised edition," depending on what the
title page says.

Republished Book

> Tolkien, J. R. R. *The Hobbit.* 1937. New York:
> Ballantine, 1982. Print.

Older books may be published by a company different from the original publishers, or a hardcover book can be republished in paperback. In this case, insert the original publication date after the title, and then give the recent publisher and date.

Edited Book

> Cox, Robert, ed. *Environmental Communication and the Public Sphere.* 2nd ed. Thousand Oaks: Sage, 2010. Print.

Add *ed.* after the editor's name. If there is more than one editor, use *eds.* for "editors."

Translated Book

> Bakhtin, Mikhail. *Problems of Dostoevsky's Poetics.* Trans. Caryl Emerson. Minneapolis: U of Minnesota P, 1998. Print.

Add *Trans.* after the title of the book, followed by the translator's name, not inverted.

Printed Articles

Articles appear in newspapers and periodicals (journals or magazines). While newspapers are usually published daily, magazines are usually published weekly or monthly, and journals are published quarterly or even biannually. The following samples are for print articles only.

General Format

Article Title:
Article titles are always in quotation marks.

Ellison, Harlan. "Strangers in a Strange Land."
Newsweek 7 Apr. 1997: 49. Print.

Publication Medium:
End with the publication medium (in this case, Print) followed by a period.

Author Name:
Regardless of the type of source, the author name is inverted. The same rules apply for all sources.

Publication Date:
For weekly or biweekly magazines, include the date (day, month, and year) directly after the title of the publication. (For all types of sources, abbreviate all months except May, June, and July.) For monthly magazines, give the month or months (e.g., Sept.–Oct.) and year.

Periodical Title:
The title of the magazine, journal, or newspaper is italicized.

Page Numbers:
End with the specific page number(s) on which the article appears. If the article covers several consecutive pages, include the range (such as 52–75). If the page numbers are not consecutive, include the first page number, immediately followed by a plus sign (such as 64+). Place a colon after the date and before page numbers.

Article in a Newspaper

> Gabriel, Trip. "Learning in Dorm, Because Class Is on
> the Web." *New York Times* 4 Nov. 2010. A1+. Print.

After the author, if one appears, list the title of the article and the publication. Exclude introductory articles *(a, an, the)* from publication titles. Add the city name in square brackets if it does not appear in the title of the newspaper and the newspaper is local. Add section letters before the page numbers. As with magazine articles, if the page numbers are not consecutive, list the first page number, immediately followed by a plus sign. End with the medium consulted.

Article in a Journal

If an academic journal provides both the volume and issue numbers, provide both in your citation. Otherwise, simply provide the volume number.

> Horner, Bruce, and Min-Zhan Lu. "Working Rhetoric
> and Composition." *College English* 72.5 (2010):
> 470–94. Print.

The volume and issue numbers (separated by a period) come directly after the journal title. The year is in parentheses, followed by a colon and the inclusive page numbers. End with the medium consulted.

Article Reprinted in an Anthology (Such as a College Textbook)

> Faigley, Lester. "Judging Writing, Judging Selves."
> *College Composition and Communication* 40.4
> (1989): 395–412. Rpt. in *Landmark Essays on Voice
> and Writing.* Ed. Peter Elbow. Davis: Hermagoras,
> 1994. 107–20. Print.

First use the basic article format with the information of the original publication. Then add *Rpt. in* (abbreviation for "Reprinted in") and include the information for the anthology. End with the page numbers on which the article appears, followed by the medium of publication.

Encyclopedia Article

> "Writing." *Encyclopaedia Britannica.* 15th ed. 2005. Print.

Begin with an author name (inverted) if one is given. (Check for author names at the beginning or end of the article.) Put the title of the article in quotation marks, and italicize the encyclopedia title. End with the edition, year, and medium of publication.

Other Sources

Government Publication

> United States. Dept. of Education. *Nontraditional*
> *Education: Alternative Ways to Earn Your*
> *Credentials.* Washington: GPO, 2003. Print.

If an author is not given, list the name of the government first, followed by the agency. The title follows, and then the publication information. Many federal publications are published by the Government Printing Office.

Pamphlet

> Masonic Information Center. *A Response to Critics*
> *of Freemasonry.* Silver Spring: Masonic Services
> Assn., n.d. Print.

Give information in the same format as a book. Use abbreviations to indicate missing publication information: *n.p.* (no publisher or no place), *n.d.* (no date of publication), and *n. pag.* (no page numbers).

Personal Interview

> Jackson, Lynn. Personal interview. 4 Mar. 2010.

Begin with the name of the interviewee, inverted. End with the interview date.

Personal Letter or Memo

> Bosley, Cindy. Letter to the author. 15 Nov. 2009. TS.

Like all sources, begin with the author name (inverted). Then give the title or description of the letter. End with the date and medium of publication (*TS* for "typescript" and *MS* for "manuscript").

Published Letter

> Tolkien, J. R. R. "To Christopher Tolkien." 18 Jan.
> 1944. Letter 55 of *The Letters of J. R. R. Tolkien.* Ed.
> Humphrey Carpenter and Christopher Tolkien.
> New York: Houghton, 2000. 67–68. Print.

After the date of the letter, give the number of the letter, if available. List the information of the source in which the letter was published, according to the correct format for the source. (In other words, if the letter is published in a book, as above, follow the book format.)

Television Program

> "A Streetcar Named Marge." *The Simpsons.* Prod. Al Jean and Mike Reiss. FOX. KTVU, San Francisco, 10 Oct. 2007. Television.

Begin with the title of the episode or segment (in quotation marks). Italicize the title of the program. Name the creator, producer, director, narrator, performer, or writer (if pertinent); network; call letters; and city of the television station (if appropriate and available). End with the broadcast date and medium of reception.

Film

> *Monty Python's The Meaning of Life.* Dir. Terry Jones and Terry Gilliam. 1983. Universal Studios Home Entertainment, 2005. DVD.

After the title (italicized), list the director(s), the year of original release, the distributor, the year of rerelease, and the type of medium (such as *DVD* or *Videocassette*) on which you viewed the film.

Sound Recording

> Pearl Jam. "Jeremy." *Rearviewmirror.* Sony, 2004. CD.

Begin with the artist's name. Then list the title of a particular song or section (in quotation marks), the collection title (italicized), the recording company, and the year of release. All of this information is available on the product sleeve or insert. End with the medium (*Audiocassette, Audiotape, CD, LP*), followed by a period.

Lecture or Speech

> Parmuk, Orhan. "My Father's Suitcase." Swedish Academy, Stockholm. 7 Dec. 2006. Nobel lecture.

Begin with the speaker's name (inverted). Then list the title of the presentation (in quotation marks), the name of the meeting and sponsoring organization (if applicable), the location of the lecture, the date, and a descriptive label (such as *Address* or *Lecture*).

Advertisement

> Kahlua. Advertisement. *Every Day with Rachael Ray.* Dec.–Jan. 2011: 22. Print.

Begin with the company or product name, followed by *Advertisement*. Then list the relevant publication information. For instance, if the ad appears in a periodical, list the information in the appropriate format and end with the page number and publication medium.

Work of Art (Painting, Sculpture, Photograph)

O'Keefe, Georgia. *Evening Star No. VI.* 1917.

Watercolor. Georgia O'Keefe Museum, Santa Fe.

Include the artist's name (inverted), the title of the work (italicized), the date of composition (if unavailable, use *N.d.*), the medium of composition, the collector or institution that houses it, and the city where it is held.

Performance

Of Mice and Men. By John Steinbeck. Dir. Martha

Henry. Perf. Graham Greene and Nicolas van

Burek. Tom Patterson Theatre, Stratford. 21 June

2007. Performance.

Begin with the title (italicized), the author of the performed work (if applicable), the director, the performers, the site of the performance, the date, and the descriptive label *Performance*.

Electronic Sources

Like print sources, citations for electronic sources require author(s), title, publication information, and date. Authors and titles are formatted in the same manner as for print sources. However, for electronic sources, the rules for publication information change. The primary difference is that all entries for electronic sources require the date on which the source was accessed. The 7th edition of the *MLA Handbook for Writers of Research Papers* indicates that a Uniform Resource Locator (URL) should be provided only when your reader is unlikely to be able to locate the source without it. If a URL appears in a citation, enclose it in angle brackets and end with a period.

Often, electronic sources originally appeared in print and have been uploaded to an electronic environment.

Journal Article from an Online Database

Edwards, Clifford H. "Grade Inflation: The Effects on Educational Quality and Personal Well-Being." *Education* 120.3 (2000): n. pag. *Academic Search Elite.* Web. 10 Apr. 2010.

First cite as a print article. Note that databases do not always list the entire page range of an article. In that case, use *n. pag.* for "no pagination," as shown above. Then list the name of the database, the medium of publication (*Web*), and the date of access.

Magazine Article from an Online Database

Stanglin, Douglas, and Amy Bernstein. "Making the Grade." *U.S. News and World Report.* 4 Nov. 1996: 18. *Academic Search Elite.* Web. 10 Apr. 2010.

Apply the rules of the previous sample entry. However, notice the difference between journals and magazines: Magazine entries do not require volume or issue numbers, and the date is not given in parentheses.

Abstract

Zsolnai, Laszlo. "Honesty versus Cooperation: A Reinterpretation of the Moral Behavior of Economics Students." Abstract. *American Journal of Economics and Sociology* 62.4 (2003): 707–12. *General BusinessFile ASAP.* Web. 10 Apr. 2007.

Include the information for the source in the appropriate format. Add the description *Abstract,* and as usual, end with the date of access.

Online Book

McCreight, M. I. *Chief Flying Hawk's Tales: The True Story of Custer's Last Fight.* New York: Alliance, 1936. *Online Books.* Ed. John Mark Ockerbloom. U of Pennsylvania. Web. 15 May 2010.

Follow the format for print books. Italicize the title of the website. If the book is part of an online scholarly project, which is often the case, include the sponsoring institution. At the end of the entry, add the publication medium and date of access.

Article in an Online Journal

Silva, Mary Cipriano, and Ruth Ludwick. "Interstate Nursing Practice and Regulation: Ethical Issues for the 21st Century." *Online Journal of Issues in Nursing* 5.3 (1999): n. pag. Web. 10 Aug. 2010.

Follow the format for print articles. After the date of publication, give the range of pages (if unavailable, use *n. pag.*) and the publication medium. At the end of the entry, add the date of access.

Website

Bioneers. Collective Heritage Inst., 2007. Web. 16 July 2010.

Begin with the title of the site (italicized). If the site has no title, offer a description, such as *Home page* (not italicized) in its place. Next, give the name of any sponsoring or supporting institution or organization, the date of electronic publication or the latest update (if available), the publication medium, and the date that you accessed the site.

Article from a Website

"GM Reports Upbeat Earnings; CEO to Leave." *MSNBC.com*. Microsoft, 12 Aug. 2010. Web. 13 Aug. 2010.

Marvin, Cate. "'Tell All the Truth but Tell It Slant': First-Person Usage in Poetry." *Poets.org*. Acad. of Amer. Poets, 2007. Web. 28 July 2010.

Begin with the author (if available) or, if unavailable, the title of the article. Next, give the name of the website, followed by the sponsor of the site and the date of the article (if available) or most recent update. Always end with the publication medium and the date that you accessed the site.

Web Log (Blog)

"Lite a Joint, Fight Cancer." *A Big Fat Slob.* Google, 19
Apr. 2007. Web. 2 Aug. 2010.

Begin with the author (if available) or, if unavailable, the title of the blog entry. Next,
give the name of the website, followed by the sponsor of the site and the date of the
entry (if available). Always end with the publication medium and the date that you
accessed the site.

E-mail

Miller, Maria. "Changes to Physics Dept." Message to
Dennis John. 23 Nov. 2007. E-mail.

Begin with the author of the e-mail. Then list the title (in quotation marks) that
appears in the subject line of the e-mail, the name of the recipient, and the date the
e-mail was sent. (If you are the recipient, write *Message to the author.*) End with the
medium of delivery (*E-mail*).

Online/Listserver Posting

Brandywine, Jacob. "Raising Standards." Online posting. *Writing Program Forum.* Northern Michigan
Coll., 26 Apr. 2005. Web. 25 May 2010.

Add the descriptor *Online posting* after the title. Then give the name of the listserver
or forum, the sponsoring institution, the date of the posting, the publication
medium, and the date of access.

CD-ROM

Trigonometry Explorer. Chevy Chase: Cognitive
Technologies, 1996. CD-ROM.

If no author is given, use the editor, compiler, or translator's name, with the
abbreviation *(ed., comp., trans.),* in its place. If none of these is listed, begin with the
title. Then list publication information (city, company, date). End with *CD-ROM.*

Online Encyclopedia

"Spanish Inquisition." *Wikipedia.* Wikimedia
Foundation, 26 Aug. 2007. Web. 7 Aug. 2010.

As with a print encyclopedia, begin with the title of the article if no author is listed.
Then list the title of the encyclopedia, the sponsoring organization, the publication
date (if available), the publication medium, and the date of access.

APA Documentation Style

The information in the in-text citation should correspond directly with the References page (the APA equivalent of a Works Cited page).

"Replacing the harmful inherited myths about our menstrual cycles with accurate information is part of women's healing" (**Northrup,** 1998, p. 113).

Northrup is used in parentheses because **Northrup** is the first word in the References entry for that source.

References

Northrup, C. (1998). *Women's bodies, women's wisdom.* New York, NY: Bantam.

In-Text Citation In-text documentation for APA involves referencing the original text in parentheses within the actual sentences of your text. An in-text citation must occur whenever a writer:

- Quotes directly from a source.
- Paraphrases ideas from a source.
- Summarizes ideas from a source.
- References statistics or data from a source.

For direct quotes, APA in-text citations should include the author's name, date (year only) of the source, and page number from which the cited material is taken. Unless an electronic source is based on a print source (as in a PDF), omit page numbers from the in-text citation when not given online. Include the author's name in the citation unless it is given within the sentence.

> "After months of exhausting research, they had finally come to understand the problem with their design" (Smith, 1998, p. 82).

Commas separate elements within the parentheses. The abbreviation *p.* ("page") or *pp.* ("pages") comes before the actual page number(s). End punctuation comes after the parenthetical citation.

Writers using APA style often include the date directly after the author's name in the sentence because timeliness is so important to researchers in the social sciences and other fields that use APA style.

> Emphasizing her point, Miller (2000) demands that "it is now time for something drastic to change here on campus" (p. 43).

If the source has no author, use the first words of the source title and punctuate the title accordingly (either with quotation marks or italics).

> "Even though most of the nation's coastal shorelines can no longer sustain a full range of sea life, the vast majority of Americans seem unconcerned" ("Dead Seas," 2001, p. 27).

If the source has two authors, use the last name of both authors. Notice that APA style uses an ampersand (&) instead of the word *and* in parenthetical citations.

> (Lunsford & Ede, 1994, p. 158)

If the source has three, four, or five authors, use the last name of all authors in your first parenthetical citation. In following citations, use the last name of the first author, followed by *et al.* and the year.

> (Sanger, Cunningham, & Toy, 2003, p. 46)

> (Sanger et al., 2003, p. 46)

If the cited material is quoted in another source, cite the source in which you found the quotation and add *as cited in* before the author name or title:

> (as cited in Smith, 1998, p. 82)

If you want to acknowledge more than one source for the same information, use a semicolon between citations within one set of parentheses. List the authors alphabetically. If you are citing more than one work by the same author, list the citations by date, separated by commas:

> (Lunsford & Ede, 2003; Smith, 1998)

> (Parkinson, 1999, 2002)

References The reference list includes the sources that are directly cited in the text. (A bibliography, on the other hand, lists all the sources that a writer has read and digested in the process of researching the project.) The first piece of information in each References entry should correspond to the in-text citation. For example, on page 437, notice the relationship between the in-text citation for Northrup and the entire bibliographic information in the References list.

Entries in a References list must follow strict formatting guidelines, but the process is easy if you know the formulas involved. Despite the differences between sources, all entries give the same type of information in the same order:

1. Author name

2. Date of publication

3. Title of the work

4. Title of the bigger work (book, magazine, newspaper, etc.), if applicable

5. Page numbers, if applicable

6. Place of publication or distribution

7. Publishing or broadcasting company

8. For electronic sources: Retrieval date (if source is likely to change) and DOI (digital object locator) or homepage URL

Each type of source (book, journal article, online magazine, etc.) may require some slight changes in the formula, but the order of information always follows the above pattern. Also, all entries (regardless of the source) adhere to a definite format.

- **Author names, inverted, come first.** First and middle names are always indicated with initials only. Unlike MLA style, all author names are inverted.
- **Dates come in parentheses directly after the author name.** If no author appears on the source, the title comes first.
- **Title of the work comes directly after the date.** Article titles are always in regular type without quotation marks, while the sources in which they appear—newspapers, books, magazines, and journals— are italicized. Only the first letter of the title is capitalized in article and book titles except for proper nouns. For newspaper, magazine, and journal titles, capitalize all words longer than three letters.
- **Publication information follows the title of the source.**
- **If the source is a print article, page numbers come last.** If the source is electronic, the date of access (if needed) and DOI or URL come last.

Printed Books

All of the necessary information for books can usually be found on the title and copyright pages, which are inside the front cover.

General Format

Title:
The first word of the title or subtitle is capitalized, as well as any proper nouns. The title is italicized.

Ridl, J. (2009). *Losing season.* Fort Lee, NJ: CavanKerry Press.

Author Name:
Give author last name and initials of first and middle name (if available).

Publishing Company:
Place a colon between the city (or state) and publishing company. End with the company name.

Publication Date:
Comes directly after the author name and goes in parentheses.

Two or More Authors

Murphy, J. J., & Duncan, B. L. (2007). *Brief intervention for school problems: Outcome-informed strategies.* New York, NY: Guilford Press.

Add any additional author names, also inverted, before the title.

Corporate Author

Federation of U.S. Midwives. (2001). *Listening to the mother.* Heathrow, FL: Author.

Use the name of the corporation for the author name. If the corporate author also published the text, write *Author* for the publisher.

Subsequent Editions

> Lauwers, J., & Swisher, A. (2010). *Counseling the nurs-ing mother* (5th ed.). Sudbury, MA: Jones and Bartlett.

Find the edition information on the title page of the book, and write the information in the entry directly after the title. Use abbreviations *2nd ed.*, *3rd ed.*, and so on, or *Rev. ed.* for "Revised edition."

Edited Book

> Beer, M. B., & Nohria, N. S. (Eds.). (2000). *Breaking the code of change.* Boston, MA: Harvard Business School Press.

Use the editor's name (last name and first and middle initials) and *Ed.* (for "editor"). Use *Eds.* ("editors") if the book has more than one editor.

Translated Book

> Freire, P. (1995). *Pedagogy of the oppressed* (M. B. Ramos, Trans.). New York, NY: Continuum. (Original work published 1970).

Add the translator's name (first and middle initials and last name) and *Trans.* (all in parentheses) after the title of the book.

Printed Articles

Articles appear in newspapers and periodicals (journals or magazines). While newspapers are usually published daily, magazines are usually published weekly or monthly, and journals are published quarterly or even biannually.

Article in a Magazine

> Appenzeller, T. (2007, June). The big thaw. *National Geographic, 211,* 56–71.

Include the date (year, month, day) directly after the author name. Do not abbreviate months. Give the volume number in italics after the magazine title, followed by issue number (if available) in parenthesis. End with the page numbers of the article.

Article in a Newspaper

Debate rages over whether Katrina is still killing. (2007, June 3). *The Salt Lake Tribune*, p. A18.

If no author appears, give the title of the article first, followed by the date. After the title of the newspaper, include any section letters before the page numbers.

Article in a Journal Paginated Continuously

Most academic journals number the pages of each issue continuously through an annual volume. The second issue does not begin with page 1, but with the number after the last page of the previous issue.

Fiske, S. T. (2010). Envy up, scorn down: How comparison divides us. *American Psychologist, 65,* 698–706.

Place the volume number in italics directly after the journal title, before the page numbers.

Article or Chapter in an Edited Book

Batt, H. W. (2001). Value capture as a policy tool in transportation economics. In L. S. Moss (Ed.), *City and country* (pp. 195–228). Malden, MA: Blackwell.

After the author and date, give the title of the article/chapter. Then write *In* and the first and middle initials and last name of the editor(s). The abbreviation *Ed.* or *Eds.* (in parentheses) should follow the editor(s). End with the title of the book, the page numbers on which the article or chapter appears, and the publication information.

Encyclopedia Article

Aesthetics. (2005). In *Encyclopaedia Britannica* (15th ed., Vol. 13, pp. 9–23). Chicago, IL: Encyclopaedia Britannica.

Begin with the author (if given) and date. Then give the title of the article. The name of the encyclopedia (after *In*) should be in italics. The volume number and page number(s) should be in parentheses.

Other Printed Sources

Brochure

> Masonic Information Center. (n.d.). *A response to crit-*
> *ics of freemasonry* [Brochure]. Silver Spring, MD:
> Masonic Services Association.

Use *n.d.* to indicate "no date," which is often necessary for brochures. After the title, add the descriptor *Brochure* in square brackets before the publication information.

Personal Interview or Letter

APA style recommends citing personal communications only with in-text citations—not in the References. In the in-text citation, give the name of the interviewee, the title *personal communication,* and the date.

> (L. Jackson, personal communication, March 4, 2010).

Television Program

> Martin, J. (Writer), & Moore, R. (Director). (1992). A
> streetcar named Marge [Television series episode].
> In A. Jean & M. Reiss (Producers), *The Simpsons.*
> Los Angeles, CA: Twentieth Century Fox.

Begin with the name and title of the script writer, then the name and title of the director and the date. Give the title of the episode or segment, followed by *Television series episode* in square brackets. Next, list the producer and the title of the program (italicized). End with the city and state (of the broadcasting company) and the company name.

Government Publication

> U.S. Census Bureau. (2010). *Statistical abstract of the*
> *United States.* Washington, DC: U.S. Government
> Printing Office.

If no author is given, use the government agency as the author, followed by the date, the title (in italics), and the publication information that appears on the title page. If a report number is given, include that information in parenthesis just after the title.

Electronic Sources

As with print sources, citations for electronic sources require author(s), publication date, title, and publication information. Authors and titles are formatted in the same manner as print sources. The difference occurs with publication information: Publishers of electronic work sometimes assign a digital object identifier, which is a kind of persistent virtual address. The DOI is sometimes, not always, located at the top of the article. If a source has a DOI, you need not include a retrieval date or URL. If no DOI was assigned, however, provide a URL. When adding the URL to your citation, break it only before punctuation and do not add hyphens. The APA Style Guide says, "No retrieval date is necessary for content that is not likely to be changed or updated, such as a journal article or book." In other words, if the content is likely to stay the same, no retrieval date is needed. Especially with electronic sources, remember the basic principle behind citing sources: *to provide a guide for finding the sources you used.*

Activity

In small groups, discuss the following:

1. The APA Style Guide urges researchers not to put the name of a database in a reference—even if the source was retrieved from a database. Imagine APA's reasoning.

2. APA invites researchers to use DOIs when possible. But much of the information on the Internet has not been assigned a DOI. How would you, then, deal with that discrepancy?

3. Given that style guides like those of MLA and APA cannot account for every emerging type of source, what should researchers do? How should writers and researches develop a uniform strategy for documenting their work?

Article in an Online Journal or Retrieved from a Database

Nolan, K. P., & Harold, C. M. (2010, September). Fit with what? The influence of multiple self-concept images on organizational attraction. *Journal of Occupational & Organizational Psychology, 83,* 645–662. doi:10.1348/096317909X465452

If the article has a DOI assigned, include that after the same information you would provide for a print article.

Pavur, Claude. (2009, November). Classical Humanism has everything to do with justice. *Electronic Antiquity, 13*(1). Retrieved from http://scholar.lib .vt.edu/ejournals/ElAnt

If the article does not have a DOI assigned, include the URL for the journal's home page after the words *Retrieved from*. If the journal is published only electronically, it may not have page numbers, in which case none appear in the References entry.

Website

American Society for Aesthetics. (n.d.). *Aesthetics on-line.* Retrieved August 10, 2010, from http://www .aesthetics-online.org

As with all sources in APA format, begin with the author's or editor's name(s) (inverted), if available, and the date of electronic publication. Give the title of the site (italicized). Write *Retrieved* and then the date of access (if the information is likely to be edited or revised), followed by *from* and the URL (no final period).

Article from a Website

Hart, P., & Jackson, J. (2006, May/June). Stossel's "stupid" schools. *Fairness & Accuracy in Reporting.* Retrieved from http://www.fair.org/

Sample Research Essays

Sample MLA-Style Research Essay

Tengelitsch 1

Samantha Tengelitsch
Professor Jones
English 111
17 December 2010

Sage Femme: An Argument in Support of Home Birth

Last Sunday, I gave birth at home. It was my third baby, second homebirth. Nobody delivered my baby; I did it—on my bed, holding on to my husband with the support of a certified midwife and her apprentice. My children were in the other room sleeping soundly. My mother was downstairs on the couch, waiting to hear the baby's first cries. Another friend, who had helped watch my children as I labored throughout the day, slept on the floor beside the bed where my children slept. The dog took little notice. Laboring and birthing at home seemed as normal as the spaghetti we had had for dinner that night.

> Begins with personal narrative.

My husband and I chose homebirth for our second and third babies and a local midwife to serve as guardian over these births. The practice of midwifery is ancient. Midwives have attended women at home for hundreds of thousands of years, with knowledge passed from one generation to the next. The majority of traditional midwives are educated through apprenticeships. They understand that birth is a normal event in a woman's life and allow this process to unfold naturally with little to no intervention.

> Provides relevant background information about midwifery.

In other countries around the world women labor and birth in the safety and comfort of their own homes. Consequently, women in these countries experience less obstetrical intervention and lower infant/maternal mortality rates. One study conducted in the Netherlands reported that "women who had given birth previously had significantly better outcomes in planned home births" (Brodsky 92). Sound scientific evidence has proven in recent years that midwives are as safe as or safer than doctors for primary care and using midwives greatly reduces the rates of unnecessary obstetrical interventions (Wagner 1226). Despite this, the United States has seen a dramatic decrease in home-based maternity care in the last century: In 1900 less than five percent of women gave birth in a hospital; by 1940 half of all women, and seventy-five percent of all urban women, had their children in a hospital (Edmonson and Kassen). While the United States Centers for Disease Control reports a slight increase in home births for the period 2005–06, they account for only 0.59% of all births.

> Uses research to argue about advantages of homebirth.

The decline of midwifery in the United States from the early 1900s to the present is due in part to misconceptions about midwifery and in part to the introduction of man-midwives (later called "obstetricians") into the birth space. Significant advancements at the turn of the century in human understanding of the anatomy and physiology of birth helped spur the *medicalization* of childbirth. In their article "The Homebirth Choice," Jill Cohen and Marti Dorsey write:

> Since women were barred from attending medical schools, men became the birth practitioners. Having never had a baby themselves, they were unable to approach women and childbirth with the inner knowledge and experience of a woman. Childbirth became viewed as pathological rather than natural. Medical techniques and interventions that were unnecessary and often dangerous became commonplace.

Midwifery changed rapidly as midwives were unable to obtain licensures and in some cases even forbidden to legally practice.

When my husband and I first informed our family of the decision to have our second child at home, the question most often posed was, "Why would you want to do that?" There was confusion over why I wanted to experience birth, including the pain of labor. And despite the evidence for the safety of homebirth, misconceptions lingered that homebirth was dangerous and that we were somehow putting our baby at risk. The opposition came for the most part from the older generation; a generation mostly numb to birth, women who were unconscious or semi-conscious for their deliveries, having been given analgesics like Twilight Sleep.

When their generation was giving birth to ours, hospital protocols called for women to deliver on their backs, their feet in stirrups, their genital hair was shaved, they were given enemas, their perineum was surgically cut, and their babies were often pulled from their bodies with steel forceps as the drugs severely depressed the body's natural urge to "bear down." It is no wonder women of this generation elected to forget the experience of childbirth. Although they were home-born babies themselves, by the time these women were of childbearing age, a medical model had taken the place of midwifery and the hospital swiftly overshadowed home as the most appropriate place to give birth.

When men entered the attendant space, the beauty and empowerment of birth was stripped away in favor of procedure and positions that were better suited for the attendant, rather than the laboring woman. Hospitals enacted protocols to ensure delivery of the baby within twenty-four hours of admittance into the maternity ward. Some of these protocols included inducement or augmentation of labor with synthetic hormones, routine episiotomy, and delivery by Cesarean. The percentage of women in the United States who give birth by major abdominal surgery soared from 5.5% in 1970 (Goer 21) to an astounding 30.2% in 2005, according to the United States Centers for

---

Provides background on the mainstream perspective of childbirth.

Description of hospital protocol for childbirth.

Provides a government statistic as support.

Tengelitsch 3

Disease Control. That is, nearly a third of babies born in the United States today are born surgically. Women are left in the dark about the looming risks of hemorrhage or infection and the ongoing pain associated with major abdominal surgery. Other protocols, such as the dreaded episiotomy, an incision made into the perineum to expedite delivery of the baby's head, are still routine procedures used in hospitals today and are a quintessential example of an obstetrical procedure that persists despite a total lack of evidence in favor of it and a considerable body of evidence against it (Goer 275).

Birth is almost taboo in American culture. The movie and television portrayal of labor and birth is so far askew from normal that it is no wonder women are choosing an intrusive approach to delivering their babies. But I hoped for something less invasive and institutional. When my husband and I found out we were expecting our first baby, we researched our options. We knew we wanted a natural birth and read everything we could find on the topic. It was then that I first noticed a peculiar trend: The books written from the obstetrical point of view emphasized what would be done to me, while the books about homebirth were typically written by women or midwives and told the stories of their births.

Makes an evaluative distinction between the secondary sources on the topic.

These books were inspirational and renewed within me a trust in the process. We interviewed a homebirth midwife, but pressure from our families and the misrepresentation of birth as dangerous in the media deterred us from having the baby at home. We choose to labor in the hospital with a CNM, a certified nurse-midwife. The experience wasn't unpleasant, though we were offered drugs (despite the fact that we had insisted on none) and I was kept on the electronic fetal monitor for short durations throughout the labor, which meant I had to be on my back. Prior to my labor, I had gone so far as to call the hospital to request a list of all procedures and standard protocols. We went in knowing what to expect, armed with knowledge and a newly inspired trust in my body.

As that first labor progressed to the pushing stage, the nurse-midwife had me push while on my back or on my side, but I just wasn't moving the baby down. Pushing felt awkward and uncomfortable. Finally, instinctively, I flipped around onto my hands and knees. I felt suddenly empowered and was able to move with the contractions, pushing as I needed. I ignored the screams of the nurses to *PUSH*! and let my body work the baby out. Within ten minutes, my first daughter was born. No tears, no complications, no cord wrap, no intervention. Just birth, as it has existed for hundreds of thousands of years: unflawed, powerful, and beautiful.

Develops argument through personal narrative (next several paragraphs).

I knew I wanted to be at home the second time around. I needed a space and a woman attendant who would respect my body and allow me to do what I needed to bring the baby into the world. I chose a midwife who lived in town and was certified with a state organization. She had already attended over 250 births and her soft voice and gentle demeanor left me feeling very comfortable. During my labor, she seemed to disappear into the shadows of the room, leaving my husband and me to do our dance.

The second birth was fast and easy. I labored in a tub of warm water and then got up and found myself once again in the familiar hands and knees position, pushing with ease. This time the midwife held onto my husband's hands as our baby came into the world. He, too, felt a sense of empowerment in catching our second daughter as she was born.

Last Sunday, we did it all over again. Same position, same bed, same midwife. All was so familiar. Candles lit the room, my children slept soundly, the dog took little notice. Why wouldn't anyone want this? The pain is fading fast in my memory, replaced with the sights and sounds of labor. The flickering of candles, the midwife's soft touch, my hand in my husband's hands and the reassurance of his presence.

Women actually experience less pain at home. During labor, oxytocin—the hormone which causes contractions and helps the baby to be born—works in harmony with endorphins—the body's own pain-relieving hormone. During a homebirth, the woman's body will release these hormones according to her needs and she will usually cope well with the sensation of labor (Wickham). The pain of labor is what guides our bodies into the position best suited for birth. Squatting and kneeling (the position I naturally assume in labor) have remained some of the most common postures in traditional cultures throughout the world (Kitzinger). As the baby's head descends into the birth canal, these positions take pressure off of the perineum, decreasing the chance of tearing. They also open the pelvis and allow more room for the baby to maneuver.

Back at the hospital, my fellow new mothers are delivering on their backs. Many are suffering from unnecessary procedures such as episiotomy due in part to the supine position and in part because this is simply the way it has been done in hospitals for the last half-century despite warnings to the contrary from the World Health Organization (WHO). In its report "Classification of Practices in Normal Birth," the WHO suggests both the "freedom in position and movement throughout labor" and "encouragement of non-supine position in labor."

In the supine, or on-the-back position, women are more likely to feel vulnerable; it's a death position, a sleep position. In their book *Women Giving Birth*, Astrid Limburg and Beatrijs Smulders describe the vital importance of a non-supine position:

> The upright position is an optimistic position, making [a woman] feel strong. She can trust her body, which has been made to give birth and deliver with her own strength. She has equal status with those around her. This is not the case when a woman is in the supine position. She

Refers to authority—the World Health Organization. The authority supports the point stated at the beginning of the paragraph.

Blends information from source into text. See pages 395–410.

The quotation supports and extends the idea stated at the top of the paragraph.

Tengelitsch 5

lies in a bed as if ill, and people tower above her, making her feel small and dependent. When the delivery does not go smoothly, she tends to surrender to the specialist and gives up responsibility. (2)

The supine position is simply not conducive to birthing. *Would you poop lying down? Of course not*! Gravity is beneficial! Upright positions encourage the baby to move down into the birth canal and are often far more comfortable for laboring women. Movement is essential in speeding up or maintaining good momentum in labor and yet, in the hospital, women are limited not only by their sterile surroundings, but also by tradition and technology. While I'm not suggesting that all medical advancements are without merit, some are simply used too often and in many cases incite, rather than prevent, further intervention.

Qualifier: Not all medical advancements are without merit.

In addition to external interventions, drugs are still a major part of the birth equation in hospitals. The majority of women are opting to say no to the pain of labor, with more than 90% of women receiving significant pain relief during their deliveries (Rooks).

Sheila Kitzinger, world-renowned midwife and birth advocate, writes, "It is ironic that the phrase 'Just say no,' invented for the anti-drug campaign, is now being used to promote drugs for pain relief" (284). Women are more likely to request pain relief and less likely to experience normal birth when they are in a space that elicits feelings of vulnerability or fear. (A hospital in itself is a place for sick people, so the association is immediately negative for many.) Drugs, especially epidural medication, leave women without the ability to move about freely and they have side effects that doctors must address. According to Judith Rooks, a certified nurse midwife:

Quotes an authority—Kitzinger. In an appositive phrase describes her credentials.

> Women who have epidurals often need additional procedures, treatments and other elements of care to deal with the unintended effects of epidurals, including oxytocin to strengthen labor, an intravenous infusion (to prevent hypovolemia and hypotension), urinary catheters, continuous electronic fetal monitoring, and forceps or vacuum to deliver the baby. Depending on which drugs are used, the women may need medications and personal care and support to deal with itching, nausea, vomiting, and shivering.

Soon the body is no longer laboring; the entire process has been augmented by the so-called "miracle" of modern medicine.

However, when women are left alone to labor as they wish, they reach into a place that is older than our hospitals and our medical invention and birth from within.

Homebirth isn't for everyone. In some cases, women need to be in the hospital setting. We are, however, the only country that relies on routine obstetrical care for all women, despite their risk factors. Perhaps if we

Concession: Homebirth isn't for everybody.

Tengelitsch 6

Concludes with appeal to value:

Home is familiar and intimate.

began treating women like thinking individuals, if we returned the trust in them, women would not feel obligated to choose a hospital delivery. They would recognize the safety and comfort of their own homes and likely opt to stay there during their births, where they can labor standing, sitting, squatting, in a tub of warm water or on their hands and knees. In a place where they are surrounded by family and friends, where their children sleep soundly in the other room, and where the dog takes little notice.

Works Cited

Brodsky, Archie. "Midwifery's Rebirth." *National Review* 11 Aug. 1997: 46+. *Academic Search Elite.* Web. 1 Dec. 2010.

"Classification of Practices in Normal Birth." *World Health Organization.* World Health Organization, 2004. Web. 19 Nov. 2010.

Cohen, Jill. "The Homebirth Choice." *Midwifery Today.* Midwifery Today, Sept. 2008. Web. 22 Nov. 2010.

Edmonson, James M., and Julian Kassen. "Obstetrical Literature and the Changing Character of Childbirth." *Dittrick Medical History Center.* Case Western Reserve U, 2002. Web. 22 Nov. 2010.

Feldhusen, Adrian E. "The History of Midwifery and Childbirth in America: A Time Line." *Midwifery Today.* Midwifery Today, July 2001. Web. 19 Nov. 2010.

Goer, Henri. *Obstetric Myths versus Research Realities: A Guide to the Medical Literature.* Westport: Bergin, 1995. Print.

Kitzinger, Sheila. "Who Would Choose to Have a Caesarean?" *British Journal of Midwifery* 9 (2001): 284–85. Print.

Limburg, Astrid, and Beatrijs Smulders. *Women Giving Birth.* Berkeley: Celestial Arts, 1993. Print.

Rooks, Judith P. "Epidural Analgesia as Used During Childbirth in the United States." *Japanese Journal for Midwives* 54.10 (2000): 9–14. *MidwifeInfo.* Ed. Nancy Sullivan. MidwifeInfo, n.d. Web. 22 Nov. 2010.

United States. Dept. of Health and Human Services. Centers for Disease Control and Prevention. Natl. Center for Health Statistics. *Births: Preliminary Data for 2005.* By Brady E. Hamilton, Joyce A. Martin, and Stephanie J. Ventura. 2006. *National Center for Health Statistics.* Web. 23 Nov. 2007.

———.———.Centers for Disease Control and Prevention. Natl. Vital Statistics Reports. *Trends and Characteristics of Home and Other Out-of-Hospital Births in the United States, 1990–2006.* By Marian F. MacDorman, Fay Menacker, and Eugene Declercq. 2010. *National Center for Health Statistics.* Web. 11 Nov. 2010.

Wagner, Marsden. "Midwifery in the Industrialized World." *Journal of the Society of Obstetricians and Gynaecologists of Canada* 20.13. (1998): 1225–34. Print.

Wickham, Sarah. "Homebirth: What Are the Issues?" *Midwifery Today.* Midwifery Today, May 1999. Web. 19 Nov. 2010.

Sample APA-Style Research Paper

Running head: FILLING IN THE BUBBLES   1

Filling in the Bubbles:
An Investigation of Standardized Tests

Kate Pottoff
Northwestern Michigan College

FILLING IN THE BUBBLES 2

Filling in the Bubbles:
An Investigation of Standardized Tests

It is inevitable. It is no use trying to escape or avoid it; at some point during everyone's academic career, he or she will be required to take a standardized test. Everyone knows the routine: The alarm clock going off at a ridiculous hour of the morning prompting a search for that early-morning coffee on the way to the testing facility. People are then directed to the proper seat, and for the duration of the day they are expected to take the infamous test. The desks are too small for comfort, the pencil tips eventually dull filling in the bubbles, and soon hands start to shake and sweat as students realize they are taking the first step towards their future.

But what if this test does not measure aptitude and, by extension, intelligence, like it is assumed to? Suddenly, the weight society places on test scores seems a little skewed. The SAT and ACT have been used to evaluate future college students for decades now, and just recently the integrity of these tests has been questioned. It is becoming more and more apparent that perhaps standardized testing, specifically the SAT and ACT, does not provide an accurate portrayal of an individual's intelligence and should be weighted accordingly by college admissions personnel.

Standardized testing is under current scrutiny for good reason. There are many known and even more unknown flaws behind the logic of standardized testing. Over the years, standardized tests have been blamed for favoring certain races and genders and hindering others. As Christina Perez (2002) argues, the SAT does little more than reinforce the gaps in wealth. Ultimately, Perez says, the SAT "tilts the playing field even further against low-income and minority applicants." Cultural biases have shaped test questions as well as format, and the project to erase all biases from the tests is an ongoing process. It is imperative that every student tested is tested fairly, especially in a country where all "men are created equal" and guaranteed equal rights. Equality is a concept that our society has struggled with throughout history. Racism and prejudice towards all groups of people have been condemned and people now expect the same rights as their neighbors, no matter what their race, sex, religion or ethnicity. Those rights should extend to the right to be tested and evaluated fairly. According to the National Center for Fair and Open Testing, many university leaders now realize that "the preoccupation with test scores hinders educational equity and has come at the expense of students' other high school experiences" (n.d.).

General scenario.

Proposes a *line of reasoning*. If A, then B, then C.

Explains that standardized tests are culturally biased.

Quotation from the source supports the main idea of the paragraph.

Standardized admissions tests (such as the SAT, ACT, GRE, and MCAT) fail to predict achievement, and they block access to higher education for otherwise qualified students. For example, when test scores are used to determine eligibility for scholarships, "students of color receive disproportionately fewer scholarships due to their lower test scores" (National Center for Fair and Open Testing, n.d.). And those who doubt the connection between test scores and family income might consider the following: Studies show that good coaching programs can raise a student's score by 100 points or more (National Center for Fair and Open Testing, n.d.). Many of these courses—which teach little more than test-taking strategies—are expensive, costing $800 or more. While the standardized test-makers claim that their tests measure "skills and knowledge learned over a long period of time" (National Center for Fair and Open Testing, n.d.), the coaching programs undermine such claims and expose one type of income-related bias.

Test scores vary by gender, family income, and ethnic group. For the SAT in 2005, males scored 1051 and females scored 1009. Those with a family income over $100,000 scored 1119, while average scores drop consistently in accordance with a drop in family income—$80,000–$100,000: 1063; $70,000–$80,000: 1037; $60,000–$70,000: 1026; $50,000–$60,000: 1014; $40,000–$50,000: 996; $30,000–$40,000: 967; $10,000–$20,000: 906; less than $10,000: 884. Scores vary based on ethnicity as well. Asians, Asian American/Pacific Islanders scored 1091; Whites, 1068; Other Hispanic or Latino, 932; Mexican or Mexican American, 916; African American or Black, 864. Results for the ACT follow the same trends (College Board, 2005). However, there is plenty of evidence to show that these scores do not correlate to intelligence or even success in college. "Colleges that have made the SAT optional report that their applicant pools are more diverse and that there has been no drop off in academic quality" (National Center for Fair and Open Testing, n.d.).

Although these biases are probably far from intentional, they are an injustice all the same. Obviously, the tests are far from perfect, favoring some cultures and even genders over others. Since these tests are not perfect by a long shot, this means the tests themselves are flawed, and we should not be expected to accept the results as a true representation of a person's intelligence. Especially in a culture where test results can determine a student's acceptance into college or make or break an applicant's future career, biased test results cannot be tolerated. If our society is going to weight tests heavily, those tests should at least be fair and unbiased.

Transition to another problem
with standardized testing.

Not only can the practice of standardized testing harm certain groups of individuals by inaccurately measuring their intelligence, it can also harm the way education is viewed in schools. Teachers have been accused of trying to "teach to the test" in order to boost students' scores. This new style of teaching can lead teachers to ignore crucial core elements of the curriculum and classify information as important or irrelevant to the test. But education is not regurgitating answers on a test; it is asking questions, problem solving, and learning to think in new ways. As David Owens (1985), author of *None of the Above: Behind the Myth of Scholastic Aptitude*, puts it, "The cult of mental measurement beguiles us into forgetting that the numbers are less important than the learning they are supposed to represent" (p. xix). To limit education down to a crash course in how to ace the SAT not only hurts students but eventually the society they live in as well by devaluing education and intelligence.

Apparently, the SAT and ACT both have their downfalls. However, perhaps the problem does not begin with inaccurate, biased tests, but with how society views testing in general. Besides these obvious flaws of standardized testing, many more lurk beneath the surface. Standardized testing presumes to measure a person's aptitude for college, and by extension, his or her intelligence, all stemming from only a couple hours of test taking in a classroom. The idea that tests measure intelligence is not a new one; it permeates our culture in every aspect. Whether a person is applying for a driver's license or taking the bar exam, tests are everywhere. They are used as a rite of passage and a measuring tool of accomplishment.

Counterargument: Challenges
the position that tests measure
intelligence.

Smeared throughout life is the notion that tests accurately measure intelligence and competence. However, to assume it is possible to measure a person's intelligence in a single isolated behavior known as "filling in the bubbles" is a stretch. Intelligence is not a black-and-white, tangible aspect of a person; it is a vast gray area, which can only be explored through avenues a little more extensive and involved than filling in dots on a Scantron. Simon Benlow (2004) shares the same view of intelligence. Benlow explores how consumerism has infiltrated academia and promoted passivity in students. He argues that students must take an active role in their learning instead and challenge themselves: "In college, students cannot simply consume knowledge. Even in its most packaged form, the textbook, knowledge must be regenerated, revised, reinterpreted and remembered to be anything beyond an answer on a multiple choice test" (p. 173).

Refers to authority, Benlow, for
support.

Benlow realizes that intelligence is more involved than memorization and regurgitation and values a more intensive view of intelligence, one that standardized testing fails to acknowledge. The majority of most standardized tests are multiple-choice questionnaires, and do not require the critical thinking and creativeness that should be considered an important part of intelligence.

The term "intelligence" refers not only to a person's "textbook knowledge" but also to a person's talents and intellectual skills. "Textbook knowledge" is material essentially copied out of students' books and pasted onto a test page. It is important information, but it is hardly brain surgery. On the other hand, intellectual skills such as creativity, cleverness, inventiveness, and problem-solving abilities all comprise a person's intelligence as well. These skills and abilities are as crucial to intelligence as textbook knowledge. However, measuring these skills poses quite a challenge. Impersonal tests cannot presume to measure these skills. Therefore, test results offer an incomplete portrayal of a person's intelligence. According to Perez (2002), "No matter how promoted, no three-hour test can measure habits of mind such as creativity, perseverance or judgment, so important in college and life." Standardized tests can measure a person's basic knowledge, but fail to factor in the other elements of intelligence.

The source blends in and directly supports the point already stated in the paragraph.

Not only does standardized testing lack the ability to measure a person's entire range of knowledge, but it also assumes people who are knowledgeable will test well. However, due to testing anxiety and improper preparation in high schools, many students have poor test-taking skills. It is easy to imagine how students with inadequate test-taking skills could be at a disadvantage when it comes to the practice of standardized testing. For example, imagine a student, Stacey. Stacey has worked hard throughout high school, performing to her full potential and working hard in all of her classes. When other students were out socializing at football games, shopping with friends, or simply sitting at home on the couch watching television, she was studying. When students were sitting in the hallway before class furiously scribbling answers to material due two weeks ago, she was already planning her approach to the end-of-the-year research project.

Uses a scenario as a support strategy.

However, when it came to the ACT, Stacey's preparations did not pan out. Time after time, she took the test, attending classes and doing test booklets in her spare time, and her score never improved. At the end of her senior year, Stacey ended up as class valedictorian with an almost perfect GPA. Although her work ethic and dedication far exceeded those of her fellow students, Stacey was rejected from many of her choice colleges, colleges that many of her peers were accepted to. Students with lower GPAs, easier classes, and a less impressive work ethic were considered to be more promising college students than she. Undoubtedly, there is something wrong with that picture. Certainly, a student's GPA and study habits should be a better indicator of future success in college than a score on a standardized test. A GPA reflects students' attitudes toward their education

FILLING IN THE BUBBLES 6

and how much they value getting a quality education. A GPA also reflects students' work ethics over an extended period of time, so it should be considered more representative of a student's success or failure than a simple score on a college entrance exam.

Since the practice of standardized testing is flawed, the weight placed upon test scores seems somewhat absurd. As Lemann (1999) recognized, "The [SAT] is widely believed to be the key to admission into a selective college, which in turn is widely believed to be the key to a life of prestige and prosperity. People can't help thinking of the score as a permanent measure of their innate worth." Although some colleges deny that standardized testing contributes heavily to the admissions process, many would disagree. According to Marklein, colleges are still promoting high standardized testing scores. She states, "College admissions deans often downplay the significance of the exam in the application process—but then tout their schools' rising average scores in glossy recruitment brochures" (2002).

Despite the hype over standardized testing scores, some colleges are wising up and eliminating such scores from their admissions process. For example, Chatham College in Pittsburgh has dropped all standardized test score requirements for admissions, and now encourages applicants to submit graded test papers, high school GPA, and portfolios. According to Michael Poll, vice president for admissions, "Standardized tests only reveal verbal and mathematical aptitude within a very controlled environment . . . but Chatham also considers qualities like creativity, ingenuity, leadership or reasoning that better indicate a successful college student" (as cited in Chatham College, 2005). More than 700 accredited bachelor-degree granting institutions no longer require a standard admissions test score for applicants (Chatham College, 2005). The National Center for Fair and Open Testing (n.d.) reports: "Schools that have dropped or sharply restricted their use of standardized admissions tests are widely pleased with the results. Regardless of size or selectivity, these institutions have seen substantial benefits, including increased student diversity, more and better-prepared applicants, and positive reactions from alumni/ae, students, guidance counselors, and the public." And in the fall of 2008, the National Association for College Admission Counseling urged colleges throughout the country to omit both the ACT and SAT as required components of admission. Citing a variety of institution-specific studies, the NACAC argued that ACT and SAT scores may not be the most reliable indicators of college success and may, in fact, skew the entire process of admission (Jaschik, 2008).

Standardized testing fails to take into account flawed testing or the idea that perhaps intelligence cannot be measured by one lone test, but yet, it is still weighted heavily by most colleges. Although the practice of

Uses sources to detail recent attitudes and developments regarding colleges and standardized tests.

Concession: Standardized testing has some merit.

standardized testing has some merit, it may not be the answer to evaluating future college students. Testing has been accepted in our culture because it often *can* measure what an individual does or does not know, but testing is far from a perfect science, and so it should be weighted accordingly.

Many people would argue that standardized testing is the most economical and efficient way of measuring intelligence and predicting performance. However, in the long run, the investment to reduce dependence on standardized testing would pay off. Certainly, portfolios and interviews, combined with previous GPAs, give colleges a more realistic and tangible representation of a person's intelligence than a stack of impersonal and perhaps flawed test scores.

In the end, standardized testing is simply inadequate as a tool to determine potential collegiate success because it fails to measure intelligence accurately. Intelligence is too complex to be measured by a test booklet and accompanying Scantron sheet. Also, biased tests fail to evaluate all people fairly. Testing has its pros as well as its cons, but higher education needs to consider the flaws. Other avenues should be pursued to replace testing, or at the very least, the weight of tests should be reduced significantly.

Counterargument: Many people would argue X. However, Y.

References

Benlow, S. (2004). "Have it your way": Consumerism invades education. In J. Mauk & J. Metz (Eds.), *The composition of everyday life* (2nd ed., pp. 151–153). Boston, MA: Wadsworth.

Chatham College implements "SAT-optional" applications policy. (2005, November 17). *College Campus News.* Retrieved from http://www.collegenews.org

College Board. (2005). College bound seniors 2005. Retrieved from http://professionals.collegeboard.com/data-reports-research/

Jaschik, S. (2008, September 22). Dramatic challenge to SAT and ACT. *Inside higher ed.* Retrieved from http://www.insidehighered.com/news

Lemann, N. (1999, September 6). Behind the SAT. *Newsweek.* Retrieved from http://www.newsweek.com

Marklein, M. B. (2002, August 27). Love it or hate it, the SAT still rules. *USA Today.* Retrieved from http://www.usatoday.com

National Center for Fair and Open Testing. (n.d.). University testing. Retrieved April 11, 2010, from http://www.fairtest.org

Owens, D. (1985). *None of the above: Behind the myth of scholastic aptitude.* Boston, MA: Houghton Mifflin.

Perez, C. (2002, March 28). Get rid of SAT, similar tests. *USA Today.* Retrieved from http://www.usatoday.com

Glossary

Academic Argument A type of argument that focuses on written text in an academic setting. Academic arguments are different from the fleeting hit-'em-when-they-least-expect-it rhetoric of consumer society. Academic arguers explore complexities to develop new ways of thinking on a topic. In academic argument, both claim and support are the result of focused exploration, a sincere attempt to understand other points of view, and a willingness to question one's own current way of thinking. (See Argument; Academic Audience.)

Academic Audience The audience for academic writing (including academic arguments). *Audience* usually refers to a collection of readers rather than one particular person. For example, although instructors ultimately read and assess student writing in college, academic writing most often addresses a broader community of potential readers—not merely the instructor and students in a class but also the community they create as participants in college life. Academic audiences are aware of themselves as an audience and are constantly thinking about the messages being sent and the way the ideas can be received. Academic audiences expect and value qualities that are not expected in popular culture: revelatory rather than familiar points; appeals to logic rather than to emotion; analysis rather than packaging; inclusion rather than exclusion. (See Audience; Academic Argument.)

Ad Hominem (Latin for *to the person*) A logical fallacy that attacks an arguer rather than examining the logic of the argument: *We shouldn't listen to their claims about social justice because those people are crazy.*

Allusion A reference to some bit of public knowledge (from history, current events, popular culture, religion, or literature). Allusions are commonly used to support ideas in formal essays, informal articles, and literary works. Allusions are also common in everyday argument, especially as presented in movies, songs, and TV shows.

You're a real Einstein is an allusion to Albert Einstein, for example, and most audiences will understand what this allusion means. In a sense, allusions are like outside sources because they add depth and meaning to an argument. By making connections to culturally shared bits of knowledge, allusions link an argument to the world beyond it. (See Support.)

Analogy An extended comparison in which two things share several characteristics or qualities, or in which two situations or scenarios are presented as the same. Usually, an unfamiliar or lesser known thing is compared to something more familiar, thereby making the unfamiliar more familiar. Analogies also can be used to bring out a particular quality: *The U.S. military faced the same kind of consistent attacks in Iraq as the Russian military did in Afghanistan. Eventually, the attacks prompted the Russians to pull out their forces.* (See Support.)

Anecdote A short account of a particular event or incident. Anecdotes are often given in the form of a brief story that supports an arguer's point. While testimony, another form of support, comes from an eyewitness ("I saw the train coming around the mountain"), an anecdote is told by the arguer as though he or she were an objective reporter of events ("The incident on the train tracks started with the train coming around the mountain"). The details in an anecdote can provide powerful support because they help to draw an audience into a specific scene. (See Support.)

Antonomasia A figure of speech in which a description of someone is used in place of an actual name, such as *The King of Pop* to refer to Michael Jackson, *The King* to refer to Elvis, or *Ol' Blue Eyes* to refer to Frank Sinatra. (See Figurative Language.)

Appeal A major form of support in argumentation that requires the arguer to *create* a connection between the audience and the topic. Appeals call on the reader's sense of logic, emotion, character, value, or need. They differ from forms of evidence (statistics, facts, illustrations, etc.) in an important way. An arguer can simply point

to something as a fact or statistic. But an appeal must be constructed out of logical steps, shared values, beliefs, or needs; the arguer must *create* the bridge between the topic and the audience. For this reason, Aristotle called appeals *artistic proofs* and forms of evidence *inartistic proofs.*

Appeal to Character (*Ethos*) Drawing attention to the arguer's personal nature, integrity, experience, wisdom, or personality. Appeals to character are an explicit strategy for building trust or confidence in the arguer, which helps the audience to accept the arguer's claims.

Appeal to Emotion (*Pathos*) Connecting the audience's emotions (sympathy, anger, happiness, etc.) to the topic. Appeals to emotion are not usually used in academic arguments.

Appeal to Logic (*Logos*) Engaging the intellectual/reasoning capacity of the audience. Appeals to logic are key in academic argument and constitute the primary rhetorical moves in all academic disciplines. (See Deductive Logic; Inductive Logic; Syllogism; Enthymeme; Logical Fallacies.)

Appeal to Need Making a connection between the topic and a basic human need (food, shelter, belonging, intimacy, self-realization, etc.). Like appeals to value, appeals to need tap into a broad layer of human affairs. They work by reaching inside of an audience, into their essential requirements.

Appeal to Value Making a connection between the topic and a general value (such as fairness, equality, honor, kindness, selflessness, duty, responsibility, economics, pragmatics). While an argument emerges from a particular situation, the claims made in an argument emerge from value systems of its participants. Appeals to value may be the most intense and abundant appeals in popular arguments about political, social, and cultural issues. In everyday life, we often use values to persuade others to accept points: Any argument based on equality, justice, duty, responsibility, security, or honesty is an appeal to value. When arguers can make the connection between a particular point and a broader value, they have tapped into something beyond their particular argument; they have called on the belief system of both the audience and the broader public. (See Ideology.)

Argument The act of asserting, supporting, and defending a claim. Argument is an intellectual and a social process. People are surrounded by argument almost constantly. It can be said that public life is argumentative—that people are vying to be heard, trying to assert their vision of the world to anyone who will hear it. But argument can work in much more subtle ways in the form of advertisements, songs, billboards, posters, slogans, and even stories. While our daily language may not be full of explicit debate, it is full of suggestions about our beliefs. When people make a subtle point about a favorite song or an interesting class, they are suggesting an entire argument, which entails a set of values and assumptions about social worth. (See Academic Argument.)

Arrangement The organization of ideas in an argument. Arrangement involves putting ideas in a particular order and creating connections between those ideas. But it also involves structuring the logic and creating lines of reasoning. When arguers structure ideas, they create the reader's journey through their argument. (See Unity; Coherence; The [Five] Canons of Rhetoric.)

Artistic Proofs Support that must be created by the arguer. Aristotle called appeals *artistic proofs* because the writer must create the bridge between the topic and the audience. Writers also use inartistic proofs (facts, statistics, testimony), which they do not create. Inartistic proofs already exist. (See Appeal; Inartistic Proofs; Support.)

Assumption An assumption is a logical connection between a claim and support. Every argument (every claim and support) contains an assumption that is crucial to its validity. Assumptions are sometimes stated and sometimes unstated. They can be obvious and easily accepted, or hidden and highly debatable. Claim: You should dress nicely for your interview. Support: You want to make a good impression on the employer. Assumption: Dressing nicely makes a good impression on potential employers. (See Warranting Assumptions.)

Audience The people receiving, or potentially receiving, a message (a written, spoken, crafted, or performed argument). Especially in everyday argumentation, a specific audience may be known—a friend, colleague, family member, employer, etc. But in academic writing, *audience* usually refers to a collection of readers rather than one particular person. (See Academic Audience.)

Authorities Experts in a given field who offer specialized knowledge. A type of support, authorities are used in arguments to give credibility to a writer's claims, to illustrate outside or opposing perspectives, to help explain a topic, or to give a sense of popular opinion or historical context. Authorities, or references to outside sources, can be used in a variety of ways, but they usually are used to give an idea credence or believability. (See Support.)

Begging the Question A type of logical fallacy that attempts to prove a claim by using an alternative wording of the claim itself: *We should vote for the school levy because it is the best thing to do.* Also called *circular reasoning.*

The (Five) Canons of Rhetoric Invention, arrangement, style, memory, and delivery. Since classical times, rhetoric has been divided into five categories or canons. (Rhetoric has been thought about and categorized in various other ways as well.) These canons are used as intellectual tools for developing, extending, and shaping ideas.

Claim An assertion made about a given topic. In argument, claims are supported or argued for. An argument consists of a main claim (or thesis) and support. Claims can be categorized as claim of fact, claim of value, or claim of policy.

Claim of Fact A type of claim that argues that a condition exists, has existed, or will exist. We often associate fact with truth (hence, with being beyond dispute), but facts themselves are always in dispute. For instance, a historian must prove that Rome influenced all the societies of Europe; another historian might suggest a region that was beyond the influence of Rome. Claims of fact include *The Roman Empire influenced all of Europe. The Earth is not flat. The Packers will win the Super Bowl this year.*

Claim of Policy A type of claim that argues that some action should be taken or some change made. Claims of policy call for a particular change in behavior, policy, approach, or even attitude: *The Confederate flag should not be flown above a state capital building. Voluntary prayer should be allowed in public schools. We should get out of class early today.*

Claim of Value A type of claim that argues that something has or reflects a particular quality (that it is good, bad, just, unreasonable, practical, unfair, etc.). It may assert approval or disapproval. Any claim that argues the worth of an issue is a claim of value; usually an adjective, or a *predicate of value,* can be found in the claim. For instance, in the following, *good, underhanded,* and *wrong* are all predicates of value: *The Packers are not a very good team this year. The governor's strategies for getting elected are underhanded. Abortion is wrong.*

Coherence The flow and connection of ideas within the text. (See Arrangement.)

Concession Granting value or credit to an opposing claim. Concessions are closely related to *qualifiers,* which acknowledge the limits of one's own claims. Conceding certain points and qualifying others are important strategies for strengthening an argument. When we write arguments, it is easy to become fixated on our own opinions and to draw firm boundaries between our own perspective (which we assume is correct) and others' (which we assume is less correct or flat-out wrong). Concessions allow us as arguers to cling less tightly to our own perspectives, which allows us to invent more nuanced points. This does not mean that *conciliatory* arguments (those that concede points) are wishy-washy. It means that they are more engaged with the opinions swirling around in the rhetorical situation. (See Counterargument; Qualifiers; Rogerian Argument.)

Counterargument Refuting the claims or positions that are opposed to those being forwarded by the arguer. In academic argument, simply projecting one's opinion is not enough. Good arguers must engage what others believe and must take on opposing viewpoints; they must *counterargue.* Perhaps other positions are unethical, unreasonable, logically flawed, or impractical. Whatever their shortcomings, opposing viewpoints must be addressed head on. Dismissing opposing positions too easily can shortchange one's argument. Good arguers carefully examine others' positions, and even try to imagine contrary points, and this helps them draw clear boundaries between their positions and others'. (See Concessions; Qualifiers.)

Deductive Reasoning This type of reasoning builds a conclusion from accepted premises or general principles. Often, this means relying on classes (all dogs, all men, all raincoats, and so on). For example: *All birds* have beaks. Polly the parrot is *a bird.* Therefore, Polly has a beak. Here, a conclusion has been built from a general premise about birds. Deduction may also rely on, or build from, a definitional statement—a statement that says what something is: *Bipeds are* animals with two legs. *Ostriches are* two-legged animals. Therefore, Ostriches are bipeds. Also, notice the definitional statement in the previous example: Polly the parrot *is a bird.* (See Inductive Reasoning.)

Delivery The presentation of ideas in an argument. Delivery is one of the five canons of rhetoric. In ancient Greece, and through much of the history of argument, *delivery* referred to the physical oral performance of an argument. But since the move to written text, it now refers to all the processes involved in presenting ideas to an audience. Although we can make a

distinction between invention (discovering and developing ideas) and delivery (shaping the final presentation of ideas for readers), the two are intertwined, deeply rooted together. As people invent ideas, they often simultaneously think about their readers and even consider certain phrases that might resonate with others. And, as people shape ideas for others, they may also reinvent them. Perhaps the most helpful distinction between invention and delivery is that invention emphasizes the discovery of what the arguer knows, and delivery emphasizes what the audience knows and how it will react. (See The [Five] Canons of Rhetoric.)

Dialectical Reasoning (*Hegelian Logic*) A process of critical thinking put forth by philosopher Georg Wilhelm Friedrich Hegel (1770–1831), who believed that all human thought developed through various stages from personal to social to spiritual. Progression through those stages depends upon a type of reasoning: First, we believe or put forward an idea (thesis); then we inevitably doubt it (antithesis); then we come to new understanding (synthesis). In other words, in order to grow intellectually, we must move beyond our initial ideas (our theses) by doubting. But doubting everything is not complete growth. We must reconcile our doubt with the original thought. In argument, Hegelian logic helps us get beyond our initial opinions (thesis statements) and into increasingly sophisticated ideas. For example:

- Thesis: School uniforms deny students freedom of expression.
- Antithesis: School uniforms do not deny freedom of expression because expression is not exclusively about clothing.
- Synthesis: School uniforms make clothing irrelevant as the sole form of personal expression.

Either/Or Reasoning A type of logical fallacy that offers only two choices when more exist: *You either agree with the policy, or you are anti-American.* (See Logical Fallacies.)

Enthymeme Statements that contain unstated premises or assumptions. *Because*

the dog is scratching at the back door, someone should let her out is an enthymeme because it contains a claim, support, and an unstated premise. The claim is *someone should let the dog out.* The support is *because she is scratching at the back door.* And the unstated premise or warranting assumption is *when the dog scratches at the back door, that means she wants to go outside.* Enthymemes are the most basic form of reasoning in everyday arguments, and they also function in formal arguments. Sometimes unstated premises, or assumptions, are not entirely acceptable, and so an entire argument can be called into question. (See Warranting Assumptions; Syllogism.)

Ethos See Appeal to Character.

Evidence A type of support that includes reference to authority, facts, statistics, and testimonies. Evidence does not require an arguer to create it but only to employ what already exists. Merely mentioning evidence, for example, simply giving a fact, is not usually enough. Arguers must also explain the relevance of the evidence. (See Authorities; Facts; Statistics; Testimony; Support; Appeal.)

Examples Particular occurrences of a phenomenon. Whenever arguers support a claim with particular versions of a point, they are using examples. An example of a horse is Secretariat; an example of a bad idea is diving off a bridge into shallow water. (See Support.)

Exigence The critical moment in a rhetorical situation; the moment that requires someone to speak or write. The exigence is created when something happens (or fails to happen) that calls for someone to speak out and persuade others to think or act in a particular way. An exigence may be something as direct and intense as a power outage, which might prompt an official to persuade everyone to "stay calm" or to "assist those in need." An exigence may be more subtle or complex, like the discovery of a new virus, which might prompt medical officials to persuade the public how to change its behavior. Exigence is part of a situation. It is the critical component that makes people ask the hard questions: What is it? What caused it? What good is it? What are we going to do? What happened? What is going to happen? (See Rhetorical Situation; Stasis Theory; Kairos.)

Facts Agreed-on bits of knowledge that do not require further support in an argument. Facts are verified or verifiable claims. This is not to say that facts cannot be disputed; they often are. But when arguers use a fact, they assume that it carries its own support. (See Support.)

False Analogy A type of logical fallacy that makes a comparison between two things that are ultimately more unlike than alike. The differences between the things compared make the comparison ineffective or unfair, or the comparison misrepresents one or both of the things involved: *Running a college is a lot like running a corporation: if you provide a better service, then you get more customers.* (See Logical Fallacies.)

Faulty Cause/Effect A type of logical fallacy that confuses a sequential relationship with a causal one. Faulty cause/effect wrongly assumes that Event A caused Event B because Event A occurred first: *the sun rose because the rooster crowed.* (See Logical Fallacies.)

Figurative Language Language that is not literal; language that redirects meaning away from the literal definitions of words. Figurative language is used to help arguers portray ideas, and, if used appropriately, it can add layers of richness to an argument. Some types of figurative language include antonomasia, analogy, hyperbole, irony, metaphor, metonymy, personification, simile, and understatement.

Formality/Informality Formality is the adherence of a text to conventions of style and format. Writing that stays within conventions and does not draw attention to itself by digressing or breaking with convention is considered formal. While many other features dictate the degree of formality, the following are major factors:

Formal Writing:
- Adheres to conventions of grammar and sentence structure.
- Does not draw attention to itself with novel phrasing or dramatic shifts in tone.
- Does not use much figurative language (metaphors or similes).
- Attempts to remain transparent; draws attention to ideas rather than the sentences, words, and phrases themselves.

Informal Writing:
- Veers away from standard conventions.
- Intentionally breaks conventional grammar or sentence structure rules.
- Draws attention to itself with unique or quirky phrasing.
- Freely uses slang or street phrasing.
- Draws attention to the writer (*I, me*), the audience (*you*), or both (*we*).

Hasty Generalization Drawing a conclusion about a group of people/events/things based on insufficient examples. This is often the logical flaw behind racist, sexist, or bigoted statements: *German Shepherds are vicious.* (See Logical Fallacies.)

Hegelian Logic See Dialectical Reasoning.

Hyperbole A figure of speech involving a deliberate exaggeration: *Look out! That puddle's the size of Lake Erie.* (See Figurative Language.)

Ideology The collection of unstated values and beliefs that inform people's understanding of the world. This collection of values and beliefs is not readily apparent to us; it is camouflaged by the sayings and behaviors of everyday life. You might think of ideology as the most invisible, most indirect or unstated, layer of an argument. Ideology is not usually directly addressed in arguments, but it does give birth to people's opinions about particular issues, and more sophisticated writers will dig deep enough to expose this layer. That is, they will try to explain the system of unstated beliefs and assumptions beneath their own argument or the arguments of others. Political ideologies include

communism, conservativism, fascism, feminism, liberalism, and so on.

Illustrations Graphic descriptions or representations of an idea. Sometimes writers illustrate a point with words only. They carefully describe the details of an idea so that an image is created in the mind of readers. In essence, writers draw a picture with words so that readers imagine it visually. But illustrations, in the strict sense of the word, use actual graphics. (See Support.)

Inartistic Proofs Support that already exists, such as facts, statistics, and testimony. Aristotle called appeals artistic proofs and evidence inartistic proofs because with appeals, arguers must create a bridge between the topic and audience; with evidence, the arguer utilizes evidence that already exists. (See Artistic Proofs; Appeal; Evidence; Support.)

Inductive Reasoning This type of reasoning builds from specific premises and leads to a general claim. For example: Two cars collided at the intersection last week. A pedestrian was nearly hit at the intersection yesterday. Today a motorcycle rear-ended a car at the intersection. Therefore, this is a dangerous intersection. When we come to a conclusion based on several specifics, we are reasoning inductively. Inductive reasoning is the primary engine of scientific research because researchers conduct specific tests or experiments to arrive at general conclusions. (See Deductive Reasoning.)

Informality/Formality See Formality/Informality.

Invention The discovery and development of ideas. Because the goal of argument is to *reveal* a new way of seeing a topic (and thus to persuade people to rethink their positions and beliefs), good invention strategies are key to success. Invention is the first of the five canons of rhetoric. (See Rhetoric.)

Inventive Research A type of research that is exploratory. It may involve seeking out opposing points of view, reexamining a familiar topic from a different angle, finding new layers in a topic, and so on. In short, inventive research is adventurous research. (See Seeking Research.)

Irony The act (or art) of saying one thing and meaning the opposite. In other words, an ironic statement means the opposite of what it says. When people proclaim, "Nice job, Grace!" after someone has tripped, they are being ironic. They really mean, "That wasn't very graceful." As an argumentative strategy, irony is a way to connect with the audience—to share a secret understanding, like a wink. Because the arguer assumes that the audience knows the real meaning behind the words, a bond develops.

Kairos Greek for *opportune moment*. It refers to the moment in a rhetorical situation that is ripest with opportunity—the moment when the right statement can have the most impact and influence on an audience. (See Rhetorical Situation.)

Logical Fallacies Flaws in the structure of an argument that make the claims invalid. A fallacy is a falsehood, so a logical fallacy is a logical falsehood that makes no sense within a given situation. (See Ad Hominem; Begging the Question; Either/Or Reasoning; Faulty Cause/Effect; False Analogy; Hasty Generalization; Non Sequitur; Oversimplification; Red Herring; Slippery Slope; Strawperson.)

Logos See Appeal to Logic.

Main Claim The primary assertions made about a given topic. (See Claims.)

Memory The fifth of the five canons of rhetoric; the recollection of prepared points. In ancient Greece, when the five canons were vital to the teaching of rhetoric, rhetors memorized lengthy arguments and delivered them as speeches. However, the rhetorical situation has changed dramatically since then. Now that we depend so heavily on written text, and less on a dramatic performance (or delivery), memory is hardly a vital part of argument.

But memory has been replaced by revision (or reseeing): we no longer need to see our argument in our mind for purposes of remembering, but since others will read it, we resee it to imagine how readers will understand it. Then we make adjustments.

Metaphor A comparison in which one thing takes on the characteristics of another: *Our economy is on the edge, and one wrong move could send it plunging downward.*

Metonymy A figure of speech that names something using only part of that thing. For example, people use *Washington* to refer to the U.S. government or *the pen and the sword* to refer to writing and military action.

Non Sequitur (Latin for *it does not follow*) A statement that does not follow logically from what has preceded it. This is the result of skipping several logical steps in drawing a conclusion: *Alphie is good-looking; therefore, he will be happy.*

Oversimplification A type of logical fallacy that does not acknowledge the true complexity of a situation: *If Bill and Lisa would just get married, they would solve their problems.*

Pathos See Appeal to Emotion.

Personification Treating a nonhuman thing as though it were human: *So the house just sat there through the years, minding its own business while the world built up around it.*

Premise Any claim that provides reasoning for another claim. Premises work like support in that they substantiate claims. But premises are single statements that set up or make an intellectual path for other claims. Premises are most often discussed as statements that lead to a conclusion or to a claim that has been proven. For instance, *if A and B, then C.* A and B are premises that lead to C: *If the rain has been coming down for two days, and if your shoes have been outside the whole time, your shoes are probably ruined.*

Proof A broad term that refers to support strategies. *Proof* is sometimes used synonymously with *support*. Aristotle split proofs into two categories: inartistic (forms of evidence) and artistic (appeals). (See Support.)

Qualifier A word or phrase that limits the meaning of another word or phrase. A qualifier acknowledges the limits of one's own claims. Qualifiers are closely related to concessions, which grant value to someone else's claims. The difference is that concessions focus on others' ideas and qualifiers focus on the arguer's own claims. If you qualify your point, you draw attention to its limitations. We often qualify our claims in everyday conversations: *I'm not saying that all politicians are bad, but many of them seem to distort the truth. Granted, some country music is good, but a lot of it just rubs me the wrong way.* Qualifiers also show up as words and phrases that make statements seem less extreme. Words such as *perhaps, seems, maybe, could,* and *might* qualify argumentative claims.

Red Herring A type of logical fallacy that tries to shift attention away from the original focus of the argument: *I might have wrecked your car joy riding, but you shouldn't have left the keys in it in the first place.*

Rhetoric A process of recognizing and using the most effective strategies for influencing thought. Aristotle defined rhetoric as "the ability in each particular case to see the available means of persuasion." In other words, rhetoric is more than a tool for changing people's minds; it is also the *study* of how people get persuaded into their beliefs. People who study rhetoric and writing are interested in how people's opinions form and change; they study the relationship between language and belief; and they examine the cultural conditions around people and their everyday use of language. In its classical origins (which most scholars note as the fifth century BCE), rhetoric was a primary field of study. In many ways, it was the glue between various academic pursuits because it focused on how ideas (regardless of content) get used, shared, communicated, implemented, and manipulated in the world. The study of rhetoric was the study of social and intellectual activity.

The study of rhetoric is still at the heart of contemporary writing classes. That is, students learn not simply about correct grammar but about the relationship between language and thought. Rhetoric is key in the study of argument (the deliberate and calculated use of rhetoric to influence or change thought). Aristotle's lessons on rhetoric are still in place. In writing, debate, communication, and speech courses, students still study the five categories or *canons* of rhetoric passed down from the ancient Greeks:

- **Invention:** The discovery and development of ideas.
- **Delivery:** The presentation of ideas.
- **Arrangement:** The organization of ideas in a coherent and engaging fashion.
- **Style or Voice:** The personal or individualized use of language conventions, with attention to appropriateness, situation, and audience.
- **Memory:** The recollection of prepared points.

Rhetorical Situation An opportunity to address a particular audience about a disputed or disputable issue (in other words, a chance to use rhetoric—to study the available means of persuasion—in a particular set of circumstances). A rhetorical situation involves an *exigence*, or an occasion when something happens or does not happen that results in some uncertainty. The rhetorical situation also involves the speaker/writer, the audience, the method of communication, and the rules of communication (whether directly stated or implied). No aspect of the situation exists independently of the others: what can and should be said (the message or text) depends upon the other elements. All elements of the rhetorical situation exist in time and place. All of the thinking and living that goes on in that place—and that has gone on before—impacts what can and should be said. Good rhetoricians (good arguers) understand how to use particulars within a setting. The ancient

Greeks called this *kairos*, or the opportune moment. The particulars of a situation actually bring an argument into being and help writers and speakers to develop ideas. And attention to the details of the rhetorical situation creates an effective argument. Making powerful arguments, then, involves not merely attention to language but also an awareness of surroundings (the intellectual, physical, and social layers of a situation). (See Rhetoric; Exigence; Kairos; Audience.)

Rhetorician An expert in or teacher of rhetoric. Rhetoricians do more than find the best language to change someone's mind; they study the whole situation (the real-life conditions and details, the rules and institutions involved, the values of potential audiences). They are interested in the relationships between what has happened in the situation, what is said or written, and what might happen. In a way, rhetoricians are part sociologist, part language theorist, part psychologist, and part philosopher.

Rogerian Argument An approach to argument based on the work of Carl Rogers (1902–1987), in which the arguer attempts to build common ground between value systems. According to Rogerian theory, arguers should first seek to understand opponents' views. Once we know the terrain of our opponents, we can build a bridge to it. The goal, then, is not to uncover weaknesses in opponents' thinking, but to uncover the key similarities between our own perspectives and those of others. Only then can we genuinely determine the nature of our own positions and effectively change how we think, which is a key element in Rogerian theory. This strategy is related to dialectical reasoning, or Hegelian logic, which attempts to find synthesis between two opposing claims. (See Hegelian Logic; Dialectical Reasoning.)

Sarcasm A type of irony characterized by a slant toward mean-spiritedness. Sarcasm is often used in a playful manner between people who are familiar enough not to offend one another with playful poking.

But in academic argument, and more formal situations generally, sarcasm should be used very discriminately—or not at all. Because academic audiences are not necessarily familiar with a writer, they do not expect to participate in much sarcasm. In the wrong situation, sarcasm can make a writer (or speaker) seem dismissive of audience's expectations or of the situation itself.

Scenarios Fictional or hypothetical accounts. As a persuasive tool, scenarios can support nearly any argumentative claim. When arguers use scenarios, they signal the audience that they are in hypothetical territory. This can involve a simple cue such as *Imagine that* or something even more subtle: *If one student were to score a 93%, another 95%, and another 100%, they would all receive a 4.0. However, the final grade would be. . . .* (See Support.)

Seeking Research Research done to find particular pieces of information, such as data, a specific historical account, or examples. (See Inventive Research.)

Simile A comparison using *like* or *as* in which one thing takes on the characteristics of another: *"You are like a hurricane. There's calm in your eye"* (Neil Young).

Slippery Slope A type of logical fallacy that assumes that a certain way of thinking or acting will necessarily continue or extend in that direction (like a domino effect). Such an argument suggests that once we begin down a slope, we will inevitably slip all the way down, and so the effects of a particular action/idea are exaggerated: *If the Supreme Court allows the police to set up informational roadblocks, it will soon grant law enforcement full license to inspect anyone at any time.*

Stasis Theory A system or approach involving four questions that help one to understand the nature of a disagreement and the precise nature of opposing claims. The term "stasis" comes from the Greek root *sta*, "to stand." Arguers ask a series of questions that help them determine the issue to be argued, the point of contention, or the place at which an arguer "takes a stand." In any rhetorical situation, there are many possible positions and opinions—and without some process of narrowing the scope, arguers might be left to simply bounce from point to point, never settling on real differences between positions. Stasis theory provides a framework that helps arguers to narrow in on a given point and to say, in effect, *"This is the point of contention."* The process involves four general questions:

1. **Conjecture:** Does it exist? Did something happen?
   (All questions related to origin and cause.)
2. **Definition:** What is its nature? What do we call it?
   (All questions related to meaning.)
3. **Quality:** Is it right or wrong? What or whom does it involve or affect?
   (All questions related to value.)
4. **Procedure:** What should be done?
   (All questions related to policy or procedure.)

An argument (even several different arguments) could emerge from each question. Arguers use the four questions (or stases) as investigation tools to ask, *Is this the disagreement?*

Statistics Numerical data drawn from surveys, experimentation, and data analysis. (See Support.)

Strawperson A type of logical fallacy that misrepresents an argument by oversimplifying it so that it can easily be proven wrong: *People against the war think that the U.S. shouldn't defend itself from dangerous forces.*

Style The personal or individualized use of language conventions, with attention to appropriateness, situation, and audience. An arguer's style is the particular way he or she uses language to engage an audience. Style is closely related to (and sometimes used synonymously with) voice. While both terms have long histories and have come to mean many different things, there is an important distinction for academic writing: Style is most often associated with a personalized set of mannerisms that a

writer carries from situation to situation (or assignment to assignment). Ernest Hemingway had a style. Emily Dickinson had a style. Voice, on the other hand, is seen as something that changes from situation to situation, sometimes dramatically. Writers can change the nature of their voices depending on the audience, topic, time, place, and shared expectations. This ability to change is key to rhetoric, and key to good argumentative writing. (See Voice.)

Support Sometimes called *grounds* or *proofs*, support gives substance and legitimacy to a claim or thesis. Support comes in various forms: authorities, facts, statistics, evidence, allusions, anecdotes, examples, illustrations, scenarios, appeals to logic, appeals to emotion, appeals to character, appeals to value, appeals to need. Through the ages, scholars have categorized and recategorized these support strategies. One long-standing perspective casts them into three main groups:

   Types of Appeal: to logic, emotion, character, value, need
   Types of Evidence: authorities/testimony, facts, statistics
   Types of Example: allusion, anecdote, illustration, scenario

While the groupings are interesting (and helpful in the broader study of rhetoric), they are not essential. Most arguments depend on various forms of support; however, there are common tendencies. For instance, arguments about value tend to use appeals, while claims of fact tend to rely heavily on evidence. Appeals to logic are key to all types of formal, academic arguments. Support gives substance and legitimacy to a claim or thesis. (See Appeal; Evidence; Authorities; Facts; Statistics; Allusion; Anecdote; Example; Illustration; Scenario.)

Syllogism A line of deductive reasoning that requires three steps: *If reason A is true and reason B is true, C must be true.* Or put another way: *A is true and B is true; therefore C is true.* Often, A and B are referred to as *premises*. The premises create an intellectual pathway to the final claim. Notice the following popular

example about Socrates, the ancient Greek philosopher:

   All humans are mortal.
   Socrates is human.
   Therefore, Socrates is mortal.

Testimony An eyewitness account: *I watched as the crescent got smaller and smaller; I was hoping to find a dark spot where I could pull off to the side of the road and take in the full beauty of a lunar eclipse.* (See Support.)

Toulminian Logic An important system for analyzing arguments, based on the work of Stephen Toulmin (1922–2009). Originating from the formal study of logic, Toulmin's framework suggests that an argument has six primary components: main claim, support, warranting assumption, backing, modal qualifier, and rebuttal. The first three are most widely discussed in the field of rhetoric; the warranting assumption is the most notable element because of its wide range of use. (See Warranting Assumption.)

Understatement A figure of speech in which a deliberately less forceful or dramatic expression than expected is used: *Antarctica is a little chilly.*

Unity The cohesive quality of ideas. If a text has unity, it develops a primary line of reasoning without significant digression. Although many different points (and sometimes seemingly unrelated points) may be addressed in a single argument, they are all directly related to the main claim or thesis. Writers use transitions between major points to achieve unity and logical connections among ideas.

Voice The writerly identity created within a text. Voice is closely related to style (the personal or individualized use of language conventions) but changes from situation to situation. When we read a text and comment about the author, we are commenting only on the identity in the particular text: *Clark is very formal here. Tamera seems curious.* This identity is referred to as the *voice* of the writer, or the presence and character of the writer as it appears in the text. All texts have a voice; it may be formal, barely noticeable, formulaic, or monotone. Some writers create a strong voice, one that comes out of the text boldly, while others keep their voices understated. (See Style.)

Warranting Assumptions The reasons that connect claims with their support. As philosopher Stephen Toulmin explains, inside every argument lies a warranting assumption, but it is often unstated. The assumption may seem so obvious to the arguer that he or she feels no need to announce it, or perhaps the assumption rests so deeply and quietly in the arguer's mind that he or she does not even recognize it. Warranting assumptions rest deeply in our thoughts. In a sense, they are part of our ideologies: the collection of unstated values and beliefs that inform people's understanding of the world. When we discover a warranting assumption, we reveal the hidden support structure of an argument and can more accurately determine the argument's strengths and weaknesses.

For example, the statement *We should not withdraw our troops from Iraq just because the war isn't going well after four years* rests on an unstated assumption: that people want to withdraw troops because the war isn't going well. People may want to withdraw troops for other reasons; people may be against the war whether it is going well or not, or they may want to withdraw troops because they feel the war has been managed incompetently. Because of an unstated warranting assumption, the audience may be led in a particular direction without realizing it, and ultimately led to a particular conclusion that is not based on sound logic or evidence.

Text Credits

This page contains an extension of the copyright page. We have made every effort to trace the ownership of all copyrighted materials to secure permission from the copyright holders. In the event of any question arising as to the use of any material, we will be pleased to make the necessary corrections in future printings. Thanks are due to the following authors, publishers, and agents for permission to use the material indicated.

Chapter 1: 10: Copyright © 2004 by NC State University.

Chapter 3: 32–33: © Bibliomania .com. Reprinted by permission. **32, 45:** Cameron Johnson, "Somewhere in the Past: Clarksville's Schools and Community Life." Reprinted by permission of the author. **33–34:** Ed Bell, "Lunar Eclipse: November 8, 2003." Reprinted with the permission of the author. **34:** Laura Tangley, "Natural Passions" from INTERNATIONAL WILDLIFE (September–October 2001). Copyright © 2001 by the National Wildlife Federation. Reprinted with permission. **37:** Lynda Smith, "Disconnected." Reprinted with the permission of the author. **37:** From THE NEW YORK TIMES, June 26, 2010. © 2010 The New York Times. All rights reserved. Used by permission and protected by the Copyright Laws of the United States. The printing, copying, redistribution, or retransmission of this content without express written permission is prohibited. **55:** Justin James, "Standardized Testing vs. Education." Reprinted with permission. **55:** Reprinted with permission from Holly Wren Spaulding.

Chapter 4: 65–66: MERE CHRISTIANITY by C.S. Lewis. Copyright © C.S. Lewis Pte. Ltd. 1942, 1943, 1944, 1952. Extract reprinted by permission. **68:** K. T. Glency, "Letter to Kohl's." Reprinted with permission. **70:** John Adams, "The Education of Ms. Groves." Reprinted with permission. **70:** Reprinted with permission from Tracy Webster.

Chapter 5: 80: Reprinted with permission from Tracy Webster. **82:** Justin James,

"Standardized Testing vs. Education." Reprinted with permission.

Chapter 6: 98: Cameron Johnson, "Somewhere in the Past: Clarksville's Schools and Community Life." Reprinted by permission of the author. **100:** Reprinted with permission from Megan Ward.

Chapter 7: 144: Quote from "Punk After the Pistols" by John Goshert. Popular MUSIC AND SOCIETY, 24 (200): 85–106. © Taylor & Francis. **158, 159, 160, 162, 163, 165:** Andrew Hyde, "The Fashion Punk Paradox." Reprinted with permission. **158, 159, 162, 164:** Margaret Mead, "Warfare: An Invention. . .Not a Biological Necessity" from Asia 40 (1940): 402–405. Copyright 1940. Reprinted with the permission of The Institute for Intercultural Studies. **161:** John de Graaf, "What's the Economy for, Anyway?" from http://www.newdream.org/newsletter/ economy_for.php. Reprinted with the permission of the author. **165:** Justin James, "Standardized Testing vs. Education." Reprinted with permission.

Chapter 8: 178, 199: Excerpted from "Pesticide Product Use and Risk of Non-Hodgkin Lymphoma in Women" by Ikuko Kato et al. ENVIRONMENTAL HEALTH PERSPECTIVES, Sept. 2004 112(13): 1275–1281. **196, 201:** From THE NEW YORK TIMES, June 26, 2010. © 2010 The New York Times. All rights reserved. Used by permission and protected by the Copyright Laws of the United States. The printing, copying, redistribution, or retransmission of this Content without express written permission is prohibited. **198, 203:** Reprinted with permission from J. Noel Trapp. **200:** Reprinted with permission from the June 15, 2000 issue of THE NATION. For subscription information, call 1-800-333-8536. Portions of each week's Nation magazine can be accessed at http://www.thenation.com.

Chapter 9: 223, 230, 236: John Adams, "The Education of Ms. Groves." Reprinted with permission. **231:** Reprinted with permission from Michael Hilliard. **272:**

Reprinted with permission from Tracy Webster.

Chapter 10: 272, 273–274: Reprinted with permission from Curtis White. **278:** Amber Edmondson, "Citizens and Consumers." Reprinted with permission. **278:** Reprinted by permission of Laurie Schutza.

Chapter 11: 303, 351: Cameron Johnson, "Somewhere in the Past: Clarksville's Schools and Community Life." Reprinted by permission of the author. **310, 314, 318:** Joannie Fischer, "A Nation Made of Poetry," from US News & World Report, Sept. 23, 2003, pp.80–84. Copyright 2003 U.S. News & World Report, L.P. Reprinted with permission. **314, 319:** © Bibliomania.com. Reprinted by permission.

Chapter 12: 346, 352, 353–354: REPRINTED WITH PERMISSION FROM PSYCHOLOGY TODAY MAGAZINE. (Copyright © 2000 Sussex Publishers, LLC.) **348, 351:** Reprinted with permission from Joel Papcun. **351:** Reprinted with permission from Joel Collins.

Chapter 13: 396: Joannie Fischer, "A Nation Made of Poetry," from US News & World Report, Sept. 23, 2003, pp. 80–84. Copyright 2003 U.S. News & World Report, L.P. Reprinted with permission. **398–399:** Laura Tangley, "Natural Passions" from INTERNATIONAL WILDLIFE (September–October 2001). Copyright © 2001 by the National Wildlife Federation. Reprinted with permission. **406:** Jay Harrington, "The Origin of Grunge." Reprinted with permission. **407:** Reprinted with permission from Tracy Webster. **407–408:** Jennifer Worley, "Fantastic Ideals." Reprinted with the permission of the author. **408–409:** Justin James, "Standardized Testing vs. Education." Reprinted with permission. **409:** Reprinted with permission from Wendy Kaminer, "Gender Bender," THE AMERICAN PROSPECT: September 2002. Volume 13, Issue 16. http://www.prospect.org. THE AMERICAN PROSPECT, 1710 Rhode Island Avenue, NW, 12th Floor, Washington, DC 20036. All rights reserved.

Index